STREAMS OF CONSCIOUSNESS

Christopher Bollas' *Streams of Consciousness* is available in two volumes

1974–1990

1991–2024

STREAMS OF CONSCIOUSNESS

Notebooks 1974–1990

Christopher Bollas

KARNAC

firing the mind

First published in 2025 by
Karnac Books Limited
62 Bucknell Road
Bicester
Oxfordshire OX26 2DS

British Library Cataloguing in Publication Data

A C.I.P. for this book is available from the British Library

ISBN: 978-1-80013-258-0 (paperback)
ISBN: 978-1-80013-259-7 (e-book)
ISBN: 978-1-80013-260-3 (PDF)

Typeset by vPrompt eServices Pvt Ltd, India

Printed in the United Kingdom

www.firingthemind.com

Contents

Preface

These notebooks are presented in two volumes, spanning the period from 1974 to 2024. They are preceded by a brief history in order to provide the reader with an account of those teachers and writers who influenced some of the ideas in this text.

Never intended for a reader's eye, many of the early entries were written in the few minutes between psychoanalytical sessions when thoughts arrived that I felt were worth noting. Most were dated and titled to provide some organization, especially when it became clear that lines of thought were emerging that needed some form of identification.

Through the years, I rarely revisited previous entries. The notebooks functioned less as a repository of ideas which might be reviewed and reconsidered, and more as a medium for thinking—rather like a conversation with an other, ideas displaced by the next thoughts that arrive.

Although the writing mind does leave traces in the sand, if thoughts are left untouched and unreviewed, not exploited for revisionist thinking, they serve a rather unique potential that lives in the act of writing itself. When I look back, I find myself looking into a curious mirror. I see the familiar guise of a writing personality but each revisiting reveals a new movement of thought, one that invites—indeed provokes—contradictions, odd juxtapositions, and neologisms. Ordinary words may take on entirely new meanings without my necessarily knowing what is meant. In such a circumstance, the writer follows the pen, and over time establishes an intriguing intrasubjective relation between consciousness and the unconscious. Our inner phenomenology enacts this relation.

In the notebooks, I refer to many of the writers who have influenced me, and the order in which they appear provides an essential link to the associative logic of the entries. They include works across the literary spectrum, from ancient texts and well known literary milestones to so-called "lesser" writers, and specialists whose works are comparatively unknown.

Were this an academic work, with the aim of commenting on the full spectrum of writers that influenced my work, these allusions would need to be fully referenced. This, however, is not what this was, the term "transformational object" came immediately to mind. Some years later, Joe Sandler said he thought it worded the experience of being inside the analytical process.

Many ideas are launched in conversation and in this section I list those who have been for me the most significant figures in the conversational world. Those not included can be found at the end of the history in the Acknowledgements.

I hope that this contextual information may help to orientate the reader. Although the notebooks were begun only in 1974, they reflect my experience in the 1960s, so we begin there.

UC Berkeley: 1960s

How did I come to psychoanalysis and where was I before I started writing these notebooks?

As a student at the University of California I sought psychotherapy to help me with anxieties and symptoms that were bewildering to me. At the same time, Frederic Crews—later famous for his *Freud Wars* critique of psychoanalysis—invited me to attend his graduate seminar on Psychoanalysis and Literature. Our analytical texts were mainly American classics, including works by Charles Brenner and Jacob Arlow. We also read Faulkner's *The Bear*. The Crews seminar became an intellectual template. Our Freud reading stayed very close to the text, going over the same passage again and again, taking in the precise wording, syntax, and flow of ideas. This allowed us to study a product of unconscious thinking in a way that seldom happens in clinical trainings. While clinicians can never share the same patient, those in applied analysis—commenting on poems, plays, novels, historical events etc.—can share the experience directly, in real time. It is a highly effective way to teach psychoanalytical thinking.

In the summer of 1966 together with my close friend, Michel Small (a UC student), who was also interested in psychoanalysis, we vowed to read Otto Fenichel's formidable text *The Psychoanalytic Theory of Neuroses* and to discuss our reading for a few hours every week. These conversations allowed two novices to share ignorance and slowly, slowly, begin to wise up.

I studied American colonial history and historiography at Berkeley. Historical time—the sequence of *events*—is a logic of the real. Study the steps of historical action and you find the material to be highly overdetermined, made up of multiple separate but related strands that share space and time.

My senior thesis was a study of the psychological conflicts manifested by the earliest settlers in Boston. I found Wilhelm Stekel's works of considerable use in translating their complex repressions into an understanding of the underlying issues they were avoiding.

I moved into psychology and history as I studied slavery and the mind of the plantation slave with Kenneth Stampp, whose book *The Peculiar Institution* argued that Black people were not cognitively inferior to white people but that their apparent stupidity was in fact an intelligent act of adaptation to their oppressors. They gave the impression of inferiority in order to protect themselves from graver violations against them.

I studied with Alan Dundes, professor of anthropology and expert on Ferenczi and Roheim. His lectures on the cultural unconscious and racism remained ingrained in his students. Using what seemed like simple childish jokes, he showed how these emerged from forced integration, for example the bussing of Black Americans to white schools. The elephant joke, he pointed out, expressed a racist fear that Black folks were going to move into the neighbourhood. (A man puts elephant manure on his lawn. "Why are you doing that?" asks a neighbour. "To keep the elephants away." "But there are no elephants near here." "You see—it works!")

The East Bay Activity Center

From 1967–1969 I was a counsellor at the East Bay Activity Center in Oakland California, where I was thrown into the deep end of intense work with highly disturbed children. Their individual plights and solitary anguish were compelling. Several of the senior staff had studied with Anna Freud in London and brought her perspectives to the work, so we had in the back of our minds the road map we call "psychodevolopment". This informed our thinking and provided us with reassuring evidence in a world in which things seemed not at all clear. The evidence was those visible psychic steps that we all travel and that distinguish a four-year-old from a six-year-old, and an eleven-year-old from a fifteen-year-old.

This was the era of Margaret Mahler and her important work on autism. Although we found these texts useful, they tended to be experience-distant, so when I happened to see a review in the *TLS* of Guntrip's book *Schizoid Phenomena, Object Relations and the Self*, I ordered it and devoured it, because it showed the reader how to use the theories in clinical practice.

The British were dedicated to being clinically effective. From Guntrip I moved on to read Winnicott, Balint, Klein, and Fairbairn. Klein allowed me to imagine (creatively invent?) the internal worlds of the puzzling children who were such a crucial part of my life.

The Bay Area was awash with the fecund world of Gestalt psychology most commonly associated with Fritz Perls at Essalen. I found some of his ideas compelling, but it was the work of the Palo Alto Group—Gregory Bateson, Donald Jackson, and Jay Haley—that I found most useful in thinking about human interaction. *The Pragmatics of Human Communication* by Paul Watzlawick, Janet Beavin, and Don Jackson, provided a very different view of what we would term "character", and over the years I maintained an interest in the gestalts of human action and interaction. I also read Austin on illocutionary acts and Searle on speech acts. (Searle was at Berkeley and played a prominent role in the Free Speech Movement.) To my way of thinking the theory of illocutionary action fitted into the realms being discussed by the Palo Alto group and, looking back, contributed to my interest in character as action.

I found Heinz Werner's text *The Comparative Psychology of Mental Development* eye-opening. It conveyed many different lines of thought that were endemic to the depth psychologies, and I think its structuralization of pluralistic thinking was foundational for me. I find, for example, that I am as much at home reading Howard Gardiner's *Frames of Mind* as any of the psychoanalytical texts. I also found clinically useful some of the predicates and practices of the Transactional school, notably Eric Berne.

University of Buffalo: literature and psychology

In 1969 I drove east to the University of Buffalo where I was to do a PhD in English literature. There I was enrolled in the "Literature and Psychology" program which was part of the English department. The program included psychologists and psychoanalysts and the monthly meetings of the Group for Applied Psychology involved people from various university departments and from within the community. Warren Bennis, a leading figure in organizational psychology attended, as did Heinz Lichtenstein, the eminent psychoanalyst and student of Martin Heidegger. Guests dropped by all the time and I was fortunate to meet Kenneth Burke whose work on rhetoric as intersubjective action (my interpretation of him) influenced my understanding of character as the idiom of a self's actions and interactions. Indeed, the issue of how our being enacts axioms from our unconscious is an area studied by many great American psychologists, amongst them Abraham Maslow and the remarkable American ego psychologist George Klein, whose work I read when I was at Austen Riggs in the middle 1980s.

Riggs inherited and treasured the interface between classical psychology and psychoanalysis. The seminar on the ego conducted there by David Rapaport during the 1950s was attended by Roy Shafer, Robert Holt, and others. Ego theory insisted that behaviour be included in the assessment of ego functioning. For me this was an interesting road to travel in searching for a language to identify character moves, motives, disorders, and transformative potentials in a psychoanalysis.

Nelson Rockefeller had called Buffalo the "University of the twenty-first century". He had put a fortune into gathering a remarkable faculty, and at the time it was the most radical and creative English department in the country. Many poets and writers from the Black Mountain School (which had closed) found their way to Buffalo, including Robert Creeley and Gregory Corso as well as the doyen of that group, Charles Olson. They joined other poets and novelists such as Carl Dennis and John Barth.

But above all it was Robert Hass who would change my way of thinking. Deeply familiar with psychoanalytical thinking, he made implicit use of it. In a seminar on Wordsworth's *Prelude*, Hass and others on the faculty taught us in depth how a poem *thinks*. This was an act of sustained immersion: we suspended consciousness to allow unconscious thinking to receive and communicate the logic of the poetic text.

At a first reading, most great poems elude consciousness. They are unconscious presentations, and they require hearing or reading again and again before our consciousness begins to gather *some* of that unconscious thinking, and then to consider and organize it. The subtitle of the *Prelude* is *Growth of a Poet's Mind* and I think this work, along with Freud's *Interpretation of Dreams,* became the background for my own views of unconscious thinking and free association.

Encountering a complex poem is remarkably similar to listening to a patient's narrative. The logic of a poem moves at times in cryptic condensations that are similar to free associative speech. The finest teacher of psychoanalytic thinking, in my view, is the astonishing literary critic Helen Vendler. As she critically examines poets and their works we find an evolution of

Freudian method that is stunning. Her analysis of syntax opens up a perspective that allows us to see how, and in what ways, character is syntactical.

Buffalo also had a strong contingent of French writers and philosophers such as René Girard, whose lectures on the "enemy twin" were complex musings on the psychic reality of the double: a forerunner of my own thinking on the borderline personality. A variety of psychoanalysts would come for extended visits. In particular, I found Guy Rosolato's detailed lecture on the movement of the phonemic (words echoing one another) highly illuminating.

Our resident genius was Michel Foucault. His English was not great and as my French was merely touristic, I found his lectures hard to comprehend. But, perhaps because my father was French, somewhere in my unconscious I *seemed* to understand him.

At Buffalo I studied Lacan's work with Stuart Schneiderman, who left the university to enter analysis with Lacan. In the late 1970s, after publication of my essays in the *Nouvelle Revue de Psychanalyse*, Lacan conveyed his appreciation of my work and his wife, Laurence Bataille, who was editor of *L'Ornicar,* asked me to contribute to the journal. Through readings and conversations I eventually grasped *my* Lacan, and I used his structural theory (symbolic, imaginary, real) as a psychodynamic reality. I have since then seen the constant interplay of the self within these differing realities and I have often found Lacanian writings inspiring because of the doors they open or the questions they ask or the puzzles they offer.

Meanwhile at Buffalo, while studying for my PhD in literature, with the kind, careful, and thoughtful guidance of Lloyd Clarke MD, head of the psychology section of the Student Health Center, I was trained on the job to do psychotherapy with students and faculty. With the authorization of S. Mouchly Small, psychoanalyst and head of psychiatry at the university medical school, I attended rounds with the psychiatric residents, and we spent time at Buffalo State Mental Hospital interviewing institutionalized male schizophrenics. On ward rounds in the hospital various psychiatrists taught us how to observe a distressed person, what to look for, and how to form a diagnosis.

I was working two days a week at the Student Health Center, and Clarke and I, with the help of Murray Schwartz (English Department), set up a training in psychotherapy for graduate students in the humanities.

The weekly staff meetings were a wonderful soup of views: Rogerian, T-groupers, encounter therapists, Jungians, existential psychoanalysts, systems theoreticians, and ego psychologists. These remarkable meetings, in which the group would concentrate on the task of discussing a new patient, were living proof of the value of differing perspectives. Every approach bore within its predicates crucial assumptions that also operated within psychoanalysis, and I would transfer ideas from these approaches into my psychoanalytical vision.

As with all university departments, Buffalo's faculty and students shared space but followed diverse schools of thought. The era of Formalism was waning, giving way to Structuralism, Phenomenology, and the abstract-hungry schools of critical theory. What we called "applied psychoanalysis" had a long history. Beginning with Freud's own analyses of literature, it found its way into anthropology (Lévi-Strauss, Weston La Barre), history (Hofstadter and Schorske), political theory (Sheldon Wolin), philosophy (Marcuse and Norman O. Brown), and even further afield.

The psychoanalytical wing of the English Department had been assembled by Norman Holland, a Shakespeare scholar who undertook non-clinical psychoanalytic training in Boston and went on to write crucial texts applying psychoanalytical concepts to literature. He was joined by Leslie Fiedler (my dissertation director), Robert Rogers, Murray Schwartz, Richard Wilburn, Jim Swann, Mel Faber and others, who formed the most cohesive graduate program in "lit and psych" anywhere.

Not long after I arrived, Buffalo discovered the British School of psychoanalysis and one full semester was devoted to the reading of Marion Milner's *The Hands of the Living God*. Murray Schwartz, gifted Shakespeare scholar, would write one of the first Winnicottian essays, "Where Is Literature?", which has become a classic over the decades.

Smith College and Beth Israel, Boston

In 1972 I left Buffalo to study at Smith College. I had applied to both the British Psychoanalytical Society and the Hampstead Child Analysis training. Anna Freud asked that I gain a "proper" clinical training and license, and she recommended Smith, where I could gain an MSW in one calendar year.

In those days the college was founded on ego psychology and I was fortunate to study with Paul Seton (member of the Western New England Psychoanalytic Society) and Donald Fern, a brilliant young analyst who died prematurely in his forties. The psychiatric social workers on the faculty were outstanding clinical thinkers and their attention to the detail of a session was grounding. My clinical placement was in the Department of Psychiatry of Beth Israel Hospital in Boston which was staffed by psychoanalysts.

1971 saw the publication of Kohut's *Analysis of the Self*. All serious clinicians were reading it and many were changed by it in vital ways. A senior Boston analyst said, when discussing a patient who some thought needed analysis, "No! The only people who need analysis are psychiatrists training to be analysts. It is not for the guy on the street." I was shocked, but at that time his view was not controversial. With Kohut evoking hope in clinicians that they really could help highly disturbed people, ego psychology gave way to new movements in America and a new view of psychoanalysis.

At Beth Israel I was most fortunate to attend Arnold Modell's seminar on object relations. A kind, shy, and brilliant man, Modell was one of the very few senior American analysts who really grasped the British approach to psychoanalysis. For me, his musings on "the intermediate area of experience" were especially resonant.

I also attended Peter Sifneos' workshop on focal psychoanalysis. He taught me many things, but top of the list was his insistence that comments to a patient must be lucid, and should connect with what they had just talked about. Although he was not, I think, familiar with the work of Bion, Sifneos was certainly into linking.

Beginning analysis and work in London

In the summer of 1973 I moved to England to begin psychoanalytic training, and in September I began my training analysis. There is nothing like five-times-a-week analysis—it is a remarkable experience—and although this first analysis was brief (about three years), when I resumed with another analyst the process was very similar. Both were members of the Independent Group, and this approach profoundly informed my view of the creativity of psychoanalysis.

Before beginning my formal analytic training, I worked as a psychotherapist at the Personal Consultation Centre (PCC) in Kings Cross, which offered psychotherapy to anyone who came through the door. It was a wonderful introduction to British culture and to those fascinating axioms that generated personality in mid-twentieth-century Britain. It was a good opportunity to study personality, and especially the schizoid phenomena that so fascinated D. W. Winnicott, Michael Balint, and Masud Khan.

The two years spent at the PCC also gave me time to find the English person within me. My father lived his first ten years in Paris, his adolescence in Argentina and Chile, and his early adulthood in the UK (in Surrey) before migrating to the United States in his mid-twenties. When I visited Paris for the first time to stay with relatives, I found aspects of my father and myself in the French idiom of personality. The same would prove true when I visited Argentina, recognising many of my father's mannerisms in the gregarious full-on lifestyle of these fascinating people.

I was slowly getting to know British psychoanalysis. At the PCC we were supervised by Geoffrey Thompson, a close friend of Samuel Beckett and Wilfred Bion. His supervisory comments were wonderfully elliptical and creative, like a music critic enjoying the mental instrumentations of *Homo sapiens*. People were an endless and fathomless surprise: "Oh my word, now, what do we make of that, eh?" he would say with great delight.

And it was through the PCC that I came to know John Bowlby. I remember sitting in his office at the Tavistock, impressed by this most remarkable and sincere scientist who had somehow landed in the fields of psychoanalysis. He provided heroic empathy, reaching across class, ethnicity, and age to actualize a hidden thread running through all of us that is deeply curative.

Politics and psychoanalysis in the community

As part of the Camden Council of Social Service, chaired by Pam Warren, our task at the PCC was not only to provide individual psychotherapy but also to be available for "community work". This was not new to me, and here I shall digress briefly to mention some political and cultural strands in my intellectual background which are frequently reflected in these notebooks.

From the age of sixteen I had been politically active in Orange County, California, especially in organizing effective opposition to landlords who rented cardboard homes to African American families in a ghetto in downtown Santa Ana. I was encouraged and supported by Arnold Hano—a writer and chair of our local Democratic Party group—who looked forward to my getting a driver's licence so I could put ideas into local practical action on behalf of our group.

culture I know, the French think through conversation. Their journal *Combat* testifies to the art of verbal and intellectual fencing. This idiom is reflected in French prose, which is less formal, structured, and predictable than the English essay. Its impressionistic, almost circular spin of ideation is, as Blanchot puts it, an "Infinite Conversation". Maybe the French idiom of writing mirrors inner speech.

I wrote three essays for the *Nouvelle Revue*, written in English and published in French: "Le langage secret de la mère et de l'enfant" (*NRP*, No. 14, 1976), "L'esprit de l'object et l'épiphanie du sacré" (*NRP*, No. 18, 1978), and "Comment l'hysterique prend de l'analyste: l'effet de la conversion dans le contre-transfert" (*NRP*, No. 24, 1981). When Pontalis invited a writer to contribute, he would include a brilliant essay of his own on the same topic. These essays were an inspiration, illustrating what a creative editor can do to challenge psychoanalysts to think outside the box.

In the following years I also got to know Janine Chassaguet-Smirgel. In the mid-1980s I invited her to lecture at the Austen Riggs Center and we remained close until her death in 2006. She was a remarkably brave thinker. Whilst contending with disturbing misogyny in her own analytical culture, she pushed on with radical thinking about anal structures that proved challenging and evocative.

A meeting with Jean Laplanche at a conference in Lisbon launched us into a correspondence. He was always kind and supportive.

I am grateful to Didier Anzieu, Joyce McDougall, Haydee Faimburg, René Major, Michel de M'Uzan, René Roussillon, and René Diatkine, for their support.

The British society and the Tavistock Clinic

I attended seminars at the Institute of Psychoanalysis in London from September 1974 through June of 1977 and qualified in August of 1977. I was taught by Hannah Segal, Betty Joseph, Herbert Rosenfeld, Henry Rey, Donald Meltzer, Irma Pick, Moses Laufer, Anne-Marie Sandler, Harold Stewart, Nina Coltart, Enid Balint, Martin James, and others. Trainees were required to have two analysands for which my supervisors were Paula Heimann and Marion Milner. The transition from Associate Member to Full Member required two further supervisions, and I went to Eric Brenman (Kleinian) and Clifford York (Freudian).

At the same time, I was also training in psychotherapy at the Adult Department of the Tavistock Clinic. Along with long-term open-ended analytic work, we also trained in brief or focal therapy, group psychoanalysis, marital/couples therapy, and organizational consultancy.

My years at the Tavistock years were sculptural. It was like the best graduate school one could ever hope for, and we were comparatively free to study topics of special interest. It was here that I learned Bion, primarily through supervision with Robert Gosling, his analysand and Chair of the Tavistock and I attended Bion's lectures there and thus gained a sense of this intriguing figure who clearly enjoyed the mischief of being a sage.

I enjoyed discussions of child cases presented by Donald Meltzer and Mattie Harris, which were discussed in Kleinian terms. The key clinical difference, in my view, between Bionian analysts and Kleinians is that Bion said very little whereas Kleinians traditionally talked a lot. However, a new generation of clinicians, including John Steiner, were introducing what would come to be known as the "new Kleinianism".

I was fortunate to participate in Frances Tustin's seminar-workshop on autism. I had read her work while I was working at the East Bay Activity Center, but her thinking came alive for me when she discussed children in treatment. At this time I also attended clinical presentations by Anna Freud. It was not until I heard her using the structural theory that I realized quite how beautiful a model of the mind and self it is.

My study of focal psychotherapy with David Malan expanded on the training I had received in Boston with his friend and colleague Peter Sifneos. Focal psychotherapy has much to teach analysts, especially in its expectation that the analyst will provide a clear explanation of the patient's thought processes and behaviour in the session.

It was also my good fortune to study "core psychoanalytic concepts" in Joseph Sandler's weekly seminar at the Tavistock. Joe had taken me under his wing and he mentored me in the years to come, linking me up with psychotherapy training programs such as the British Association of Psychotherapists. He was a lucid thinker who believed in growing psychoanalytic theory from the core.

I came to appreciate Jungian analytical perspectives through supervision with Judith Stephens—a Jungian analyst—and Rosemary Gordon, a friend and gifted analytical practitioner.

Italy and Sweden

In 1978 I began my tenure as Visiting Professor of Psychoanalysis at the University of Rome, and for the next twenty years I would visit the University Neuropsychiatric Hospital for Children (known as "Via Sabelli") three or four times a year, for a week at a time. I also visited Aquila, Naples, Venice, Turin, and Milan, but Rome became my analytical home, a refuge from the warring psychoanalytical factions in London. The meetings there were non-partisan, searching, and jovial. Most of the essays in my early books were presented first in Via Sabelli.

In 1983, Ulla Bejerholm, a visionary Swedish psychoanalyst who lived in Malmö, invited me to attend and conduct her annual conference in Arild, in the south of Sweden. She, too, had worked at Beth Israel in Boston and had been part of Sifneos' workshop, so although we had not met before, we shared a common background. For the next thirty years the Arild group invited me to lead seminars and workshops for three days at a time. The group had about twenty-five members; most people attended over decades and we grew older and wiser together.

During this same era, I was invited by Arne Jemstedt to conduct seminars in Stockholm. Reared as they were in an interesting mix of existential psychoanalysis, ego psychology, and object relations theory integrated with their own mentality, one found in the Swedes a remarkably distinct perspective that cast new light on my own work. They are responsible for the best contemporary cultural journal that is psychoanalytically based, *Divan*, that has published some of my essays and placed them in interesting contexts.

Bion and Winnicott

In the early 1980s Parthenope Bion asked me to edit a volume on her father and I travelled to Turin to meet with her and discuss his work. She and Francesca Bion were sorting through his papers and were in the early stages of setting up the first Bion conference in Milan. Parthenope's knowledge, grasp, and deep understanding of her father's way of thinking and practising changed my understanding of his work. Our discussions of "O" and the mother helped me to embody Bion's categories and to see how his visions could be brought into the consulting room.

In the early 1980s Clare Winnicott asked me to be one of the literary editors of the Winnicott Trust. Invited into the 1952 Club—a group formed by senior Independent analysts—I was able to present developing ideas and to have invaluable guidance from its members, notably from Margaret Little, who had been an analysand of Winnicott and was a leading figure in Independent Group thinking. Clare Winnicott also invited me to join the "Hood Study Group" convened by James and Catriona Hood, two analysts from Scotland who had worked closely with Winnicott. We were joined by Margret Tonnesmann whose grasp of Winnicott and clinical acumen were appreciated by all of us. Our group would pick a theme, for example "use of the object", and spend several hours spinning it round through our minds. It was a most intellectually enlightening group experience.

Austen Riggs and the University of Massachusetts 1985–1987

In 1985 I took up posts as Director of Education at the Austen Riggs Center in Stockbridge, Massachusetts, and as Professor of English at the University of Massachusetts. One of my responsibilities was to invite speakers for the monthly Friday Night Lecture, attended by members of the Riggs community and local townsfolk, including a fair number of psychoanalysts from Boston and New York. The visiting speakers would spend the week at Riggs, with a few days at the University of Massachusetts where they would give a seminar led by Murray Schwartz, who was a dean at the university.

The staff at Riggs were the most inspiring group of people with whom I have worked and it is impossible to trace their influences on my thinking. I owe a great deal to Daniel Schwartz, Jim Sacksteder, Gerard Fromm, and Betty Homich for supporting my work. To Erik Erikson, Otto Will Jr., Martin Cooperman, and others, I am grateful to have learned from people whose use of ego psychology, object relations, and the unique American "school" of psychoanalysis (the "aw shucks, what do I know?" trope exemplified in Mark Twain) created a fascinating intellectual grasp of the stunning clinical challenges of working with psychotic patients.

Workshops on unconscious thinking 1988–1998

During this period I offered seminar-workshops in New York and several other American cities. Most of these were on "unconscious communication". We met in small groups of eight or nine people to listen to a case. This was presented without describing the gender, age, or circumstances of the patient, and with no additional comments from the clinician. The words of the session were the one shared, objective reality. No questions were allowed, and no theoretical formulations. Every few minutes I would intervene to ask the group for their free associations. Gradually a tree of associations would grow, and after seventy-five minutes the presenter would take fifteen minutes to track these, informing us of striking connections. Only then would we hear the age, gender, and other details of the patient. This form of study, based on the unfolding chain of associations, illuminated what Freud meant by "propinquity in time".

For sixteen years I met three times a year in Chicago with four study groups of nine colleagues each. I am grateful to the gifted analysts and psychotherapists who took part and represented that "can-do" mentality of the American grain: licensing degrees of individual clinical inventiveness that was often very creative. On each visit I dined with my dear friend Ernest Wolf and his wife Ina, and as the years passed I found Ernie's accounts of why he chose to follow the works of Heinz Kohut compelling and moving. His theory of clinical empathy chimed with some of my own ideas about the "celebration" of the analysand.

Supervision and clinical discussion

Psychoanalysis as a practice is usually discussed by analysts through the individual case presentation. In London in the 1980s, I enjoyed collegial clinical discussions with my cohort within the Independent group, and I found the exchange of views with Michael Parsons, Jonathan Sklar, and Roger Kennedy especially important. For some years we met monthly as "The Spanish Club".

In the 1990s a group of European analysts came together and met in Stockholm, Zürich, Tübingen, and London, to constitute a study group that aimed to examine unconscious thinking and communication in analytical sessions. Many clinicians were to be involved over time, including Arne Jemstedt, Eva Schmidt, Sarah Nettleton, and Peter Wegner.

The influence of conversations with colleagues was formative, including a few dear friends whose influence on my thinking and practice is too deep and ramifying to identify. Nina Coltart and I became life-long friends and on vacations, over dinners and innumerable teas (really an excuse for meeting up), there were hardly any nooks and crannies of psychoanalysis we did not discuss. Nina's understanding of the role of silence and the positives of present absence—how it elicits very early ego memories—influenced my way of thinking and practising.

Marion Milner was a close friend for life and we visited one another regularly. Joyful and naturally playful, Marion opened the door to endless conversations about the aesthetics of pleasure, the joy of being in analysis, and she was another important influence on my concept of the "celebration of the analysand".

Enid Balint, who had accepted me for training (and insisted early on that one day I would write) was inspiring. In time we became very close friends and we travelled together in the States in the 1980s. When I returned to live in London, we met up for enjoyable discussions of ideas, especially her disagreements with my thinking that were based in particular on her view that there was no such thing as the self!

My own reading of Freud was somewhat offbeat at the time, and I was also developing a clinical theory that was rather different from that of the mainstream of colleagues in Great Britain. Many people found this hard to grasp, so I was surprised and grateful when, in the late 1990s, Sarah Nettleton came for supervision and immediately understood the gist of what she would later term my metapsychology. She had previously been a pianist and I was to find in subsequent years that musicians tend to understand sequential thinking, and easily grasp what Freud means by the logic of free association.

Writing

My job at Riggs allowed me time to write and it was there that I put together the collection of essays that became *The Shadow of the Object*: *Psychoanalysis of the Unthought Known* (1987). It was after the publication of this first book that I began to enjoy writing. Between 1989 and 1999 I published four books of essays: *Forces of Destiny: Psychoanalysis and Human Idiom* (1989), *Being a Character* (1993), *Cracking Up: The Work of Unconscious Experience* (1995), and *The Mystery of Things* (1999).

While I was at Berkeley I had written some plays (to the amusement of my friends), but these were lost in a fire. At that time I could not bring myself to continue, but in 2004 I decided to return to fiction, with the first of three linked novellas: *Dark at the End of the Tunnel, I Have Heard the Mermaids Singing,* and *Mayhem*. I also produced a volume of plays, entitled *Theraplay* (2006). I found that writing fiction allowed me "to stage" psychoanalysis, enabling me to explore complex psychic issues in a new way.

When I resumed "proper" analytic writing, my main aim was to illustrate and explore how we can listen to free associations. I rethought Freud's theories—he had many on free association—and elected his concept of the immediate chain of ideas: that one finds this form of thought in the leaps from one topic to the next. What seems insensible—in this leap—reveals a remarkable "chain of ideas" if patiently noted over time.

The Freudian Moment (2007) confronted extremes in practice that threaten the intellectual freedom released by Freud's discoveries. *The Infinite Question* (2009) used close study of clinical material to show the complexity and logic of the free associative narrative. *China on the Mind* (2013) was prepared for a Korean analytical association that disinvited me when it was clear I was going to refer to ancient Chinese texts. I pushed on and turned the lectures into a small book that reflected the struggle of this Western person to comprehend the Chinese mind which, paradoxically, seemed curiously familiar.

Meaning and Melancholia (2018) took many years to write and is something of an end-piece, although events since its publication naturally invite us to continue to think, speak, and write in protest about the pathology of our times. By the time these notebooks morphed into a book-in-waiting, sometime in 2022, I was no longer using them as a form for writing-thinking, but rather as a means of addressing the catastrophes of our era. What will become of human thinking? Is *Homo sapiens* approaching its end?

Who knows?

But in the meantime, these notebooks are some of my traces in the sand.

I preface the *Notebooks* with an essay published in 1974 but written in 1973 before my emigration to the UK. It organizes and indicates many of the interests that will occupy me for the next fifty years and is a good point of embarkation.

Acknowledgements

I have many people to thank for conversation and support, some of whom are mentioned in the Brief History and I shall not repeat their names here.

In addition, I thank Adam Phillips, Jacqueline Rose, Vincenzo Bonaminio, Anna Hobart, William Cornell, Adriano Giannotti, Elizabeth Spillius, Emmanuel Calamaro, Lars Bejerholm, Ulf Trigg, Jerome Bruner, Italo Calvino, Juliet Mitchell, Joseph Scalia, Stan Zuckerman, Darlene Ehrenberg, Pearl-Ellen Gordon, Jean Baker Miller, Sara Flanders, Emmanuel Ghent, David Scharff, Jill Scharff, Ernst Prelinger, Bernard Leach, Malcolm Bradbury, Naohiko Tachi, Marion Soloman, Jim Swann, John Dings, Sharon Olds, Laurie Ryaveck, Whitney Davis, Mona Simpson, Patrick Fieri, Kelli Fieri, Amneris Moranis, Adam Limentani, Muriel Dimen, Bruce Reiss, Kevin Popp, Camille Norvell, Gretchen Schmutz, Ken McMullen, Leo Stone, Leo Rangell, Alan Spivack, Greg Gorski, Jan Witkoski, Alan Tansman, Erich Winter, Ben Churchill, Andrew Lanyon, Peter Shoenberg, Laurence Gerlis, Barrington Cooper, Carlos Fernandez, Francis Lemon, Marge Champion, William Shirer, Salomon Resnick, Sonia Langlands, Rosemary Gordon, Eleanor Bertino, Jack Peirce, Ignazio Matte Blanco, Harold Searles, Peter Giovacchini, Anthony Foty, Anne Friedman, Syd Arkowitz, Dennis Duncan, Alex Pollock, Al Alvarez, Mary Sue Moore, Anne Alvarez, Stephen Grosz, John Lahr, David Aronovich, Roger Lehmann, Gabriella Mann, Itamar Levy, Anna Bouvet-Chagall, Manoel Berlinck, Naum Gabo, Hans Loewald, Albert Solnit, Gabriela Goldstein, Victoria Hamilton, Anish Kapoor, Anthony Molino, Karla Hoven-Bucholtz, Jean Sanville, Joel Shor, Hedda Bolgar, Carol Morgan, Camilla Bargum, Jim Grotstein, Peter Giovacchini, Camilla Burgum, Woody Faigen, Richard Jones, Veikko Tahka, Ritta Tahka, Teija Nissinen, Edward Corrigan, Peter Schoenberg, Dirk Hammelmann-Fischer, Joseph Scalia, Leslie Gardner, Sergio Lewkowicz, Martha Nussbaum, and Oksana Yakushko.

I thank Kate Pearce of Karnac for her wholehearted, intelligent, and astute guidance of this book to publication. I thank members of her staff in particular Anita Mason, Aimee Dexter, and

Gilbert Courbanally for their work. To Nick Downing for his editing of this text and to Leonard Rosenbaum for the index: thank you.

My thanks to Steven Groarke and Arne Jemstedt for "having a look" at the text and to Sarah Nettleton for her unfailing support for this project which included her reading it through and commenting on the introduction.

I thank Suzanne King (Bollas) for her tireless and patient support even when it seemed fated to pass away before delivery.

Lastly, I thank all my patients over these fifty years for teaching me how to be an analyst. It is awful that I cannot name you and ask you to take part in what was always a collaboration between two people: only one of whom is present in this text. I remember each and every one of you—even your dreams!—and you have never left my mind. To have been your psychoanalyst was a great privilege and I shall always be grateful.

Note to the reader

Most quotations from Freud's texts refer to the *Standard Edition*, for example, SE10, 21 (*The Standard Edition of the Complete Psychological Works of Sigmund Freud*. London: Hogarth 1957, Volume 10, p. 21).

Every effort has been made to track down references I make to the works of other authors. However, after several house moves many of the books to which I refer have vanished. Where it has not been possible to locate quotations I reword them, so the author's ideas are acknowledged even if the specific source is not given.

The only changes made to the original text are details of punctuation and the occasional omission of a fragment that was unclear or insignificant. All references to analysands are, of course, fully anonymized, and they are few and far between as these were never intended to be clinical notebooks.

The index does not include all authors. So many are referred to in the text that I felt this would be overwhelming. It is intended instead to help the reader track particular areas of thought, such as "the structure of evil", or issues of analytical interest such as "hysteria" or "perversion".

To recap the history (see above)—in short—from 1973 through 1975, I was working at the Personal Consultation Centre in London. I began my psychoanalytic training at the Institute of Psychoanalysis and was in five times a week training analysis. In September 1975 I joined the Adult Department of the Tavistock Clinic where I undertook a training in adult psychotherapy meant to prepare the students for duty in the NHS as consultants, a promise that was abandoned by the government.

In 1977 I opened my private practice in North London. I qualified as a psychoanalyst in 1977 and left the Tavistock in 1978.

From the late 1970s I was teaching literature—at Richmond College in London and psychodynamic theory at the North East London Polytechnic. From the late 1970s through the late 1990s, I taught regularly at the University of Rome and in Stockholm and Arild in Sweden. In 1985, I took up a post at the Austen Riggs Center (as Director of Education) and at the University of Massachusetts (as Professor of English). In 1987, I returned to England and resumed analytical practice.

A short history on the period 1990 to 2024 can be found in the preface of volume two.

Character: the language of self*

Contemporary psychoanalytic theories of externalization when linked to Freud's formulation of the repetition compulsion suggest that the recurrent patterns of a person's behavior are, in fact, reproductions. Freud regarded reproduction as a special form of memory and his idea that repeated patterns are embedded in a subject's character suggests that character is the embodiment of memories that will be repeated, rather than reflectively recalled. Character, however, is not simply a form of memory, but reflects the subject's unconscious interpretation of himself which he represents to the world through his behavior. Character is viewed as a special form of speech which is an invaluable resource in psychotherapy if the clinician develops a notational vocabulary to decipher the semantics of character. Current developments in communication theory, particularly in semiology, provide a conceptual vocabulary for the clinician's discovery of the hidden language of character.

For some time now psychoanalytic theoreticians have relied on a few discrete though often interrelated ideas to describe the externalization of internal psychic contents and structures into patterned forms of behavior. Some of the classical concepts are transference, acting out, projection, the repetition compulsion, and, in some cases, sublimation and substitution. More recently, Bychowski's (1967) "release of internal introjects." Lichtenstein's (1961) "identity theme," Giovacchini's (1967) "externalization," and Khan's (1966) "happening" explore an old idea of new terms: man's external behavior expresses his internal world in some form.

These modes of externalization are, I think, self-explications, a communicative resource—the person's way of telling us about himself. Freud's (1914, 1920) exploration of the idea of the repetition compulsion has laid the foundation for broadening that compulsion, it seems

---

* Originally published as Bollas, C. (1974). Character: the language of self. *International Journal of Psychoanalytic Psychotherapy,* 3(4): 397–418.

to me, to include all patterned forms of repetition specific to each individual. That is, man projects, transfers, acts out, displaces, or sublimates in(recurrent styles)that are specific to him, as the atmosphere of a novel is specific to its author. Freud (1914) laid further significant groundwork when he linked the repetition compulsion (with his notation that repeating is a form of recollecting) to character. He provided, thereby, a frame which I shall use for my argument that "character" is not simply a form of recollection, a telling by showing (mimesis), but is(a personal hermeneutic—an interpretation of the self's history.)The original definition of "character" is sign, or mark, and, I think, the etymological meaning of the term is significant. For character as a sign, or more accurately, a system of signs, is a form of meta-language. To understand a person's character, which I regard as a mimetic evocation of the repressed, we must comprehend the signifying feature of a person's character: his system of signs. Thus, I hope to link the study of character to the field of semiology, and to indicate what I think is the contribution of semiology to psychoanalysis. I make this connection because semiology, as the study of signs, bears within its linguistic model a new conceptual language that can add to our understanding of character. It is my intent, further, to suggest that a generic idea of externalization (as I call it "the inside out") resides within the idea of character, if we appreciate that an adult person's character is an(interpretive mimetic evocation of his past)and if we appreciate how, it signifies this mimesis.

Why do I make this inquiry and develop what to some may appear to be a peculiar if somewhat scholastic emendation of—or shall I say rumination—on the theory of character? Psychoanalytic ego psychology, with its focus on defense, adaptation, and synthesis, and with its concern with the stages of development and the person's growth through these stages, has tended, it seems to me, to focus too much on the psychological function and dysfunction of man. There is not, for example, within ego psychology, at the present time, a theory of communication specific to the individual. Man, and his center—the ego—we know does not simply defend against impulses, adapt to realities, synthesize conflicts, and interact with others. Above all, man communicates. He speaks. He acts. And his speech and acts are always involved in some form of communicative process. It is my view that within the psychoanalytic theory of character lies the seed for a theory of personal communication: the subject's interpretation of himself.(For, as I will argue, the subject's interpretation of himself is his character,)and his character bears the several themes or meta-themes of the interpretation. It will be my task in the following pages to illustrate how I think the idea of(character, once linked to the theory of the repetition compulsion)becomes a foundation for future exploration of the subject's interpretation of himself.

Several concepts—character, repetition, remembering, interpretation, and communication—will need to be worked into one another in order to appreciate this paper's central idea, itself a collation of parts, that (1) a person's character is a subjective interpretation of the self, (2) a character's style, the specificity of a person's "ambience", is a potential language, (3) the potential language of style can be realized by the psychoanalyst if he regards a subject's character as a mimetic evocation of the repressed, and finally (4) the psychoanalyst needs to develop a lingual appreciation of the mimesis by valuing some of the concepts developed in this paper.

penumbra

First, I will present a brief history of the psychoanalytic contribution to the inside-out (as it applies to my idea of the mimetic evocation of the repressed) in order to link psychoanalytic theory with what I believe falls within the penumbra of hermeneutical phenomenology: semiology, communication theory, interaction theory. Such a history is intended not only to nudge psychoanalysts into recognizing the clinical usefulness of semiology and communication theory but to appreciate the potential contribution psychoanalysis can make to the languages of man, a contribution that I think is necessary to enrich the somewhat rigid and superficial qualities too often found in the literature on communication. For, as always, where the behavioral scientist develops categorical indexes for the observed (as *langue*: cf. Poole, 1972), the psychoanalyst can move one step further toward the interpretation of the found, adding to the phenomenology of the data his invaluable hermeneutical skills.

Freud: reproduction, recollection, and character

Everything in psychoanalysis begins with Freud. In 1912 he nearly provided a generic theory of translation when he linked the repetition compulsion to character.

> It must be understood that each individual, through the combined operation of his innate disposition and the influences brought to bear on him during his early years, has acquired a specific method of his own in his conduct of his erotic life—that is, in the preconditions to falling in love which he lays down, in the instincts he satisfies and the aims he sets himself in the course of it. This produces what might be described as a stereotype plate (or several such), which is constantly repeated ·constantly reprinted afresh—in the course of the person's life, so far as external circumstances and the nature of the love-objects accessible to him permit, and which is certainly not entirely insusceptible to change in the face of recent experiences. It follows from our earlier hypothesis that these cathexes will have recourse to prototypes. will attach itself to one of the stereotype plates which are present in the subject: or, to put the position in another way. the cathexis will introduce the doctor into one of the psychical "series" which the patient has already formed.

Freud argues that a person's "specific method", created by "innate disposition" and external influences, forms a "stereotype" in him which he perpetually repeats and reproduces. This "stereotype" is an internal pattern that sponsors recurrent behavior. In the transference, he argues, libido will "attach itself to one of the stereotype plates which are present in the subject" and in turn the patient will introduce the doctor to one of the psychical series which the patient has already formed. When the patient weaves the figure of the physician into one of internal series, he attempts to synthesize in a dialectical interplay the outside (figure of physician) with the inside (the series or cliché.) We know this to be transference, and, to some degree, transference occurs in all interpersonal transaction.

Though for the most part Freud defined the compulsion to repeat in terms of the person's negotiation of a traumatic experience, here he locates the compulsion to repeat in terms of the duplication in behavior of internal psychic structures (i.e., "stereotype"). In the paper "Further Recommendations in the Technique of Psychoanalysis, Recollection, Repetition, and Working Through" (1914), Freud says of this "compulsion to repeat" that "in the end we understand that this is [the person's] way of remembering." Repetitive recollecting is a behavioral reenactment that replaces reflective recollecting (memory) but that, nonetheless, is a special form—albeit unconscious and unknown—of memory. When memories become dissociated from the subject through characterological absorption he will repeat them without knowing his repetitions to be a recollection. As Freud (1914) says:

> We have learnt that the patient repeats instead of remembering and repeats under the conditions of resistance. We may now ask what it is that he in fact repeats or acts out. The answer is that he repeats everything that has already made its way from the sources of the repressed into his manifest personality—his inhibitions and attitudes and his pathological character traits.

Freud follows up this initial connection of serial reproduction to character in *Beyond the Pleasure Principle* (1920).

> The "perpetual recurrence of the same thing" causes us no astonishment when it relates to active behavior on the part of the person concerned and when we can discern in him an essential character trait which always remains the same and which is compelled to find expression in a repetition of the same experiences.

So, while the subject transforms memory into act and thereby loses consciousness of the ontology of his actions, the therapist, according to Freud (1914), must translate the characterological behavior (lingual sign) back into memory and consciousness:

> This state of illness is brought, piece by piece, within the field and range of operation of the treatment, and while the patient experiences it as something real and contemporary, we have to do our therapeutic work on it, which consists in a large measure in tracing it back to the past.

In order to "trace" the reproduced character trait "back" to memory the analyst needs to appreciate the message encoded in the act, indeed, must comprehend in the first place, as Freud argues, that as reproduction is a special form of recollection one of the tasks of analysis is to understand and translate the unconscious language from the self into the conscious memories of the self.

Fortunately, many of Freud's colleagues agreed that the repetition compulsion could serve as a comprehensive (generic) idea to explain patterned repetition of behavior, a move toward linking repetition to character. Abraham (1911) confirmed through his clinical and cultural studies that various psychic states in the mature person are patterned on the form and the content of early experiences", and that "man is compelled to repeat his early experiences." Ferenczi (1915) noted that "behind this pleasure in repetition there is also a peculiar pleasure in rediscovery."

Reich: the forming of character

Certainly, one of the first significant explorations of character after Freud appeared in 1933 with the publication of Wilhelm Reich's book *Character Analysis*. Reich found Freud's tendency to explain character traits from an instinctual bias too narrow and argued that character is *"an integral formation* both generally and in terms of typological transmutations." Character, according to Reich (1933) develops as a *"chronic* change of the ego which one might describe as a hardening" (p. 155). He argued that the instinctual conflict did not determine a character trait but that *the way* the parents handled a child's instinctual conflict determined the trait (p. 159), thus removing the trait and the repetition compulsion from the social vacuum of discrete libidinal conflict stages. In doing this he placed the repetition compulsion in a relational context—a context not inconsistent with some of Freud's writings. Reich's summary of his connection of character to parent–child relations is worth quoting in full:

> If we once again briefly review the basic character structures sketched above, we see that they all have one thing in common: they are all stimulated by the conflict arising from the child-parent relationship. They are an attempt to resolve this conflict in a special way and to perpetuate this resolution. At one time, Freud stated that the Oedipus complex is sub-merged … but it resurfaces in a different form. The Oedipus complex is transformed into character reactions which, on the other hand, … constitute reaction formations against its basic elements: … The basic infantile conflict continues to exist, *transformed into attitudes which emerge in a definite form*, as automatic modes of reaction which have become chronic and from which, later, they have to be distilled through analysis. (p. 167)

Though Reich's work is regarded as a classic in the psychoanalytic canon, it has spawned few disciples in the Western world. Studies of character, neglected in Europe and America, have appeared primarily in Arab and Japanese psychoanalytic circles, where the idea of character may be of interest for cultural reasons. Fourteen years after Reich's work on character was published in Germany, however, Erich Fromm extended Reich's findings in his work *Man for Himself* (1947). Like Reich, Fromm criticized Freud's focus on libidinal styles (p. 65) and suggested a new metaphor (a mimetic one) to describe the expression of a subject's character.

> Closely related to Freud's concept of unconscious motivation is his theory of the conative nature of character traits. He recognized something that the great novelists and dramatists had always known: that, as Balzac put it, the study of character deals with "the focus by which man is motivated": *that the way a person acts, feels, and thinks is to a large extent determined by the specificity of his character* and is not merely the result of rational responses to realistic situations; that 'man's fate is his character'. (p. 64, italics mine)

But when Freud linked the idea of repetition to character, he did more than simply argue that the repetition compulsion expresses character traits. He argued that repetition is a *form of recol-lection*, so that if we are to make sense of a person's character traits (henceforth to be called his *personal style*), *we must see the "style" as itself a form of recollection.*

xxxiv CHARACTER: THE LANGUAGE OF SELF

Loewald: repeating as remembering

Hans Loewald (1971) is one of the few contemporary analysts who has made use of Freud's idea that the repetition compulsion is a form of recollection. He writes:

> Repetition in the form of action or behavior and affect is a kind of remembering, albeit unconscious, and remembering as a conscious mental act is a kind of repetition. If one adheres, as psychoanalysis does, to the concept of unconscious memory, repetition and recollection can be understood in terms of each other, depending on whether we focus on the present act, in which case we speak of repeating, or on the past prototype in which case we see recollection. Indeed, it can be claimed that to understand repetitions ("reproduction as an action"-Freud) as a form of remembering, and to understand remembering as an act of repeating, as a "reproduction in the psychical field" (Freud), *is one of the cornerstones of psychoanalytic psychology.* (p. 59, italics mine)

Loewald sees two forms of reproduction: passive reproduction and active re-creation. "Everything depends," according to Loewald, "on how these early experiences of childhood are repeated in the course of life", to what extent they are repeated passively suffered again if "actively" rearranged—and to what extent they can be taken over in the ego's organizing activity and made over into something new—a recreation of something old as against a duplication of it" (p. 60). Where Freud regards the repetition compulsion as in the service of instinctual experiences, Loewald follows Bibring's (1943) focus on the ego's function as the synthesizer of reproduction.

One of the functions of analysis, according to Loewald, is to transform passive reproduction into active re-creation: to help the patient recognize he is personally involved in these patterns, "that the unconscious he becomes aware of is his unconscious, or that he dreamed the dream he had" (p. 62). Loewald stresses that psychoanalytic theory must note that it is not simply the privilege of a neurosis to repeat its past but of the "normal" human life to find itself a "sequence of repetitions of some crucial prototypical events" (p. 64).

Loewald, to my mind, helps the patient to see that his behavior is speech and that he is the actor-speaker. The repetition compulsion in Loewald's hands takes its rightful place as a symbolic form: a mimetic re-collection of early subjective experience. Unexpressed in conscious memory, the past is continually presented to the world in the form of the subject's character: in stasis it is emblematic like a rebus; in action it takes the form of a mimesis.

Inside-out: theories of recreation

The idea of a mimetic structure in aspects of external behavior derives from Freud's concept of the repetition compulsion, the replication in action of an internal psychic phenomenon. Thus far we have seen how the repetition compulsion is embedded in character (Freud, 1914; Reich, 1933) and how character traits—a mimetic language of the self—reproduce memories unknown to the subject (Freud, 1914; Loewald, 1971). A review of psychoanalytic literature,

I feel, will illustrate how many analysts take this connection of the repetition compulsion to seriated enactment (the mimetic evocation) for granted without acknowledging the theoretical implications of their assumption. I will review an important sample of such writing to indicate how a tacit recognition of a mimetic evocation of the repressed has emerged in the writings of psychoanalysts, a recognition that I will try to make explicit.

In a series of articles Gustav Bychowski (1956, 1959, 1967) has argued that in psychotic states the ego releases its introjects and the subject finds himself in an external object world of his own making. Though Bychowski's concern is to explore the extreme manifestations of such an event in terms of psychosis he does provide a generic frame. He believes (1959) his studies demonstrate:

> The extent to which relations, existing between the child and his parents, find their first replica in reactions prevailing in the psychic structures; subsequently, these reactions become imbedded in the ego and are projected onto external persons, representing, in the last analysis, substitutes of the parental introjects, that is, the original parents themselves. (p. 248)

In his paper "The Archaic Object and Alienation" (1967) he argues that archaic objects (an archaic image of the self, and/or original love-hate object) "exert a powerful impact on the behavior *and on the entire existential style of the individual*" (p. 385, italics mine). Bychowski (1956) describes a patient, A. who externalizes his introjects.

> Now in the course of his analysis A repeats the process of externalization in everyday life and in transference. On a dance floor, in a classroom, or in a restaurant he is constantly harassed and at the same time attracted by characters consisting of real individuals fused with internal images. Their position reflects deep ambivalence which he had experienced in his relationship with his parents, his older sister, and the playmates of his childhood: they are coveted, painfully longed for, and seemingly unattainable friends, as well as hated persecutors … We see that real individuals serve as points of materialization of internal images, including the image of the self. Yet, in periods of intense analytic working through of early object relations, when A is alone in his room, the internal images, set free, come to haunt him as in his childhood. (p. 331)

Where Bychowski focuses on psychotic externalization, Eric Berne (1961) creates the framework of a larger theory which describes a process similar to Bychowski's but which makes itself available to all forms of human transaction. Berne's structure is the somewhat inflexible idea of "scripts", where he argues (1961) that the script,

> is an attempt to repeat in derivative form a whole transference drama, often split up into acts, exactly like the theatrical scripts which are intuitive artistic derivatives of these primal dramas of childhood. Originally a script is a complex set of transactions, by nature recurrent , but not necessarily recurring, since a complete performance may require a whole lifetime. (p. 116)

William Murphy (1965) amplifies Bernes' mimetic metaphor:

> The vicissitudes of the present call forth various roles on the part of the patient. These are roles that have been played repetitively and, although they may appear to vary considerably, they tend to show definite structural patterns based upon past experiences. Another and more complex way of stating this is that a persons patterns of relationship with *objects, persons, himself* and his *body image* tend to be similar and to be repeated many times over the years with only minor variations. In this respect a patient is the author, audience and director of the play. While he is versatile enough to take any of the main roles convincingly, he needs other persons to complete the cast. (p. 13)

Following in Bernes footsteps, Laing (1969) extends the dramatic metaphor but rids it of Berne's often simplistic and stereotyped formulations. A person is not simply handed a script which he then dutifully performs for the remainder of his life: he internalizes, according to Laing, (a "family" (the family *created* by the subject) which undergoes modulations and other transformations in the process of internalization")(p. 17). At all times Laing sees the "family" however as the primary internal structure that (generates the individual's style.) In this way, he differs significantly from those like Heinz Lichtenstein (1961), who sees the repetition of external pattens as formed in the earliest stages of mother–child relation.

In his illuminating paper "Identity and Sexuality (1961) Lichtenstein argues that each person has *an identity theme* that is based not on identifications but on the mother's unconscious imprinting onto her child. The mother, argues Lichtenstein:

> does not convey a *sense* of identity to the infant but an *identity*: the child is the organ, the instrument for the fulfilment of the mother's conscious needs … (The mother imprints upon the infant not *an* identity, but an "*identity theme.*") This *theme* is (irreversible, but is capable of variations,) variations that spell the difference between human creativity and "a destiny neurosis". (p. 208)

Lichtenstein's subject manifests in his personal style an *identity theme* formed in the earliest months of his life, the subject's (mimesis will therefore constitute we may say *a telling* of the earliest relations in his life. It is this identity theme that Lichtenstein sees as the substance of the repetition compulsion,) for it constitutes a sameness within change, a core-self which will find or achieve many variations but remain irreversible in its theme.

In the 1960s a new series of papers written by Masud Khan (1966, 1969) focused on the *peculiar way* several different *kinds* of patients expressed internal structures through a manipulation of the outside world. Khan's intent is to try to discover the semantics of such manipulation, to discover in these patients the meaning implicit in their arrangement of themselves-to-the-world and the-world-to-themselves. Writes Khan (1966) of a schizoid patient:

> By making the object *special*, they become special themselves. … This projective re-living of the self through making others sponsor one is typical of the schizoid character. (p. 308)

> One gets the vivid impression that all these *happenings* were a way of "remembering" and actualizing experiences that these patients had lived through at crucial stages of their lives *vis à vis* significant objects … (p. 309)

Khan's patient creates a climate which allows him to relive part of himself, such that the reliving is a way of remembering (Khan's focus here and his other works is on pathological style as re-collection; my attempt is to make this connection—style to reminiscence—generic to all people). In another paper (1969), Khan found that the peculiar perversions of one of his patients allowed her to activate and mimetically represent a latent and unknowable part of herself—not as he argues, an alter self, but a "collated internal object" which consisted of "aspects of her father, aspects of her mother, and essentially the mother's dissociated unconscious and an amalgam of self-experience from very early childhood, as well as what her mother phantasied her to be" (p. 562). It is important to Khan's craftsmanship as a therapist to permit the patient to *act out* (a classic mimetic metaphor) on occasion within the therapeutic setting. Here, it seems to me, Khan finds the way a person sets up the "props" of the session to be a clinically useful means of informing the patient as well as the therapist. For in attending to the way a patient locates himself within the therapeutic space and in permitting subtle or even gross manipulations of the therapist, the clinician can witness the patient's mimetic evocation of the earliest object relations: the self, prior to verbal expression.

Though she has significant doubts about the usefulness of permitting acting out in analysis, Anna Freud (1968) admits that such experiences reveal very early object relations *not available* to a subject's memory. She writes:

> The "forgotten past," especially so far as it refers to the pre-verbal period, has never entered the ego organization in the strict sense of the term, i.e is under primary not secondary repression and, therefore, is not recoverable in memory, only apt to be relived (repeated, acted out, in behavior). (p. 167)

The point I wish to make here is that acting out, which I regard as a species of a person's style, is somewhat like a dumb show: a drama without words. Much of what we regard as a person's *style* is nonverbal made up of an endless series of patterned and therefore typical modes of behaving—a kind of mimetic pageant. Bychowski's release of introjects, Berne's scripts, Laing's scenarios, Lichtenstein's identity theme, and Khan's happening are all different forms and even styles of the subject's presentation of his past in everyday life. They are modes of re-presentation: Berne's of family memories, Lichtenstein's of dyadic "memories," Khan's collated internal object a mosaic interpretive recollection with unconscious subjective meaning. More than likely an individual expresses himself in several of these modes, representing dyadic and triadic issues alongside one another, collated to use Khan's example, in an interpretive mosaic. It is crucial to our future work as clinicians, I think, to be tuned to this appreciation of style and to develop a vocabulary of the verbal, paraverbal, and nonverbal cue system to help us organize what we see.

Toward a semiology of self

Arguing that "psychoanalysis has yet to concern itself with a 'psychology of style' " (p. 449), Victor Rosen, in his article, "The Relevance of 'Style' to Certain Aspects of Defense and the Synthetic Function of the Ego" (1961), feels that "'style' is best defined as a progressing synthesis of form and content in an individually typical manner" (p. 447). In a statement close to Lichtenstein's idea of the identity theme as sameness within change, Rosen claims that style is "invariant" and the "hallmark" (p. 449) of a person's individuality. He then turns to the complicated task of deciphering the discourse of personal style.

> The development of a manageable notational system is one of the problems that confronts a study of individual variance in style. Until such a system is available within the framework of psychological discourse it will be difficult to know whether this feature can be described in terms of the vernacular of current characterology or whether style in expressive activity reveals fundamental aspects of human personality in the manner postulated for example by the students of graphology. (pp. 449–450)

Rosen does feel that stylistic phenomena occur in the clinical hour "in the individual variations of speech, mimetic expression, manners, dress" (p. 450), but he notes that analysts focus on other material and are without a system of notation with which to make sense of the mimetic cues sent their way.

In another paper (1969), Rosen turns to the study of semiology to find such a system of notations—a vocabulary able to describe personal style. In doing this, he borrows from the terms set by Ferdinand de Saussure in his *Course on General Linguistics* (1916) and locates himself within the field of semiology. At the core of semiology is the distinction between the signified and the signifier. According to Roland Barthes (1964), a modern student of Saussure, the components of a *sign* are the *signifier* and *the signified* (p. 35). "The plane of the signifiers," argues Barthes, "constitutes the *plane of expression* and that of the signifieds the *plane of content*" (p. 39). To a semiologist every function of man is pervaded with meaning such that his use of objects, for example, is a semantics: "as soon as there is a society, every usage is converted into a sign of itself" (p. 41). Thus, man may wear a raincoat to protect him from rain, but such an act does not foreclose the fact that the raincoat is a sign of rain—that the coat is a signifier and the rain the signified. Semiologists point to the existence of a human "notational field" (p. 35) and argue, correctly I think, that such a field is composed of a variety of typical signs: verbal, iconic, graphic, gestural, and vestimentary—to name only a few.

A problem I find with current studies in semiology is the tendency to categorize signs according to social rather than intrapsychic codes. *Some* of the social semiologists have created a notational system, however, which could be used by clinicians in the study of personal style as mimetic evocation of the repressed. One of the most useful systems, it seems to me, is Goffman's (1971) "tie-signs." Goffman believes that an individual externalizes his meaning through "intention display" (p. 11), a series of rituals which have "a dialogistic character" (p. 63). Tie-signs are signs (which express the subject's experience of another person in a relation.) They are part of his "ritual idiom"—not a language but an *idiom* (p. 225), not a series of messages but (a source of evidence) (p. 195). Tie-signs. however, are a form of personal semiology. Writes Goffman:

> Through quite minor acts of deference and demeanor, through little behavioral warning lights, the individual exudes assumptions about himself. These provide others with a running portent, a stream of expression which tells them what place he expects to have in the undertakings that follow, even though now little place may be at stake. In fact, (all behavior of the individual,) insofar as it is perceived by others, (has an indicative function,) made up of tacit promises and threats, confirming or disconfirming that he knows and keeps his place. (p. 344)

Where Goffman focuses on the personal idiomatic expression of tie-signs, Ray Birdwhistell (1956) develops a system of *kines*. "A kine is the smallest perceptible unit of body expressivity. A kinemorph is a series of kines strung together in significant recurring sets" (Poole, p. 61). Birdwhistell seeks a language of specific body cues. "All kinesthetic research rests," he writes, "upon the assumption that, without the participants being necessarily aware of it, human beings are constantly engaged in adjustments to the presence and activities of other human beings" (p. 61).

Birdwhistell. however, tends to collapse the *idiomatic use of kines* into language categories and the individual's style becomes lost in his modern equivalent of the nineteenth-century dream book where symbol A, like kine A, *equals* meaning B. In a brilliant new work, the English philosopher Roger Poole (1972) has taken Birdwhistell to task. Using Saussure's distinction between *langue* (languages) and *parole* (speech), where language is the cultural grammar of which the subject is a participant, and *parole* is his individual speech, Poole argues that Birdwhistell's "reduction of the particular gesture to the general rule of grammar" has "squashed back" the *parole* into the *langue*. Poole finds that for Birdwhistell the "objective, given observable gesture, the signal, the facial expression, is taken as being sufficient for purposes of analysis" but, Poole argues, "the gesture *itself*, the signal *itself* is not *sufficient* for the purposes of analysis. One has to get behind the gesture to the originating subjectivity for whom that gesture has a meaning, a specific meaning. The meaning transcends the sign in which it is enclosed" (p. 65). Poole insists on our using kinesthics not simply to form a larger language (a *langue*) but to discover the meaning within the subject's idiomatic (stylistic) use of the gestural language. (We discover the subject's pattern, his stylistic use of the kine (or his use of tie-signs) and interpret what we find to inform us of his meaning.)

Semiology and communication theory, tempered and enriched by the wisdom of Poole, provides the clinician with an educated eye for the patient's multilingual means of informing him about the "originating subjectivity" behind the gestural code. We can now state the following:

1. Communication theory can help the psychoanalyst decode a person's gestural ambience toward a clinical meaning if the psychoanalyst appreciates that such signs are not simply indicators of ego function—and thereby placed in a nosological index—but such signs are

highly specific clues to the intrapsychic life of the person. A person's character has, as I have argued, semantic as well as functional implications.

2. Given the phenomenology of a subject's character, the psychoanalyst can enrich his clinical understanding of the person if he understands that (a person's character is the unconscious interpretation of the self) and can be valued when brought to consciousness as the essence of this person's (statement from himself to others.)

3. Such interpretation of the self is (not only an intrapsychic event but is to be understood as an unconscious communication to the other, often a telling by showing (mimetic evocation of the repressed) of something not known to or understood by the subject) Though the signifier may be witnessed (as symptom or mimesis) the signified is the unknown, the unconscious "originating subjectivity" behind the signifier.

4. The patterns of the self are repeated and constitute what we have called a person's character, but psychoanalysts have failed to acknowledge the depths and complexities of a subject's character.

5. A person's character is not merely the random collation of its parts (i.e., of dyadic or triadic object sets, wishes, introjects, cognitive structures, learned patterns, etc.) but, as a whole, a totality, it has meaning. (Character, then, is the dialectical synthesis of unconscious interpretations of self and significant others,) fashioned in critical developmental stages according to structural (ego, id, superego) interplay, (within the frame of an interpersonal process that allows the subject to internalize and identify with external objects.) To see a person's character as an interpretive recollection of his past is to recognize it as a positive hermeneutic—to appreciate it as a source or resource of the self as creative-reflective voice. To regard character, then, as in the past, according to libidinal stages (i.e., oral, anal, phallic) or nosological type (hysterical, obsessional) is crudely to overlook the individual parole and to crush it back into a collective langue. Character is not an end product in stasis: it is a communicative resource of the self and, as Freud argues, its "traits" are *compelled to find expression* in the here and now.

Clinical hermeneutics

Let me simply suggest as a preliminary formulation three clinical means of developing a hermeneutics for the therapist. Ultimately, such a notational vocabulary must wait for refinements already in the process of development and, as Rosen argues, we have much to learn from the literary critic in the art of interpreting discourse: the finding, the discovery of the story contained within the subject's character. Here then are a few organized working notes for the clinician: a set of tools for hermeneutical discovery of the person's subjective interpretation of himself, known popularly as his character, and presented to us as a mimetic evocation of his repressed unconscious—a modern psychopathology of everyday life. As clinicians, then, we observe and note the following:

1. Created arrangement of self: the atmosphere of "self." We ask: how does he appear in terms of the in-self? We look, thus, at how he wears his clothes (vestimentary signs), and locates

himself in and uses space (spatial signs). We regard his recurrent body movements, typical body positions (i.e., gait, posture), and body signs (kinetic signs). We note if any self-sign signals specific affects and if they recur (i.e., a body gesture followed by a sigh, or a frown, or a "sag" effect.) Finally, as in all cases, we look for the convergence of these variables and ask: how are they collated into a mimesis—what is the person's interpretation of the in-self?)

2. Created arrangement of self and other: (the atmosphere of the dyad.) We ask: how does he appear in terms of the from-self? We look and ask: (a) How is he relating to the other and what is he telling to or asking of the other (i.e., tie-signs)? (b) How does he involve the other (induction signs) and what are the assumptions of the subject about the other's position in his world (script signs)? (c) What feelings does he evoke in the other? Here the affective shifts in the other are sources of evidence (from reactive to countertransference signals).

3. Created arrangement of discourse of self to others. We ask what his recurrent speech forms are (i.e., cliches, phrases), such as, "You know" (perhaps indicating symbiotic omnipotence), "I guess" (passivity). We note superego signs: i.e., "should," "must." Or id signs: "want," "need." We look for forms of speech accompanied by iconic signs (i.e., "I never should have" accompanied by a matronly frown) which may, if repeated and recurrent, indicate primitive identifications. Such forms of speech are a meta-language—a second tongue which speaks out from regular discourse because it recurs in a pattern of its own. Again, we ask as we stand outside of our data: what is recurrent? What is being re-collected? What about this person's characterological speech is a mimetic reminiscence?

Certainly, this is too schematic and, as such, a distortion of the therapeutic finding of a patient's character as it is revealed to us in psychotherapy. So, I will illustrate a fraction of what I mean by providing two very brief clinical vignettes that focus solely on one aspect of the patient's ambience: his mimetic evocation of the repressed.

Case I

Mr. N., a thirty-two-year-old medical student, was referred to me after three months in a hospital for what was described as acute paranoia. When he entered my room for the first time I saw a good-looking, fashionably dressed youth, who moved toward his chair with a gait of expectant familiarity. He reached for the ashtray, lit up, slouched into comfort, spread his legs apart, rocked his feet on the heels of his cowboy boots and surveyed the space. His assumption felt to me as if I were the stranger here, and that he was perfectly at home, as if he had captured the clinical space rather than entered it. Yet he was remarkably friendly, trying to find us together on familiar terms. "What was my first name, call him G., did I know H., the fellow who referred him?" Then a few warnings: "be real not cold like the 'shrink' whom he saw. In hospital, did I always say little, how long would I be here?" And so on. To log all of his gestural cues would prove too exhaustive for this paper, but at this first interview I noted an emergent trend: apparent familiar gestures emptied out into space in spite of the object world, marked by warm and genuine smiles, and expectant glances, a curious dysynchrony of obliviousness and reaching toward. I felt divided.

On the one hand I found him charming and intriguing—he looked like Bob Dylan—and quite intelligent, yet I felt he was embodying the unexpected. So, I wasn't very comfortable with him and felt he was throwing himself out to me without our being together. I discovered that with others the mimesis was clearer: he had a tendency to disarm people by a charming familiarity, was a great flirt with women, and more than an occasional nuisance to the authorities. After therapy began, a clear mimetic pattern emerged; he would involve himself with a woman and act out against a male authority, to the point where he was in considerable danger of being expelled from school for being a "bad character." After the third month of treatment, he said he felt he was "wrestling inside with a demon" and as he said this he mimed ever so slightly a wrestling gesture. He had used the word *wrestle* recurrently and feeling that the word was a sign and that the mimesis signified something important I pointed out that it looked as if he were wrestling at that moment. He laughed but looked anxiously and expectantly at me as if I had discovered something forbidden. I mentioned that he seemed troubled by my remark, again he laughed, but said that "funnily enough" he used to wrestle a lot and, looking away from me, mumbled something about he and his mother wrestling. In the course of the next few sessions an oedipal drama (with complicated homosexual and paranoid trends) emerged where he used to wrestle with his mother on the floor in full view of the father, this lasting on and off from age six to fourteen. The wrestling "match" itself was a mime that juxtaposed sexual desire for an inviting other with defiant fear of a disapproving and potentially retaliative other. As we explored his recollections of this drama the props fell into place with his character traits. In the presence of a male he had to almost sprawl and expose his sexuality, and try to exact from the male-other a tacit approval that this behavior was acceptable. Even so, his apparent emptying out of his desire left him expecting disaster. In his work life his most precarious moments were those when a teacher disapproved of his treatment of a female patient, prompting the youth to challenge the knowledge and authority of his mentor. In the therapy, by interpreting at the oedipal level we were able to translate his character traits back into memory so that as he became aware of his authorship of this mimetic script, he in due course understood the drama he re-created and experienced a great relief when he stopped forcing "this scene" as he called it, upon himself and others. It is my feeling that the success of the bringing into awareness his authorship of his character and what he was telling us depended on my appreciating his characterological cues. Where his traits of exhibited desire, flamboyant and defiant seduction, expectancy and provocation were the signifiers, the signified was the repressed oedipal struggle. To most people his behavior was simply "out of place" or incomprehensible, but I took his gestural language seriously, to signify a memory through mimetic reproduction, and I waited with him to provide the translation. To my mind, most clinicians do what I did, but they have not appreciated, it seems to me, the rich theoretical backgrounds—provided now in semiology and communication theory—to their actual clinical experiences. While metapsychology will by its very nature continue to extrapolate *from* clinical experience toward abstraction, an appreciation for the language of the self—a micro psychology—will move always with the material of the sessions toward a meaning with the patient.

Case 2

Mr. Y., a twenty-four-year-old student, entered my office for the first interview bearing the vestimentary signs of the hip life: long hair, leather jacket covering a turtleneck sweater, wide-belt corduroy slacks, sandals. Yet he seemed burdened by something, as if the rather stooped body gait, slow motion hand and head movements, holding in of the air he breathed, belied his gay vestments. Was I seeing a "dude" depressed or a depressive trying to become a "dude," I asked myself? In the first interview I noticed a slight but present string of gestural structures which I thought might be a mimesis. He would clasp his hands together on his lap, take in air and hold it before letting it out slowly, part then unpart his hair, and reach into his pocket to produce a handkerchief which he would use to blow a nose which often—as I would see later—had precious little to contribute to the ritual. This mimesis collated several normally unrelated events: clasped hands, holding of breath, parting/unparting of hair, blowing of nose. The young man informed me that he was here because of impotence; he "couldn't get it up" as he said, and in the course of telling me his history he noted the lifelong debility and mental illness of his mother who died fifteen months before, roughly the same time Mr. Y. no longer found he could "get it up." During the subsequent months of therapy, the mimetic gestures continued, often in tandem with his recurrent cliché, "I can't get it up", and the dichotomy between his hip vestimentary cue system and his stooped and lifeless body expression. Then he appeared with a dream. In the dream he was kneeling beside his mother who was lying in bed (in fact, she was often in bed and it was his lot to provide for her) and he was unsure whether she was breathing. This changed to a feeling that she was, then to a wish that she was dead, that she should not get up, followed by a rush of guilt and remorse, a futile attempt to pray. Then as he blew his nose and cried to indicate the finality of his mother's death and his grieving response, he stated that he felt slightly phony, as though he didn't know whether to play the part of the bereaved son or to feel greatly relieved. In this dream and in the subsequent associations and recollections we were able to see how his character and specifically his mimetic evocation of the repressed as a lingual representation of his characteristics told us prior to the dream of his confused wishes and fears. Indeed, the mimesis seemed an uncanny replication or oracle of the dream to come: the clasping of the hands a gesture of failed prayer, the holding of breath, a reversal of mother's giving up the breath, the parting/unparting of hair a sign of his not knowing whether to play or not to play *the part* of the grieving son, the blowing into the hanky a sign of grief, even if that isn't what he felt. His symptom—impotence—seemed to be the missing presence in the mimesis, represented by the cliché, "I can't get it up." As he transformed the mimesis into memory, he was able to recall that immediately after his mother died he was terribly afraid that she would come back from the dead, and this fear left him feeling that he would never be himself again (i.e., never potent). Soon he reported a troubling fantasy that his erect penis reminded him of his dead mother and prompted him to state spontaneously: "You know I never could help my mother when she was alive, she just lay in bed all the time, and I think it's better that she is dead, better for her and all of us." He felt relief as he repeated several times, "I couldn't get her up, I couldn't help her to want to live, could I?" I tried, for a long time

I tried, but she just wouldn't get up." As he exclaimed how relieved he felt, his face registered the passing of a great burden in his life, he concluded: "But now I don't have to be weighed down anymore." He felt that he had failed to help his mother and his subsequent relief with her death had intruded itself into his psychic space as a motivated neglect of her that sponsored her death. Not being able to "get it up" represented a lingual displacement of the helplessness over getting mother up that had manifested itself in his heterosexual life, where to try to get it up really signified the enormity of his struggle to make mother's life worth living. He began to "fail" his girlfriend as he had "failed" mother and his impotence signified, in part, his previous struggle to give life to mother. In time, we discovered some of the pathogenic fusions of grief, guilt, dread, and potency, into his characterological position (condensed and represented in the mimetic evocation of the repressed) and we worked toward a liberation of his affect into language. He regained his potency, was able to be with his girlfriend without experiencing intolerable anxiety, and continued with his studies.

By attending to his mimesis as an important signification of his character—what his lingual pointing toward an unconscious signified—we were able to appreciate how his self-state (the ambience of his being) reflected a complicated interpretation of himself *vis à vis* mother. I don't wish to overstate the bearing of this recognition on the therapy, for truly such epiphanies in therapy can develop only after the necessarily lengthy time it takes for the therapist to value his interpretation of the patient's language of the self, and not only are many interpretations (given or not given) discarded but once the essence of the patient's character-ological statement is revealed the period of working through is only just begun. Practically speaking, I think the advantage of regarding the material produced by the patient as self-reflexive statement is that it facilitates the entry of a person's whole being into the therapy, where the "material" is the patient and not a comfortable dissociated matrix of the stuff of the unconscious. The patient's "material" is not an intrapsychic "happening," a pure culture of wish met by defense but is this person's interpretation of himself which he has translated into the very essence of his being.

Summary

In summary, the repetition compulsion constitutes a re-collection through reproduction. The self recalls the subjective "past" unconsciously by re-presenting it. Such reproductions are structurally patterned and recurrent: they are typical of and specific to the subject who has lived the "past" that he reproduces. This "past" is embodied (given body) in his character, and the character trait—an enacted idiomatic expression of the self—is the subject's interpretive reading of this past. The person's traits constitute part of his personality: the synthesis by the ego of the past in terms of the present—emblematic in stasis, kinetic in operation. A person's character is not, then, simply the sum of its parts or the product of negotiated survival of libidinal stages. It is the subject's interpretation of his past—a re-collection of experiences (extra- and intra-psychic) and relations as transformed by the subject, bearing the characterological signature of his experiential hermeneutic.

References

Abraham. K. (1911). Giovanni Segantini: A psycho-analytical study. In: *Clinical Papers and Essays on Psychoanalysis*, 210–261. London: Hogarth.

Barthes, R. (1964). Elements of semiology. In: *Writing Degree Zero + Elements of Semiology*, 9–11. Boston: Beacon.

Berne, E. (1961). *Transactional Analysis in Psychotherapy*. New York: Evergreen.

Bibring, E. (1943). The conception of the repetition compulsion. *Psychoanalytic Quarterly, 12*: 486–519.

Birdwhistell, R. (1956). Kinesic analysis of filmed behavior of children. In: *Kinesics and Context*, 47–50. London: Allen Lane.

Bychowski, G. (1956). The release of internal images. *International Journal of Psycho-Analysis, 37*: 331–338.

Bychowski, G. (1959). Some aspects of masochistic involvement. *Journal of the American Psychoanalytic Association, 7*: 248–273.

Bychowski, G. (1967). The archaic object and alienation. *International Journal of Psycho-Analysis, 48*: 384–393.

Ferenczi, S. (1915). The analysis of comparisons. In: *Further Contributions to the Theory and Technique of Psychoanalysis*, 397–407. London: Hogarth.

Freud, A. (1968). Acting out. *International Journal of Psycho-Analysis, 49*: 165–170.

Freud, S. (1912). The dynamics of transference. In: *Standard Edition, 12*: 97–108.

Freud, S. (1914). Further recommendations on the technique of psychoanalysis: Recollection, repetition and working through. In: *Standard Edition, 12*: 123–144.

Freud, S. (1920). *Beyond the Pleasure Principle*. In: *Standard Edition, 18*: 7–64.

Fromm, E. (1947). *Man for Himself*. New York: Fawcett.

Giovacchini, P. (1967). Frustration and externalization. *Psychoanalytic Quarterly, 36*: 571–583.

Goffman, E. (1971). *Relations in Public*. New York: Basic Books.

Khan, M. (1966). Role of phobic and counterphobic mechanisms and separation anxiety in schizoid character formation. *International Journal of Psycho-Analysis, 17*: 306–313.

Khan, M. (1969). Role of the "collated internal object" in perversion formations. *International Journal of Psycho-Analysis, 50*: 555–565.

Laing, R. D. (1969). *The Politics of the Family*. New York: Vintage.

Lichtenstein, H. (1961). Identity and sexuality. *Journal of the American Psychoanalytic Association, 9*: 179–260.

Loewald, H. (1971). Some considerations on repetition and repetition compulsion. *International Journal of Psycho-Analysis, 52*: 59–66.

Murphy, W. F. (1965). *The Tactics of Psychotherapy*. New York: International Universities Press.

Poole, R. (1972). *Toward Deep Subjectivity*. New York: Harper.

Reich, W. (1933). *Character Analysis*. New York: Noonday.

Rosen, V. (1961). The relevance of "style" to certain aspects of defense and the synthetic function of the ego. *International Journal of Psycho-Analysis, 42*: 447–457.

Rosen, V. (1969). Sign phenomena and their relationship to unconscious meaning. *International Journal of Psycho-Analysis, 50*: 197–207.

Saussure, F. D. (1916). *Course of General Linguistics*. London: Peter Owens.

The Notebooks

1974–1990

1974

[undated]
[untitled 1]

Let us imagine that all neuroses and psychoses are the self's way of speaking the unspeakable. The task of analysis is to provide an ambience in which the neurotic or characterological speech can be spoken to the analyst and understood. It is not so much [a question of] what are the epistemologies of each disorder but what does psychoanalytical treatment tell us about them? We must conclude that it tells us that all conflict is flight from the object and that analysis restores the structure of a relation so that the patient can engage in a dialogue with the object.

The style of the obsessive–compulsive, for example, is in the nature of a closed cognitive and active world. If obsessive–compulsive behaviour is memory, what is being recalled? It seems to me that obsessive–compulsive behaviour is a mimetic caricature of rigid mothering. It is caricatured self mothering which [may] recall [interpret] the mother's handling of the child.

How else can we account for the shifts in disorders if we don't take into account the paradigms which generate them? Insofar as we know that patterns of mothering vary historically, can't we assume that each disorder remembers the primary object relation? Indeed, why else does psychoanalysis go back to childhood when presented with conflict? Because it is understood by most to be functionally derivative of infancy.

The only problem is that the philosophical assumptions of this hypothesis remain unappreciated, to wit, all disorders speak the individual's past and they ultimately speak the subject's interpretation of the past and therefore are a form of remembering. The advantage of this to the person is to value his disorder as a *statement* not simply a dysfunction. This is the difference between the hermeneutic and functional traditions[1] of psychoanalysis.

A symptom is a way of thinking. Remembering is a way of thinking. Symptoms are some form of the subject's thinking about himself. Psychoanalysis is a way of two people thinking together about one person's thinking.

A patient brings a mood, thought, confusion, a blank—collages of himself—and the analyst provides the space. The therapeutic alliance is simply: we are thinking and working together. The transference and countertransference: we are feeling for each other together.

25/10/74
[untitled 2]

"A" connects the death of her father with menstruation. Bleeding announces the death of the girl. Perhaps this is a breakdown of a notion of the self. Bleeding also heralds the death of the girl's relation to her father. Does her melancholic retreat mirror her experience of his disappearance?

It's curious that psychoanalytic theory for all its focus on grief has no theory for joy. Joy would be manic denial of "x": love, a regressive reciprocal delusion with the object.

It is comparatively easy to be with the object[2] but what is difficult is to be in the moment between subject and object or to be without the split between subject and object that is the moment.

We try to serve up ourselves and our others into time, and, the futility of not finding an entrance through time's gates leaves us in despair.

We abuse the energy of the moment by diverting it from itself into another temporal dimension—the future—and thereby we lose its privacy and the solace it holds for us. If we rob the moment of itself we become time's fool, our being, its own mockery.

The moment brings us tenderness and nurturance. In the moment we breathe together, see, touch, wonder, sense, and we know no thing about it. Rescued from doing, the moment is the sacred space of being. We are hushed by its embrace into tranquillity and ever so briefly into eternity.

There is an illness within psychoanalysis and this illness is in the nature of a predisposition. The analyst is predisposed (at the mercy of prejudice) toward finding a certain kind of "other" in the person which is really a collage of the analyst's predisposition. Thus he looks for anxiety, grief, rage, and disturbed thoughts. This *is* the person he is looking for. It is tragically significant that psychoanalysis *does not* concern itself with joy or love or transcendence or the ontology of faith. Joy becomes manic defence, love is regression to reciprocal delusion, etc.

If the self flings itself against the woman/mother in rage, then we might be able to say that he wishes to kill her. Now, why? Why try to kill the object that created one? To kill is the opposite of to create—yet, curiously, if in one's omnipotence one can kill the object, then one can create it as well; or, so goes the logic of delusion. To kill the mother may simply be the dark side of the effort to create her, a phoenix wish, out of *our* ashes will be born a new creation. In this sense, is destruction the first step of creativity?

If depression is a way of self holding, then obsessive–compulsive may be a form of self maintenance. If anxiety prepares any self to be vigilant, then depression may console the self. How do these affects serve the self existentially, i.e. as self-in-the-world? Do they happen to the self or are they the self's way of doing something for itself? Too often, depression is seen as happening to the subject. Helplessness leads to self holding or existential slump.

12/11/74
[untitled 3]

It seems that classical psychoanalytical theory provides a more Sartrean framework, as we are responsible for our actions: they emerge from our own conflicts. The Winnicottian vision sees us mostly as victims of poor mothering. The mother is herself the victim of a culture (of men) that fails to comprehend the enormity of her task. She is the *worker* par excellence, the most oppressed and her oppression can lead to alienation from her child. (See Marx's concept of the worker's alienation from his object in the *Economic and Philosophical Manuscripts*.)

That is, there is inherent in the mother–child relation a great deal of pleasure (biological) for the mother which the father cannot experience and never will, but the mother's total abandonment by her mate (who may have to abandon her for work) leaves her bereft and necessarily inconsistent. This isn't new. But how does one salvage the mother for the patient? Particularly for the female patient?

In infant observation³ I see with "my mother" both devotion and derangement; that is, the child is both source of great pleasure and of [mental confusion]. He is almost an objective correlative of madness for the mother: waking in the night, in rage, in need of instant gratification and pre-genital pleasures. Must she deal with the infant as an objectified representation of a repressed—mad—part of herself: an object that gives and takes away? Further, she is abandoned by the father, as if he says, "not tend to the madness" (cf. Sylvia Plath).

Indeed, the male phantasy—perhaps like the female phantasy of the infant—is that it is bliss. So the mother expects bliss and finds instead an oscillation of bliss and madness. By madness I mean that if we had a patient who awakened in the night, who was preoccupied with wild thoughts etc. we would think of madness. So the infant is de-ranging. By being left with the infant the mother may be left with the feeling that she is mad rather than the situation being crazy. This comes from being alone with the infant.

Winnicottianism is often myopic. Klein allegorises madness. Classical analysis ignores it. We must speak of *it* (mother–child) as a *mad scene: everything is maximised*. The nudge comes with this. Does the father and the culture bear with the mother's dilemma or does it abandon her to it?

16/11/74
[untitled 4]

It is important to further the fact that the task of the mother is to contain inside herself the mad scene of the mother–infant relation. We must appreciate how she has to contain it (especially the rage, the exhaustion, the tedium) and how in the place of rage she must substitute dosage of firmness; in place of exhaustion her somatic presence; in place of tedium her inventiveness. Thus out of internal chaos she must provide things for the infant that do not come necessarily from the mother–infant relation, but from her own ego reserves. Again, this task is to hold the mad scene and in some ways we speak of the capacity of the mother to bear a psychotic-type experience. This is similar to my idea of the impact of the examination on the student.[4]

[18/11/74]
[untitled]

To what extent does melancholia prevent damage to the other by making the conflict an internal one? What are the object relational or psycho-sexual determinants? From the context of the mother–child paradigm, the child cannot fully express rage against the mother, so much rage is withheld. If it were outside, then the child could repair damage to the mother: i.e. "I am sorry." To what extent is melancholia a remembering of an object relation? To what extent is depression "held unacted rage" and mania "un-held acted rage?" Freud on melancholia:

> In yet other cases one feels justified in maintaining the belief that a loss of this kind has occurred, but one cannot see clearly what it is that has been lost, and it is all the more reasonable to suppose that the patient cannot consciously perceive what he has lost either. This, indeed, might be so even if the patient is aware of the loss which has given rise to his melancholia but only in the sense that he knows *whom* he has lost but not *what* he has lost in him.
> "Mourning and Melancholia", 1917 (SE14, 245)[5]

So, isn't this <u>what</u> exists unconsciously from the past? It is a past object, lost in the present object, hidden by the self.

The mother–infant relation is less a relation than it is a plenitude of psycho-affective-cognitive paradigms.

Freud:

> We see how in him one part of the ego sets itself over against the other, judges it critically, and, as it were, takes it as its object. (SE14, 247)

If the self splits, so that one part takes another for its object, then can't this be a compensatory relation, making up for loss of the primary object?

25/11/74
"Silence as protective shield"

Some patients who experience the other as invasive organise defences against invasion. It is a hardened paranoid strategy. In analysis, an interpretation—or even a clarification—is experienced as an invasion. In such cases, the patient needs the security of an unintruded upon space, a solitude of self, and the first therapeutic task is to help the patient set up this space. It means listening to the patient, though not interpreting. It means constant reassurance that the patient must first speak to himself, or know himself inside before sharing this self with the analyst.

The classical idea of resistance as something that must of necessity be overcome does not necessarily hold, as a resistance in this case is prerequisite to the forming of a psychic space in which the patient holds himself. The task of analysis at this point is in the setting up of the space. Also, all associations spoken by the patient though not interpreted must be carefully remembered by the analyst.

The analyst shows by example how he can hold and how his holding is not an unsharing (because of his silence) but a holding space toward eventual sharing. This presents unique problems for the clinician who must not do what is his custom. (I do interpret with "A". Yet they are not content interpretations but self state interpretations. I am after affect, the patient's self reflection, and awareness of personal tradition, or ontology.)

How does the self deal with its care? The area from which the ego decides?

This "core" is the psychic region of implanted paradigms: of self to self.

As an analyst I am aware of being invested with paradigm potential by virtue of the transference. I exist as a transferential (?) transformational object.[i] Therapeutic change necessitates that "I" be taken into the "core" as a paradigm and the preparation of the patient for this is essential. This does not lie in the plane of interpretation to the other, but as object for the other.

"A" receives my interpretations as if lost; that is, on her level she is unprepared for language, as language feels too far ahead (developmentally) of her psychic position.

What do I say to her?

1. I pare away non-care statements (i.e. trivia etc.) but do not suggest I am asking after anything.
2. When she associates I ask where she—and I use her first name—is. I do not ask her to tell me, but ask if she has heard from herself.
3. I have come to understand historicizing of the self in event terms is an invasion or losing of the self into the "they".[ii] I am convinced that this is a resistance induced by the therapeutic process and accounts for long periods of the patient's providing material, faithfully analysed by the analyst, "understood" by both, but not leading anywhere.
4. The core is hidden by virtue of splits and dissociations.

---

[i] First use of the term "transformational object".
[ii] I happen to be teaching Heidegger's *Being and Time* at Richmond College, London.

7

[undated]
"Gilgamesh"

Isn't it possible that insofar as Freud considered dreams a special form of thinking that Enkidu's dreams are a way of thinking about his future? The idea of dream as prophecy may contain a wisdom that as subjects can determine their future so too can they dream it. Seeing a dream strictly psychoanalytically subjects it to dissociation from its potential as referent to the future. Psychoanalytical interpretation of the dream too often removes it from its place as potential determinant of future time. Indeed, Gilgamesh takes Enkidu's dream very seriously and the dream is viewed then with probably more true regard than the dream of psychoanalysis. So in a sense there was extraordinary respect for the dream as a way of thinking.

[undated]
"Examination anxiety"[iii]

This anxiety partly signals the danger of imminent rage in the self and fear of the destructiveness of rage. The anxiety itself often materialises in omnipotent brooding or withdrawal which is really a reaction to the anxiety over rage: a way of removing oneself from the enraging object, in this case, the exam. The steps:

1. I am being challenged by the exam: in a rage over being challenged and anxious over the challenging material. Withdrawal into compensatory omnipotent control over the challenge. Struggle on anal level: material can be seen as faeces and the struggle is over giving up of faeces. Oral: the material is the good breast and the exam is the bad breast, or, the examiner is the bad mother. On the oedipal level, the material is the mother and the exam is the father.
2. How does this theory of anxiety specifically differ from the psychoanalytic theory of anxiety, if it does?
3. In this examination anxiety we do not see the anxiety per se, but the defences against the anxiety which is an attempt to control the rage which threatens to overwhelm the self. (In some ways the rage is projected onto the examiner who is then feared.)
4. Those students who fail an exam because of "misreading" the instructions really represent a subtle way of substituting their omnipotence for the exam. They are saying "I ask the questions of myself and I answer them."

Further, there are four types of exam failure.

1. The drop out.
2. Poetic dispersion.
3. Misunderstanding/misreading.
4. "Choking up".

[iii] These notes derive from working with a young adult who was a brilliant and gifted student who always failed his exams.

The student who is frozen or "chokes up" is a reversal of what he would like to do to the exam, namely to choke it. He turns the aggression against himself which is acknowledged in the expression "choked up".

4/12/74
"A"

She returns to her poetry class after dropping out for two weeks. The teacher, a warm woman, says that she was struck off but will allow her back. She shows concern. "A" says that each Monday night—the evening of poetry class—she had started on her trip to the class but couldn't make it. She has a fantasy that the teacher provides her with a private space with her own writing materials, in which to write poems. The teacher is in the background and unintrusive.

"A" has cancelled her trip to Austria with her mother, whom she imagined could not go without her. In fact her mother has decided to take a cousin with her and will go anyway. I say this is her mother's way of acknowledging her failures to "A" by providing her with her absence and showing her that she can go without her. (The mother had until this time been cripplingly dependent on "A".)

She had an attack of hysterical paralysis in the train station and has also gone blind for limited periods of time. Today she says that she got up in the morning and "could not see". This links in her associations to being with a close girl friend who is blind, and she says, "I feel that she is in a kind of dark rind." In the previous week she had the fantasy of jumping into the "dirty Thames" and diving down below the darkness to a "clear area" where there were "living things". I said it seemed she was going back inside the mother's body, past the barrier of bad feelings, and into a good place. I wonder to myself if this dark rind around her is some kind of protective shield.

[undated]
"American literature"

American writers speak the true self, while the country doesn't listen. Melville tries to identify with this American false self—the external explorer and conqueror—but fails and the true self breaks through.

18/12/74
"Character and speech"

I left out of my essay[6] that the move from character gesture to language begins in the paradigm of the infant–mother relation where the infant's gestures are spoken by the mother. Thus the paradigm of our becoming is always addressed to the "other" who after infancy will be absent. In character disorders we have often noted how the character disorder projects himself into the other or how the other experiences the character's illness. It seems that this represents the speech-style of the character disorder: to get the other to do the speaking (and often the feeling) for him.

So many schizoids attach themselves to florid hysterics (as with "B" and his girlfriend) who speak all their gestures. Inevitably such a marriage merely "bespeaks" the fixation point of the schizoid character whose space is intruded upon by an impinging object that aggressively speaks the schizoid before he can speak himself. Though this fills an emptiness he experiences inside himself, at the same time it confirms paranoid dread about being invaded. Hence the autistic withdrawal of the schizoid.

The essential point is that ontologically our character is spoken by the other (mother). This is why analysis is ideally suited for character disorders as it is the analyst at first speaking for [this aspect of] the person.

[undated]
"B: masculine and feminine"

He talks about sex and connects his withdrawal from his girlfriend with his fantasy that she has a penis. He talks of a feeling that he has a special intuitive knowledge of women. I interpret:

1. With his girlfriend he has given up a phallic-masculine identification and become a good little girl. This is part of his psychic compliance with a mother where he interpreted choice of being with mother or father as the choice between being a boy or a girl.
2. The anxiety is fear of castration. The result is regression to feminine identification where he adopts another's projected version of the masculine world.
3. His current anxiety is that after trips to his home a masculine identification was consolidated with his father and his withdrawal from his girlfriend (ucs. Mother) is an effort to develop the phallic self, in hiding. But this venture creates castration anxiety (from the mother) and the temptation is to regress to earlier levels for safety.
4. His psyche is split between a female and a male self that is further split between:
   a. Good male self, identified with his father and with phallic organisation.
   b. A bad male self which is a projection—creation of the mother—and which he experiences when in the feminine position.

[undated]
"Ahab"

What is absolutely essential is to keep in mind that Moby Dick is an invention, a projected object. The horrid irony of Ahab's effort to break through the "pasteboard mask" is that he is the object behind the mask! He is the originating subjectivity. Does Melville make this irony specific?

The five phantoms loosed in chapter 47 are the loosening of Ahab's internal objects: or the objectivization of internal selves. Rage permits the dissociations to be loosed though never integrated. Rage—especially in the search for the whale—is a loosening of or an exorcism of internal objects.[7] The whole point of the trip is to exorcise the phantoms and to put them into the whale.

1975

[22/1/75]
"Ego space and ego objects"

There is a need of any self to create in objects a memorial field and for the field to be a correlative of the subject's ego space. Is there an ego shield?

[23/1/75]
"C"[i]

His psychic world is divided between an autistic self and a self involved with an object (a damaging woman) where there is a fusion and a loss of ego sense. I say that he seems to have solved his fear of annihilation from mother by giving up his identity to his mother. "Yes, she ran everything." He says that when he thinks of the women of his life (who exist mainly as internal objects) that his own ego "melts away" into the confusing internal object. Autism seems to be the defence against this loss of identity.

[27/1/75]
"C"

He arrives and is silent for 15 minutes. He says, "I stifled myself last night." More long silence. Says, "I'm frustrated. I want a woman." Long silence. Reports a dream: "I am in bed sleeping with a vague sense that my parents are in the room and I am feeling stifled. I want to cry out to them,

---

[i] "C" begins three-times-weekly analysis. He is in his late twenties and arrives for analysis because he is unable to function: collapsed in his room, unable to go out into the streets, quite paralysed.

but I can't make words. I can't make words. Finally I can only make a grunting sound, hoping they will hear me. I walk into my parents' bedroom and mother is in the bed. My father comes towards me to help me. Both my mother and father are talking at the same time and the lights are on."

I say I think the silences of the session recapitulate the inability to speak in the dream: there are no words. The dream is about a child's imagination of parental intercourse and his feeling is that he is being stifled by it, wanting to speak out, but only able to make the sound he hears. He tells me that he slept in the same bedroom with his parents. He and his cousin would play a game called "bed sauce" in the morning, when they would tunnel under the parents' bedroom mattress and rip up the bed, jumping on the springs. "A person could get killed under the bed," he concludes. I say that as a child he seems to have interpreted parental intercourse as violent and was frightened they were destroying one another. The game was an effort to master this fear, yet it also acted it out.

[undated]
"D"

"D" is sent away by her mother at six months to live with a friend till she is five. She returns to live with mother until ten but then is sent away to live with a relative until she is fourteen. These details emerge only after patient has been in long silences which seem to me to express some fear of invasion of her privacy. A memory of sitting on the front porch at fourteen comes to mind and she says "I would like to have taken myself out", meaning that she would like to have gone out into the world on her own.

She talked about how overly compliant she was with her mother, but as she is an exceedingly composed person I ask her if she has not also been too reliant upon her "executive self", leaving her private self in states of need and rage etc. She alludes to having been in exile, in order to avoid the anxiety of compliance. As she has talked about her mother's madness, I say that her style of mothering herself—where she takes executive care of herself but fundamentally neglects the true self, as she is not animated and does not seek gratification—leads me to wonder if she has absorbed mother's style. Is this a form of remembering of her early life?

[undated]
"Transference"

Transference as "*Umwelt*" [surrounding world]: the way a person uses space and objects in that space. This plane of expression may be juxtaposed to the verbal plane. The structure of the *Umwelt* speaks the way a person was held by the mother. A patient's sprawl may express unholding; "A"'s jittery brittleness the nervous mother, "C"'s massivity the child as faeces, as he drops hunks of himself onto the floor.

[undated]
"Character and me-ness"

As an addendum to my paper on character[1] I can argue that the style of the self antedates the knowing of the self (consciousness) and that when a person falls in love with another it is because they are captivated by the me-being of the person: her style or what is revealed beneath the executant self.

We are first the object of the other and therefore we know ourselves as "you" or "Christopher" and our self has been verbally characterised thousands of times by the parents as well as conditioned by them. This self is prior to the "I"—the self as executor of its own being—and is later known to the "I" as "me" insofar as the "me" embodies the former self state of being the other's object. Semantically "me" is always an object once the self has found its subject as "I". The task of contemporary psychoanalysis is towards the "me", and in order to get there the analysand as "I" must take the "me" as object—a kind of narcissistic holding—in order that "me" can communicate to "I" and be further integrated with it.

In Winnicottian terms "I" corresponds to the false self—although it isn't—and "me" to the true self, whereas the truth of the self lies somewhere in the gap between the two!

"Me" always involves the other.

"I" does not.

Self reflection is "I" thinking of "me".

[March 1975]
"Character and body ego"

Character traits in stage one are the language of the body ego or the ego as body. The body ego is the "me", as it is formed through the mother's "stimulus cast". Thus the body always has a position as an object, of the other (i.e. the mother), and even of the self (i.e. "my body"). Often when people say—"me?"—they point to their body. "I" is more in the realm of conscious intentionality. The body-me is formed in a corporeal and psychical stimulus cast so that "me" is also a verbal object of the mother. Does the verbal and stimulus/physical "me" converge or are they separate? While being held and adequately cast is there a verbal *"anlagen"* to the sensory experience?

[undated]
[untitled]

It is one of the ironies of existence that you can only love the other after you have lost the other. With ego development the fusion with the other is lost, a necessary precondition for recognising the other's separateness, but nonetheless a losing of one's [fused] self.

[undated]
"The Castle"

In some ways Kafka's book can be seen as an attempt through fantasy—sometimes paranoid—to deny the emptiness of the castle. To ward off the vivid reality of a "discouraging environment". Such an environment would challenge one's sense of self unless he defined himself *negatively* so that he pushed against it and it against him. Others are united by the fact that they were all gazing at him and this raises the point of the castle being K's point of unification, like the mother is to the child. By looking to the mother the child is not integrated but feels integrated. Indeed without the integrating potential of the mother the child faces annihilation.

In this regressed village Kafka created the illusion of the castle to provide the villagers a pseudo sense of unity. The political metaphor: a state which gives its people a sense of identity but which fails in basic provision. I should like to call the castle the corporeal domain of madness in the village, rather like a sanatorium, for the ruins of the civilisation which feeds it.

[March 1975]
"A"

1. Imaginary reading of her: You expect people telepathically to hear you thinking "I need" or "I want". Then you experience their inaction as a failure, a rejection of you, and finally as an abandonment of you, whereupon you shift from feeling need to feeling hate. "I hate you." Then you globalise: i.e. "everyone has failed me, I hate them all." Finally, "life isn't worthy of me, I will kill myself."
2. "The existential set-up." In reality you give no one a continuous sense of your being. You don't share yourself with them. In fact, you confuse the object, derange it—a result of your then murderous feelings toward it—but suddenly you feel panic or permit a sudden expression of pseudo-need; you cry in their presence, but because they know nothing about you they cannot help. They don't know they are being set up by you to prove your point: i.e. "you see, when I really need someone, they fail me. I have tried, I have expressed myself, but they are too stupid, too uncaring to comprehend my needs. Life isn't worth living."
3. This schema is a delusion, it existentially enacts a distortion, with set 1 effecting set 2: hatred leading to a theatrical proof. Nonetheless the "I just get along at work. People don't care" bears the "they should care" in it when in fact people experience you as uptight, a shit, a nuisance, etc. etc.
4. She expresses rage over a fat woman sitting next to her on the bus, but follows this with an expression of fear that the bus will come, everyone will get on except her, and this leaves her terrified. I say that she feels murderous towards the fat lady, fears that if she expresses her murderousness the streets of London will be empty, as people will leave the city to get away from her.

[undated]
"Heidegger: being and character"

"That which remains *hidden* in an egregious sense, or which relapses and gets *covered up* again, or which shows itself only 'in disguise,' is not just this entity or that, but rather the *Being* of entities" (*Being and Time*, 59).[2]

1. This being is Poole's[ii] "originating subjectivity"[3] and can be linked to Winnicott's "true self".
2. It is also the "me" of the self; the "I" is any motion (psychic) which acts on the assumption of itself: an "I", so that "I" may be declared.
3. Psychotherapy must concern itself with the *emergence* of being so that a person's being may be lived and so others may *know* the being of the person.
4. "A" shows herself for what she is not. Her behaviour reflects the absence of Dasein.
5. Character, then, is being—or true self, or "me"—but often reveals itself not as the thing-in-itself but through the language of character which stands in for the thing-in-itself, but which it is not; may indeed be the opposite of the thing-in-itself.
6. Character is not the language of the self, but the being behind the language, the signs only acting for it, or, in its place but not constituting it.
7. Am I talking about the motions of the ego? Ego is hidden, but so are id and superego. No. Ego acts in response to something; it creates signs from the being of the thing-in-itself (conflict or whatever).
8. "Being and the structure of Being lie beyond every entity and every possible character which an entity may possess. *Being is the transcendens pure and simple.* And the transcendence of Dasein's Being is distinctive in that it implies the possibility of the most radical *individuation*" (BT, 62). Amazing! In psychoanalysis we so often focus on appearance, though some do go for the being: i.e. heading for the true self; or, in classical analysis heading for root conflict.

[undated]
"Frustration, language (symbols) and the schizoid patient."

"L"'s patient, at age 14, has an affair with a man old enough to be her father, an affair that lasts until she is 31. It is a secret. I say to "L" that it seems that her patient keeps secrets because her identity lies in the space of a secret: *the structure* of the secret space holds the absence of identity. Yet at 14 she finds a need gratifying object, which suggests:

1. She does not daydream about pop stars in adolescence, that is, she does not experience frustration which necessitates symbolic expression and the gratification of need.

[ii] English philosopher Roger Poole.

2. Her actual gratification means that she has the thing-in-itself and having the object prevents a need to symbolise it.

3. "L" complains that she can't free associate, or claims to have no recall of her past. Actually she cannot free associate since the thing representation has not found a symbolic expression. Yet she "spits up" memories and provides occasional information. This is really "free dissociation",[4] the eruption of the unconscious into consciousness. In this patient there is a split between the id and the ego, such that the ego's representational function has been impaired and the id's needs are gratified unconsciously: the unexpressed need finding the unrepresented (actual) id object. An id object is an object not sought symbolically through ego processes. The ego's functions are actually unconscious and in the service of the id; supporting primarily the function of a split between the ego and the id. In "A"'s case, she cannot express, or, has no sense of the expression of internal states in symbolic ways. Only body feelings are stated (pain, ache, etc.). "B" also. Or vague affective remarks: I am sad, I am empty, I am hollow. There is a lack of context for the analyst, as if this person has no being-in-the-world.

An irony. This person *can* express in symbolic terms, but has no sense of this capacity. What does this mean? They can represent other people's self states.

It is simply that their id speaks itself, through unconscious ego processes, though it is not experienced as the self speaking.

Is it that there is no one who creates a stimulus barrier in the child's world; a failure of a mirror function that holds the child as it gives the child *back to himself*? The mirror holds the self while it gives the self back to itself. In these patients there is a different sense of "me". There is no sense of continuity of self. Everything is in the now. There is no sense of time, of a good future. There is no capacity for holding or frustration. Their "me" is often emptied out into the world in the form of projective mechanisms.

Giving persons "back" the "me" from its id projection is finding the "me" inside the self from which a sense of identity emerges.

Existential historicity: a person discovers their character and their personal history.

Mirror function. This person seeks holding environments—in others—in order to have the self mirrored back to itself. They can only find the self through the other. They are held while they are given back to themselves. Hence they use others for omnipotent needs, no gratitude to others for provision of mirrors.

A mirror holds a person's image while they have time and space in which to discover themselves.

They don't free associate as the ego gives up through splitting of contents of the id that are lost from the self.

In free association, the thoughts are held in a way that a person knows their potential use. They know it bears potential meaning and that it comes from the "me".

March 1975
"I and me"

Heidegger: "'Worldhood' is an ontological concept, and stands for the structure of one of the constitutive items of Being-in-the-world" (BT, 92).

If "I" (or Dasein) is experienced in terms of the Other,[5] then "I" is still an object even though grammatically it is subject.

It can be stated this way. Each "I" begins first as a "me". This is its essence; the self is constituted out of the "me" experience, out of being the other's object.

[21/4/75]
"B"

He searches for his cigarettes but does not complete the gesture, and then mutters to himself. I help him complete the gesture. [I said he seemed to be looking for something and then he went ahead and found his cigarettes.] This shows that he cannot actualise the needs of the true self. Mentation is in the way. He substitutes actuality with ego entertainment [his mutterings] as his true needs are not met as he doesn't actualise them due to internal inhibitions, but he finds a substitute in ego entertainment: looking at himself, mutterings, etc. etc.

I take up masturbation as space between actualisation and inhibition, in its use of the Imaginary and the Real. Actualisations are completed in the Imaginary.

Women are object fulfilments of id needs. He uses *Hustler* centrefolds (solely for the id).

He comments: "I keep getting in my way", which I pick up as the "I" that gets in the way of the "me", where me is the domain of need and desire, and where the motion is spontaneous, while the "I" is the executive organ whose action is calculated.

The "I" [here] seems to be the in-heritor of the mothering style: it sets the limits or outlines the scope of environmental facilitation of id need. (Once, the mother seen as auxiliary ego, as outside the child.) The "me" is the true self whose needs may or may not have been met. Health is the "I"'s labile capacity to represent and meet the needs of "me" or just to represent. Otherwise, frustration ensues and "me" is enraged—in rage—which is a secondary reaction to the failure of "I".

"I and me".

The "I" may make any statement about itself, but its being ("me") may totally contradict the "I". We may call "I"'s opposition to "me" deception, denial, reaction formation and so forth, but the distinction I/me should be held as the constitutive frame of the problem (rather than mechanisms of deception etc.) as ontologically this split (I/me) lies at the base of the problem.

"Me" discloses itself through mood. See *Being and Time*, pp. 174–175. Mood is the inexorable "presence" of the "me", primordial, a priori: before the "I". The schizoid lives primarily in the space of mood which has no language as it is prior to language. Mood is the "there" of self.

17

"A child's tone of voice"

A child's tone of voice may be altogether different from other tones he uses: at school, with friends, talking to the mother. We often say of X that he is speaking in baby language, that it is regressive. It is the child's way of holding onto the mother through tone of voice.

[29/4/75]
"Character"

Our being—with another's character—is primordial, in the domain of what psychoanalysts call the countertransference. Character is the language of any person's Dasein: his existential mark.

Being the object is being grounded in existence *first*; that is, before the necessary illusion of an "I". (There is no "I" without a "thou" and "they". The "me" is grounded on the primordial matrix of "thou" and "they".)

The being of a person's character speaks through mood, the parole of the "me"; or, via use, where "I" acts from the motion of the "me".

The existential characteristics of understanding are prior to those of cognition. In this sense, the unconscious is primordial understanding.

As we are trying to get a person to understand their unconscious we must do so as to give them their unconscious as primordial to them rather than as a dissociated text to be interpreted. This gives them back to their own Dasein.

[undated]
"Sulking"

The person, usually the child, who sulks loses original despair or vulnerability by discovering the use of their despair against their parent. Anger comes into the picture. Sulking becomes a strategy and the original despair is lost. It is a form of aggravated grief.

[undated]
"Depersonalisation and Heidegger's theory of anxiety"

For H depersonalisation would really be ontological anxiety, a way of seeing one's being and in-authenticity. It is a way of "not being at home" and the self may flee from this. As such, the psychoanalytical idea of depersonalisation is really, for H, a personalisation, in the sense that the self sees itself as-it-is; the facticity of the self (the observation of the self) prompting an ontological dread caused by a sudden wrenching out of the everyday. For H there are generative features to depersonalisation which are not appreciated in psychoanalysis which focuses exclusively on its dysfunctional meaning.

[23/6/75]
"The enigma"

"A"'s enigma of today about her father's death—which leaves her with her sister—is to see if they could get along. It leaves me with this:

Being the enigma places the other in an irresolvable double bind. On the one hand, being the riddle announces the subject's separation from the other. Not being understood creates query space, or interrogative space. Yet, as understanding permits separation (once understood, both can go on to other things), enigmas force fusion. It forces the other to think of the subject, hence the other is denied separation at the very moment it is feeling it.

The underlying anxiety is of being left; the other turning completely away from the subject.

[25/6/75]
"Reaction formation or identification?"

"P"'s false self bears generative and real character traits. But his character was born not of identification with positive character traits of the parents—or their introjects—but out of reaction to his impulses. That is, his need is reacted to by character traits of giving; murderous feelings toward his father by consistent rescuing of others; omnipotence by selflessness. These positive traits are real, but these traits though imbedded are still repressive (or reaction formation traits) against impulses that are still there. As such, these traits are rather like symptoms and it explains why such a "good person" can have such a sudden breakdown. Fundamentally they have a true self image that is horrid; "P" sees himself as a "black star" (dense, dangerous, giving off no light): this is his true self. This leaves him in his secret life not believing in his character traits or false self. (Actually his character should speak this dissociation and does.) Importantly, there are those people whose self is formed from identification with aspects of a parent which modify instincts and structures them. There are those whose self is not born of identification but only out of reaction to the instinct.

This may come from parents who are not existential models of the corrective statements they make to the child. Their description of the "good boy" is fiction; just words. They don't speak to a reality of their internal life. There is nothing for the child to identify with except to accept the dissociation between the parent's words and their true reality.

For "P" the parents were never really there to be identified with; only their words. Hence he used the superego prohibition to gain protection and control of impulses that threatened to disrupt the rigid family. But using the superego's words this way is not identification, it is a counterforce, or counter cathexis and the person remains aware of its not really being him.

The fear of himself, then, is a fear of his impulses. His overcontrol is an attempt to cope with his impulsive self.

[undated]
"On relations"

I said to "F" who is upset over not liking a woman at work—and with another woman who also dislikes her—why not accept your dislike of her? I focused on her unsuccessful attempts to reverse dislike, to be inauthentic with this woman.

I said, "The sad fact of modern life is that we often don't 'get along' with people, we 'survive' them."

I exclude, of course, friendships.

I spoke of this being a problem because of the fact that customs that had defined our roles in relation to the social other have dissolved leaving us to our true feelings about the other. Manners, defences, protocol, roles, protected the self against this modern problem.

[undated]
"Enigma 2"

The enigma contains its own unintegration, concealed behind its form. Being the mystery is bearing forth one's defiance of understanding. At the same time, the observing subject remains as a confused object within the other and the other carries the subject with it, denying separation.

All of this is a remembering of a primary relation, of child to mother where mother's actions were enigmas to the child, leaving the child with a confused image of the mother who was there as impenetrable yet whose impenetrability, her distance, her being the riddle (often speaking or holding ambivalently) left the subject wondering about them afterward; hence, no separation. The subject can only wonder in the presence of the enigma. The psychoanalyst must express his wonder as it is essential to his establishing himself as a witness to the enigma, thereby recreating or re-enacting the original position (of mother and child) and thus able to translate it.

[1/8/75]
"The enigmatic character"

It is important to differentiate this from the borderline, and, it is closer to the schizoid and narcissistic character. It is a subject's specific use of themselves wherein they indicate to the other an alive internal self and then withdraw it, thus frustrating the other. All of this is a memory—a mimetic representation—of this early failure with the mother. The mother is there, promises to contain the subject-child who, just as the child actualises the true self, is "let down", literally, by the mother.

It is important that while this is a memory it becomes a strategy for self and other. The drama of showing/withholding mimetically represents failed actualisation but also as the child was enraged over the mother's failure, so the subject learns how to do this to others.

Object relations become a theatre of the past.

I need to focus on the clinical development. As a clinician I was increasingly frustrated. These people are silent, yet on rare occasion suddenly reveal a true self that fantasizes. In one way they are punishing me as other: which installs an anorexia in the therapist. In another way, they have a genuine fear that if they actualise themselves (in fantasy) they would be "let down", a metaphor which carries a mime in it. With one patient it took two years, and only after I was hurt by her, before the sadistic defence gradually yielded toward her imagining my presence.

Include, now, enigma as distance and its denial. Not being able to forget the object, they are denied the competition of the cycle of the instinct linked to its partial actualisation into relationships which include reparation and sublimation, so that the object of the instinct (the mother) can be forgotten (as in Winnicott's use of an object). They are stuck with unactualized instincts and needs where actualisation leads to relating and playing so that the aggressive component (etc.) can be worked through.

[undated]
"Melville's ethics"

At a time when the other is sought outside, as a deity, an idea, or history, Melville's hero points toward the struggle to find other as the unconscious self. In a sense as man has destroyed culture (collective dream/play space) he then assumes the responsibility of it and comes to a point of wisdom: culture always reflected him; he created it, it came from him. The sacred, profane, shared, etc., all experienced as outside; Melville says we must experience an inside other.

Thus he has in *Mardi* and in *Moby Dick* a transitional metaphysical and psychical moment between other as outside (the whale) while Melville gently proves it to be inside the self. It is important to see this as Melville's ethic. Outside, there is neither solution nor absolution; nor is either ever possible. Insight, the seeing into the self, to witness and behold the other as inside is the shock of re-cognition that Melville asks of us. It is the venue of the psychoanalyst as well, but the psychoanalyst—after Freud's metapsychological works processed the other and ethically disowned it.

Free association, which was a way of access, against the resistance of man, became a means of disowning the other by processing it. A novelist like Melville searches inside himself, comes to the point of seeing and holds the fundamental fact of the internal other.

[27/09/75]
"Descartes"

Descartes proves he exists, as thought or thinking, but he doesn't know what he is as a result of his proof. He constitutes a dissociation of human sensibility.

By denuding himself of all assumptions, Descartes places himself in the tradition of what was to become existential thought, in the place of man for whom the question was existence itself.

Descartes decomposes himself (and his culture) and reassembles himself according to reason.

The Third Meditation reveals how Descartes takes an autistic position: he empties himself of culture and context. In Heidegger's sense, it is a falling into Dasein, almost pure being, totally depopulated of They.

By necessarily placing his world in doubt, which leads to the proof of his existence, Descartes has annihilated his environment, an attack or measure of such violence that it leaves him with a dissociated self; hence, his finding the schism between mind and body.

This extraordinary dissociation is what distinguishes Descartes from Montaigne.

[undated]
"Freud's *Studies on Hysteria*"[6]

Because Freud sees the hysterical attack as "hallucinating the same event" (SE2, 4) which precipitated it and because he sees that external events "determine the pathology of hysteria" the way we must define it is the illness whereby the person creates a theatre which presents the original trauma. Hence Hamlet is an hysteric. The precipitating event produces a phenomenon. In this sense the person is really just a medium of the translation (event to phenomenon); the person, himself, the conductor.

Freud also writes, "in other cases the connection is not so simple. It consists only in what might be called a 'symbolic' relation between the precipitating cause and the pathological phenomenon—a relationship such as healthy people form in dreams" (SE2, 5). So the person's *symbolic capacity* is what differentiates him from being simply a medium or conductor of experience to phenomenon. Thus the symbolic capacity complicates matters, makes man fuller, less like a conductor.

Freud also says that it is not the event, per se, which traumatises the person, but the fright the event may create. He says what therefore must be considered is the capacity in the person to be traumatised. Without knowing it, this "capacity for conversion" is really a reference to the health of the ego. Today there is more focus on the strength of the ego.

Freud says that it is not that the trauma continues to act as an agent provocateur but that the "psychical trauma ... acts like a foreign body" which "long after its entry must continue to be regarded as an agent that is still at work" (SE2, 6). This "memory" seems to function as an introject. Clearly this is what Freud means as there is hardly a better definition of an introject than this.

Freud saw the continued presence of memory due to the failure of the person, when the event occurred, to have "an energetic reaction" to it. He didn't blow off steam. Thus the hysteric is compliant to the event, and isn't this what we notice about hysterics, how compliant to events they are?

So insofar as hysterics suffer from reminiscences what they are also recalling is the memory and their compliance—even, we must say, their grand indifference—to the event. This is the hysterical style.

Freud says that the failure to react to a trauma may be due to the nature of the trauma, social circumstances that make a reaction impossible, or because it was a matter of things a person wished to forget and therefore was a repression. The first and second causes are "Winnicottian" as the subject must comply with external reality. It seems, really, that the defence must have been dissociation. In a way, though, Freud is really writing of two hysterias, one out of compliance with a forbidding external reality and the other out of repression against the subject's own wishes.

He argues that the basis of hysteria is the existence of hypnoid states. The ideas that "emerge in them are very intense but are cut off from associative communication with the rest of the content of consciousness" (SE2, 12). This is "*dispositional* hysteria" (12) whereas trauma producing splitting is "*psychically acquired* hysteria" (12–13).

What causes the hypnoid state? According to Freud and Breuer the ideas which are "cut off from associative connection" can form connections with other ideas which are also cut off forming "a highly organized rudiment of a second consciousness, a *condition seconde*" (SE2, 15). This is the hysterical theatre. But philosophically, what agent in the self does the connecting? In a Winnicottian sense does the hysteric internalise a play scene which at one time existed between the child and the parent, which was part parent and child, more a mixture of fantasy and reality, thereby confusing the analyst as to the mix of reality and fantasy in the hysteric's delusion?

Was this play, now internalised as a private theatre, an attempt to create a relationship which perhaps foundered because of the discrepancy between the hysteric's idealised image of the parent and the reality of the parent?

Hysteria: theatre in a hypnoid state, with the hysteric the indifferent director and the analyst the interested observer.

Obsessional: theatre is an assembly of irrational acts which distress the subject who feels compelled to carry them out. The obsessional is an actor without a script in an irrational play.

Psychotic: flight into theatre to deny the existence of reality.

[30/10/75]
"The dream"

There are two contradictory views of dreaming in Freud. One is that the dream disguises meaning by being fairly unintelligible, or intelligible but meaningless referentially. The other is that the dream unifies discordant thoughts and desires and brings them together and does so through creative combinations. In this sense the dream is not so much disguising as bringing together incompatibles.

Yet, nowhere in Freud do I find him pondering on the existential motive of the enigmatic dream. Such dreams, because they are so bizarre, are remembered by the person the following day. They are bizarre in order to be recalled. This is the private self's way of asking to be included in executive self functioning. So, in this new function of the dream, the dreamer is dreaming not simply to protect sleep, but in order to represent unforgettable images that will engage the self the following day.

This accounts, then, for the neglected activity of *remembering the dream*. Therein, the dream is puzzle to the self; the "work" of the dream has been considerable. It represents unconscious feelings and ideas, in protected form so that if the executive self wishes to, the "I" may encounter and interpret the dream. See *The Epic of Gilgamesh* for a vivid portrayal of how the dream is enigma to be presented to the executive self for consideration.

The analytic use of dreams pays tacit attention to the function of dreams, to protect privacy and yet offers its contents to the "I" if desired.

One of the critical functions of remembering and thinking about a dream is to be in touch with, or touched by, the private self and to have an ongoing tradition of integration of the night time self and the day time self. The dream functions as an integrative space between all that we appreciate and know about night and day.

The significance of "A"'s relating the "ornament dream" to me is that it integrated her with herself—though painful and even psychotic—and also brought me into her private region without the disclosure of the dream feeling like an invasion of herself. Dream interpreting is a mutual process where two people discover together the gift of the private self, so that the unconscious or private self is integrated at the same time into ego space and interpersonal space.

[10/12/75]
"On good interpretation as poetry"

It is the form of an interpretation that is most effective. We must know that our best interpretations are poetic in their structure and delivery, so that the form holds words in such a way as to *deeply* affect the patient. In the same way, poetry rather than prose gets to us in a deeper way.

1976

[untitled]

Out of the debris of our dying culture (early twentieth century) comes a new mythology and a new language. We see this early in Baudelaire who finds the symbolic inside the city; we discover it in Barthes (*Mythologies*) who creates a new mythology. It is godless. It is *ordinary*. As Barrett points out in *Irrational Man*, cubism is the ontologizing of the banal object, because out of the debris only objects are left.

The psychoanalytical experience is, in free association, the use of the ordinary (i.e. trivial language) to re-mythologize the person, to find his myth, his culture, *through* the debris. From the debris of his own words, which up till now he has found barren, a wasteland, he discovers meaning and then his own myth.

The analyst is the person, par excellence, who carries the person through the wasteland of the self, and who *holds*.

Where has the debris come from?

From an explosion in the 19th century of human value and belief. We are commodities, objects-to-ourselves, defined by use or function.

The death of culture. Debris. Playing with debris (Dadaism). Creating a new language.

The analytic process: death of the old self; debris and the sense of dislocation; playing with the debris; searching in anger, despair; through reflection, finding one's self.

Barrett says that before man is a being, he is a "being-in" (111): taking Heidegger's point about Being in the World. In modern man this Being in, or the essence of our being, has been lost. It can be re-found in psychoanalysis.

In Coleridge's "Dejection: An Ode" and in Marx's *Economic and Philosophical Manuscripts* we see man expressing his sense of loss of being-in the *actual world*. We have seen this earlier with Pascal, though in his situation it was as much the losing of a spiritual world: being in a world of spirit. Being-in spiritually (mythically) and Being-in actually (materially) have been severed. It is this loss which writes the "Wasteland" and founds existentialism.

Out of this comes man and world as debris, cut up in Dada and Joyce, and now a new myth of man emerges. What is the new man?

The silence of the patient comes after despair over the word. They have said, perhaps, a great deal, but begin to have a feeling of despair over the word. This despair sponsors a silence; it is silence in the face of the unthinkable; the absence in the core of a person over a truly spontaneous sense of being-in the world. Their speech has been a narrative account, a construction, often beautifully or bravely rendered.

The patient of today can speak only for so long. Speech is an effort. It is an attempt to hold off the void. (Pascal). The silence denotes emptiness and the absence of the other. The analyst must be absence coming eventually into presence through holding.

We focus on the mother as the cause, but in fact, she is all that is left of one who gives meaning, breathes life into the other, and so we focus on her. She can never make up for the void in the culture. Our search into this relation, solely, is a misdirected one.

Character and creation. Our being does have voice through character. To hear it is a task, painful, awful. It is the voice of our emptiness yet through the transference—the analytic paradigm—our character changes.

In *Moby Dick* the myth explodes (capitalism, Protestantism). We are left with Bartleby, mute among the debris—dead letters. *The Confidence-Man* remythologizes by manipulating the ordinary into the fantastic. He picks up debris and maps the fantastic.

After 1914 man learns, according to William Barrett that the solitude of being a self is irreducible regardless of how completely we seem to be part of a social milieu. Man is no longer contained in a social fabric. But with our patients the tragedy is that each must fashion a life out of a wasteland.

In the 1960s politics, group movements, the therapies, communes etc. were all attempts to fashion cultures. The Beatniks (Kerouac etc.) were the first.

It is silly to say "counter-culture" as there was no culture there in the first place.

Each of us carries within our own debris. It is our past: a past not held within a familial, social, and cultural container to be given recurrently back to us. We don't know our past. We only have images, memories, pictures etc. We bring this flotsam to the analyst who gathers the pieces; he gives form to our content—if we can trust him to do this—we find our past. This is the analyst as the <u>transformational object</u>: the one who gives form to our content and thereby trans-forms the content itself, by giving it meaning.

Out of the debris of our past emerges our own mythology. Why have I been so moved when on one bright day I witnessed from a 10,000 ft. peak of the Sierra Madre a tiny train thousands of feet below crossing the California desert? Why should this experience be so close to me, seem to hold me? It was a question, in fact, that I had never asked at the time. Its essence evaporated into the diversions of my life, though now and then I recovered it.

In analysis I found two things about myself. One was that, as my father had gone off to war when I was three months I did not see him until I was nearly two. I was overly eager not to see my mother disappear as well. At nursery school, it was my fate to stand up high on the steps of the slide—not to go down—in order to watch in the distance for the first sight of my mother who would come to collect me.

So being up high and searching for something vital and joyful was part of my personal idiom: the creation of my myth of significance and order.

The other mythical object was the train which has always filled me with sadness and, strangely, contentment at the same time. So it was in my analysis that I discovered that it was by train that I left my birthplace and my father and also it was to the train station that every day my grandfather took me to see the train go by. Perhaps he did it out of his own love of trains or perhaps it was because I indicated my desire to see trains and he, in kindness, facilitated this wish. What the myth of trains gave to me in analysis, with the understanding of the essence of the aesthetic experience on the mountain top, was how an experience visualised for me a deep myth: searching for recovery from my mother, longing to be re-united with my father. The experience of looking on the mountain top *was* me.

[24/1/76]
[untitled]

To take Freud and Winnicott, both say that depression is the mood of our civilisation. Why is it the common mood? We must go beyond psychodynamics and recognise (through Heidegger and Camus) man's ego ideal: to be immortal (Gilgamesh). We have dealt with this historically in several ways: 1) the Hellenic, which is to be struck by the finitude and to mark our time with knowledge of our world: to be here, in the real; 2) the Hebraic, to develop laws of metamorphosis from this world into the other, thus achieving a faith which attempts to transcend the depression and anxiety caused by the ego ideal of immortality. How do we see this dilemma in modern times?

With my patients there is a chronic sense of *not having time in which to do it all*. To do what? They do not know. They realize that this angst has meant living outside of life and that there has been a loss. They do not worry about being mortal, or particularly, about achieving knowledge. What they desire is to create a personal history within a spectrum of time that achieves the status of a personal myth for them. This comes, perhaps, from the capitalist-historical myth in America of the self-made person. Nonetheless, the sense that they do not have time to create themselves is their basic anxiety or that they are failing to do so or that someone has hindered them. They seem to have inherited the personal intrapsychic idiom, the "spirit" of progressive liberalism, that given motivation and intelligence and the right environment we can improve ourselves.

Perhaps *this* is one of the cultural transmissions given to the child from the mother through play: the toys (world) as progressive tool for the parent's aspirations for their child. Each child is the transformational myth of the parent and it leaves the child-person with an inherited sense of a myth of self renewal and creation.

New jobs, new beginnings, are like new sets of toys. The past is *broken*; it is debris.

If we have as part of our psyche the spirit of liberal-capitalism then we also have an inherited personal to cultural discontinuity. The self created legend of liberalism—the progressive fashioning of a new and better world—lies in ruins around us. The myth continues only in the individual attempts of each of us, but the disparity of our myth amidst ruins has, ipso facto, made us *suddenly not of this world*. Alienation, so to speak, is a sense of not being in the world.

If Pascal could not face the silence of the empty spaces, we cannot find the silence or the space amidst our cultural debris.

The semiology of our culture has become so abstract (the language of the city) that our intellectual and cognitive self is precocious by its very need to adapt.

Except for the delinquent, who refuses to abide by the signs and prefers to ruin or to live amongst the ruins. Our culture is no longer a dwelling place for man as integrated, but a socio-scientific laboratory with man as its subject.

Nature, or living with nature, cannot be viewed as a concrete aim. As metaphor, it meant a world in which man could feel an integrated participant. One aspect of the myth was of dwelling with the earth, to give place to the physical, and in the rites of spring and themes of renewal, a place for man's sensuality. All of this is now gone. It is there only in its remains, only after it has been fed through the computer of the ad-man who retransmits it as abstract sign.

[25/1/76]
"Free association"

Is this technique a destruction of narrative form, or, does it acknowledge the breakdown of narrative form and find the person through bits and pieces?

[26/1/76]
"Transformations"

The mother–child relation is an aesthetic, in the sense that the mother gives form to her infant's fantasy and affect. The analyst does the same with the patient.

The mother is thus a transformational object: the one who transforms the subject's subjectivity. To define: aesthetic, structure, transform.

[undated]
"Nouvelle Revue de Psychanalyse article"[i]

The dream object (self as) is a secret: a covenant. The self is the mother's object of transformation and the subject holds himself. The secret as fantastic.

1. Time. Self as incubus or cocoon. "Arrival" in future, future thought. Revelation.
2. Self as thing to other and by identification of self; hence watching of self. Receiving of self.

The mother dreams actually—she creates an ambience of the fantasies—where the self is constituted as a place (imaginary) in the mother's discourse. He does not know himself, he hears of himself through the mother.

Special problems in analysis can be the fact that analysis can structure the bearing of oneself without knowing from within. Analysis can become another narrative reverie. The problem is to reverse the patient's passivity and to stop them reporting selves as "stored object".

Self as shared secret.

The embodied secret.

Self as secret.

The patient feels that the risk of leaving the timeless dream-object-identity is to cause a catastrophic depression in the mother. There is a feeling not simply that the mother will die, but that the mother will die because she *lives* in her fantastic world. Concomitantly, by identification with the mother, there is a fear in the patient that he will die should he challenge this.

[undated]
"The external world"

"B"'s relation to it as the mother's knight errant, without aim. The external world is something one enters in order to accomplish something or get something for the mother *in order to return to her*. Thesis: world as transition to fulfilment of mother and self. Thus world success is not gratifying in the present tense, but material for a future in which the gratification is shared with the mother.

We are born as a thing or an object, but not as a self. The mother will give birth [to the self] at a later date.

[undated]
"Character as culture"

The idioms of the mother–child space are a culture: of gestures, feelings, sounds. Thus body language, affect, sounds (music) precede culture proper. Also the ways of handling the world (primitive defences) are the culture of the ego, as it is structured during this time.

---

[i] Notes assembled to prepare an essay for the *NRP*.

This subculture, domiciled in the unconscious, voices itself or utters itself in the person's character. Character is utterance. Character as a process may continue for a long time—as process, it is the self's integration of internal and external states into an existential stance—but its earliest formations find actualisation through the language of gesture, affect, early defences (the phenomenology of introjection, projection), and the structure of the ego.

1. Use Heidegger on existence as structure.
2. Illustrate how this culture *becomes* the culture of psychoanalysis as the transference is its utterance. The analytic space as it resembles the mother–child relation facilitates the person's speaking this culture. The transference *object relation* is composed of early projections, projective identifications, etc.
3. Elsewhere, note that groups and communities have a character—again speaking through preverbal signs: body, affect, mood, projection, introjection.

[3/03/76]
"The primary repressed unconscious"

I shall argue that Freud's primary repressed unconscious should be revised in terms of the mother–child relation. The primary repressed unconscious *is* the discourse of mother and child, which remains repressed and unconscious because it is not easily translatable into language proper. Derivatives—what Bion would call transformations—of the primary repressed can enter preconsciousness if the mother and child find articulations for the primary repressed unconscious.

Aspects of character utter the primary repressed unconscious, particularly in the subject's traits of self expression, and his use of objects (Winnicott). What often shows up in the transference, is, indeed, the primary repressed. That is why the transference space is its best potential space for speech as transference is enactment (not recollection) or re-enactment. The language of transference is in the subject's use (anxieties, desires, expectations, defences) of the analyst-object.

[8/3/76]
[untitled]

The child's signifiers are id needs but the signified of the need are responded to by the mother, so they are involved in a communication and an object relation. As the mother attends to the signifier through the signified, the baby's id finds expression through an ego (an unconscious).

[9/3/76]
"Character and the unconscious"

The unconscious is not a reservoir of energy. It is composed of the language of the mother and the child. It is a great deal instinct, but when the instincts are modified through recurrent behaviour patterns (see Escalona[ii]) and the baby is relieved, then he experiences a structuring experience that is functional but also carries a meaning in that each set utters something.

In "The unconscious" (SE14, 1915) Freud writes "the system *Ucs.* is at a very early moment overlaid by the *Pcs.* which has taken over access to consciousness and to motility" (187). This "overlaying" is really not apt, because the early dialogue of mother and child is not so much overlaid as transformed (Bion) into new terms. That is, new symbolic equations are found to speak older ones. The symptom can be transformed into a new speech.

Think of "B" who was on all fours in the garden, gets up, is giddy, and doesn't know what to do with a kettle (she had to come in as it was dark outside) telling herself to compose herself. She reports this as a *scene*; it is the theatre of her drives. Actually it is in her character, her way of mimetically representing something that feels ill because it is a communication that is not understood. I interpreted (transformed) her character into speech: "you are on all fours like a baby, playing in the garden. It becomes dark. You feel you must go in, yet you want more time to play. You make yourself angry and when you come into the house you are full of rage and feel like smashing the tea kettle (i.e. 'I don't want tea, I want to play outdoors!') breaking chairs, but you become the threatening then coaxing parent to yourself."

She was immensely relieved for many reasons, but primarily because what had been a symptom was translated into intelligible utterance. The relief came through the transformation, but not before I had regressed to the level of symbolic representation of the symptom. I was able to understand it (like mother) and to transform it. Thus I linked with her unconscious as other and brought her to herself.

Freud (1915): "On the one hand we find that derivatives of the *Ucs.* become conscious as substitutive formations and symptoms—generally, it is true, after having undergone great distortion as compared with the unconscious" (193).

So, the subject and the symptom are transformations of the unconscious.

Freud: "The content of the *Ucs.* may be compared with an aboriginal population in the mind" (195). The unconscious equals the discourse of the mother and the child: i.e. "the aboriginal population." Thus my use of the term "the primary culture" can be linked to Freud.

Freud says in *The Interpretation of Dreams* (SE5, 565–566) that the satisfaction of a need is originally often connected with a set of mental (mnemic) images previously the object of satisfaction or specific movements—gestures—which led to satisfaction. Lacan calls this the psychic motion of desire. But this is also the language of desire as the gesture which must be met by the gesture of the mother.

By implication, the capacity of the person to make use of the unconscious will depend on the level of transformational integration of the infant's language (primary discourse) into the new equation of secondary discourse. This is an equivalent to Winnicott's notion of good enough

---

[ii] Sybille Escalona, American psychoanalyst engaged in infant studies.

mothering where through this mutuality the mother facilitates the infant's need-fear discourse into symbolic discourse. Secondary discourse, then, feels meaningful as the transformation has brought results and also it means that the internal life of the infant is linked to a new discourse that can speak it.

But the primary discourse does not disappear. It becomes the subject's character. Character traits do communicate to people and perhaps this unconscious to unconscious communication is more effective, is deeper, than the secondary. Freud writes in 1915, in the paper on the unconscious: "It is a very remarkable thing that the *Ucs.* of one human being can react upon that of another, without passing through the *Cs.* This deserves closer investigation, especially with a view to finding out whether preconscious activity can be excluded as playing a part in it; but, descriptively speaking, the fact is incontestable" (194).

Why is it more effective? Because the differentiation between need and its symbolization is less marked so that a person responded to *on this level of primary discourse* is *held* by the other, like a mother holds a baby. We could call it an event within a symbiotic space, but actually this communicating is what constitutes deep empathy and intuition.

So, is there a need, then, to communicate on both levels? Perhaps. Goffman[iii] indicates in his studies of interaction rituals[1] that people respond to each other on this level. This level is primary discourse.

[undated]
"The hysterical theatre"

My patient experienced a genuine trauma intruding into the analytic space. She dealt with the trauma by trying to convert it into theatre, to deny its reality by declaring it to be a fiction. She then insisted that I accept it as a fiction. By this exploitation of the real into theatre the hysteric reverses her position from passivity (victim of trauma or impulses) to activity: creating a drama to obscure the trauma, perhaps creating others as victims. Rather as Hamlet creates a play to disguise, yet present, a trauma to himself, thus reversing his passivity (his delaying) by being active through making the other into a victim.

[14/3/76]
"Character"

We have regarded the ego as a structure, which it is, but it is also a hermeneutic, or, structure as signifier. The signified will be the differing character traits.

"Trans" [transformational object]

What is the mother to the child during the early weeks of life? She is transformational.

The question to ask is what is the mother, as an object to the baby? How does she experience her? Reconstruction in the transference suggests that she regards her as one who transforms

---

[iii] Erving Goffman, American sociologist.

both within external reality. This paradigm continues as the paradigm of the unconscious: where condensation and displacement are the psychic syntax of the two.

So what is the clinical use of this knowledge? The words of the psychoanalyst, the space as structure, the structure of interpretation (as poem) is what counts at this level. To listen, to hold, and to interpret, so as to give new form.

[16/3/76]
"Transformational object"

In adult analysis the patient becomes aware of the analyst's style of using words, forming sentences, of transforming her (the analyst's) and the patient's experience into language. This is the psychoanalytic aesthetic and each patient will appreciate this aesthetic, though not uncritically. Thus, I have found that with a given patient if I introduce a new word or phrase of some metaphorical colour he will note it, either as pleasing or displeasing. With all patients we are corrected as our words fail to give correct form to their experiences and they will give us another word. This symbolic reciprocity is again the psychoanalytic aesthetic.

[undated]
"Hysteria"

Does the hysteric have an autistic core, or a centre from which their theatre distracts? It is as if they are far removed from the core of their conflict—*la belle indifférence*. Their theatre becomes an extrapyschic culture of affect and object relating where they choose to live rather than within themselves.

Their theatre is their peculiarly vivid domain of fantastic object relating. Behind surfaces they feel are their fantasy connections to reality, and it is to the order of reality within the fantastical that they attend.

Theatre is play which demands witnesses who accept that play speaks to a truth beneath the convention of reality. See Hamlet's play.

But in the case of the unconscious theatre of the hysteric, she is attempting to divert from the trauma.

"B": the truth of trauma is only imagined. She tries to get me to be the audience to claim that the trauma is to be her own theatre. So is this pointing to the trauma? Obviously not. She is defending against the private experience of a trauma by gaining an audience. Why defend against the private experience? Lack of ego capacities?

The hysterical defence against privacy is against what?

Functionally, she cannot hold her self. The internal is *lived out* in public space. Because the outside world is seen as the only conceivable holding space. The failure is with the mother. So is the theatre a flight for coverage from the mother to the father and to others?

[undated]
"Pregnancy"

While pregnant the mother dreams about her own mother. Thus she and her baby are in utero; or, she is the baby. Pregnancy is transitional.

There is a period of grief as the mother, just before delivery, gives up her old self. Thus the child is born of the death of a mother's previous self. He or she will constitute an aspect of *the mother's* rebirth.

A mother is also being exiled by a culture which idealizes her role, denying the painful and isolated aspects of pregnancy. She is therefore placed on the mythic-Madonna level.

In the postpartum some mothers are depressed by the baby's lack of communicating. I want to say this is a period of stillness which confronts the mother after the death of her old self and the birth of the child. It is a curiously necessary reflective position; a period of awe and dread over the infant's enclosedness and unrelating. "How can I speak to you? Reach you? We are so silent together."

[25/3/76]
"The aesthetics of being"

1. Pregnancy
2. Mother and child
3. Formation (creations of) character
4. Semiology of character: language of self
5. Human aesthetics
6. Psychotherapy and aesthetics

I will focus on pregnancy and delivery and the past from the points of view of the discourse of myth. I will distinguish between child as myth and child as reality. The mythical child is the fantastic child composed during pregnancy and the mother gives birth to this myth. The child is seen as a transformation of the self. Death of old self. The *stillness* after birth is due to the sudden realisation of the child's reality and his unrelating as myth-object.

Some argue that good mothers give up idealised notions of themselves and get down to hard work; they practise at it. In fact, they give up the divine plane of myth for the real. But she will always handle or speak her unconscious needs and the very privacy of their relation. The idiom of their discourse reasserts the secret culture.

From myth to secret culture?

I will focus on the phenomenology of their discourse. *Meeting places* in their village: feeding, diaper changing, etc.

Then the experience of the infant and of the mother. Transformation of his needs (Bion). Her style. Being an object of her style. The maternal aesthetic and appreciation of it.

Myth --------------------- Culture ------------------------- Reality (History)

Of mother/child

Play

Roles and possibilities

Ch: 3. The formation of character. Internalisation. Play. Structure as signifier. Entry into the world. Triangular space. The space where both parents create transition. Rite de passage (second birth). Culture of the world.

Ch: 4. Semiology of character.

Character utters: myth, culture of the mother/child, history. These are its discourses.

Private theatre.

Theatre of being.

Autism of the theatre of being … no receiver/and … the absent mother.

[undated]
"Formation"

Move from the region of myth or tragedy (the mother/child) to the domain of the family (comic space). How will the hero fit inside the comic aesthetic? Comedy (family) is a true test of ego capacities. The individual (character) will be lost for a while in the madness of the moment.

[undated]
"Madness and the comic"

The comic space permits a psychosis. Identities are confused; sexualities are mingled. It is the nightmare, awakened from. Opposite of the analytic.

[undated]
"Comedy and the daydream"

The therapeutic sequence has the structure of a comedy as one person enters, reclines into dream state, experiences anxieties, dreads, desires, joy and emerges toward the end.

How is this so?

Are all therapists comic muses? Oberon?

Entry into the family is entry into the comic space as all children will grow out of the family. Family space is where the child and parents can cross identify actively and be lost and found again. It goes on all the time and assumes a pitch during adolescence.

[chapter]
Lévi-Strauss views kinship systems, its language as an avoidance of incest. To work from similar notions of a system working as a way of avoiding something I want to argue that the mother's creation of a discourse with her baby is to avoid death, either death somatically or psychically (autism). In the first place, she has thought of dying during childbirth. In the second, until the child is able to [be self sufficient], there is always a threat to their life.

But, most important, all babies are born autistic. They are not choosing to live in the human community. Language is used by the mother who translates the baby into the human village so he can survive in the human world. It is done to avoid autism (the non-being of the human). Thus, feeding becomes the first potentially non-human contact (animals feed) where the mother tries to create a food discourse. She utters to baby sounds of gratification (yum, mmmmmmm, or yes, that's right) or some typical verbal or preverbal sound schema that is inherited by the baby as part of his feeding.

So character will speak the varied discourses of this culture; indeed, each person's character bears the mark of their all coming from different countries (differing cultures of mother and child) speaking the voice of that culture.

To what extent can I compare the language of the mother child culture to the totemic or to *bricolage*? What are the Signifier/signified (S/s) relations and what order are they: i.e. totemic or caste?

They seem to revolve around need or desire and the body. When the mother names the baby or names his action how does she do it? Some are nicknames: "Nibbles", "Pooh", "Puff", "Hopper", "Chips", because she associates the baby's name to a body activity or to some characteristic of behaviour which another name captures.

"Chips" refers to Mr. Chips: i.e. to absent mindedness.

The mother's discourse, assigning at random names according to her associations or to the baby's activity corresponds in some ways to the baby' arbitrariness.

Does a person's character embody or personify in some way this form of thinking? If true, the mother captures some essence of the baby and assigns a name to it. Then the baby acts this sign out as an adult: feeling themselves to be a nibbler, a poo, and so forth.

Why?

Because as an internal structure it will be spoken. It is a memory. It is a primary state of being something to the other (see Lichtenstein[2]).

Also, other names may be "idiot" or phrases like "we don't understand you" in which case the child—as with "A"—becomes the enigma.

It must be seen as not victimisation, but that a mother may pick up some essence of her baby and name it or she may project some part of herself. So the baby–mother discourse will have essences of both. This may be rapport.

To what does each mother address herself; from what is her discourse constituted? If she responds to her baby's need, discourse will be of need and gratification. If she reacts against the baby's need out of disgust, or fear of cannibalisation, she will introduce the discourse of disgust and so forth. If she demands of a baby a schedule or whatever, she introduces the discourse of coldness and obsession where the baby is not her object. In each case—and I must list the others—the child will grow up in this culture and will speak (through character) a discourse derived from it. From this discourse we will be able to infer the mother's assumptions.

Although the baby may react against the discourse, we may eventually sort out what discourse he is defying.

[29/3/76]
"Comedy and the hysteric"

The hysteric places her distraction into comic space. That is, a complicated triangular situation, endowed with trauma, may be converted into the body but displaced into a mode or style of living that embraces the comic.

The comic mode is to deal with fantasy or trauma by regulating the real, itself, as ordered in the fantastic. Hence the hysteric lives in a fantastic domain. By investing the real with the comic she negotiates the difficulty of coping with *deep personal fantasy*, creating a surface level of comic existence.

It is comedy not tragedy because it is guided or ordered within the fantastic rather than the historical. All tragedy is grounded in history, in the irreversibility of the real. "B"'s symptoms are her comic place. She knows she will emerge from them, yet she refuses to look deeply into her self.

Her *belle indifférence* is a trivialisation of the true conflict; it may lead to the true conflict; it may lead to a dissipating trivialisation with her real life, as reality will always seem to her merely a theatre into which she acts out her dreams.

"B" takes a deep unconscious memory and "acts it out". She creates a theatre. This is her memory of it, but it is also the use of comic ordering to negotiate a trauma. I must focus on the self living inside the fantastic, the vividness of symptomatology, where most of her lives, whereas—so far as reality—she feels in a daze or clouded or not there.

Significantly, the therapist must know what it is like to be with the hysteric in her comic space. Do therapists function as Oberons? Our identities and perceptions will be radically and continually challenged.

We must permit them initially to make full fantastic use of us in the transference; only to be gradually brought into the real, while our function of containing reality must also be existent.

[undated]
"Sexuality, the comic, identity"

Does the hysteric come to a preconscious vision of sexuality (where the ego cannot process the id) except to externalise the conflict into a managed space, a comic space? It is placed in a space between the hysteric and the other, in such a way as there is a gap between the self (hysteric) and the other (mother, father, the analyst) which recreates the original trauma: the perception and/or phantasy of something which interrupts and forces a gap between the self and the other.

"B" sees the birth of her sister, which leaves a gap she fills with the theatre of her conflict. She involves us; becomes a riddle (an enigma) which unravels as we become involved in the answering of the riddle. Thus she involves us in the conflict, bridging the gap in the object relation. When we become involved in the conflict, in the transference and the countertransference, and through interpretation and symptomatic phenomenology, we enter the comic space. This means de-rangement (identity diffusion etc.) as it is her way of recalling ego incapacity to cope with unconscious phantasy and experience.

In the transference she will create the ritual idiom of her private theatre (symptoms, character style) because it has been her ego-self's way of holding. When we enter the theatre there will be a specific dread of yielding self holding to regressive dependence on the analyst, but it will come as we become involved in the comic space, bridging the gap. They need the ego capacities of the other (the parent or the analyst) to permit a yielding of their own pseudo-ego capacities, to regress into dependence, to experience the core trauma/phantasy/experience and the other's capacity to remain. This holding of a space where the self can enter, disintegrate in generative ways and re-integrate (from id diffusion to slow integration of ego capacities) is the magic of the comic space.

[undated]
"Aesthetics and psychoanalysis"

The Kleinian view of art as reparation to a damaged object is wrong as it doesn't understand the following.

The first human aesthetic is the baby's experience of being transformed by the mother. She is appreciated as one who provides structure symmetrical to his needs. As the infant experiences how he changes the mother, a sense of mutuality will develop.

This leaves the person looking for transformational objects.

Gratification in reality and sublimation mitigates the need for the transformational object.

The artist, however, continues to seek transformation, but narcissistically. She tries to create a form (painting, poem, score) which will hold and transform her id/ego needs and expressions. What she searches for is deep subjective rapport with her created object, a rapport that has the object transforming her. She may achieve such moments (normal narcissistic states of fusion) but always she will experience the failure of the object. Then she attacks the form, attacks, re-creates, attacks, re-creates. The depressive despair is our recognition of the unmagic of the mother (Klein's depressive position) but the depression mutates to resigned acceptance of the impossibility of the object, as it is the loss of the transformational experience; hence, attack on the object for betraying its promise to always be a form which continues to transform id/ego needs.

[undated]
"Aesthetics of community"

Each community of people (take London) will be a group functioning according to a structure which is idiomatic: its aesthetic. It will have its own history. It will have its own myths and legends. It will have its own locations for expression of rage, need, despair, community—so that each of these spots is not only what it is (functional) but what it means (semiology) to the people of the community. Each community will have its own sentient hierarchy: a matrix of authority built around usually strong characters who determine the fate of the community.

It is the task of the community consultant to analyse and appreciate the particular aesthetic of the community and how its aesthetic (symmetry of arrangements) holds it together and gives it meaning.

The DHSS or Local Authority social services do not correspond to community groups: obviously, they cannot.

The task of a community council is to analyse dead ends in the community and to bridge the gap between a DHSS, the Local Authority services, and the community.

I cannot take up, now, the larger and perhaps more significant problem of the break-up of community. But communities do break down, often by alteration of the buildings by architects etc., faster than the capacity of the community to assimilate, or, through the infusion of new populations who are not from the area.

One solution for coping with radical social change in a community—enabling it to absorb the new and maintain the old—is the play space, be it the playground for children or a shopping area, and so forth. Where there is an ambience which, of its own accord, permits mixing.

The other is the community festival which permits cross identifications so that the new may not be seen as an impingement but as an assimilation.

As communities undergo rapid social change, they need spaces to deal with the psychic stresses within the community, particularly playgrounds, parks, discos, libraries, where the violent denial of change can be eventually transmuted into aggressive encounter and play.

As for the other who comes into a community, leaving behind his old one, there may be a feeling of "lostness" and bewilderment. This very real response to rapid social change has a generative possibility; that is, the play space or festival permits and contains confusion—and can permit the other the bewilderment that he or she may feel until they sense the structures (community) putting on the festival.

It is the task of the community consultant to analyse the character of the community, to note future changes and traumatic effects, to facilitate the community's dealing with them, and through psychoanalysis and group theory both understand and plea for spaces which will absorb the shock and facilitate assimilation.

[5/4/76]
"Aesthetics and psychoanalysis"

I will focus on the rapport between the subject and the object. This recreates the first human aesthetic. It is the special rapport that differentiates artist from others. Naturally, such rapport cannot be maintained; each artist will become alienated from his object and therefore alienate himself. The other theories of aesthetics—i.e. reparation, mourning etc.—are really the different reactions of the person to the loss of rapport: the loss of the transformational object.

[6/4/76]
"Aesthetics"

In a poem, though the content of any two lines may be opposed, the rhyme (form) will unify them. In modern poetry it may be rhythm or patterning. This is a dialectic of the whole: but, the form contains the destruction of the content; it is the rhythm of creation which shall contain the themes of terror or depression, etc.

[21/4/76 St. Ives]
"The recurrent dream"

"A"'s letters are tracing the evolution of a dream, what we have thought of as a recurrent dream. The recurrent dream may chart transformations of the self. Each dream has its own culture and, curiously, its own *history*. So, even though dreams are timeless as the unconscious, the chronology of the dreaming person is its own history.

[undated]
"Hysteria"

The hysteric becomes an event. She entertains a comic position which is essentially to be an event for the other rather than to relate to the other. She presents herself and asks for witnesses. The witness is her frame, "in" which she is contained and according to which she can loosen herself. To the other she assigns discriminative functions which she may demand (as attentive listener) or feel persecuted by. She may feel manically triumphant or a paranoid victim.

She must be accepted, by the hysteric contract, as an event to be taken seriously and not as a serious event; so, she wants attentiveness, discrimination, but not critical judgement, as she is exposing in her theatre acutely private aspects of herself. The witness *will know this but* because of the hysteric's insistence on willing suspension of disbelief, she feels protected.

The hysteric can feel particularly bitter when her comedy enters history—then, she can be smitten with remorse and bitterness. The world has taken her at her word, has acted upon it, without seeing it as a characterological aside, a comic interlude, which escapes history (consequence) and permits the hysteric to dance before the world (re: a little girl before father; or, Feiffer's[iv] "A Dance to Spring!").

Without herself as a mad event which is to be indulged, the hysteric feels suicidally cut off from her own internal reality which she must see through the eyes of the other. Hence, her concern after her presentation for the description of others. Was I alright? How did I appear? What do you think?

Then, there is the feature of her speaking about herself, not as a person, but as an event. She creates herself as an occasion, as Mrs. Dalloway fashions her party.

The process: splitting apart, bringing together. Disintegrating reality and re-integrating it in her own spirit. Her blend of creativity.

[iv] Jules Feiffer, American cartoonist.

[1/5/76]
"Character as aesthetic"

Character is an aesthetic insofar as it is a form: the person's form of the self. Interpretative form of recollection embodied in style of self which I could see as an aesthetic. Character as form shows up in diagnostic assessment insofar as concepts (hysteric, borderline, obsession and compulsion) are derived from observation.

[9/5/76]
"Metaphysical psychology"

Is it the eventual affirmation of the negative? Is *Moby Dick* an affirmation of brotherhood, through the destruction of isolated fanaticisms? Ishmael lives to share a narrative with others, unifying men through discourse, while Ahab uses men to fulfil the fantastic demands of his private culture.

[undated]
"Hysteria"

Marcuse discusses desublimation and the contraction of libido. Because the tension between what is desired and permitted is dissolved he argues that the reality principle no longer demands considerable sacrifice. Thus, the disappointment of hysteria as frustration is not sufficiently there to force symbolisation.
    Other reasons for disappointment:

1. The emergence of adolescence which de-sublimates (de-symbolises) the hysteric. Immediate gratification.
2. The disappointment of the family as a space for the gathering and expression of symbols. Whatever father or uncle symbolised for Dora (desire, etc.) family members no longer symbolised, so that expression of desire emerges in or outside the family in "technological reality": in cars and other objects.

[undated]
"Psychopathic kinship system"

Culture today. The family as symbolisation of desire and obligation is shattered and the child is almost instantly "released" into culture, unmediated by the family.
    This culture, where technological reality predominates, institutes a system of "Happy Conscience", and becomes a matrix or kinship of anarchic desires which because of their unmediated history (in a family if the super ego is internalised it mediates) have reached a perversion: being is translated from desire to technology or gratification(s).
    While no one appears to themselves or the other as *desiring* anything, they live in a world of plenty and are vigilantly adept at stealing the wanted object.

[13/5/76]
"Instinct and desire"

Instinct is of the id, desire is the ego's experience and expression of the instinct. Instinct may achieve reality through impulse, but this is not desire. Desire is the responsibility of the self, but instinct may be felt by the subject as not self.

I saw a young and brilliant student for consultation. He had had two analyses for some time and he had developed a certain facility for candidly reporting what fantasies or feelings cropped up in him. He was a teletype machine for his intrapsychic processes. What puzzled me was that although he could report himself with ease, he seemed bereft of desire. Yet here he was reporting fantasy and impulse one after another, looking at me inquisitively, for some interpretation. At one point he said "I am having a fantasy that I want to grab psychotherapy with you, as if not having it means my being excluded." Yet when I asked *why* he wanted therapy he could only respond in a slightly contemptuous manner that his previous group therapy had ended and he had a year that was free—open for therapy he meant—before he returned to his home in another country. I asked what he would like from this year in therapy but he seemed confused by the question and said that he was at that point having an impulse, which took him by surprise, to demand treatment from me, even though he didn't know why. I said it seemed to me that he was telling me about impulsive events occurring in him without feeling the agent of the event. He wondered what I meant. I said, "as if you are approached by an urge within you which you permit to carry you along without owning it, sharing in the responsibility of the urge." He agreed and was quite surprised by this differentiation.

It seems to me that he was at a state of development where instinct had not been integrated into that part of his ego functioning that one might term self identification; the process in normal narcissistic development where the person identifies with their instincts, through reflection and self empathy (brought about by ego capacities of delay and differentiation) so that instincts, owned by the ego become desires.

I think it is wrong to regard desire as the representation of instinct, because this patient's impulses (urges) and fantasies expressed the derivatives of the instincts. They were, however, as fantasies and urges, split off from his ego functioning.

Desire is the instinct integrated into the ego, and, when assimilated with ego capacities of generative narcissism [it becomes] the necessary dialogue in the person between representatives of the id, ego, and superego owned by the self.

Instinct is representative of the id; desire is representative of the ego. Instinct will reach intrapsychic symbolisation; desire is the ego's symbolisation through the word.

Instinct -- impulse/urge
Desire -- wish

Impulse is a happening or an event felt as not me; wish is a symbolisation of instinct not felt as an event but as a wish. Impulse is a happening or an event felt as not me; wish is a symbolisation of instinct which is not felt as an event but as a wish.

The reporting of fantasies, or impulses *objectively*—to assist the analysis—may impede the development of desire, which assumes psychic ownership of the internal stimulus. Thus, interpretation at the level of impulse may preclude it from becoming a desire. This may [foster] a self state which is objective to its internal world but fails to develop a subjectivity. Subjectivity depends on the persons situating himself as the one who experiences desire.

Mood may be unconscious desire; or impulse (instinct) which is already being processed by the ego but is not yet a desire. However, it shares with desire the nature of being owned by the self.

Is the wish the activity of desire?

Does wish suggest a fantastic activity, an activity within fantasy whereas desire moves toward reality?

The impulse is impersonal to the subject (indeed, sometimes unwanted and therefore repressed) but the desire is personal.

How does the analyst help develop a person's subjectivity? That's the question! *The associative analysis increases self as object to itself.* How do we develop a person's intrasubjective discourse that can increase their subjectivity, which is a rapport with one's internal objects? What is this rapport?

The impersonality of an impulse. Does the patient report a fantasy in an impersonal way? That's not the question I want to ask. How does impulse become desire? And, how does desire facilitate ego richness? My most distinctive point is the difference between the impulse person, or the person who reports impulse and the person who desires. What does the absence of desire indicate? An unintegrated ego? No, maybe to desire something one must have a tradition of having impulses met and gratified by an object in such a way as to link the impulse with the object, so that desire anticipates gratification.

[17/5/76]
"Character, fate, myth"

My notion of character is really about a myth, a person's unconscious myth, that becomes his fate. The internal world is simply the frame of the myth and its grammar. Each myth will be different and each myth will take something from reality.

[undated]
"Fate and subjectivity"

"B" only reacts to her instincts. Sum of reactions. Fate, or the notion of self as an object, rather than self as a subject, which isn't fate. Fate is denial of subjectivity. "B"'s loss of her mother was her fate and everything since feels like fate. Fate denudes the subject of a sense of subjectivity.

[undated]
"Dream, reverie, comedy"

The hysteric's sense of theatre is a reflection, after the instinctual; it is an ego confusion. An impulse, fantasy or idea sets off a confusion of the ego where the hysteric's splitting is a trying out of voiced identities (or parts) in order to survive the anxiety. But the splitting also threatens the ontology of the self—a sense of continuous well being. There are depersonalised elements.

The hysteric dissociates her mad scenes from her sense of self. Hence her need to extract permissiveness and forgiveness from those around her. All must comply with the fact that she is theatre, or, it was theatre: hence it is dissociated from her reality and those who surround her.

[28/5/76]
"Aesthetics"

Aesthetic appreciation is prior to creativity. It is the earlier experience as it is the appreciation of being in the first human aesthetic.

[14/6/76]
"Freud"

The dynamic unconscious, the preconscious and the conscious are the aesthetics of "lost experience" of the self: into repression, into the preconscious, or even consciousness.

[undated]
"Integration, the analyst, comedy: on therapeutic aesthetics"

When the patient discovers that the analyst is the integrator then the patient can dissolve. So right away, we have the disintegration that is typical of comedy:
    Disintegration -------------------------- breaking apart
    Analysis -------------------------------- unifying
    The patient can disavow their own cognitive functioning.
    Comedy is the interplay of instinct (or desire) and identity (or self).
    The desire.
    The object (other of the desire).
    The composition of the self. (Desire and other?)
    Analysis has the promise of the flow of comedy.
    The free associative state is the comic mode. It facilitates the expression of desire (and fantasy) and also dissolves the "I" into its fantasies. Into the night forest of fantasy.

[undated]
"The theatrics of hysteria"

Is it the presentation of an image? Is the hysteric's space a *dream space* with the witness the integrative victim, the container?

The hysteric places dream into reality and becomes the object of her own dream.

In Act 5, Scene 1 of *A Midsummer Night's Dream* Theseus says of a poet (true also of the hysteric):

"The poet's eye, in a fine frenzy rolling,

Doth glance from heaven to earth, from earth to heaven,

And as imagination bodies forth

The forms of things unknown, the poet's pen

Turns them to shapes, and gives to airy nothing

A local habitation and a name."

The enactment of the hysteric's dream gives it a place in reality. The person who witnesses it is not related to even as a victim. He is a prop or frame of her theatre, he gives her dream a place in history. The fantastic is printed into the real where the hysteric exhibits herself as victim of desire.

Does this place her acting-out into the space of perversion? Probably not, as perversion is the opposite of repression.

The hysteric invests reality with the force of the dream. This is a link with comedy, where the dream often disrupts reality according to the disavowals of the unconscious rather than social discourse.

[22/6/76]
"Hysteria"

Is the hysteric, as Laing[v] said today, living out the logic of her internal life as an episode (or event) to *implicate* others in lieu of an incapacity to believe that others will willingly listen to her?

[1/7/76]
"Hysteria"

The hysteric relives mad scenes that she contains. In this sense, Freud was right about re-experiencing an event in symbolic form. He saw it in sexual terms, as a trauma, but also, I believe as due to a loss.

The hysteric contains family imagoes retained through vivid memories which she associates with each imago, and borrows from them aspects of their identity to actualise her own inner states of being. Thus she does not experience her own traumas or emotional life as such, but as something of an event, a personal happening, what I term her "theatre", because she is borrowing and collating past events and imagoes to speak for her. In this sense she is the unconscious

[v] This entry refers to a talk R. D. Laing gave at the Tavistock Clinic on 22nd June 1976.

45

comic muse who releases her "characters" who are in the form of an allegory as each role often represents an idea (which is the definition of allegory). Can we call the hysteric's madness, comic allegory?

I think we have reason to believe 1) that she contains memories which are not abstracted from experiences, but picture images of the past, almost eidetic (due to the fact that as she expresses the scene, she expresses it in her theatre) and 2) she cannot interpret her experience: and loses its essential meaning to her. She can only re-present it or identify with some feature of it.

Why does the hysteric implicate others? Unconsciously she is longing for omnipotence at the centre of mad scenes in order to control what, in fact, as a child she did not control. To manipulate others is to give her a pseudo-control over the "events" of her family. There are manic components. She assumes a pseudo-omnipotence over an event which replaces her subjectivity, but once the event is released she assumes also the position of an object within the event.

[undated]
"Watching television as mass conversion"

Where has hysteria gone? Toward a mass conversion where the enervated region is the brain. Watching television immobilises a part of the body which becomes dysfunctional in familial reality, according to its previous function. The family becomes mute and no one knows that life lived with the television is not really going on.

[undated]
"Hysteria and the analyst"

Analysis has a comic form to it and a formal comic evolution, an evolution according to the rules of comedy: first a sense of order, then disorder, and then a catastrophic challenge to the first sense of order and meaning, and finally a resolution.

As Donaldson[vi] maintains, one of the comic conventions is that beneath the surface of a respectable figure is a fallible or devious one.[3] The hysteric feels compelled to indicate this, flaunting her "other" and challenging others to do the same. This is "comic inversion".

[8/7/76]
"Politics of hysteria"

The hysteric threatens an inversion of an entire social pyramid: once the law of the father is proved to be a sexual transgression, the pyramid is overturned. Freud blames "lower order" working girls for seductions. Donaldson: "Levelling comedy is comedy of unmasking, comedy which reveals unexpected and embarrassing brotherhood in error" (7).

The hysteric levels the social order to achieve a community of ego weakness in the face of instinct.

[vi] A literary critic who wrote on comedy.

[undated]
"Hysteria and the secret"

Is the theatre of the hysteric the evolution of the secret (shared in puberty with other girls) into drama? Does the analyst become the other who shares the secret? The secret as complicity?

[undated]
"Unveiling and the vagina"

The vagina, like the penis, is symbolic of fantasy. It signifies that which evokes the sexual fantasy. The woman who lifts her skirt (unconsciously to show the vagina) is lifting the curtain onto the scene which evokes a fantasy (image) from the audience.

Specifically the vagina is a sign of what the other's fantasy will be about. This unveiling of a woman elicits the discourse of shared phantasy between man and woman, woman and woman, man and man, or man alone, or woman alone. To introduce the sexual or to point toward the curtain (veil of defence) is the hysteric's way of eliciting the imaginative in the other for her own purposes. She knows it to be socially incursive, almost as in the medieval sense of man's belief that apprehension must be mental: from or to God, or later, rational rather than imaginatively evoked by the genitals: the passions, the irrational, the mad.

The hysteric will often deal with this aversion by displacing the genital drama upwards into identifications where she characterises genital fantasies.

Donaldson (13) suggests (to me) why hysteria has disappeared. Comedy is only effective when the victim (i.e. a judge) is still held in high repute. Thus as long as Viennese society believed in patriarchy the hysteric's comic abuse of this remained usable. But as the father's authority dissolved, comic inversion ceased to be a counterpoint but became descriptive. It had lost its comic disruptiveness.

From that point, the hysteric seems to have taken herself for her own joke, as the position of women became far more respected, so that, ironically, the parody of self—hysterical theatrics—became almost a shrew comedy, challenging women.

[undated]
"Hysteria and image"

"B" creates an image, or a theatre, to distract and to control others. But if she believes that her mother doesn't internalise her, then she concludes that the only way she can put to mother aspects other than her own emotional and internal experience of living, is to create a theatre in front of her mother.

Charles Lamb said that we fear being infected by the representation of scenes of disorder. The hysterical theatre as infection. Laughter as infectious.

[14/7/76]
"Hysteria and intercourse"

"B" creates a theatre because she is convinced she isn't internalised by the other. Hence she constructs a vivid presentation of the self (she externalises her self) to match the fact that the other deals only with externalisations. It is a meeting within a projective space or theatre; an effort to overcome the despair of being one-dimensional to the other (to the narcissistic mother) who doesn't internalise the infant but who stereotypes it in one dimensional space. The hysteric theatre is an attempt to force the other into witnessing aspects of an internal life, as witnessing replaces mother's empathy which is lacking. Thus the hysteric seeks witnesses to madness rather than empathy.

[22/08/76]
"Hysteria and comedy"

Comedy as freedom. Dora is a comic satire on the bourgeois drama of Frau and Herr K and Freud uses her as the comic foil. The semiology of Dora is her pointing toward the duplicity of her father; her symptoms—like her father—are comic identifications, her way of pointing out her father.

[28/08/76]
"Attachment to mood"

"D"'s attachment is not to his mother, but to the mood of the family; a pathos of being. It is a fixation to an affective presence—a state of being—rather than to a psycho-sexual state or to an object. Not to an object because the objects are diffused into a mood: family gloom, etc.

Why to a mood rather than a person? Because the mother only offered a mood, not her person.

Why attachment, not identification?

What do parents offer of themselves?

[10/09/76]
"Character structure and subjectivity"

In analysis we attempt to analyse the structure of the self in order for the analysand to achieve subjectivity.

If there are splits in the ego, dissociations etc., then aspects of the self are disowned, decreasing not only self knowledge, but the sense of self.

There can be a depletion of self so that generative reflection, looking into and being with oneself, becomes impossible, as the self is split into parts and located in projected spaces.

[11/09/76]
"Theory of criticism"

The difference between theories of art as imitation or as human invention may find a point of convergence in the fact that the mother is imitated (as the aboriginal structure of nature) and also created (through the facility of illusion and her own ego function as auxiliary and transformer).

The mother is subjectively experienced *à la Bion* as a transformer—she is a transformational object—which like Krieger's[4] aesthetic object promises transformation. The transitional object takes aspects of the mother with the self, so the self becomes the agent of transformation.

[undated]
"Descartes"

When he says that the "I" needs no material thing nor the body, Descartes disavows the other and the body as other. In a way, the schizoid position is to regard the body as the disavowed other; the narcissistic is to embrace the body as the only other. Descartes describes his breakdown on p. 100.[5] This is a work about breakdown. He severs dependence on the other and repudiates his body. He wants certainty, but depending on mind, which raises and solves problems. His breakdown is the God of his delusion.

[undated]
"Toward Kant"

Hume's attack on cause–effect was an attack on the Newtonian assumption of "Universal Causality". Such a doctrine had made free will moot, as every human action is presumed to be completely determined by antecedent events. Kant's attack on Hume really seems to be in order to establish that there is *some* link of self to outside. In modern psychoanalysis it is as if environmentalism was said to have been solely responsible for everything, then this is attacked, and out of it comes Kantianism/Kleinianism.

In a way, Kant argues that every experience is an experience of a consciousness which organises and unifies experience into a whole.

When Hume poked fun at the existence of self—asking from what impressions could such an idea evolve?—Kant argues that if there were not this unification of experience, there could be no knowledge and no experience. He concludes that unification presupposes a principle of unification, and this is the ego. The self, argues Kant, is not to be found amidst the substance of experience but can be found transcendentally among the conditions that comprise experience. The ego, he concludes, authorises all our experiences; it is the agency that has experiences.

The self is a *condition* of experience, but as such a condition, it transcends possible experience. If it is to be considered an object, the self is a noumenal object. The empirical ego is the only ego that can be known. It is the transcendental ego as it appears to me; that is, as phenomenon. The transcendental ego = self-in-itself.

[04/11/76]
"On a character serving in a restaurant"

I am watching a young woman who is the waitress (wife) in an artificially lit Italian café that serves sandwiches to the English. The surroundings are without character, rather like the set of a television film, suggesting its impermanence. There is little here, except the come and go. The first time I ate here, she paid me no attention—flung the food on the table. Yet, tonight, I have discovered her use of herself as a character. She dissociates from the surroundings, defying the anomie by being a character. She throws her hands through her hair, punches out the orders, laughs or teases the locals—yet, she is totally self contained. I find this interesting as I am reminded of Marx's theory of alienation. She deals with it all by labouring her character: *it* becomes the surrounding of the self, and she looks no further.

1977

[17/01/77]
"The environment"

Kleinians do implicitly recognise the clinical nature of the environment when they devote themselves to matters of technique. They are fastidious. They feel, as clinicians, that they do matter. So, the environment does count for a great deal.

[24/01/77]
"Dreams"

The dream takes from the subject's experience of life and makes it into a private narrative. See Freud's Grotto dream. We could call this day residue but the point is that life is made into a narrative, where it allegorises the subject's experience of living and places the subject in the allegory. It is, then, the subject's most recurrent fiction of the self. A fictionalising of the self.

[25/01/77]
[untitled]

At one time when we believed in demons affecting us, in our lived experience, we were personifying the cosmic dreaming. We were, that is, the personified agents of the dreaming God. Trying to grasp our meaning through the exegesis of meaning inside the Other: we were allegorical representations. If we acted one way, it meant one thing to us, but another when valued as an agency of God.

[28/01/77]
[untitled]

Angus Fletcher[i][1] argues that, in a way, a dream in literature is a space where the internal world of a character may be actualised, whether known or not, to the author. Dreams are the language of the self. In literature it is also the language of the author's private self. Think of the construction of a dream. Who does the constructing? In literature we know who the narrator is. Do we in dreams? Are there points of view, styles, and recurrent imagery?

[28/01/77]
"New technique"

Where do we British Independents differ from other groups?

1. Silence. Not seen as a resistance. The wish to sleep is not a blocking out of analysis, but the opposite: a character recognition of trust in the analyst.
2. Non-interpreting.
3. Creation of an ambience.
4. Direct statements to the patient's private self.
5. Use of the dream as an avenue to providing a patient with curiosity about the self.
6. Interpretation of patient's free associations when the analyst feels through the patient's tone, or the associations or anything else, that the patient is being unreal to himself.
7. Use of countertransference, e.g.: "It is my feeling …" or "I can only share with you what I feel, as we have no evidence per se."
8. The facilitation and development of transference that is not interpreted until it is developed.
9. The use of vignettes of one's own life at critical moments of entrapment for a patient to free paranoid fears of isolation, to give him recognition of the analyst as a person, based on our recognition of the patient's relation to a one dimensional parent.

[undated]
"Dream"

The dream text is not a narrative. It is a drama. The secondary narrative emerges in telling it to someone.

Freud's Irma dream. He takes lines from the dream, like a literary critic decoding poetry. He calls the day of the dream the "dream-day" so the dream is the interpretation of the self during the day. It is the narrative of the Other (as unconscious). The Other's narrative of the experience of the whole self during the day. The poetry of the true self? The space of the true self? The narrative point of view of the true self?

---

[i] Literary critic with whom I studied at the University of Buffalo.

Freud ponders how "psychically indifferent experiences" (SE4, 170–177) in dreams take the place of "psychically significant ones" and this leads him to his theory of displacement. In fact, this is allegory, but allegory from the significant to the banal.

He comments on the dream condensing all sources which have stimulated it into the unity of the dream itself. This is the dream work, but it is also the narrative work. There is something about the work of the dream which is at the foundation of the work of creativity.

Freud's connection of dreams to literature, where he says that creative writing is due to the habit of dreaming and we may trace literature to the dreams of the night before. Freud interpreted the dreams in *Oedipus Rex* and claimed that the tale of Oedipus is an imaginative reaction to these two common dreams.

Latent contents are equal to "dream thoughts" (SE4, 277). If this is the case, then there is a dream thinker. The Other thinker, or, thinker as Other.

Confusion of dream with reality. Jones argues in *On the Nightmare* that people confessed to witchcraft because they had dreamt it and could not distinguish the dream from reality. Jean de Meung believed that such experiences as night flying and so forth are due to the vividness of certain dreams. There was considerable anxiety over erotic dreams and nightmares. So, the Other is sexual evil, as the case will be according to the repressions of the ego.

Abyssinian proverb: "When a woman sleeps alone, she sleeps with the devil."

If the dream in *Paradise Lost* proves that the erotic dream, or the dream of transgression, is to be assigned to Satan, it means that the dream is denied its place as a voice of the self. This would also be true of *The Epic of Gilgamesh* and most dreams up to the novel, where the dream is viewed as a subjective voice.

Desire is the place of the dream.

Transgression is the place of the dream.

Is the dream in literature a deconstructive act? It throws us into seeing the technique of the book, unless the allegory of the dream is consonant with that of the fiction.

A dream within literature may be like a dream within a dream: see Freud in the dream book on this. It is a dream within a fiction. A literary device.

In *Paradise Lost* the dream is the space of erotic transgression. The laws of the day are violated.

The early allegorical dream, where the dream allegorises political or cultural issues is not private. It is a literary device used to get past censors that are religious etc., and provides the self with space to think about eros or evil. The distinction to be made is between the dream as political allegory, or the politics of the dream, and the dream as authentically private, where it is enigmatic allegory.

Perhaps one way of telling is that in political or religiously constructed dreams, the dream is interpreted by someone in the work itself, whereas in the modern novel, it is left uninterpreted, as an open text to the reader.

Some argue that the dream, insofar as it symbolises eros and evil serves as the location of the repressed within the text. As if the dream in the text corresponded to the repudiated text. The text, itself, would be manifest content; the dream, the latent content.

One could say that the specific sexuality of the biblical accounts is made manifest in the dream. The work derives consciousness of its own sexuality, but places it in the dream sponsored by Satan.

In Freud's point, that dreams use a "method of representation by means of identification" (SE4, 321), we can distinguish dreams as allegories, but also ask that in dreams, true dreams, there will not be spelled out logical connections. A real dream would be a puzzle. A dream as a literary device would use conventional allegory and would be assumed to be public or shared and not private.

Freud (SE4, 323) believes all dreams are of the ego, so the ego is represented in the dream. To establish an authentic dream, is the person of the dreamer in the dream? If the dream is a political allegory and we cannot link the dreamer to the dream, then the dream is a disguise for a political, moral, and theological allegory. I would consider this to be an inauthentic dream. It shares with the dream only the use of the dream space, as a location for the representation of the censored, the taboo. It uses the sanction of the dream to make a political, moral, theological public position.

[undated]
"The dream of the text"

The text dreams insofar as it sponsors associations to itself. If we regard Freud's point that dreams are constructed through juxtaposition, we could say that the sequential movement of a text's imagery, thematic, and aesthetic, is its way of dreaming or being dreamed. This is different from saying a text is a dream, because a text is not. It bears the author's conscious intent and makes sense. But we can see it dream if we note the unconscious syntax of imagery, theme, and aesthetic.

Joyce and Faulkner, amongst others, have grasped this and share the textual space with their own conscious intentions and the text's dreaming.

[04/02/77]
"The dream"

How does the dreamer *use* the dream space? Given that it is a recognised psychic region, what use will be made of it? In literature and in life? It can be a simple space of wish and gratification (as in childhood). An allegory: i.e. this is a political, moral, theological, or a dense fragmented dream. We must ask 1) what is *left out* 2) what does the dream style (use of dream) say about the dreamer? *Gilgamesh* uses the dream to create a dialogue between human frailty and the search for immortality. Thus, we may ask how this dream space is being used.

In the dream there is a two-person relation. If we regard the unconscious as the Other, then the dream is the language of the Other, who speaks to us during the night. It is much more akin to the other self than to the notion of the unconscious.

[undated]
"Dream"

In the first place, the dream is a kind of literature. The Other scripts a hieroglyphic text and the conscious self re-reads or reviews the dream, as it occurs and later in the day recollects it. Thus the dream is a space where the Other's voice is heard through fiction, with the dreaming self a witness to a fiction about the self. As such, the dream in literature owes much to this special province of the self.

[undated]
"Dream"

Part of the function of an allegory, argues William Empson in *The Structure of Complex Words*, is to make the reader feel that two different areas of being correspond to one another and indeed that there is some intrinsic hidden reality to this.

The above can be said of ourselves. Only for the most part, by the 19th century do we become an enigma, and, as such, so does the dream. This may serve to distinguish what happens to the dream in literature. The original dream was an allegory made to match cosmic allegory. The 19th century was to match it with the self.

Allegory, even as a convention, unleashes unconscious conventions. It is the poetic license. Of course, the conscious conventions may be obvious, but the use of imagery, the symbolic, utilises the discourse of the unconscious.

Fletcher[2] writes that "as far as imagery is concerned then, the art of allegory will be the manipulation of a texture of 'ornaments' so as to engage the reader in an interpretive activity" (130). In that sense, the dream is there to engage the dreamer in an interpretive activity. This means that the unconscious—the Other—provokes the self into some form of reflection. In ancient times, as human meaning was determined by heroic deeds (what one did or did not do) then dreams were often interpreted in terms of action or fate. This space (prophecy) was the domain where the subject reflected upon his personal meaning.

[undated]
"The dream"

The dream in literature is an allegory. What cannot be evoked by the conscious self is placed in a dream space. In Sumerian literature, the omnipotence of predicting one's future is in the dream, as the subject would transgress the laws of his culture if he arrogated this task to the conscious self. Renaissance allegory places the erotic in this space.

For Freud the dream is an event all of itself, with its own laws which, if understood and applied, can make available to the interpreter its meaning. Freud's respect, however, is for the ingenious workings of the dream. In fact, he has discovered his own discovery of dreams and the unconscious is impressed with his own hermeneutic capacity. What is the dream to Freud, in the context of another question: what is the dream to an author? It is not so much what the dream contains, but how clever the dream work is that enlivens Freud's interest in the dream.

For Freud, the dream must contain desire. Each dream must be the fulfilment of a wish, even if such fulfilment means to fulfil the wish to dream. If we regard the dream as the locus of the taboo in one's life, I think we may argue that the absence of desire in Freud's life shows up in the dream. He wants one space to be free to wish.

Also, at times Freud maintains in his theory that the thinker/dreamer is always in control of the dream allegory. Freud's wish is to control; the ego is to be imperial.

[undated]
"Dream of the text"

The dream in literature, to be considered a genuine dream experience, must be a dream about the text itself. The experience of being that provides the material for the dream must come from the text and should actualise in dream-code some repressed or split off feature of the text.

[undated]
"The text dreaming"

The text would have to undergo an experience of its own dream. Like the dreamer, the text would have to be confused. It is not simply the author who has the dream as the dream elements are already in the text at hand. With Stubb's[ii] dream I must see what holds up to the dream and then what occurs after the dream.

The point is to establish the composition of the dream space, in literature or in life. It is an area of

1. Wonder or terror
2. Actualisation
3. Enigmatic meaning
4. The place where the thinker is the thought of himself, or, the thinker the participant in the thought

The dream in literature must be a region of wonder, separate from yet reflexive to the rest of the text. It must be the dream's text, as it must use and pit itself against the text, in order for us to consider it as a dream. A space in relation to the context of events in the fiction. Is it an allegory within an allegory?

What is the difference between a vision and a dream?

I am concerned with a text which has a dream, a moment when the continuity of its presence of mind is interrupted by a dissociation in its consciousness, in a space that I have called the dream space. The text can have its own dream if at this moment the cumulative experience of imagery making, of plot construction, of characterisation, breaks down into a self reflexive dream process.

[ii] In *Moby Dick*.

This is rather like a breakdown, but a breakdown of a very special kind. In such moments the author yields, under the demand of the text's unconscious logic, to the text's (and his) need to share a dream with each other. (So, the author shares a dream with his text!) We could say that this moment will be more available in the modern novel, where the author already has found an intimacy of rapport with the text, where he uses more the idioms of his own internal psychic structures than the conventions of literary creativity. Even so, few authors—as Poulet[iii] insists[3]—achieve a level of sincerity toward their own text. I should say, an intimacy where the text is the container of unintegrated subjectivity, and where the author's Other is not an alienated *moi*, but a subjective object.

To the person writing or dreaming, writing (or textualization) and dreaming are processes of thinking about being, not products. We must, as E. Said[iv] argues, reacquaint ourselves with writing as a process, not a finished product.

This can also happen because an author, like Melville, needs to dream within the text; though the experience of the dream will be in the textual space, will use the history of the text for the dream material, and, as such, will be the text's dream. If an author, like Melville, yields himself to the text, then we can say that the text will dream him, or dream about him.

[23/02/77]
"The dreaming text"

Perhaps every text dreams, in the sense that we can see dream elements (allegory, metonymy) but not see all that texts actualise in the dream.

The dream will make sense only in terms of its con-text, nowhere else, as in the author's mind for example. The author empties the imagery but the dream thinks about what is already placed in the text and thinks about the future of the text.

The author occupies the position of a mediating ego, between id and superego.

[28/02/77]
[untitled]

Every text contains a dream, but not every text actualises the dream into a reality. Only where the author gives over to the Other [does] the text [dream].

[undated]
"Character"

In a clinical hour we may choose to take up the discourse of the unconscious as conflict. This is the narrated text. However, character reveals itself as another level of signification by its handling

iii George Poulet, French philosopher and essayist.
iv Edward Said, literary critic, author of *Orientalism*.

of the narrative. Thus style, point of view, recurrency (the synchronicity of the text's themes which render them extra-textual) must be referred outside the text of free associations to the discourse of character.

Transference and countertransference are part of the discourse of character.

The discourse of character comments on the spoken text of free associations through mood, irony, point of view, transference, and may interrupt the text or create gaps in it.

Character is always the gap in the discourse of the subject. Like the way patients handle the poetic text, character handles the free associative text; harmonizing with the declared or contradictory or raising questions. What a person says does not reveal the character, it's how they say it. If we don't take it up at the character level our interpretation of the free association conflict will remain superficial. Winnicott's technique takes place at this level. Analysis can take forever if it takes place at the level of text of fantasy rather than the handling of character.

Hesitation. Silence. These are the discourse of character, as we then become aware of the narrator narrating.

The features of character:

1. Style (form, irony, paradox, sarcasm and ego defence).
2. Recurrence (of themes and of imagery).
3. Point of view. The person's perspective in relation to the reported material.
4. Mood.
5. Transference.
6. Countertransference. What is split off and placed in the other? And our reaction to the person's character.

[undated]
"Character: technique of analysis of"

The analyst must "interpret" character within its own terms. He must speak to the person in and through silence(s), body perceptions, and so forth, which is the holding function of the analyst, a feature of his management of the clinical situation. The analyst suspends interpretation of thematics and focuses instead on another level of reality.

The mother's discourse—of mood, action, soothing, behavioural cueing, idiom of fitting—is the origin of the silent discourse of character.

We wait in silence with a patient. When a patient is silent, to ask how they are feeling or where they are may be a mental impingement. The person will usually show how a thought arises in them through body movement. They may be moving toward a need for speech and the analyst may say "yes?" and help them along. This is not an impingement but a facilitation. What is discussed here belongs to the same phenomena that are described by Winnicott in "The capacity to be alone".

[undated]
"The dream in literature"

The dream in literature, if genuine, is somewhere between the text and the reader. Or before author and text and reader as a shared event, which invites interpretation and is unique. It is distinct from the other events of the text as it is the text's dream, to be shared with the reader. It is an offering of the text's way of thinking and it appeals to the discourse of the unconscious. As an event in literature, the dream is a gesture of recognition that literature has evolved from the dream. So, the dream in literature is a phylogenetic act; it honours the origins of the process that now contains it.

[03/03/77]
"Technique"

Winnicott's notion of the continuity of being for the infant is also the task of the analysis. What does the analyst do (or not do) to preserve continuity of being? Much emphasis must be placed on the analyst not doing, and just being-with the patient.

Khan's writings—"On symbiotic omnipotence"[4]—follows the path of cumulative trauma, and he examines how the patient affects the analyst in the countertransference, which he understands as the patient's re-experiencing the relation to the mother. There is a discourse of character, which speaks in the internal world of the other, no doubt because the patient does not believe in the empathy of the other but situates himself inside the other. The analyst holds while this happens.

The infant cannot register in consciousness or in fantasy what constitutes the cumulative trauma. If the trauma were due to the child's own projective fantasies then at least the trauma would be available to the person's thought processes and memory. But the experience is dissociated in the ego and also in the thought of the child partly because the mother traumatises but appears not to. Therefore, the trauma is registered in the silent discourse of character which is dissociated from fantasy or consciousness. The mother gives to the child her own system of meaning: her hermeneutic. The child may respond to this hermeneutic—it is the only hermeneutic he can respond to. The discourse of the actual trauma is disavowed from the very beginning. It finds no symbolic equation and, indeed, the equation finds a deceptive discourse.

[07/03/77]
"The dream"

The dream challenges our notion of reality. By using day residue it takes reality and turns it into fiction.

The dream in literature is a spot in time when the origin of the future process—the dream—is given its due and also as a direct extra-literary communication.

Is it a symbolic fusion of self, author, text: something in between, as if something pops out of the text, though it is part of the text; in a place in between the self and the text, or author and text.

The dreams of Gilgamesh are a symbolic discourse which is appreciated by its people, as their myths, legends, etc. use dream thinking. The dream, then, is part of the culture. By the time of [x] the dream is lost from us. It is dissociated. Thus it may once have felt like a special gift to one's potential understanding of the sacred (in myth and legend) as its discourse was similar to them. It integrated man with myth and legend as he bore elements of the mythic in himself at night.

Also, as people understood so little about how to control their natural environment (e.g. subject to the floods and droughts etc.) the logic of the world seemed animated by spirits.

The "Parliament of Fowls" [Chaucer] is about the dialogue between a text and a dream, or a text about a dream and a dream. Literature and the dream are fused.

In allegory, a person stands for moral or immoral qualities. In myth, the mythical God also stands for qualities. In myth, one usually stands for many, while in allegory the relation is one to one.

Mythical and allegorical personification represent two different modes of thinking and they come together in Chaucer. Chaucer begins with dream, then the dream yields to vision, then to a society of allegorical personifications. He creates a continuity from dream to social discourse. Contemporary literature may try to do the same, to link the dreaming self with the living self, who is radically removed from imagination.

Today we suffer the blank person, the subject without imaginative presence. The person who translates any phantasy into immediate active discharge. The dreaming self is emptied into a manic reality self: or a person who empties thought into reality-activity, giving the latter a fantastical logic, unknown to himself.

The novel as a culture's dream.

American fiction may be the culture dreaming about itself.

How does American fiction dream?

[13/03/77]
[untitled]

The desire of a dream is to provoke understanding. The dream veils itself into a riddle so that it will catch the imaginative fantasy of the dreamer. The dream desires to provoke free association.

We can say that psychoanalysis evolved around the dream. The hysteric with her dream-like veils (symptoms) lured the Odyssean Freud from his scientific travels into the domain of the dream—desire and deceit, defences etc.

The dream tantalises the dreamer.

All writers are tantalised by the veils of the imagination which they guide carefully into literary convention.

A dream in literature is genuine only if its associations are rooted in the text. It must be the text dreaming.

A dream in the text occurs as the text regresses to more archaic regressive organisations as an attempt to elicit the other's attention. The main property of the dream is its unique effort to change the terms of discourse in order to catch the dreamer.

Stubb's dream is dreaming about the central masochistic wish of *Moby Dick*: to be harmed by the object; to achieve intimacy through conflict.

Some writers, e.g. Kafka, find in the dream a feeling and a fantastical world which may correspond to their day-time world, so they use the dream as a place in which to live.

[12/03/77]
"The dream and Kleinian technique"

Klein treats the session as a narrative fiction. A fiction, like the manifest content of a dream, fictionalises the latent dream thought. The Kleinians regard the narrated session as a metonymic representation of the true thoughts which underlie it, and, of course, their interpretations are geared to translating from the text back to the thoughts.

At the centre of their theory is the transference, essentially a belief that all narratives are metonymic speeches about the analyst, and all objects in the narrative are taken as symbols of the analyst.

[undated]
"The dream and fiction"

Does all fiction take place as a form of dream work: the creation of the Other's text?

Manifest content = Veil

Latent content = Absence.

When we interpret a dream we are reaching out for what is absent, as the manifest content asserts an absence, not a presence.

The manifest content, as text, is a veil created by the dream work. The child creates the veil. The adult thought has attracted the child-impulse which then transforms the adult thought into child hallucination (i.e. child's play). The text is the veil of hallucinated desire; the child's *creation* of desire. Freud does not appreciate the aesthetic of the created text; he wants to break through the veil to the "true" thought that underlies it. He wants none of this child's play as it distorts the "truth." He does not care for invention. On the other hand, the dream theory is an invention, a genre of criticism: of dream fiction.

In fact, the enigma of the veil—like the artistic work—provokes the interpretive gaze. It is child's play as communication, the child enacting his desire through condensations, displacements, symbolisations. We can only find the desires by working with the play which is essential to the interpretation.

Freud is after the meaning of the thoughts, not after the aesthetics of the dream. So he ignores the reasons why certain images recur, or how the mother child relation creates a world for its subject and what the dreamer's experience is of aesthetic transformation. He takes the dream and breaks it down into pieces, asking for its source-meanings (deconstructs it) but does not have time for the world of the dream. Thus he does not put dreams next to one another to glance at the subject's dream world.

One of the most important things about the dream is being captive to an enigmatic discourse which continues to dwell with us. Indeed, the impact of its aesthetic may be far greater than the meaning we derive from an interpretation of it.

[09/04/77]
"Psycho-somatics"

One of the earliest links is to the child's fear that if he has a bad thought or does something wrong, then he will be physically punished.
Mind (thought)
Fear (of physical harm)
In the adult, cancer is the hand of God the Father.
It is the castration of the body.

[21/03/77]
"Fiction"

Culture as fiction. Not to say that what we experience is not real, but that we narrate reality and we use reality to construct a narrative of being: from the cultural, familiar and personal points of view.

[23/03/77]
"Dream experience"

The dream experience is a form of thought: as poetic construction, a dramatic experience. And the telling of the dream text is a narrative, with the interpretation a form of literary critical endeavour.

The associations within the dream, of image to image, are not based on the image but on the word that lies behind the image: i.e. "sand" may show up in the dream as a desert, but the word may also associate to sea, so the next frame of the dream may be of a beach. In each case the word is hidden behind the veil of the image. The word, itself, is a veil for the thought it contains.

For us, it is a text; for the dreamer it was an experience.

[01/04/77]
"The blank self's dread of experiencing fantasy"

The transformation of need or wish into thought is because fantasy leads to catastrophe. What catastrophe? It leads to a wish, then to no gratification, then the transfer of wish into violent thoughts (e.g. attacks on the mother or on the self) which is a catastrophe. He says he really just wants to sleep or be dead. I had said he wants to live in an area of no thought. Here sleep is rest from the need of the mother. Sleep for "E" as a baby was more gratifying than wakefulness. Is it why his narcissism (or self love) is like a somnambular state of being? Is he is trying to avoid the experience of desire and its thought as this will lead to catastrophe? He tries to create the illusion of self gratification.

A phobic dread of the internal world. He needs to be apparently oblivious to everything: to thoughts, to interpretations, not because of their content but because of the dread of the processes of thought and fantasy themselves.

Fantasizing is hallucinatory in the infant, sponsored by hunger. But if the infant is not gratified, the accumulation of this process leads to a dread of the experience of fantasy.

[01/04/77]
"Two types of narcissism"

Fantasy is more immediately gratifying than object relating. We are always disappointed in object relating or living as it seems to drag against the quickness of getting something through fantasy. "D" gets more from fantasies on an omnipotent level. He has experiences in order to store material for his fantasizing, though this is unconscious. The process of fantasizing is so gratifying that, as living involves delay, life is regarded as an obstruction.

"E" and "D" are opposite ends of the narcissistic spectrum. For "E", fantasy is dangerous as it leads to the experience of nothing which evokes memories on the unconscious level of frustration, while with "D" fantasy is exhilarating as the wish-completion is gratifying and not depressing, as it is with "E". "E" tries to live on a plane of reality as fantasizing is dangerous. "E"'s is the narcissism of someone who gratifies himself against the experience of a wish as he tries to distract himself from desire, while "D"'s narcissism is of someone who lives in the fantasy so as to distract himself from life. For "E", the semiology of the wish means nothing.

[15/04/77]
"Self and other"

"B" is captured in the image of the other; or herself as other—a fundamental alienation. Akin to the Renaissance notion of the soul's imprisonment in the body. This other does not seem to be the internalisation of an other, but the construction of a false self, fashioned out of a negative image: the opposite of the mother. This other served her as an infant, but has imprisoned her as an adult.

[18/04/77]
"Dream"

Even in the dream when the subject appears to be acting according to his own volition the subject is guided by the Other. In fact, in such moments the dreaming subject is both subject and object: subject of his own apparent desire and object of the unconscious Other who facilitates and directs the motion of events.

Indeed, in "X"'s killing of the cats dream he is made to perform actions as the ostensible subject that are deeply repellent to him. This forcing of the subject's commission of an action is one aspect of the Other's play on the self.

"X" is always the obvious victim of his subjectivity, never prepared for the gratifying (e.g. the lake dream) or frightening (killing the cats). His ego abandons him and doesn't make essential connections. But, isn't it the logic of dream construction—as a psychotic set-up—to leave the subject in rather dire subjective straits?

[undated]
"Perception"

"F" tells me that she does not hear the noises that a colleague of mine made upstairs, noting that it is because "F" has more of her own life and is less concerned with what goes on around her. This follows my bringing up the primal scene after she opens the session in anger with her boyfriend, whom she accuses of ogling the girls. I say she wants to own and to control his sexuality, as she had wished to control her father's sexuality, partly to prevent the birth of her sister. Her reporting a diminishment of fury over the noises upstairs has something to do with the fact that the dynamics behind perception, once interpreted, give her back perception for her own living.

[19/04/77]
"Aesthetics of reading"

Being held by the text. Cradled. Story-telling to the infant. The text cradles us and allows us to dream … "it". The state of reading: can we accept it? We are at the intersection of two discourses of the text: one secondary, the other the logic of image and metaphor, etc. We are in both states and when with the image we are in the dream space. We move in and out of the text. We are torn by the text. The reading subject is split by the two discourses of the text.

Is the reader de-centred? Is Norman Holland's[v] search for a unifying theme an effort to deny the splitting of the subject?[5] The content of the "identity theme" denies the split in the aesthetic of the reading experience. When does the text invite us to its play? Through the image alone? Probably through a quality of its aesthetic.

There must be two types of play. In the novel, I expect we go into daydream around certain events and themes within the text. Elsewhere we become dream with the text through its aesthetic. We are dreamed by the text. It is the image which invites us to a meeting. Think of Ishmael before the image of the word—"whale"—in the Spouter Inn. In some ways this is more of a space where the text actualises the logic of the dream than in Stubb's dream.

---

[v] Literary critic who focused on how readers transform texts according to their psychic history.

In the thematic, we take from the text. In the aesthetic, we are played upon by the text.

[26/04/77]
"Melville"

The core fantasy seems to be of a desire for an object to be plundered. In *Moby Dick* this was the whale, but this leads to annihilation. In "Bartleby" there is a desire for the experience to be provided by the other (the employer), with a dead ending in the brick wall prison. In "I and My Chimney" there is an attachment to the object as inanimate and under the fantasy control of the self.

What can we call this cluster? It is a private phantasy: an autistic phantasy that materialises within the fiction, but isn't made explicit as such. In "Bartleby" it is addressed to the other. In *Pierre* what do we make of the episode when the character crawls under the rock, to be born again? Is that another cluster? Is the fictional space a place where Melville can have this phantasy? An autistic voice?

[undated]
"Deep grammar, ego structure, character, paradigms"

Character is the utterance of ego structures which are the internalisation of set situations (paradigms) established in the infant mother relation. Such structures are like a deep grammatical structure (Chomsky): a set of rules that generate a grammar of being. All character utterances are memories, re-enactments of preverbal paradigms (when communicating took place in inter-relating) but are also dynamic events, as the structures themselves were rules of being evolved from experience. In a sense, character is language of the self speaking to the other.

Ego structure is an internalised set for the handling of id and superego needs, vis-à-vis an object.

In the earliest months, is the object (mother) felt to be the ego? Ego as other: an undifferentiated matrix of self and infant?

[undated]
"Setting"

The setting arouses expectation on the part of the subject in the dream. This emerges through the imagery of the setting and expectation is object relational.

The "I" of the subject in a novel—the "I" that we are induced to speak—is both the subject and the object of the book. In reality, it is the object of the author's "I"; to the "I". The originating subjectivity of authorship is Other: indeed, when we read through the "I" we are being led.

The ego convenes a meeting which takes place as a dream setting and [implicit to] this dream space is the notion of Other: always absent, a meta-object, but present in terms of its artistic creations.

[02/05/77]
"Melville"

Literary perversion.
Idiot event.
Burlesque.

Are there certain fantasies of the text that are not thoughts per se but ritual enactments of ego structures? Deep memories, paradigms, of the subject's experience of the other?

Is an allegorical personification a character? Insofar as this structure speaks structurally, it is.

The idiomatic arrangement of character structures is the voice of character: the interpretation of self.

Does character speak in fiction more uniquely as the other becomes a phantom (death of God) eliciting a mute yell from the subject—as the voice of character? All character is utterance to an absent other, and with the death of God, this absence provokes deep language cries.

In some characterisations—especially sagas—we must ask what is left out? The character may be noble, set against a surrounding world that is very violent. This is the split off voice of character, which in the 19th century is joined to the self. Character defends the self against the internal world.

How does character relate—i.e. to us, the objects around it? Such use, does it reveal idioms?

The absence of a specific character language, particularly the person who seems to be strong and induces our projective identifications, creates a dream space for us. Character is the container of the reading subject's pure self. We are Other.

[undated]
"Dream"

In normal thought when we often address ourself—"I think you should …"—the self is reflexive: both subject "I" and object "you". There is the interpretive "I" and the interpreted "you", something the dream does as well. When, however, the "you" is in the dream it is from the point of the object that it takes an illusion of being subject. It continues to be object, but does not know this. To this subject the "I" is the objective other who dreams him.

I am arguing that there are two sources of a dream expression. 1. is the voice of the dreamer's desire or day thoughts and 2. is the expression of the subject's ego memories—or character memories—which occur in the establishment of the dream setting: how the subject is handled by the dream.

There is a thought or a wish in the dream—as in life—and this is processed through the idiom of the subject's character (ego structures) in the dream as in life. The thought or desire will be transformed by basic ego structures (paradigmatic attitudes and defences) or handled by them. A defence is an aesthetic transformation of desire; it is also an aesthetic inheritance from object relations of attitudes: how the other will receive our desire, etc.

Defences are partly based on the subject's attitude or interpretation of the object's feeling toward the subject.

[03/05/77]
"Character in fiction"

Does character in fiction depend on what the hero deals with or transforms? Where are the events of being? Character has to do with the idiom of transformation: an interpretation of the self. Where is the locus of transformation in fiction: in the author, or, is it yielded over to character?

What is the relation of character to the author's use of character?

Character in fiction is a type of speech which may or may not occur in fiction. It is an interpretation of the self. If it is only a rhetorical device, it will only be interpreting the self as a rhetorical act. However, if the self experiences an internal world and relating, then character speech may occur as a reading of that self.

Rhetorical versus psychological character.

How do we experience the character in fiction? Or, how do others [other characters in a novel] experience the character in fiction? He is set up in others and in the reader. Is the text, the Other for the character? Does it reply to him or hold him?

Does character reflect the mental process of the text? Is character an interpretation of being inside the text? Where text is the psychical process, does character interpret this?

[undated]
"Character"

Character in a text expresses something. Invariably, it is the discourse of structure, of handling by a self, and is a different hermeneutic. A character may say "I love you" but the formality of his being may say "only at a safe distance do I love you." This speech is the discourse of character and is a subjective interpretation of the self rather than the professed themes uttered by the subject. Think of Heidegger's notion of the existence-structure of the self. Ishmael and Ahab transform the subject "I will hunt the whale" in different ways. Their style of handling is an interpretation of the self. It will speak fundamental paradigms of transformation of need, desire, fear etc., of instincts and relating to the object. When an author releases different characters into fiction he is releasing varying ego structures in himself, different selves, to personify aesthetics of being.

"The Aesthetics of Being: Character as Discourse on the Self".

We cannot decentre character from the crucial reality that there is an interpretive presence in character. The structures of character are idiomatic internalisations of self-object (and self as instinctual presence as object) relations. These are matters of choice. Ishmael and Ahab make choices derived from their different ego structures.

By releasing character the author uses different styles of transformation of desire and relating to the other.

In fiction, each character embodies a character memory.

Does any of it have to do with the experience of the text? In the sense that an author may release his internal world into the text, characters are different modes (ego structures) of handling and interpreting these themes. This handling (transformation) is the aesthetic of character.

Ego structure. The infant experiences the mother. On the basis of the infant's experience of the mother he makes choices about handling the mother.

In *Moby Dick* Melville puts one ill and one healthy ego structure alongside one another, in the juxtaposition of Ahab and Ishmael.

The mother's handling of her infant is an aesthetic and points the way to her notion of the baby's body and self. Her handling complements the baby's emergent ego (handling) functions. As the mother handles instinct and impulse, so the baby internalises her paradigms. This is the internalisation of an interpretation of the self.

[undated]
"Metaphor as secret"

Metaphor takes a word which applies to one thing and transfers it to another because it seems a natural transfer. This occurs in Melville's pyramid fantasies where clusters of metaphor sequester hidden meanings. The chimney has hidden spaces and is a metaphor of secret places. Such an act is at the root of fiction. Keeping the source a secret, yet communicating from it. Is it some deep ego structure that finds symbolic equations for itself?

[undated]
"The transformational object"

How are we handled and our needs, affects, object attitudes transformed by the other? Transference experience is memorial. It is an existential memory.

Character is a beseeching of the transformational object.

[undated]
"The self as transitional object"

The sense of self is a transitional object (of one's subjectivity) and the idea of self is in transitional [space]. "Y" feels that to marry "X" is to risk "being taken over, my self being invaded" and I think her dread is that the other will arouse her needs, desires, hopes, and sexual instincts and she will be overwhelmed by libido. Her sense of self is an adopted reaction formation to the libidinal self, a buffer, or false self.

The sense of self, or the identity of oneself, is diachronic and synchronic. It is the notion of one's aesthetic of being, over time (as history) and without time: what transcends it. It is the moment when the subject takes himself as his own known object which he sees as interpreting and regulating his being. Sense of self gives the subject a meta-object that stays with the person through all encounters and mediates the absence of the one (mother) who provided this sense of being. It is a mediating presence—an aesthetic notion that is body ego and other things. It is the sense of its presence rather than a cognitive knowing (or defining) of it that is crucial.

[10/05/77]
"Sensuality"

Is the subject's acceptance of the other's desire gratifying? It is a generative narcissism, an aliveness in the self, a readiness of the self to accept the language of desire (rather than to split it off, whether genital or not).

Sensuality is integration of all zones.

Sensuality is self comforting.

Sensual arousal or sensual experiences are different from sensuality which is a quality or an attitude of the self (or ego) toward itself.

Sensuality is generative narcissism.

[undated]
"The treatment alliance"

What is the unconscious alliance? The patient may be consciously obstructive but, in associations to interpretations, unconsciously at work with the analyst. Such an alliance may be due to a split off part of the self which does use people and situations.

[undated]
"Character and ego structure"

In my theory that the ego is constructed out of the internalised rules of being (with mother) I am stuck over the representation of early paradigms. Is it an aesthetic representation: the way the person handles the desires? Does this express the basic rule? Of course, it is not a literal repetition of it, but an attitude of the self derived from the basic rule. Is, then, repetition of behaviour an interpretation of the self?

Yes? Or, character expresses ego structures which is a grammar of being and relating. (Being constructed out of relating.) This language—expressed as idiomatic recurrency of the handling of desire—which is an aesthetic—is an interpretation of the self's history.

One of the signs of health in this situation is the degree of ego transformation, or success of such transformation into symbolic equations, an idea not far removed from Hartmann's[vi] theory of sublimation, except the latter is to do with the transmutation of instinct or libido and I am concerned with the transforming of deep ego structures.

[vi] Heinz Hartmann, an American ego psychologist.

We must look first to patterns of behaviour. Particularly to a pattern of behaviour around a function. Or in the transference. We must look at the formal properties of each ritual to gather its idiom, etc.

[undated]
"On not interpreting"

A patient like "X" needs an extended period of no interpreting. This is not supportive psycho-therapy as the analysis facilitates regression and does not patch up defences. It is a period when the analyst fits in with the patient's basic fault.

The hysteric communicated a multifaceted symbolic order. She meant everything and to reach her she had to be interpreted. The schizoid's symbolising is dormant and he is in paranoid withdrawal. Any discourse is compliant. Interpreting has to be suspended as it is felt to be an invasion of the self. The defences are never against the content of an interpretation, but against interpretation itself.

To be the dummy who interprets is an ideal way of managing the hysteric who abuses the blindness of the analyst. With the schizoid character there is no belief in the life of the object and an analyst who only interprets silently mirrors the depersonalised narrative of the schizoid. To be dummy is to fail the psychological requirements for cure of the patient, though sadly, some analysts prefer to remain faithful to analysis, even if it doesn't fit the patient.

The real technique with such patients is to know how to use one's character, one's animateness (play, humour) in order to give to the patient doses of internal life.

[17/05/77]
"Character and ego structure"

Identifications in Freud's theory—i.e. *Ego and Id*—is not identical to my notion of grammar. The grammar of the ego is based on earlier paradigms of being with the other. I think rules are determined from this, but not identifications.

Grammar does not predetermine psychic conflict; it is a way of "talking" about conflict, an aesthetic of handling all future relatings: i.e. oedipal, etc.

A grammar is an introjection. The grammar is internalised or the internalised is the grammar and generates a language. The language will be patterns revealed in speech. These patterns are forms that, when realised, will comment on the content though it does not form the content like the form of a poem structures the poetic content. Instead, form and content are concurrent; and this form is a pattern that reveals a paradigm, a rule, etc.:

Patterns:
Oedipal
Oral, anal
Idioms

How do I distinguish between an idiom—the content [figure] of the pattern—and pattern as structure?

Ego grammar = defence and object relation.

In some cases—borderline for example—the grammar is not formed; the paradigms are not set, and the object relations (as introjects) are still there.

I must distinguish between early grammar and internalisation of voices etc. Grammar must be early structure. It is the language which gives one the vocabulary for speaking about other situations, etc.

Paradigms are patterns that when taken in become rules. Rules of handling instincts, relations (internal and external), perception, cognition. In this way it is an aesthetic grammar, as it is a way of transforming all the above.

A rule is experience interpreted.

It is not an imprinting, so the rules can be based either on actual or projected (imaginary) experiences.

What are the paradigms of character handling? Are they handling contents or themes? It is one discourse commenting on another.

They are patterns of the self that express the self aesthetically. Self as an aesthetic is the discourse of character, generated by the grammar of the ego that is based on the internalisation of relations that are abstracted into basic rules.

So, in a way, the aesthetic of character is a transformation of ego grammar into ways of being. In this way the subject re-experiences his or her basic paradigms of being for that person, etc.

In analysis the grammar can be restructured by regression where, as Lacan puts it, the cure is when the patient can talk about himself to the analyst. Is that a new discourse?

What is the person speaking? Speaking the early paradigms of being, while there are thematic comments on new experiences, i.e. oedipal or latency, etc.

I will have to distinguish periods of the accuracy of this grammar. When is it over with?

How we see character in the analysis, particularly in transference situations:

Patterns of associating

Recurrency

Transference patterns

Tone, affect, rhythm, point of view

Patterns of behaviour are print-outs of paradigms. Expression of a grammar through the discourse of behaviour patterns.

1. Relating and experience
2. Rules, grammar, paradigms
3. Patterns of being
4. Patterns in being
5. Being as a pattern

Ego grammar is composed of paradigms of the mother–child relation, that is printed through the discourse of character.

This discourse is actually the printing of the paradigms through behaviour patterns, so the grammar of the ego has few transformations. The structure is symbolised or the paradigm is symbolised through new structures.

Ways of being.

[undated]
"Transference"

There is a difference between waiting for the transference to emerge (as pattern) and interpreting everything said as a transference manifestation. In the second, I am not sure anything is allowed to emerge.

[undated]
"Orgasm"

Forepleasure is relating to the other and involves intimacy, but orgasm is that ultimate trust in the other that allows the destruction of the other. See Winnicott's notion of the destruction of the object. Without the forepleasure (build up relating to an object) there can be no orgasm. Genital primacy is objectless. The other, paradoxically, is of no concern, as the act is to discharge excitation.

The pleasure principle is about the discharge of excitation. It is as if Freud is really talking about anxiety rather than sexuality.

Genital primacy is love conceived by a committee … of psychoanalysts.

[undated]
"Transformational object"

The transformational object is that object for any subject who seeks basic paradigmatic situations.

If the paradigmatic situation is one of establishing rules—a grammar—how does transformation take place? In the original setting the infant experiences "x" in relation to the self or the mother and then the mother transforms the infant's need. The nature of this transformation is a paradigm, a pattern, from which the infant establishes a rule: [to become] a piece of the ego's grammar.

So, it is a dialectic of what the infant brings to the mother and how she transforms it.

[27/05/77]
"Character and ego grammar"

Character is not an abstraction of an experience into a basic rule; it is an enactment of the paradigm. It may be sponsored by ego grammar (the internalisation of basic rules) but it is the language of grammar; the *parole* rather than *la langue*.

Character is the enactment of the paradigm, and therefore, is always an address to the other: the de-differentiated ambience of the infant's unconscious processes and the mother's unconscious processes. It is the enactment of the rule.

How does this fit with the idea of a symptom?

The grammar is put together in order to give structure to the idiom of the self's experience and history. It must occur in order to thrive within culture. It is an aspect of the internalisation of the dialectics of experience.

Character is enacted paradigm. Ego grammar is abstracted paradigm, into rule. Character is speech. Ego is structure, or grammar.

Transference is the re-experience of the paradigmatic situation, where the subject anticipates dialogue with the transformational object.

To show how structure is not simply a fantasy, recall "M", whose fantasies are on the oedipal level, but whose discourse is pre-oedipal. No, it's important to realise that character is thematic. Yet, it is revealed through a pattern of being, so it is an aesthetic. There is a structure that transcends the fantasy.

The ideology behind my quasi linguistic model is the notion of the semiology of the self; that however we may focus on our function and dysfunction, there is no functioning that is devoid of communicating. To see structures as grammar rather than functional capacities (though rules do establish functions and capacities) leads directly to the semiological aspect of living rather than the biological or systemic aspect, which fails to grasp the uniquely human aspect of the language function.

Defences—projection, splitting etc.—do not create rules; rules establish the defence. A rule may be a defence (I think). Experience or the paradigms derived from experience (perception) determine defences. Kleinians seem to feel that defences determine the rules.

Insofar as rules are based on paradigms they are rules about the handling of the instincts, the self, the object etc.; so the grammar is an aesthetics, a form-structure that is social (as form) and idiomatic.

How does the grammar move into speech? It has to do with the handling of a percept. Not all language is character. There is speech of cognitive style, symptom, etc. The problem is to differentiate what becomes a rule. I think I must say this ego grammar is a system of thinking about one's experience that will develop from the experience of being.

Let us say that a person does not believe or has no experience of sexual impulses being transmuted into desire. If he has impulses he may dispose of them according to a number of defences (splitting, isolation, repression) which may reflect what avenues were available for him. Problems can occur if the other desires him and so forth.

Desire or impulse may be deferred to material things: to play things.

[undated]
"Dream"

Does the dream withhold its secret from us, or do we withhold the secret from the dream?

The ego's aesthetic accomplishment is to transform the dream thought into dramaturgy.

The way the dreaming subject is handled in the dream is an ego memory. Or, whatever the expressed wish, the aesthetic of the dream setting and the poetics of its drama is a transcription of the ego's experience of the desire or the memory or the anxiety. In this sense, the dream puts the person into the position of being identified with the original ego experience, or, if that has changed, of being identified with the present ego attitude.

The analytic hour and the dream space are similar because both are regressed occasions, where the discourse is similar.

[undated]
"The discourse of handling"

impulse
need
dependency
excitement
erotic arousal
fatigue
anxiety
despair
loss
confusion
failure
frustration
request
play
invitation
refusal
desire
celebration
success

[undated]
"Conflict"

How do we talk about an addiction to a psychic conflict, so that people are over focused on whatever occurs to them? Conflict gives focus which holds the self together. There must be a complaint, which binds the self to other and also where the self experiences sensation, while the same experience doesn't hold true with pleasure. There is a relation to the pain—a narcissistic anguish—which pushes out other objects, etc.

[undated]
"Character in fiction"

Is the ego structure of the presented self. What does, say, a tragic figure utter—formally—that a comic figure does not? In a play, how does one figure represent different themes from another figure?

[20/06/77]
"Dream: Other to other"

Is the dream the Other's address to the other? A secret message to the transferential object? In this sense, it is the sequestered and regressed
    self addressing the primary other: the mother.
    Ironically, we occupy the position as this other to whom the dream is addressed when we recognise the dream as a communication and act as an interpreter.
    The Other assumes us as other and asks of us the fulfilment expected of the other.
    "The ego's place at the Other's play: to dream"
    "To dream: the ego's place at the Other's play"

[undated]
"Splitting"

Splitting is a defence against anxiety etc. But if we regard the mother as serving as auxiliary ego to the infant, then aspects of the infant's self care are already split up between infant and mother with mother taking a fair share of it. But this does not leave the infant in the paranoid–schizoid position if the infant is subjectively fused with the mother. The paranoid–schizoid position can only occur if such a relation collapses and the mother's provision fails the infant.

[undated]
"The transformational object"

In analysis the patient looks for an ego experience with the analyst. The analyst like the mother goes on being and provides the patient with an ambience and a process of facilitation and transformation where transformations of ego, id, and superego may take place. This aspect of the analytic relation is not the transference of a fantasy or id need, but the establishment of an ego expectation. The true self's experience of the analyst's being.
    The analyst should be aware of this aspect of the transference, as the analytic relation induces a deep memory of the basic paradigmatic relation: infant to transformational object.

[15/08/77]
"True self"

An example—fairly non-pathological—of true self's dissociation. Meeting of two people. "A" asks "B" about his holiday. "B" cannot link this question to his true experiences of the holiday and is too concerned with the mechanics of executing the relating, thus preventing actual discourse, at least about the true self.

[undated]
"Ego, subjectivity, alienation"

How the person's subjectivity is the experience of ego processes. How ego forms before the "I". How the other (as mother, world) constitutes the ego before the dawn of "I". Subjectivity as I see it is the last arrival in the formation of self experience.

In the dream, the person as subject (as dream experiencer) is confronted by the ego's use of the subject to declare memories or desires.

The unconscious is like an other.

This difference between ego and subject can constitute a fundamental alienation and crisis in the self. In narcissism there is fusion, with no difference. In schizophrenia, there is maximum alienation.

[31/08/77]
"The 2 mothers"

"N" breaks up the continuity of nascent relating to me in the transference by absences, as he goes off craving his girl friend. That is, he expresses an unconscious idea that desiring someone is a breakdown in being. I put it to him that the mother who left him (for holiday) breaks up the tradition of the mother who supports his being. The latter he can (or could) take for granted, but when the mother leaves, he craves her and this shift changes his relating. Unconscious relating = disaster.

[undated]
"Character versus subjectivity"

Character is memory. It is an aesthetic of being that forms and transforms experience according to an unconscious hermeneutic. It is mute in the sense that the receiver is absent (except in analysis) and the subject who enacts his character is blind and deaf to his aesthetic.

In a sense, character reserves an interpretation of being that may be at variance with the person's subjective notion of their essence. It is a clash between the discourse of character—which speaks through the aesthetic of being—and the voice of desire: the subject's play of the imaginative possibilities of self.

This is, perhaps, best illustrated in a person who is (as existent-structure) a certain way. He handles himself and others in a certain style. A syntax of being and relating. Now, all this may be unknown by the subject and, indeed, at wild variance with his own "internal world" or, at least, his experience of the world.

It raises the question: what is subjectivity? Or, can there be a genuine subjectivity without hearing from the discourse of character? I think the discourse of character is a mute speech. It means "listening" to one's silent speech, almost as if we bear with us a shadow self[vii] who prints in an aesthetics of being a dialogue with an absent object. In psychoanalysis, this absent object may re-appear in the transference.

In fiction, at least the modern novel, character may exist alongside consciousness; in particular, the consciousness of the author ... or the world of the novel. What is the discourse of the self? Does the consciousness of the author grapple with the violence of character; or, is it remedied by superficial placing in indexical tongues (sociological matrices) rather than as an idiomatic—unconscious—discourse of the ego: the impersonal self?

What novels do I know of where the subject grapples with character? *Moby Dick, Crime and Punishment*. It means a conscious confrontation with the mute determinacy of one's idiomatic discourse. Character is autistic, in that the receiver of the discourse is absent (the object of all characterological defences) and the language is, thereby, a dead language. It is the fact that character is a dead language—a language no longer spoken between the original speakers—that gives critics the sense that character is conservative, or inhibiting.

Most novelists only understand the effect of character—that is, linking it with mute determinacy—and this principle is then re-printed in a novel, in social terms (cf. Goffman),[viii] but that is not the truth of character, which is deeply enigmatic and aggravating.

Many novels are an attempt to escape the enigma of character by a manic-omnipotent staging of character, giving to themselves a control over character—"characterisation"—that is a denial of the very experiences of one's character.

Recent psychoanalytical studies of the self—in particular, the borderline and narcissistic—are concerned really with a patient whose primary speech is character, whose "subjective" life is blank or chaotic and who refuses to be informed as a subject, of themselves as a character.

Character is destiny if understood, and fate if not understood.[6]

Few authors permit this determinacy to be with them. Their act of omnipotent creation defies destiny. Yet some writers do: Melville, Shakespeare.

[undated]
"An example of management"

It becomes clear with "D" that in creating her "ecology" she forms an early environmental failure. At present, the environment fails her: at work, in relationships, and so forth. She is only just

---

[vii] Unfortunately, I was ignorant of Jung's work.
[viii] The American sociologist Erving Goffman.

included. She is remembering an early situation, as she brings internal anguish into contact with environmental objects (loss, boyfriend, loss of country) as this link (as opposed to intrapsychic processes of guilt, compulsion, etc.) recalls the early failure.

In treating her, I become aware that we need to remember her family, and to do this, whenever she mentions a brother, I name him. Whenever she mentions her mother's job or her brother's work, or wherever a person lives, I name the place or ask for its name. I do this because her family life is an encapsulated group memory, linked intra-familially, but then again, not linked.

[undated]
"Guilt"

"A"'s addiction to guilt works this way. It is as if she is attached to a phantom internal object that criticises her, but in fact, looks after her. The fact that guilt cannot be resolved by clarifying its source is that it is an internal attachment to the overlooking absent parent. She installs a mother inside her. When her mother gave birth to her sister—and sends her off to live with her aunt—"A" is full of rage. Later she will hear her internal mother reproach her for her murderous gestures toward her sister. This is guilt proper. But, the hearing of the mother becomes a denial of separation (ergo, some guilt is denial of separation) as she keeps the mother with her after the separation. The omnipresence of guilt in her adult life is her way of remaining attached to the primary object—a denial of separating, of experiencing freedom from guilt, of freedom from the object. She seeks to feel guilty as it fuses her with the object that causes the guilt.

[09/10/77]
"Rage and the self"

Rage over separation (see Miss Churchill in *Emma*, or Ahab) can create a self which, though weak of ego, can still construct the appearance of strength—or independence—out of this rage.

[undated]
"Ego and id"

As Freud says, the superego is the father, the mastering father, and the ego will always be submissive to it. Freud's theory of the mental apparatus is actually the allegorising into psychical agencies of the European patriarchy. The id must be the mother. The ego is the child caught between and mediating and the superego is the dominating father.

[undated]
"Cure"

Freud's first model of cure was of enlightenment: the discovery of an unconscious memory. His analyst was an explorer-adventurer. His second model of the analyst was of master: the dominance of the id that is now viewed as dangerous.

The therapeutic alliance shifts as does the politics of the late 19th and early 20th century, from exploration to conquering. The ego becomes the besieged city by the 1940s with "enemies", and Hartmann imagines the ego as a city with areas free of conflict. Klein's reconciliation is to view the subject as endowed with a death instinct, linked up to evil. So, the 19th-century view of the explorer-adventurer (an enlightenment view of man) regresses in psychoanalytical theory to a medieval view of Satan (the child) and the sacred body of the Christ (mother). A new allegory is enshrined.

Ego psychology is functional and the economic view reflects the post war—particularly American—world of the well functioning machine, particularly the economy of the id. What does the id demand? How can the ego simplify it?

Winnicottianism is an attempt, along with Lacanianism, to restore 19th-century aesthetics. They are modernist: a true self is looked for, or, the "Other" who one addresses as object of the self's search.

[undated]
"The self as toy"

I have seen a couple in marital therapy who quarrel over small details: fixing a boiler, or the car. They speak in childish ways to one another. I think some couples use "toy" language and speak like children. The self as a toy: a depersonalised object.

[15/12/77]
"Denial and paranoia"

A patient denies memory and both severs and dissolves linking, so he has no internal, accrued sense of self. He has no tradition upon which he can rest. His unconscious motivation is to deny the absence of a transformational object and to reject *what is*, to use the semiology of the self as a reproach to the other, who must feel guilt.

But, the attack on linking leaves him without structured psychological means of living-in-the-world. To survive, he uses paranoid vigilance—to scan the environment—instead of psychic insight, to know the self. Hence, paranoid thinking is a defence against anxiety surrounding survival of the self, that occurs when there has been an unconscious subversion of psychological insight. That is why he is not concerned with knowing himself or with insight, but only with how I feel about him and whether he is in trouble or not.

[15/12/77]
"Schizoid love"

"P" seduces a woman so he can find an object in whose presence he can mourn.

1978

"Manic state and the true self"

A manic state is an actualisation of the true self, contained within the athletic denial of the manic mood. It is, nonetheless, one means whereby a deeply dissociated part of the self has access to actualisation in life. It is not living, however, or being lived, as the rigor of its actualisation is more of a maddened computer print-out of its being than a leisurely enactment. Also, manic states rely on a depersonalisation of the object (which no doubt facilitates the true self's emergence) that is replaced by a narcissistic self object acting as audience.

[undated]
"Melanie Klein"

I think Klein's theory of the paranoid–schizoid and depressive positions is a description of the core psychodynamic of the adult, not the child. Because, the child has the actual care of the mother and long periods of sleep which mitigates the core conflict. However, the core conflict of her model is there, but does not come to full expression until adolescence when the adult experiences this conflict.

[undated]
"The grammar of the ego and the character of the self"

1. Establish the ego as a structure based on paradigmatic transactions from which operational rules—cognitive, defensive, relational, social—have been derived, to constitute

the grammar of the ego. This grammar evolves psycho developmentally, but has a deep or primary structure.

2. Character is the idiom of the self's state, expressed in being and relating, and is the surface manifestation of the paradigms.

Problem: if I choose to say ego = grammar, and if I say that character = syntax, it makes it look as if character is a read-out of the ego, when I mean to say the ego is the aesthetic; or, a grammar which gives structure to a syntax, which is character.

1979

[16/01/79]
"Projective processes, maturation, and illness"

I am beginning to believe that projection is more a ubiquitous feature of adult life than of the life of the infant.

1. In the adult, it is expressed in perception, probably mostly in terms of groups (where it is validated consistently).
2. It is less a feature of infantile life because the infant has a mother who looks after the baby, holds it, and receives projective processes.
3. Projection increases in adult life as the person gradually separates from the mother.
4. This process is tempered through marriage and family life where—through projective identification—members *hold* one another's projections.
5. But without these frames, or in spite of them, the human subject projects aspects of the self more as life goes on. This indicates:
   a. Registration of absence of a holding environment.
   b. Loss and separation.
   c. An attempt to reconstitute self–other (mother) relation.
6. So, in adult analysis, we make the mistake of saying we learn through the adult about the infant's projective processes. We are witness to adult illnesses.

[24/04/79]
"Dream"

Freud's work with Frau Emmy reveals how he tried with the hysteric to banish the image of a memory through "lengthy explanation". He does the same thing with dreams, trying to convert the image into discourse.

[undated]
"The experience of the patient and the text"

Being with a patient's discourse is listening to a narrative. A patient telling me about his desire for a woman on a raft in a pond is like reading Joyce. The point is, what is the analyst's relation to the woman on the raft?

[16/06/79]
"Mother's disillusion as the creation of father's space"

It is the task of the mother to create a space for the baby-child through disillusion, in her as an object of infinite supply. In that space will come the father with his reality orientation, with his moralisms, his education, his fatherisms. If the mother does not create this space through disillusion with her, or if she regards the father as a threat to herself and her baby, no area will be created in the infant for the reception of the father, or the reception of him as reality.

It is an oedipal example of the baby who gets the mother.

The analyst must disillusion the patient's idealisation; then, create a space for the reception of the father-object—and, the relation (at a willing level) to the outside world.

The area of reality is an area where as dis-illusion occurs—as illusions go—reality enters, through ego masteries and the "hands" of the father (and mother) as a tactile compensatory thing.

The toy = object of illusion and reality.

The mother, as Jacobson[i] says, must dispel herself into subjective objects. She must illuminate them. From primary maternal preoccupation to primary external preoccupation.

[24/07/79]
"Violence"

The imagery of violence bypasses the affect linked to aggression.

[undated]
"Interpretation as the analyst's fantasizing"

Some patients, who present you with a sequence of their fantasy life, do so to sit back and watch you, as they try to get the analyst to enact the fantasy via interpreting. The analyst then lives out the dissociated patient's fantasizing.

---

[i] Edith Jacobson, American psychoanalyst.

That is, we live for them through our interpreting. And particularly a Kleinian who takes a patient's reporting of the ordinary and translates it into a fantasy. It can be a countertransference enactment of a disorder in the patient; namely, a schizoid split from the play of desire.

[01/09/79]
"Compliance"

"X" is always compliant. This is re-enforced by the fact that he creates a demanding object representation with which he must comply, but through his compliance he then resents the real object for accepting!

[01/09/79]
"Gift giving, tokenism, and the fetish"

In giving a gift, "X" gives the other a fetishistic object that symbolises the absence of his whole object relating. (i.e. this token = my relation to you as my part object). And it also serves as a gift to the other: "you now have me as a fetish object as this—part object—is my use of the other." That was his function in relation to the mother.

1. He gives an identity theme.[ii]
2. Giving, he realises is a reaction formation.
3. Giving is self reflexive.

This giving is saturated with a kind of intense mournful affect. This prints the unconscious script of his mother giving birth to him, but as a token of her previously lost child, who becomes the symbol of all those lost possibilities in her life.

The mother had lost a daughter in childbirth, so her love of "X"—that is, her mournfully solicitous care of him—is the mourning of the lost child. "X" is the trace, the token, of the lost child (= lost possibilities for fulfilment). He then gifts himself to others, with accompanying affect of great sadness, because he registers:

1. His own loss of the mother's true care.
2. Her use of him as an object symbolizing loss and grief.

This is enacted by him in life. As a child he was like an object to which the parents went, as a wailing wall. His presence linked them with their grief, as by projective identification they had put their lost possibilities inside him. In life, he functions to evoke in many people those lost parts of themselves that create intense moods of sadness and need for consolation.

His relations to ordinary healthy people—in whom he evokes these "moments"—are usually brief, and intermittent, as he only sees them on occasion. They may cause embarrassment. Or, when he does this to an ill person, it evokes intensely ill parts.

[ii] 'Identity' theme is a concept by Heinz Lichtenstein.

Implications for the theory of the transformational object.

An ordinary mother—who of course unconsciously interprets her child's meaning to her—does not place the child's activities within her own narrative. That is, the mother allows the child space in which activities or presence is independent of conscious narrative. With the mother who transforms activity or presence or character into her own identity theme, or idea of things, the child remains in that symbiotic relationship where being and doing are always allegories of the mother's interpretation. A good mother does not overdose a child's play or presence with references to, from, or about *her* being, even when it is quite obvious that a child is symbolising his identifications with her. The good enough mother's transformational function is her silence, her un-interpretive function.

[undated]
"Fantasy"

Fantasy is the psychical representation of a lived experience.

[04/10/79]
"Bisexuality"

"D"'s phobia about involvement is somatised in homosexual situations and relationalised with women. With a girlfriend, it has to do with sustaining tenderness, bearing frustration and depression. When he is with a man, he is concerned with holding an erection, or the opening to his anus. It is a depersonalised use of the body, a more concrete attempt to symbolise phobic dread. Because it is concretised and somatised there is an illusion of omnipotently dealing with the problem.

[undated]
"On the non-communicativeness of the text"

Each text is private. Mute. That personage for whom the text was a living shell is either dead or ordinarily unavailable, even if alive and communicating. Critical activities are attempts to live with this fact, and the best critical endeavours are those when the critic knows that each text is deeply private and its unconscious "life" forever unknowable.

The text's non-communicating to the critical process (no exegetical footnotes) is a positive contribution. This absence gives the text a presence and a demand for unknowability that enables critics to play with the illusion that they can know but never really challenge the privacy of the text.

[undated]
"On clear thinking and the need for confusion"

Sometimes a person can think so clearly about something that although the other has understood the meaning perfectly, there is a need in the other to create momentary confusion or muddle.

Why? Envy and so forth aside, it can be because the clarity has bypassed that mutuality necessary for shared discovery.

The other does not have enough time for the emotional experience to be linked with the clear thought; by being confused or argumentative, time and space is created for the experiential-integrative need to be asserted. It is often the case that brilliant people have this effect on the other. And the other appears to needlessly hinder or fail to celebrate the brilliance. In fact, they are the object of precocious handling, have been surpassed in terms of the holding environment, and need to create muddle in order to understand.

This is the positive side of that behaviour that appears to be conservative, resistant, and reactionary (i.e. resistance).

Anytime this happens in the clinical setting the analyst should ask if the patient's confusion is not a necessary defensive need to create a space for understanding.

Often brilliant thinking annuls the inviolate solitariness of the thinker. As if phobic dread of emotional surrender gets channelled into a certain violence in clarity: a clarity that in fact refuses collaborative thinking with others.

Hence, it can be a refusal to relate, so that even though the thought appears helpful and clarifying it induces confusion that is in fact the unconscious effort of the other to be included and to experience the processes (internal) that led to the thought.

Often the brilliant thinker simply produces yet another clarity that reproduces the same effect.

The total effect on the other can be to induce a sense of futility. Confusion is refused; misunderstood as a sign of incompetence, rather than an invitation for relating, and the thinker compels the other in the countertransference to know what it is like to be with a precocious other, who interprets need as weakness and who celebrates thinking as it ensures her of the independence of her child from his and her emotional life.

The other alternative to confusion is to ignore the clarity and proceed as if it were not happening (a negative hallucination). This can develop into a "bilateral monologue"[iii] where each speaks; a mother and child speaking, but not relating.

This happened with my father, on occasion, whom I tried to engage through my confusion. I stalled in order to create possible forms of new relating and of course it was doomed. But also, his kind of brilliance compelled a certain stupidity or slowness in the other, thus fashioning in the other a capacity—for slowness etc.—that he has dissociated from himself. Eventually, through identifying with the slowness in the other etc., and by empathising with their difficulty in coping with him, he is able to accept this slowing down of himself.

It is also possible that the brilliant subject projectively identifies actual confusion into the other, but that is different from my point of view.

---

iii A term coined by Gregory Bateson.

"The borderline object"[1]

The borderline object is objectively absent. The baby creates the object, or the object becomes or emerges from the affective states created by its absence.

The borderline patient's hate, despair, and self degradation is an object relation.[2] The baby's experience of the object is its own undifferentiated affect.

Because the mother did not provide good enough presence, this "object" was not mitigated. Paranoid states of object relation are actually affective states that determine the object representation. The borderline object is almost always the projective identification of the patient's affects or defences, although, the trace of the real object is present in the borderline's anticipation of invasion, impingement, smothering, and being dropped.

1980

[25/01/80]
"Depression is anaesthetic against real (mad) feelings"

Anaesthetic statements—e.g. self-reproaches—are tablets, screening out mad thoughts. That is why depression is reassuring, although it is an affect of dissociation from mental life. A patient says that his depression "is a stopping", and that is the secondary gain that partly motivates depression.

[undated]
"The analytic process"

The analytic process uses a procedure that occurs in other settings, particularly in religions—e.g. in Zen—but it uses the process to be reflective on itself. That is the analysis.

What do we name this process that occurs in all the above settings?

The person feels himself to be inside an evolving and progressive experience of transformative potential linked to a person (or cult leader, priest, or analyst) who is assumed to have arrived through the same process.

[27.06.80]
"Moods"

Language of the baby. "X" speaks in moods. Parents were privately withdrawn into their moods. It's a form of communication, and has effects. The mother cognises and then transforms the baby's moods.

How does a mood differ from an affect?

The mood in "X" is a somatic representation.

A mood may coerce the other.

It is preverbal and, indeed, competes with verbalisation.

A mood may be composed of different affects simultaneously. It is a use of affect that suggests the person is coercing the environment, hence relating to some object or objects.

Moods (or mood speech) are often spoken through affective response or unresponse, or paradoxical response to something spoken by the other. "A" may say to "B" something very simple or straightforward, like "your radio is too loud" and "B" may reply "fine, I'll turn it down", but may express something very different in his mood, like "fuck off" or "oh shit, I've angered you again" etc. Now "A" may address the mood and try to transform it into speech. "A" may be unsuccessful, not because he is incorrect, but because "B" prefers to speak through mood. It is coercive and secretive. It ensures privacy but has an effect.

[undated]
"Character"

Unconscious fantasy or play is a life instinct (as even schizophrenic delusion is an attempt to relate to the world through fantasy) and character is—as is personality—on the rim of death-in-life. Each person's finiteness is announced in the limitation of being. The autistic process is like a death instinct. Where we speak of life and death in terms of man, we mean in terms of the self: that which is life enhancing or that which destroys the self.

[10/09/80]
"Interpretation"

We sometimes rid patients of affective experience through interpretation. "X"'s description of his date with a woman who went off, leaving him the next day feeling no sense of identity, non-existent, requires my recognition of his pain and the understandability of his sense of no identity.

[undated]
"Self as object"

The way you know who the "mother" was is to observe how the person handles themselves as an object. In that relation is the mother and her child.

[21/09/80]
"Envy and the protective shield"

"X"'s apparent envy actually amounts to incessant impingements from within. He cannot hold his own experiences because his work—his continuity in being—is interrupted by constant assaults. This may be a structural problem, as the child did not have an illusion of omnipotence, allowing a core self to develop: hence his feeling of being incomplete.

Envy for "X" is hunger; the other possesses the breast, as his younger brother has the mother's breast.

The mother gives him an illusion of omnipotence, then takes it away, gives it, then takes it away and does not build up a reliable protective shield.

His day is often interrupted by his own interests, where he goes looking at an art gallery, or a museum, all of which is a breach in self management due to the incapacity to hold himself, against impulses.

[10/11/80]
"Mood experience as an alternative to object relatedness and relating"

"J" goes through a sequence of moods in the presence of the external or internal object, but actually—though intense affect states are involved—keeps great distance from relating. She keeps herself unintegrated, to allow for full temporary experience of a sequence of moods linked to but not in relation to an object: i.e. linked to an associated experience 'vis-à-vis' the object.

With "B", for example, she says she feels indifferent to him, then talks about how she dreads return of a nurse, then discussed her father and how if he wasn't anyone, then she isn't anyone, and that sort of thing. I understand these thoughts as potentially sensible as they can link up—i.e.: "I feign indifference as it is my way of saying 'screw you'" etc.—but she refuses to be integrated in full. My interpretations of the object relational potential of the moods is quickly picked up by her, suggesting that she knows what is up, but that she preserves an illusion of total unintegration, to enable mood experiences.

In fact, she wants to prevent integration in order to preserve an atmosphere—composed of moods—that was her way of experiencing mother, father and family. Partly the mother and father were deeply private, although the father could be related to through pseudo flirtatiousness. Fundamentally she kept her distance from relating (implying trust and dependence). She substituted intense affective experience—associated with and actualised in the presence of the object—for relating. Relating meant invasion of her privacy.

I liken it to a girl reading romance fiction which makes no claims on her but allows her to hang experiences around the object (novel). This is how she relates to father and to mother.

In the transference I tell her that in the early months she needed to actualise a sequence of moods in my presence, in apparent relation to me—e.g.: grief, longing, contempt, hate, affection, irritation, confusion, identification—but that she keeps a great distance.

"F" does something similar. She orbits an object with a temporary mood experience. But for her, each orbit allows for the cessation of a previous orbit. The essence is to prevent a full and sustained affective relation to the object out of an anxiety over being swallowed up and destroyed. Her hyperactive mood life sustains her phobic stance.

Moods are all-encompassing or often constitutive and correspond to the baby's living-inside experience. Immediate experience.

The need to exist inside the experience of a mood. "J" establishes the priority of the baby's experience of the world. "J"'s regression is back to the level of psychic experience where thinking is only partially organised and where she can live closer to ego states and instinctual traces.

Analysts link affects and sensations, saying in the beginning they are very close. "J" does seem to be attempting to live inside affective experiences, one aim of which is to provide herself (body ego) with sensation. Such sensation, a function of mood, substitutes for thinking per se. It reflects "J"'s need for more of a body ego holding experience. Mood (here) is a sensation-affect holding environment linked to but not in relation to an object. Rather than the use of reflective thinking mood is a means of looking after the self. She does not think about herself and an other or a situation. She establishes a mood derived from the self, the other, or a situation and lives inside it.

Unconsciously I think she wants to live through a period of experiencing affect-sensory states, as an infant re-experiencing her object, with me functioning as an auxiliary ego—doing a lot of the thinking, remembering, differentiating—in order for her to have or to establish a core self which is absent.

Her trembling states in sessions—unlinked to either her material or my interpretations but incurable except within the transference to me—were establishments of the body ego self, needing to be shuddering like a baby. I kept the room warm as a way of managing the situation.

"J" differentiates between "those intense feelings" and "my own feelings". She feels that unless there are intense feelings there "is nothing happening".

[undated]
"Transference"

1. Premature interpretation pre-empts transference affect.
2. Militant interpretation negates reality.
3. Translations as *not* transference.
4. Translations (i.e. here and now) as idea of reference or narcissistic.
5. A premature transference interpretation interferes with the process of free association.

Transference translations are paranoid and can create a negative transference, as the patient is constantly bound to the analyst. They can also create a sense of being supported in the midst of a system.

Some transference interpretations are ideas of reference within the countertransference. Some analysts take a patient's material as if it were a dream about the analyst, and the analyst's interpretations become prolonged, extensive associations that actually require an analyst to interpret them. Such an analyst is, of course, absent.

Some Kleinians do not realise that the transference is a form of relating to an absent object (mother, father, etc.) through a present object (the analyst) who sustains an illusion of being the absent object. If the analyst does not in one way or another, over time, link himself to the absent object, this is not a transference interpretation but an idea of reference. It is paranoid because it decontextualizes things in order to enhance the analyst's self-significance.

Also, the Kleinian is almost competing for the transference object with the patient, getting "there" first. This can create a kind of rivalry.

[undated]
"Doubt as the facilitator of wish"

"P", so long as she is in doubt about whether to go to Fiji or stay in England, allows for a maximisation of wishes. She can wish for anything as nothing will link with reality as she does not know where she will be.

Doubt functions, here, to suspend reality orientation in order to allow the person to live in a temporary area of pleasure or wish which is protected.

[17/12/80]
"Transference"

When "M" tells me of a dream about Lily (a colleague) where he has positive feelings, I don't interpret this or the transference as he needs an experience of the object (Lily) in his own right. If I were to make a transference interpretation it would be unconsciously synonymous with the mother who refers all the toddler's play back to herself. This possessiveness prevents object cathexes and leads to guilt. In order to be preserved they must be kept secret from the mother.

In analysis, when patients are prevented from developing an object world—and most attempts at transference interpretation do this—real relations to objects must be kept secret from the analyst. This inspires a sense of guilt in the patient who feels the analyst is being betrayed.

Such transference interpretations become a kind of hyper-intellectual activity, arresting nascent affects and object cathexes, and links to the primary object. In this sense, the analyst enacts the role of a vigilant mother, determined that the infant's life be solely arranged around the analyst-mother.

Some patients test what they construe to be evidence of the analyst-mother's narcissism. When discussing some detail from life they wait for the transference interpretation, and sometimes try to do this to themselves.

Some transference interpretations become a form of molesting. The patient's nascent realisation of affect, object cathexis and self state within the transference setting is constantly molested (broken up) by the analyst's interminable reference of the above to an aspect of inferred behaviour toward the analyst.

Were a mother or a father to do this to an infant it would involve the child in a tie-up into the world of the parent's psychic reality that would obliterate the child's perception and relation to reality.

It is important that the father, the mother, the husband, the work setting, and the ordinary affairs of life be related to by the analyst frequently enough as non-transference. Otherwise, as reality is superseded by pure psychic reality, the analyst's interpretation becomes a form of delusion, in which reality is ignored in order to confirm the singularity of the truth of psychic reality.

As with all delusions there is—beyond the psychic reality—some kernel of actual reality (worldly reality) to the deluded transference interpretation. The problem is the failure to include the broader context.

1981

[02/01/81]
"Transference"

One problem of transference translations is that the patient simply goes on reporting their life, the analyst translating it into the relationship, and the process itself becomes a dissociation, a splitting off. Even if the patient acknowledges the analyst's remarks as correct, something is wrong if the patient fails to develop a true orientation to their unconscious that is self-reflective. Sessions reported by analysts of work with such patients reveals a process in which no self reflection, hence self knowing, appears to develop.

[02/01/81]
"Reconstruction"

The analyst who does not reconstruct does not allow for those moments when a patient dwells memorially with the parent of childhood. This evocative process frequently involving a de-repression or a de-dissociation accompanied by release of affect, allows for a psycho-developmental maturation in relation to the parental internal objects and the corresponding self representations.

To be sure, when a patient is reliving a relation to a parent in the transference, this would often be an inopportune time to reconstruct, as it would be perceived unconsciously as a cop out.

[undated]
"Mastery and the death instinct"

The identification is with the certainty (and thus the mastery) of death: with death's mastery over life.

[19/01/81]
"Simple mindedness"

"X"'s parents sent her into care when she was 7 months old and she was sent along with her 4-year-older older brother who was already in care. She recalls the parents saying "It's so nice to get married as then you can have children." The mother looked forward to her house and cleaning it up. The father said of the Christmas meal once: "Don't bother going to any trouble; we can just have a snack before we go." After Christmas Day the mother said, "It's so nice to have Christmas, because it means the warm weather is coming."

Such simple-mindedness defends them against feeling and thinking.

[04/03/81]
"On the patient's use of the analyst's first name"

I know, of course, those situations where a patient uses my first name and it is a subtle form of contempt. But with the change in my technique I have discovered—now retrospectively—that many of my patients call me by my first name. In several situations I not only do not feel irritated, I feel pleased, and I feel it is essential to the patient's relation to me.

The analyst's first name, the speaking of it, the possessing of it, is an act of intimacy akin to the baby's insistence that he has some prior claim on the mother. The first name is like a transitional object in that the first name is loveable.

When "P" says "Christopher!" when phoning me, it is spoken in such a way that this "Christopher" is her subjective object, as much as it is mine. I am aware of my name being as much her possession as mine, and I find in the countertransference a mixture of surprise and pleasure that my name should function for her in that way.

Her developing use of my first name signals my becoming her subjective object and is evidence of her use of me.

To analyse this would be akin to the mother's removal of the transitional object by cleaning it! My last name is reflecting my lineage which is impersonal to the patient: they have no contact with my family. But the first name, which specifies me, allows them to express and develop their relation to me as their subjective object. To analyse and thus subtly insist on use of my last name is to refuse the patient this necessary period of using the analyst.

The analyst's countertransference is an important diagnostic clue as to whether the use of the first name is an act of contempt or affectionate use: i.e. subjective object relating.

On the other hand, the analyst must not say initially to the patient "go ahead and call me by my first name" which would prevent use. The analyst must allow for the patient's appropriation of the first name.

I think any patient who uses the first name straight away is doing so defensively and this may need to be taken up.

[31/03/81]
"Moods"

"K" does not convey to me her needs. For example, my mistake, after which I say that it is difficult to assess how I am of use to her; who I am to her. I know I am important to her, but my significance is privately held, not put out, shared by her, so that we know of her dependence on me. Attachment is impersonal; dependence highly personal. I think she does not want to articulate need because:

1. It will dispel a powerfully magical relation to the object.
2. Insult her wishes.

Instead she communicates through moods. She nurses her rejection by me through mistake of interpretation and withdraws from me, compelling me to feel a mood of uselessness. They are nonverbal communications. Very powerful, very secretive. She associates it with her adolescence.

The adolescent's moods convey more to the parents—often—than their description of events. Their moods are very powerful and effect the parent's moods, so that frequently the adolescent is in a deeply nonverbal mood discourse with a parent whilst appearing to be separated in and through their overt statements.

"D" conveys his father through his moods; yet, does he know it is his father he conveys? I doubt it.

[25/03/81]
"L's moods"

"L" talks about how no one expressed their feelings, although I think their feelings were expressed in body states *cum* moods: "I feel a little slow", "I feel better", "Your father isn't feeling well". Affective and psychic states are transformed into body-mood states.

[31/03/81]
"*L'emprise*"[1]

The child (and Ahab) must create subjective objects.
   Why must an object be an expression of the subject?
   What is an object when it is subjectively held?

The obsessional's *emprise* is to give aseptic structure to the instincts by controlling the objects.

The manic moment infuses all objects with subjective frames of reference, as the manic person is attempting to transform his environment.

[undated]
"The true self exposed"

The schizoid does not really have a false self. To protect themselves they remain silent or comply, but dread exposure.

[undated]
"*L'emprise*"

Is also for the subject to be captured. The object of capture is usually human.

When is the child the object amidst his toys? When is he captured in the imaginary? Always! For whom, for what, and why does he possess the object?

Ahab is a perfect example of the subject's apparent possession, yet capture by the other.

A spell holds two in interlocking embrace.

[undated]
"Theatre of hysteria"

How "T" uses laughter. How she causes me to laugh. How it is a way of discharging through the other. It gives her a false sense of communicating and appears to be the result of an internalisation, but is not.

How her sulking or her bad moods is a way of getting something inside the object (other).

The hysteric communicates through senses. Senses in the other.

1. We see her
2. We hear her
3. We laugh
4. We cry
5. We are shocked
6. We are angry

These senses substitute for mental representations and true internalisation. Seeing is not knowing. Nor is hearing. In some ways, hysterical "flightiness"—the desperate shift to other means of capturing the object—actually prevents the other from cognising the hysteric's communications. The hysteric reproduces the mother's narcissistic movement away from momentary attentions to the child; namely, the mother's interest in the child as visual and auditory object. The hysteric does not feel internalised and uses language for its effect.

The hysteric captures the object but is trapped by the assumptions made about the object.

The hysteric's "grasp" of the object is aggressive. She captures the person in her theatre.

[25/04/81 Vitiana, Italy]
[untitled]

How does a mood capture the other? The hysteric's moods (of refusal, seduction) envelop the other who is unwittingly an accomplice.

A mood is an effect of the person's momentary bearing.

When does a person use a mood as an alternative to speaking?

An ebullient mood is accompanied by speech, but it is somehow transcendent of the person.

[26/04/81 Vitiana]
"The hysteric's craving for emotionality"

The hysteric seeks experiences that provide emotionality, as an alternative to internally nurtured or generated emotional realities. This need for an "emotional fix"—the psychological flip side of the hysteric's externalisation—is preverbal.

And each hysteric can be "fixed" by that emotionality drummed up by her own externalisation. It is this relation that leads most lay persons to identify the state as hysterical.

Like her mother, she mirrors—reflects or refracts—rather than internalises persons. No one's presence is taken in. Presence is amplified. A loud mirror. People avoid reflection in the hysteric, as the hysteric's mother amplified the child beyond their psychic capacities.

With "T", after "Z"'s interview (a colleague), I did not wish to come within her gaze. If when she looks I do not reflect back what she demands, then I am victim of her isolated self-amplification. Likewise, what I say to her may be amplified and fragmented.

Again, note how when thinking of the hysteric, I think of auditory and visual processes; so much so that right here I am less concerned with what they say than with their choral accompaniment: the operatic feature.

The hysteric must possess her object; it must be captured, although it cannot be related to. When one of my hysterics has captured me—as her analyst—she enjoys listening or imagining in my presence. Only after she discovers that I exist for her in spite of her energy to capture me does she experience a depression, or, more accurately, a non-experience. The body of the other is hyper-cathected, at a pregenital level, and captured, as the infant captures the body of the mother—by crying, excreting, laughing—but the other is not an internalising container.

The hysteric paralyses the object as she needs it to be in one place to receive her.

[undated]
"Self penetration into other as an alternative to phallic penetration"

"D"'s fear of genital penetration is due to a fear of mutilation, so he implants himself verbally into a woman. But he says he tends to listen more to women and links this to his mother whom he listened to. What I think is that as a boy he was denied ordinary exhibitionism, i.e. his mother did not celebrate his phallicism but substituted it with her own penetrations of him through discourse. This links up with his fatness as a boy and his dread of undressing at school. The mother also said at one point that she thought he might have a mastectomy.

The point is that in the boy the evolution of a sense of self and phallic exhibitionism are consonant and the boy needs to be able to penetrate the object. Perhaps the girl needs to have the object appreciate her receptive capacity, so that the mother or father's appreciations of her offering of her receptiveness—giving the impression that girls are more sensitive and grown-up than boys—is actually an ego expression of a sexual aim: to be penetrated and impregnated.

Is the girl's wish to possess the secret, girls enjoying sharing secrets, an early form of enacting the secret of impregnation?

Back to "D": in manic states he saw himself as bisexual, which is an aspect of his grandiosity, that he is everything.

Ego orgasm[2] is alternate to sexual orgasm and sustains in "D" his female identifications, although the male self feels castrated.

[24/04/81]
"Hysteria"

"G"'s notion of the affect being repressed is seemingly the opposite of the other side: hysteria (considerable emotionality). The affect is repressed because the parent does not listen to the child; does not offer a space for the child's elaboration of trauma through play into speech.

Freezing up of the self—see Freud's paralysed hysteric who has repressed affect—is also typical of the hysteric. They either freeze or unleash their internal world. They live, that is, either in terror of the effects of extreme affectivity, or inside the effect itself.

Through hysterical enactment she paralyses the analyst in the countertransference. The analyst's task is to survive paralysis in order to speak and be understood; not to retaliate or dissociate.

"T" places me before an object that represents the infant's object, one that functions according to projected instincts and parts of the self. But the object is not mitigated by anything. She is "my" projection; my impulse life is there before me, out of control. In certain ways, the hysteric is tauntingly and defiantly saying "come now, you—rational man—don't tell me you don't know who I am, what this is! It is you!" And with surprisingly deft control she can suddenly recompensate herself. Indeed, if I act rashly as a counter to her, in the form of "please sit down"—an impulse in me registered through her over employed defensiveness— she scorns my impulsiveness, tearing me to shreds.

In the countertransference I become frightened—irrationally so—of derivatives of impulse. I say to myself "Oh Christ, she is going to scream" or "Now it will happen; she will break one of my pots", etc. and I become the medium of fears and move further from an attempt to understand and more simply toward "getting by" or "getting through" the hour. In other words, I dissociate myself from her inner predicament and focus primarily on her as an external predicament, an object that I must dispose of, and in that moment she has evoked her mother in me.

"G"'s self is an object that is the only one she has within her total possession. When someone asks something of her, she feels something (her self) is being taken from her.

[01/06/81]
"The self 'in' the other with reference to loss"

The infant is mirrored by the mother and father. The self—as it is registered, interpreted, and stored in the mother—is "inside" the mother.

If there is a separation then the infant loses the mother, father, and the self deposited in the mother.

"G"'s reluctance to answer a man's questions about her has to do with her unwillingness to know herself through the other. We all come to know our self through the other, as we are mirrored back, but "G" refuses this as she assumes loss is too painful. It would be the loss of the object and of the self.

[undated]
"On the obsessional's thought"

With "T" I have up till now analysed his obsession about his future in terms of omnipotence and grandiosity, but it is clear that he has a relation to his thoughts or a relation to the THOUGHT. I say to him that I imagine a boy who kicks a ball against a wall. At times he enjoys the arc of the ball (manic and joyous thoughts) which = the part of him who arcs in his thought into the future, transcending his situation. But he becomes enraged with frustration and then THE THOUGHT (= the ball) is kicked in rage against the wall; the aim is to destroy the wall.

This done, the ball is focused on as it has survived the damage, comes back to him and is part of him, and so he continues. I use this metaphor and he tries to get me to explore its history or bring in other interpretive elements, but I stick with it. Now, he has a relation to THE THOUGHT which is as if the THOUGHT were a concrete object that can be attacked, hugged affectionately, or viewed as a key to transcendence.

[10/07/81]
"Self consciousness as desire"

"G" says she cannot tell me about her sexual thoughts because it would make her self conscious. But in her masturbation fantasies she is in front of a group of male onlookers who force her to masturbate. Now to be self conscious is to direct attention onto the self; it is exhibitionistic; it is not intimacy and desire for the object is not an expression of it. She does not say "Bollas, I thought A, B, C, about you"; she blocks this out and forces everything back to herself, leading the other to glance at her: "What is the matter with you?"

She discharges sex tension by laughter, laughing in a way that discharges desire.

I see in her a little girl who expresses desire through self consciousness by bringing it back to her through exhibitionism. Exhibitionism is a form of narcissism when the person does not feel desire or a need for the object. "G"'s parents were not available, hence she had to take her self as her own object of desire.

[undated]
"Omnipotence"

In thinking of "Z" who talks so much to his girlfriends, he is cancelling out the external world by converting her solely into an internal object. After talking to her about so many subjects she is like an internal object and it is as if he is talking to himself.

This is how he converts one reality (yielding to experiences with the real object) into another: omnipotent mentation.[3]

How mentation replaces experience.

How this blurs boundaries and is his baby self being with the mother.

I take up in the transference how he needs to talk and talk to me in order to convert me into an internal object.

[undated]
"Self as object, 'X' lives inside the cosy mother"

When she anticipates going somewhere or doing something she starts to worry and this mentation is a relation to the worry mother.

There is a cosy mother and a worry mother.

Both are defences against separation.

Her mother transforms a life experience into an anticipatory mental experience. "X" in her self-as-object relation interferes with just getting on with life or experiencing life by interfering with potential experience, as she converts these possibilities into anticipatory mentation.

She finds in the worry mum a person who says "I will look after you always" and so she uses this and enacts it in the transference relation to me.

"I pretend to them to be wonderfully happy, but it is a conspiracy; in fact, I am not happy and they know it." All of this is said to her mother and her father but it is part of an internal dialogue of "I pretend". She refuses life in order to make this complaint.

[undated]
"Presence as material"

Some patients *indicate* material by subtle changes in their *presence*. This nonverbal element must be picked up.

[undated]
"Female fetish"

The fetish is the body of the man.

[undated]
"Character limitation as resistance"

The preservation of a resistance within the person, in their character, that results in a form of not knowing.

[undated]
"History"

The fact that we can never know what really happened to our patients, or that versions of the past change, does not mean that we are not addressing real history. Knowing about the past is of course subjective and versions change according to the person's changing point of view. But does this mean it is a projection? No. It does mean that as a person changes *different aspects* of the past are focused on. Perhaps only bad aspects of the mother or the father are recalled, while in analysis the better features develop. Does this mean it is all according to projection? No. It means that affects or unconscious motivations bias the selection of the remembered.

[undated]
"The true self, and the self-as-object relation"

Once the self-as-object relation is analysed, once the pathology of an internalised relation is analysed, then aspects of the true self are restored. Inevitably this is desire in action. With "E", I know that she enjoys me, but she presents me with a depressed self. She wishes to engage me in this pathological system.

[24/10/81]
"Negative identity, omnipotence, negative therapeutic reaction, and the self-as-object relation"

"Y"'s refusal to create play spaces and other potential spaces is due to her pleasure in destroying possibilities, a destruction that sustains an illusion of great power, as she can omnipotently refuse to allow for creative possibilities. It is also a feature of her pathological self-as-object relation that a covetous mother who supports her sulking ("never mind *them* dear, you and I can do without them") looks after the child part of her.

"E" does the same, in that she is *refusing* possibilities, and, as it were, saying "With my nanny present I need nothing." In the transference, she has incorporated me as a lover-object, prematurely, and omnipotently, relating to me in an intimate way.

[24/11/81]
"Countertransference"

I think when the countertransference becomes crucial is when the essence of the material is pre-oedipal and structural. It is when as *the object* of the patient, the analyst is in the position of being like an infant looked after by the mother-analysand.

It also tends to assume significance when the transference is not so clear.

The analyst is also attempting to cure himself in the countertransference. In this sense the countertransference is the analyst's transference, and the classical view is correct.

[undated]
"Nostalgia is affect in search of memory"

"O" reports in a session that his mother told him she would rather that she died than him. It is one of the few times he actually reports something she said. I note this as a realisation of the mother in the session. Then he becomes reminiscent, talking about his father, grandfather, and the death of the grandfather. Only now do I realise the defensive function of his affect: namely, what has emerged is a depression, a childhood depression that can only be cognised through attachment to memories. What is repressed is the anxious child who feels left out by the mother.

[undated]
"Childhood rituals as indicating absence of mother"

"O" recalls that as a child going to school he imagined string was attached to him and that he could find his way back home as a result. He also had to say certain things in order to protect objects.

I say that he had to engage in this magical thinking because he did not feel safe as a child. He did not feel protected by a good internalised mother. Hence he had, as a child, to engage in magical and cognitive attempts to provide his own maternal care. What these symptoms indicate, I say, is his failure to internalise the good mother. She is not there and he is left to his own wits to construct a maternal holding space. I think obsessional symptoms in children express this relation to the self-as-an-object where the child has to provide through artificial magical means the presence of a maternal care system.

Paradoxically, the very rigidity and terror of the rituals reflects the child's experience of the maternal holding environment.

Ritual, then, is the trace of the mother's obsessionality. It "holds" people in a system bound by meaningless activities.

[29/11/81]
"Countertransference"

The increased use of countertransference is due to a recognition that (1) some patients do not associate etc. and can only be understood primarily through the analyst's feelings and associations and (2) in the analysis of almost all patients there comes a crucial stage when it is through the countertransference that one can understand them best.

Increasingly, countertransference means not only what the analyst feels and his awareness of feeling, but, also, how in many cases countertransference is an illness—a situational pathology occasioned by the patient's transferences—and the analyst must cure the illness in himself in order to cure the patient. Therefore, the analyst's analytic relation to himself as an object is a very important means to understanding.

The analyst must develop a new relation to interpretation when working with the counter-transference. As, for example, with "E", when—on the basis of a strong feeling in me that in the most subtle of ways she was withdrawing—I indicate to her that what I am about to say to her is nothing I can possibly substantiate, but something of potential use and I feel we must work from it, even though it may be at the moment incorrect. I say that she is withdrawing from the analysis. Now, if the analyst works cautiously then this kind of intervention allows the patient to identify with the analyst, to include in the field of "the analytic", feeling-states that are not necessarily understandable.

Sometimes analysing why one feels the way one does is extremely helpful.

Countertransference really is nothing more nor less than that experience of being the patient's object. In so being, we are ultimately also to become the object of the patient's mother and father.

Are we sometimes something of the baby's object? An affect object? Like the baby's enraged mother-object? Or the baby's sleep protective-object? When we are nearly asleep, are we the baby's dream screen, our own thought quite minimised?

Are we ever an autistic object?

We are occasionally the transitional object.

With "X" I also used my countertransference to be aggressive with him, both to cure myself and to enable him an aggressive experience. There is, perhaps, as much a need for an aggressive experience as there is for the experience of being understood.

[20/12/81]
"Countertransference"

Annie Reich's position, that countertransference interferes with the analyst's ability to develop free floating attention is a misconception. The countertransference—those unconscious processes always at work in the analyst—is that-which-is-placed on the screen of the analyst's neutrality. Neutrality is an important concept but never an achievable aim. Nonetheless, as an aim it is exceedingly crucial to the creation of and attendance to the screen, as the analyst witnesses or analyses the patient's evocations in the analyst.

An analyst at home with work in the countertransference is more analytical, and the counter-transference does not interfere with the work, but the opposite. There are two sources of associative material: the patient's free associations and the analyst's internal free associations, that become organised in the analyst over time and in relation to the patient's transference: this is the nature of a countertransference.

The idea that the analyst's neutrality means an absence of internal affect states is simply impossible.

With increasingly disturbed patients it is frequently the case that the affective core of the patient's free association takes place in the analyst's countertransference. Rather like the baby-child who is known to the mother in terms of what she feels.

How does the analyst differentiate between what the patient puts into him and what he projects onto the patient? Langs'[i] offer one way: take note of the patient's associations and ask to what extent it is from the analyst 2) the analyst analyses himself 3) the analyst sees to what extent the countertransference fits with the transference.

By countertransference I should state that I definitely do not mean the analyst's transference to the patient, but the analyst's state of mind evoked by the patient.

The patient creates an atmosphere in which patient and analyst work. This complex atmosphere biases the analyst's private moods and thoughts. It is extremely subtle and important.

---

[i] Robert Langs, American psychoanalyst.

1982

Those analysts who say countertransference is the pathology of the analyst, to be settled by self analysis, are rationalising away the difficult task of relating the analyst's feelings to the patient's transference. It is a form of acting out: turning away from the unconscious interaction with the patient.

Furthermore, to say that the analyst's feelings, fantasies and private thoughts are not appropriate is to close off half of the available material for analysis: the analyst's attention to his own inner material and his linking of it to the patient's transference.

Additionally, patients whose illness has taken the form of a structural flaw of ego formation will tend to express the conflict through the way they relate to the object. Neurotic symptoms are ego dystonic and, like dreams, can be presented to the analyst. Ego defects cannot be so presented. Each patient acts it out on the analyst and depending on how effectively the analyst reads his subjective states, the patient will understand in time. An analyst who knows that as the blank screen, the screen is more effective if it has sensors; if it can record subjective states; if it can register, that is, the dissociated elements of the patient by virtue of the patient's effect on the analyst.

On the other hand, I never consider my subjective state unless I link it to the patient's subjective state. Any use I make of it will proceed on that basis.

Where does the analyst receive the patient? From what area of the mind does interpretation come? One classical view presupposes some aseptic area of the mind, cleansed of unconscious processes by virtue of the analyst's psychoanalysis, such that he can provide the patient with classical analysis, as if this phenomenon were somehow derived from a special area of the mind. The whole idea at best is a special form of arrogance; at worst, patently anti-psychoanalytic.

There are two distinct, though often—particularly retrospectively—related countertransferences:

1. Those feelings, thoughts, etc. that the analyst believes are inspired by the patient and can be linked to some action by the patient.
2. Those feelings that overcome the analyst, are present in him, but which he cannot link to an aspect of the patient.
3. Those feelings he knows are somehow derived very much from his own psychopathology.

So, by countertransference I focus on *counter* and I take it to mean that which is in the analyst as counter to the patient's transference. If we mean the analyst's own transference to the patient and his objects, then in the word countertransference the emphasis must fall on *transference*. Analysts could italicise one or the other in order to indicate to the reader roughly speaking what kind of countertransference is meant.

If a patient is in love with the analyst and the analyst loves the patient and both know this, then this is *the truth*. Is there some way for patient and analyst to discuss it?

If they know they hate?

If they know they are confused?

If they know they feel at a loss?

I work frequently from what I *sense* rather than what I know. For example, "C" is telling me a dream and associating, but I feel that she is thinking of something else and I say so. I don't know that she is, but I sense it. This is not intuition, as in I have a sense of some*thing*. I don't really know what is specifically on the patient's mind.

It is accurate to say that there are specific types of countertransference.

1. When the analyst transfers to the patient, when that is, the patient becomes an unconscious transference object.
2. When the analyst transfers to one or another of the patient's objects: a wife, a parent, etc.
3. When the analyst is compelled by the patient to live through the patient's early life, through repetition compulsion.
4. When the analyst is given a mental function, as a part of the patient's mind: as a superego, for example.

[undated]
"The child at play"

When the child plays with the parent he needs parental participation because he needs an other to accompany his psychic life. Reality is then internalised as a partner to fantasy. Parents who do not play with the child fail the child and foster dissociation.

[undated]
"Transference illusion/delusion"

Sohn's[i] way of working with patients is to:

1. Take their accounts of self and other—e.g. wives, events in their life—and inevitably link them to himself.
2. When the patient does talk directly about the analyst to him, the patient's experience is treated as a delusion: the expressed feelings about the analyst are treated as projections.

So, when the patient is not talking about the analyst, the analyst relates it *to himself,* inviting the patient to engage with him. When the patient does, the analyst *refers it away,* by referring it to past historical figures or to parts of the patient's self. This puts the patient in an impossible situation, a borderline one, in fact.

[undated]
"True self/false self"

Clinically, I wonder if one of the earliest manifestations in some patients of the true self comes through resistance, almost as a form of antisocial tendency. I think here of aggression, in terms of its positive value. Maybe "M", for example, must break me down because the analyst is too well equipped, too competent, and she must destroy me in order to exist more spontaneously.

Perhaps when analysts insist upon being analytic they invite such attacks, as it is the only way the patient can create a space of their own making.

[21/01/82]
"Countertransference"

Actually I think that when I say to a patient, let's analyse the analyst's position, I am making it clear that I am analysing the effect of the transference, yielding a new or extended source of material. So in a sense I am analysing the transference, as I am quite sure that my mood is a result of the patient's presence.

In fact, I think it is true to say that when I get a registration of countertransference, I am very pleased. So many of my patients are incapable of verbalising or of associating, that when I am aware of feeling something, and I analyse it to myself to ascertain its link to the patient, I am very pleased.

---

[i] Leslie Sohn, gifted British Kleinian analyst.

[undated]
"Countertransference"

How with "E" *the material was in me*, as I knew she was presenting me with a false self, a false illness that could be analysed. She even gave me links, without her ever being inside the clinical situation. How I felt an absence and how I had to live with this.

Her absence = the true absence of her father who was present in a false ebullient and charming way; how she was false as a child; how she is a person of nascent health and how it was the health—her aliveness that I missed: knowing, of course, that it was there to be missed. I would not have felt this with another patient.

How my approach deepens transference regression as the patient is in an affectively present holding environment. How with some persons I work only classically, as I do not think this situation warrants it.

How after a while (six months to two years) the patient finally allows the evolution of the true self, in a state of regression to dependence.

Their emerging love, after a time, and then gratitude.

[undated]
"When we see our parents in our child"

I am thinking of how in Sacha,[ii] when I am with him, I see my mother, and of how through Sacha I feel much fonder, more forgiving of her, as something very decent about her emerges through him. Of course, I suppose I passed this on (unconsciously that is) so I am part of it.

I now see as I did not before just how the child is father (and mother) to the man, as you see your parents and yourself in your child, and it is a special form of transference.

[04/03/82]
"Self-as-object"

When "M" talks to me in her dialect—her plaintive tone of voice—she is acting out an element of herself, or more importantly of her mother, in order to objectify it, to watch it, perhaps to attack it. It is a self-as-object relation because here the self is false, indeed not the person at all, and may be someone else entirely.

[13/03/82]
"Self-as-object"

Start with Freud's idea that the ego is originally a body ego and possibly the idea that the relation to the body is responsible for three-dimensionality. Perhaps we are made particularly aware of our bodies, as in illness or pregnancy, in older age, and in the anorectic. Recall "S"'s way of rubbing his

---

[ii] My son, then almost four.

hands together, of the autistic child's fear of the body, which is an other to him. How frightened of the body contents, such as faeces, or how worried about blood and tears they are.

Some people are able to observe the mad self. This is particularly true of the hysteric and the obsessional; the former an intense witness to what they create, the latter would appear to be object of demands to do the irrational.

[undated]
"Self-as-object and schizophrenia"

When someone is delusional and projecting the self into objects, there is a loss of a relation to the self as an object. For some reason it is abandoned. In health, the intrasubjective holding environment is crucial to well being.

What has happened?

The self is no longer there to be spoken to.

The "you" is now external—as a persecutor—the same "you" that was formerly an internal object. The ever present pronominal locus of a part of the self being spoken to all the time.

[16/03/82]
"Speaking the self in analysis"

Each person has never been known so well by an other as they are by the analyst. Through this relationship, by speaking to the analyst about the self, aspects of the self, split off parts and so forth, are found, and in the telling, experienced.

The analyst must appreciate the value of the patient's need *to reflect* and to use the analyst's sentient neutrality, to find through speaking what is lost (undoing of repression) and what is felt. The analyst's interpretations often interfere with this.

[16/03/82]
"Self"

I have a subjective experience of being "inside" my own character. This total relationship (I am inside my character) is the self. Self is composed of Being as experience of subject and object. In Being, I am subject and object.

Self is a relationship in which a person's being is constituted out of a unified opposition: one is both subject and object. A subject with a self as object and as an object with a self as directing subject.

[16/03/82]
"The child as object of the self"

Each parent parenting a child is parenting a part of the self. For the mother, literally so.

"K" wants a baby. Yet her baby is a "rat" (patient's association); it is a negative narcissistic object reflecting her own baby self; or representing the greed within herself. She believes she cannot give birth to this. She has a dream of a room or a flat which she loads up with objects, splitting the door and dividing the room and opening it up to me to see inside, showing a baby and a mother.

She developed a false self to adapt to a mother and (in phantasy) the true self (baby) went back into the mother's body. As an infant she was not seduced out of autism into object relating, but I suspect it was in sleep and in feeding that she found her most enjoyable moments. To this day she sleeps a great deal. For the separation is an abortion. She lives inside people and then, after a while, aborts herself.

I think she is in direct competition with the baby she wants to have. The baby aspect of herself is saying: "How dare 'you' have a baby. What about me??" This is an unconscious intrasubjective dialogue. The self is both mother and baby.

So, in the self-as-object relation, parts of the self are mother, father and baby-child. Perhaps this dichotomy, this bipolarity, emerges from the fact that the first union—mother and child—was a situation where subject and object existed in a merged or fused state.

So, the relation to the self as an object derives from a dual-unity (mother–child) and the experience that one's being is composed of two presences, one active the other passive, or one mother and another child, etc., etc. comes from the original fact of being-with the mother and simultaneously identifying with the mother's management of the self as an object.

[undated]
"Self-as-object: patient on the way to talk to the analyst"

"K" says: "I am talking to myself about telling you something." The patient on the way to a session is having to talk to the self—indeed to ask the self—about what is new, and what to say. This relation is an important part of the psychoanalytic process. It creates an *a priori atmosphere*, prior to the session, when the patient is *in session with the self,* attempting to get to the core of being.

In fact, the person "entering" analysis is simultaneously "entering" an intensified relation to the self as other, which is spoken to, implored, and waited for. Many patients are waiting for news from the self.

[undated]
"Telling the dream"

In reporting the dream as an object the person addresses the self as Other. In that the dream is Other.

[18/03/82]
"Self as object"

I point out to "B" how her own care of herself is Victorian, censorious and cruel. I take examples of how she berates herself and say "if one of your children approached you and said all these things about themselves, I am sure you would respond in an empathic and understanding way, yet with yourself, you are the opposite."

I show her how her way of being enacts her "mother"'s handling of her: she is a "dirty girl" who drove the mother away from her.

[undated]
"The management of time"

How does each person manage time?

And if we realise that the person arranges time and space and is simultaneously the object of, or, *in* such designs, the person creates a holding environment in which they exist.

[undated]
"Evocative aspects of words in analysis"

"O" wants me to use such words as "nappy" or "mother" or "feed" because it creates or evokes feelings in him. I think it is a nostalgic reason which defends against other feelings. RECOLLECTIVE ADDICTION. The *need* to recollect as a defence.

[08/04/82]
"Self"

To what extent is the self actually the "inherited potential" that Winnicott speaks of, which becomes—through maternal care—the "continuity in being"?

[17/04/82 San Diego]
"The integrity crisis"

Whereas the *identity crisis* had to do with the question "who am I?", the person amidst an integrity crisis knows who he is, has a sense of self, which in essence is the very basis for the crisis in which he lives, because he lives with little relation between his inner self and his *personal environment*, that world created by each individual for personal habitation.

[undated]
"Self-as-object"

Who do you talk to when you talk to yourself?

[15/04/82]
"The secret self (and how I discover it) in countertransference fantasy"

Only today do I understand "S". He tells me he is at a castle where they are making a film, and that he visits the library where he looks at 17th-century books on portraiture. He decides to describe the situation in great detail, so vivid is it that I have a fantasy. I imagine him looking at these books and a colleague coming up to him—a fellow technician—who says "S, come on.

What the hell are you doing, looking at these books? Let's go!" and "S" replying "Well, actually, I am a portrait artist. My work is in the National Gallery."

It turns out the patient is a portrait artist in his spare time but it is a secret. Now this I discover through my fantasy, which says something about the uses of countertransference and how it is that he must first be imagined before he can be understood. I must dream him. Previously I have tried to understand him, to analyse him, but I have not imagined him. The fact is that he is living out a fantasy that he contains an other self, a secret self, and it is a prince and pauper fantasy. That is why he can not celebrate his painting because if he does then he loses the pauper/prince fantasy because he no longer contains a secret self. The magic of Superman is Clark Kent's secret! It is not in what Superman does, it is in what Kent conceals. This is the power of fantasy.

Fundamentally, it is an oedipal problem. The child keeps the secret that he is actually very powerful.

When I imagine (through his colleague) talking to him I am engaged in an empathic rapport with him: it is through my fantasy that I suddenly understand his fantasy. He has prepared the way by providing me with very beautiful imagery. He creates the space for imagining and I have the fantasy.

[20/06/82]
"Countertransference"

In my countertransference paper when I say that the analyst must analyse the patient and the analyst, I do not stress sufficiently that really such a psychoanalysis must be an analysis of two as if they were equals. Also, I need to point out that to see myself as the other patient is not necessitated by inappropriate countertransference states but by my recognition that I am the source of a significant portion of potential material. Furthermore, the emphasis on dramatic countertransference states, such as hate or envy, detracts from the truth, as the most prevalent inappropriate countertransferences are not severe interruptions of sessions—such that the analyst cannot work—but quiet misperceptions of the patient's internal reality. These are dynamically relevant as such misperceptions are part of the patient's transference recreation of his early environment. So I am able to see how the person is part of a quiet even secret pathology.

The above is extremely important as countertransference is defined as that which occurs in the analyst's mind while with a particular patient. The analyst cannot afford to assume that he is rational or analytic, even when certain of his interpretations are quite logical. He must be prepared to be analyst of his own analysis of the patient.

[undated]
"America's children"

The child I am thinking of has no linkage between nascent moods, thoughts, and articulate differentiated verbal representations. Indeed, there is a deflating and frustrating stereotypic speech—crude, uncategorized—and <u>this is a transference</u> in which the child re-presents a parental world that has failed abysmally as a transformational object. The child has never enjoyed generative mirroring where the parent empathises with their nascent moods and articulates them from the true self. Instead, there is "tele-speak"; simple, crude, translations into convention-language: i.e. "oh, you are just low", "you will feel better", "come on, snap out of it", etc., phrases that doom the mood to extinction and fate the child to a banal pseudo-adaptive conclusion.

As patients such people compel the analyst to feel a certain countertransference, as the patient speaks in a kind of crude speech and the analyst endeavours to transform crude speech into facilitating articulation. Each time the analyst tries to do this, the patient uses crude speech: "yup", "I guess", "I dunno", to deflate the analyst. In such a moment the analyst's experience is like that of the original child who experiences a dismissingly crude response to the effort to relate.

     infant—child----------------------mother
     (in need of rapport)   (untransformative) frustrating)

     Analyst
     (in need of understanding etc.)-------------patient
                                       (uncooperative, language deflating)

My experience with the woman on the phone in (a state in the USA) is a countertransference to the deflating mother. This was the experience when I was trying to articulate how I was different and in a sense I was trying to make myself known. She kept responding, by saying, "You either have to be" or "If you haven't been supervised by a licensed X", all of which had a terribly deflating effect on me because I wished to communicate, but I could not get through.

This brings to mind how frequently in America, particularly with medical psychoanalysts, when I was being imaginative and creative—particularly when developing something through articulation—someone would say "that's too fanciful" or "fuzzy thinking". Inevitably this is deflating. I think they *lack* the ability to contain and transform: they may have little space (internal) for reception, digestion, and facilitation of "free thought"; but they do have an impressive system for the classification and the categorisation of experience.

Thus they can relate to the phenomenon of objectivity or scientific method as if it were the other to whom one talks. That is, many have replaced communicating with a narcissistic relation to a dead object (the scientific method) into which they put the data they find, and, persons can act like this to and for each other. Therefore, if I am presenting feelings or thoughts, the listener may already be putting me into a machine <u>composed of categories functioning like inter related working parts.</u>

Hence the psychoanalytic obsession with systems and categories (etc.) in which no one listens in order to develop relating. They may listen in order to place the communication into an internalised matrix and will print out the answer.

The speech they speak can be <u>deadening.</u>

[08/06/82]
"The projective shield and healthy denial"

The mother protects the child from premature recognition of certain facts of life and screens out potentially destructive stimuli. This protective shield function is a paradigm and the infant identifies with this selective screening out, by noticing only what it can process. In a way, as the infant becomes aware that maternal function is an act of love, then self protection—protective shield to self—is also an act of love, and so some forms of denial are acts of love in relation to the self.

[30/06/82]
"The analyst's love of the patient"

Good technique amounts—as far as the patient is concerned—to being loved. Thus the positive transference is a response to analytic love which is the unconscious equivalent of parental love. If we hide behind the idea of "empathy" (etc.) we miss the point: i.e. we love the patient.

[11/07/82]
"Self"

I have a subjective experience of being "inside" my character. This total relationship (I am inside my character): is this the self?

[25/07/82]
"Transference"

One effect of "here-and-now" transference interpretation is to compel the patient into a symbiosis (a paranoid symbiosis) as a defence against the complexities of life in the clinical situation. As the analyst refers everything to himself, the patient's sense of self (or even sense of uncertainty which has been valued) is subsumed into the analyst, so in order to find himself the patient must look into the analyst (etc.). This is the symbiosis. Transference experience must ordinarily precede transference interpretation.

[03/08/82]
"Transformational object"

The analyst functions as a transformational object particularly through clarification and interpretation, transforming confusion into understanding, bewilderment into clarity. This *action* on the analyst's part evokes memories of the mother's and father's function and leads to the positive transference which is based on ego love, whereas the eroticised transference is not.

Is it possible to think of this as primarily the therapeutic element, even the psychotherapeutic element of psychoanalysis? Who knows?

The point is that the analyst transforms affect and idea in the patient, and, even when introducing a painful interpretation, the analyst presents an object to the patient that takes him out of himself.

Frequently the aim of an interpretation of the transformational object is to evoke feelings in the patient. This may be regressive insofar as this was the discourse between mother and child: emotional experience.

In the early phases I work fundamentally as a transformational object, trying to facilitate a necessary regressing specific to the clinical situation in which affect is the primary medium, the patient feels understood, and the patient becomes more infantile, and earlier structures become paramount.

[undated]
"Self relating"

I assume:

1. Each person is both a subject and an object in the idiom of self relating.
2. Ego structures, defences, and the unconscious means that a significant portion of an individual's life feels as if it is determined from elsewhere, and the person is therefore an object.
3. Each person unconsciously transfers elements of the maternal and paternal care system, influenced by the distortions of the infant.

[28/08/82]
"When the mood is the object relation: on fretting"

"S" preserves a relation to his mother–father by fretting. Fretting denies separation and preserves attachment to the parents. The mood (of fretting, hoping, being self critical) is *the effect of the object*. The way of preserving the object by holding on to the effect of the object, like humming songs after a rock concert is a way of preserving a relation to the rock group after separation from them.

In other words, we preserve the object and our relation to it by preserving *the effect* of the object on us, bearing this in our moods.

This is the opposite of projective identification. It is more a kind of introjective identification, in that the subject preserves the object by maintaining the effect it had in the first place.

"S" preserves his parents by holding on to their effect on him. His moods of self indictment, hope, and the yearnful relation to time *is* the relation to his parents. So, a mood may be an object, or more particularly, an object relation.

[01/09/82]
"When mood is relation"

"X"'s despair, or sullen sulking. He says he is aware with his girlfriend of wanting to maximise his pain in order to affect her, and that he has a magical belief that if he is sufficiently distressed then he can communicate that to her and somehow this will have an effect.

Actually, his way of being intimate with his parents was in the complicitous sharing of sadness and forlornness together. Each abandoned the other. Each grieved, sulked, and partly consoled the other. They did not love vigorously, argue with vigour, engage one another, or intellectually inspire one another.

"X"'s *personal idiom* of grief, anticipatory mourning, and sulking is an object relation.

With his girlfriend he tries to use their loss from each other as a shared grieving and through this shared grieving to become intimate with her, thus becoming or involving her in his object relation.

It is not accurate to say that infants and children have mothers and fathers. They have two worlds. The world of the mother and the other world of the father. Through these worlds they see and experience reality.

[02/09/82]
"Mood as object relation"

A mood is not entirely like a simple affect. It is the affective expression of an object relation. It is an environment, or, the moods to which I refer are self created climates of being in which the person exists and invites the other to exist in a particular way.

Frequently a mood is an aspect of self relating that recreates a relationship.

[03/09/82]
"Problems of aggression, compliance and paranoid organisation"

"X" has difficulty being aggressive. Indeed he says that expression of anger and aggression is the equivalence of violence. That is because as he cannot speak up he imagines aggression, and in his omnipotence he obliterates the object. Thus he always finds an internal violent solution caused by internal objects.

But as a child he was the object of parental neglect.

In his relations to people he is over adaptive and over compliant. He does not express himself, but what he does is to become the passive object of the other: their *tabula rasa*. He stores up information, data of those moments when he was wronged as the object, and he stores this up with the imagined Armageddon in his mind; that day when he will *list* the wrongdoings to the object, in court, and the sheer evidence will obliterate the other.

He does not want to speak up for himself when angered, for a number of reasons, one of which is that to speak is to blow one's evidence, to lose one's power. This is the paranoid strategy. By bearing the grudge, or by collecting evidence against the other, he enjoys a sense of security as he smugly collects data against the other. He knows that in court he can point to good behaviour on his part, to his overly helpful disposition, and to a list of awful wrongdoings, mistakes, and so forth by the other.

This leads to
   a. a sense of triumph
   b. a sense of security
   c. a sense of fate.

All this is related to the future Armageddon.

It is also inspired, however, by anxiety as he is desperately afraid of being wiped out by the environment.

[17/09/82]
"Rage is not anger!"

Persons who have outbreaks of rage are discharging themselves of anger. Rage is much closer to an anxiety attack. It is self-cancelling and an indirect attack on the self. It undoes anger. The expression of anger engages the object, while rage does not.

[20/09/82]
"The adolescent and the 'household'"

At the moment of apparently discarding the parents, the adolescent's use of the house reflects an interesting regressive use of an early parent. The house becomes a kind of collated object or collated alternate of the early mother. It is barged into. The adolescent leaves debris behind him (= faeces that will be cleaned up by the mother); he crashes up and down the stairs, forcing the house to groan, as if pushing against it, and enjoying its benign authority and constant availability.

[20/09/82]
"Mood as an object relation"

"S"'s dreamy mood—when he is frustrated with reality—is his way of recreating an idiom in his being that prevailed when he was living with his mother and father as a couple: he is the boy daydreaming. The mood, then, has to do with the preservation of an object relation and that is one of the dynamic reasons why he will not give up the daydreaming self.

Does mood have to do with *preservation*? Does it differ from affect, in that through a mood a person is unconsciously preserving a relation to early objects?

Does "D"'s wistfulness and forgetfulness enact a memory of his loss of his father and his nursing his grandfather? By preserving a mood, is the person indicating the necessity of an important object relation?

"I"'s pessimism and coldness—his prevailing mood—is an attachment to his father. Sure, it is negative; but it was his relation to his father, so is he relating to his father through the mood?

Indeed, mood is relating through affects to internal objects. It is the quality of relating that distinguishes mood from affect.

[27/10/82]
"The ideal"

Here and now interpreting is a negative hallucination: the removal of history.

Temporal narcissism: it's all about you and me.

Denial of time.

[27/10/82]
"Moods"

Through a mood a person accomplishes a kind of psycho-somatic state. A psycho-somatic being.

[30/10/82]
"Hypercathexis of self as fetish"[iii]

"O" misses his girlfriend. I say that he misses the image of her, or loves the memory. It is a masturbatory omnipotent love.

During the week he recollects several times the fact that she gently touched him on his jumper.

I think, given that he did not sleep with her, given that he tantalised her, that he needs to cathect his body-image-self and have accomplices, because this investment functions as a fetish. It is an organisation that is prerequisite to any intercourse. When his girlfriend actually touches him he feels anxious, as if all his potency is drained out of him, and this is because she attempts true intimacy. As the highly valued, not-to-be-touched object, the fetish is removed on actual touching.

"O"'s hyperconscious self awareness is a narcissistic-fetishistic organisation; the body self functioning as the mind's fetish object. Remove the narcissistic fetish and immediately an anxious depression ensues.

[01/10/82]
"The third party in the narcissistic relation"

"E" withdraws from her boyfriend and from me and induces a pursuant mood. This is repeated. She uses her beauty as the object of desire which she withdraws from the other, in effect saying, "You cannot have me. I have me. Sorry." This mirrors her sense of what her father did to her. It also comprises her sexual identity in relation to men.

[13/10/82]
"Transformational object"

Example of internal parenting.

A mother sees her child making a mess. For the child, it is the behavioural represen- tation of pleasure. The mother, however, is cross and yells at the child and takes him away from the mess-making activity. This is a transformation from the child's point of view, and it is one performed by the mother. Now, instead of feeling pleasure and joy, and his unselfcon- scious-going-on-being, the child is upset and anxious. He cries or approaches the mother for consoling. If she expresses further anger and does not accept the child's solicitations, the child's state is transformed again, now into despair and lonesomeness. But, if the mother consoles the child, expresses her own regret over her outburst, she transforms the child's state back into

---

[iii] These are early considerations of a personality whom I would eventually term a "trisexual".

relative quiescence and this transformational object is one that the child can internalise, as even when creating a bad transformation of the child's state, the transformational object can correct a bad transformation and so catastrophe does not ensue.

Schizoid children cannot internalise the parenting process, as to do so would be to take in a process of self-state transformation that leads to the experience of catastrophe. So, the child freezes himself. He becomes overly conscious, relates to his parents as fixed-place introjects (usually as distressing objects) so that ironically pleasure from a parent is confusing as it destabilises the child's defences!

Narcissistic and schizoid characters have frozen their internal worlds into "known bad scenes" and the dynamic interpersonal aim of such characters is to keep a distance from people, unless they "fall into" a self object relation.

Borderlines have never actually linked their internal chaos to an object; at least, not during their early development. They "know" the object only through the affective chaos created by the object. In some ways, borderlines search the object world for persons into whom they can empty or locate their intense affective chaos: hate going to person A, love to person B, anxiety to person C, bewilderment to person D and so forth.

[20/10/82]
"Reverse mentation"

"T" uses his mind to dismantle the known, through a kind of apparent obsessionality.

I say that he wants to find rest by discovering a powerful lady who will take over his mind and think for him, dominating him but allowing him to rest. He says, or asks, intellectually about this—i.e. why does he do it—and says he is not sure he wants rest, but perhaps peace. The point is, however, that he is trying to dismantle my interpretation and I note to him this transformation.

We use our minds—when our mental processes serve us—to develop the inarticulate towards meaningful knowing. Mind or mental process is a transformational object. With "T" and in cases of reverse mentation the person dismantles knowing.

In "T" it is the child undoing recognition (and articulation = positive mental processes!) of needs, affects, and perceptions in relation to mother. In order to adapt to her he felt he needed not to know his needs, desires, feelings and perceptions.

His fantasy of where his positive mental processes lay is inside the other; the woman who will dominate him. [The patient's erotic life imagines being dominated by a powerful woman.]

His mentation is useless to him. He alters self states from relative sentient knowing into sterile mental abstractions and transforms himself into emptiness and futility.

[untitled]
"Here-and-now transference"

The here-and-now transference is a narcissistic circuit. It is a simple step of narcissistic imperialism. Instead of the patient saying "I"—as that which solely composes the world—now the patient and analyst say "us" to the exclusion of external reality. But it is the defensive use of the transference interpretation which is its narcissistic element. On the positive side, it is like a nursing couple. On the negative, it is a negation of both psychic reality (which it forecloses) and the interplay of mind and reality, where the analytic couple = mind, and that which the patient presents is sometimes external reality (out looking) and sometimes reflective inner looking.

[09/11/82]
"Search for disturbance"

The person for whom peaceful being is not possible.
    To create or find disturbance is to discover the familiar amidst the unfamiliar.

[19/11/82]
"The perverse transference"

"O" has pseudo dialogues with friends. They are set situations in which she can predict how that friend might respond to any situation. If she treats one friend badly then another friend will say "you *are* monstrous" allowing "O" to cry, which then allows that friend to say "I'm sorry." The function of these pseudo dialogues is to release affects and states of mind. But always dialogues are occasions for pre known experiencing. They are sensations. Of remorse, vituperation, dread, need, and so forth. But they are not real and the only real catastrophe for "O" is how to help herself when she is in true need of communicating and true need of help.

    Equally, what I have characterised above as typical of her in external dialogues is typical of her intra subjective dialogues, where differing parts of her total self seek to be discharged of their contents. Of the analysis she can say to herself "Why do you *go* to this man?" "He helps me." "It's all a load of shit!" "No, it's not; it is helpful." In fact, she does not know the truth.

    Now how is the transference perverse? By occasionally appearing in a session– or a group of sessions—with a scrap of material, she gets me to make an interpretation. However, she then tells me how she has either lied or omitted a significant portion of the truth. The effect is to make my interpretation useless and, over time, to give me a sense of unevenness in myself. I may think I know why she is silent; indeed, I've interpreted it enough. But *do I* know what she is doing? No! I tell her all this and that it is an attack on the analysis and she says that she does have a view of me as indecisive ... which is true! I am indecisive with her, having changed my mind many times about what she is up to. In the countertransference I have become the unreliable object, except for the fact that I do say all of this and it has become the object of the analysis.

[26/10/82]
"Excitement and the false self"

"O"'s "torment" in which she attempts to confess secrets to me is part of an effort to use the idea of secrecy as a substitute for the self. In fact she is frightened that reporting to me from herself will result in a loss of identity ("I keep secrets") and a confusion that is becoming a depression.

The aim is to use the illusion of presence—of an exciting-as-yet-undisclosed x—as a substitute for the true self. In fact, *there is nothing there*! Hence, analysis of her resistances, correct as it has been—re her anxiety and guilt—was not enough to undo the perversion in the analysis, because through the perversion she maintains an illusion of personal presence. In fact, her fantasy is that upon disclosure, the other finds nothing.

I think this stems from the occasional-exciting-view of the mother. Apparently the father used to say to her that she might be "lucky" to see her mother that day. The fact is, however, that this preserves the illusion that the mother in her full presence is knowable and enriching. In fact, in this family the parents teased each other, endowing interactions with a false promise: "you only see part of me; come, catch me." But this pseudo excitement, perfected by being a little "nutty"—or eccentric—was a defence against unrelatedness and internal confusion and desultoriness.

"O" picked this up and she too became "nutty" (and quite phobic) and therefore interesting. To be interesting was her ambition. But she has been such only by teasing her objects. She goes away in order to preserve the illusion that she has something to go back to. In the transference she presents as this figure with bizarre, exciting objects, only just beyond the pale of disclosure. I am meant to be excited (and impotent). In the countertransference I do feel frustrated, angry, and futile. I have also unwittingly colluded with her in that I have believed there was something there! Her perversions led me to believe this. But the function of perversion in her is to create the illusion of presence, about to eventuate into shared meaning (orgasm) but withdrawing the secret, giving me the sense of something taken away. In fact, there is nothing there at all, except for the structure of the perverse. She has internalised the effect of the mother.

1. Here I am: surprise!
2. You want me, don't you!!
3. I do have riches.
4. But not for you: not now!

"O"'s exclusion from the mother is the reason, I think, for the heightened primal scene fantasising. She is led into a belief that if she could spy on mother in bed, she would come by the secret mother.

This mother used her sense of the child's need to tease the child: to enhance her—the mother's—depleted narcissism with the child's always unsatisfied need.

Therefore, not the object, but the effect of the object—excitement, loss, promise—is cathected. The object is not known; it is only re-experienced: the same way each time. And this is true of "O"'s sessions! She is *the same* each time!! I do not know her.

In perversion, the false self is a ritualised illusion of presence, designed to affect the object. The passive experience of trauma, once experienced by the child, is now reversed and acted out: she arouses people and leaves them, inducing trauma. But she lives in a world in which the use of self to excite and then sadistically misuse the other's true need is already a ritualised phenomenon. As everyone knows this, it can all be acted out, and rarely does this lead to real trauma.

With the analyst, however, the perversion is not completed: the analyst registers his knowing of absence, his experiencing of frustrations etc., and by bringing this to the patient, the patient is put in touch with herself. When she says to me "Oh, poor sad man, why does he try?" she is really recollecting her early childhood. I think her telling me this story of how she talks to herself about me is a turning point.

Also, her most meaningful encounters with me are in the absence of me. In her car, on the way to session, she is with me. I think her masochism is an effort to create the illusion of meaning, i.e. "if I am worthy of such punishment, then I contain evil, I am there!"

[30/11/82]
"Self as object"

"S"'s transference to self:

1. His mother did not take notice of or facilitate core areas of the self.
2. He repeats this in his relation to himself as an object as he neglects core self.
3. But the child's response is rage, manifested in:
    a. His dismantling of his own self care system, as the self care system is associated with the internalised maternal care system. The dismantling is part of a regressive demand: "I refuse to be in my care; I destroy everything; I insist everything be for me."
    b. As when a child, he lives inside a compensatory grandiose world, made up of dreams and so forth. This is opposed to mother's reality.
4. Transference–countertransference:
    a. When I try to focus on core areas of the self, areas of health etc., (or when anyone does) he destroys my efforts, including my perception. Thus he becomes an appalling negative force, as I stand up for the good core areas of the self.
        i. In my countertransference I think often of giving up and just doing maintenance therapy (false self) and in this moment I am like the child he was, facing the maternal negative force.
        ii. But what keeps me going? I do see in him recognition of my effort and some meaningful alliance. There is, thus, some good mother in him somewhere.
5. By trying to kill himself he is killing the mother's child. It is her child he wishes to kill.

[18/12/82]
"Celebration of the patient"

Example: a child, "P", is in treatment at age 11. The two parents are well-educated professionals and very controlling. In therapy she draws a big institution-like house with a television in the basement. (She suffered an outbreak of symptoms when she saw a monster's face disintegrate on a TV program.) And then she did not want to go to sleep. In therapy she draws a spider web and a spider and the therapist says, "You have put something fearful, like black spiders with their cobwebs." P says, cuttingly, "Really I wanted to make a big bicycle, but I can't manage."

Now the therapist's intervention is not correct. Let's say that the spider = representation of the mother's genitals and genital instincts, or sadistic instincts. In other words, THE INSTINCTS ARRIVE in the form of the spider. When this happens, the therapist must *celebrate* the arrival. I would say "Ah! A spider!" with some neutral surprise, facilitating elaboration. Maybe I would have said "What does the spider do?"

"P" created another drawing of a boy on a horse, very erect. But the trace of a beautiful girl can be seen: she erased it and replaced it with a boy. I would have said "What a beautiful girl! Why is she erased?"

We know from "P" that her mother was easily enraged (the disintegrating face) and I reckon the TV was a screen memory of "P" seeing her mother's face change into rage etc. over "P"'s instinctual life, lived out in play.

The child therefore needs *celebration* of instinctual life before the anxieties are interpreted, otherwise interpretation alone simply recreates the distanced parents.

With adults I have celebrated:

1. "X"'s manic metaphors during his manic periods: "Well, what you say is extraordinary", or "Well, I do admire your beautiful analogy", and then proceed to analyse, but I have affirmed and celebrated a potentially healthy side of the mania.
2. "X"'s aggression: "Ah! Okay! I am trounced by you! You are enjoying this!"
3. "O"'s sadistic fantasies: "Well, I do laugh, because frankly it is hilarious" which celebrates the arrival of his sadism.
4. "C"'s clothing: "But you know you are a strikingly handsome person and why shouldn't you enjoy your looks?"
5. "I"'s apology for being aggressive: "But why shouldn't you be aggressive! Why shouldn't you have a go at me? I won't disappear and I shall, I assure you, continue to say what I think!"

In other words, it is my view that if we are to analyse we must also include areas of health and we must facilitate the arrival of new self states (splits coming into session) by greeting such with a certain celebration: "Ah! I am a dummy am I?" "Ah! So at last we hear from your needy self. That's all right, isn't it?"

[20/12/82]
"Here-and-now transference interpretation"

In the 1960s "here and now" was a catch phrase both demanding immediate gratification of demands and in some cases shedding the self of complexity. In the therapy circles it was used by encounter therapists to counterpoint psychoanalysis, which was seen as too embedded in the past.

The irony that this catchphrase is now so avidly a part of the psychoanalytic lexicon, points to a narcissistic need in the analyst for an equivalent immediate gratification: the need to feel meaningful. The narcissistic demand is further elaborated in the fact that history and reality (other contexts) are displaced by the analyst who insists he be the narcissistic object: i.e. "all your references have to do with you and me." The fact that some patients resist this narcissism and become enraged is only the analyst's projective identification of their own narcissistic rage into the patient. The patient's "negative transference" is then analysed; in fact, it's the analyst's unconscious analysis of a split off portion of himself: that self that would be enraged if narcissistic needs were not met.

[20/12/82]
"What's on your mind?"

How inappropriate this question is! With "X" whose silence and vengefulness was so evident, for me to ask the above was to ignore her being.

"Let me comment on your being or presence" should be *the other* means of confronting this situation, as the patient is registering their state via their being.

1983

[20/01/83]
"Grief orgasm"

"L"'s lamenting, paroxysms of anguish and use of confession in front of a woman, is a sexuali-sation of loss and grief. It gives pleasure; there is a forepleasure—a build up—and an orgasm. The orgasmic moment is when he is *slapped*; that is, the moment of rejection. He does this, also, to himself. *Relief* follows, but not gratification.

The infant's needs for oral gratification are not met; instead, frustration builds up into tension-anguish, occasioned by a sense of loss. Relief comes with the eventual return of the object, but not an object-mother that can gratify the needs; only one that recreates libido need and sets up loss experience as alternative to gratification.

This is a kind of conversion experience, from libido to loss.

[23/01/83]
"Klein's technique"

Small children engage in "bi-lateral monologues" (Gregory Bateson), in that what they say to each other has no link with what the other says. What MK did not realise was that she was unconsciously acting out the infant's idiom of being, as her interpretations have little to do with the child's thinking, but the child allows for it precisely because of this fact.

"Here-and-now transference interpretation"

The analyst creates a situational illness in the patient, so it is in the here and now, but it is not an examination of transference. It is an examination of the patient's ego response to illness created by the analyst.

Transference—the establishment through object relating and usage—of the analyst takes time before what was there and then becomes here and now.

"Self reflection". I want the patient to address the self as an object. To relate to that self. If I speak too much, *translating* the patient to himself, I interfere with the patient's reflective relation to himself. Reflective thinking may be very different from analytical thinking. Psycho-reflective psychoanalysis.

[undated]
"Here and now"

Radio transmitter. The "on the scene" comment of the here-and-now analyst is like some on the scene reporter *announcing* the session, in a play by play manner. It is spoken *to* the patient as if the patient were not there, and needed a report, like the radio announcer who must report the scene to those not there.

Here-and-now interpreting destroys:

1. psychic elaboration and creativity
2. symbolic sublimation
3. intermediate object usage
4. self experiencing
5. self reflection
6. self analysis
7. individuation
8. self and other limitations (of being one person or one patient, instead of being always two people).

1984

"Trisexuality and hysteria"

The hysteric as trisexual aims to reassert the preference of pregenital object choice, from the vantage point of the other. That is, she desires the other's pregenital desire of her. This involves the mother and father as male or female genital elements.

In choosing the self as the object of desire—of everyone's desire—the hysteric *defeats* sexuality and converts it to sexualised admiration.

The promiscuous person—Don Juan or an hysteric—aims to cancel sexuality and to substitute it with self love. They defeat the oedipal space and *become a memory*.

To be the memory of the other's desire is the triumphant aim of the trisexual, who thereby asserts the priority of early object love: the immemorable. Such persons feel they have lost something. They are insistent that this be registered and in their object relations they compel the other to lose them. This amounts less to a loss of desire itself, but a conversion of desire into sweet memory and familial company. This "family" is not the past oedipal family, but the preoedipal family that congregates—in the toddler's mind—around himself.

[3/2/84]
"Control over the passing of time"

"Z" must offer himself to a woman—as a listener etc.—in order to control the interaction. He cannot let go and allow for *things to develop* in their own right. As a child his experience of the passing of time was not good. So he takes charge. He controls "it" by being aggressively maternal: he looks after either others or himself with aggressive comprehensibility.

If a child has experienced losses, departures, etc.—traumas of event—he may no longer have a sense of time passing as a good object.

[18/2/84]
"Memory & recollection"

What kinds of memory are there in psychoanalytic reconstruction?

Simple memory: the retrieval of facts.

Unconscious memory: the de-repression of a memory.

Structure as memory: I construct from the way a person is organized some conversation about their original experiences.

Structure is memory. But is it always memory of the mother or father? No. Because we also experience Self, and Self is too complex a phenomenon to be totally understood in terms of other.

We also remember structure formation itself. That is, some dreams, phantasies etc. are "memories" of ego formation. An anxiety state may be a memory. Some of these affect states are memories of affect & self states of early mental life.

[14/3/84]
"Hysterical conversion, paralysis & affectivity"

What is the relation between enervation and histrionics?

The hysteric was a *paralysed* child. Immobilized by a dominating parent.

In the transference–countertransference they become that parent and immobilize the therapist.

To be sure, their own way of "speaking" to the mother is by borrowing her histrionic style of externalising the self (what you see is what you get).

[15/3/84]
"Self analysis–psychoanalysis"

Contemporary psychoanalysis—indeed psychoanalysis from the very beginning—is an incomplete act. Freudian analysis, or that act committed by F, is an analysis of two, not one. I will hold that an analyst's self analysis is an ongoing feature, a vital feature, of the act of psychoanalysis. In many ways the increasing interest in countertransference is, in fact, the re-emergence of the analyst's self analysis, conducted in relation to a particular patient.

Freud's analysis of himself was an outcome, a development of his analysis of his hysterical patients.

It may well be that some aspects of his subsequent technique, particularly the blank screen, acts out an impasse in relation to the hysteric. It may be an enervation in the analyst.

[undated]
"The hysteric"

Emmy von N: in her body activity (hands) also <u>sounds</u>—a clacking noise: strangulated movement.

SOUND (affecting Freud's sense of hearing) she acts the fidgety child and also the censorious mother. F says her mother was severe.

She is also the 13th of 14 children! So this affirms the likelihood that she would have <u>to act in</u> front of the mother in order to get attention as mother cannot internalize her.

Note: The hysteric is <u>a sight.</u>

The hysteric is <u>a sound.</u>

[undated]
"Self analysis"

I was reading DW's chapter on ocular psychoneuroses in children and how a child's symptom reflects underlying symptoms. I can recall when I was about 7 or 8 that I complained to my parents that I was having difficulty seeing. They took me to an eye doctor who said I had 20–20 vision. I was also feeling a depression at the time. As I thought about this it suddenly became clear that I was asking to be like my father who wore these very impressive black reading glasses. Had this imitative wish been understood I think a lot of the anomie would have been worked through.

Strangely I developed the same symptom at the U. of Virginia at 19, and it was probably an acting out of a wish to be like Jack Peirce.[i]

[undated]
"Differentiating the transference"

We can say that a patient at any time may be transferring, i.e. speaking:

1. to a parent
2. to a part of their mind
3. as a parent to a child
4. as a part of their mind
5. a unit, an environment in which no object is clearly defined—an assemblage that existed
6. a bizarre object

---

[i] Jack Peirce was a forty-two-year-old graduate student who gave up dairy farming in Blue Hill Maine to gain a PhD at UVa in politics. He became a substitute father figure and close friend until his death in the early twenty-first century

[undated]
"The death instinct"

"X" attacks the holding environment. When she is deadly silent she is:

    I TR (1) The mother who departs and leaves the child half dead.

    CT (2) I feel deadened and am that child.

    II TR (1) The deadened child turning to nanny and saying "you are not good enough".

    CT (2) I am the not good enough nanny.

    III TR (1) Enacting the death wish against the mother. She identifies with the deadly element and cultivates it. The dual-unity is meant to be destroyed.

    CT (2) I feel hopeless.

    Klein's theory of the death instinct is *partly* wrong because it does not take into account the fact that a death drive aims to first destroy an object—the mother—that cannot be destroyed, and the death drive is then turned on the self because this (the self) can be destroyed.

[2/3/84]
"The classical setting is for the analyst!"

Bion's concept of the analyst's need for "reverie" suggests that the silence, the absence of judgment etc., the sound, the right temperature, is essential for the analyst's reverie.

    The analyst needs to be silent in order to allow thought to come to him.

[29/3/84]
"From dream to film"

When I give to "X" my interpretation about his sundial dream, he listens, but instead of thinking through the interpretation he proceeds to associate visually to the visual elements of the dream. It is as if this act is in defiance of thinking, but in a curious way it is creative.

[undated]
"Klein, Winnicott, Bion, Lacan"

MK from paranoid schizoid to depressive

    DW from false self to true self

    WRB from beta to alpha

    JL from x to the speaking subject.

[undated]
"The here and now"

This constant translation is a deadening not elaborating phenomenon. Its predictability is more like fantasizing.

If the patient's material is <u>like</u> that of a dream, the analyst's translation is like that of fantasizing. This reflects the analyst's need.

[3/5/84]
"From where does the analysand speak?"

In listening to "X" today I "solved" a long standing problem. I often knew in the transference to whom she was speaking and why, but she has always spoken <u>to me</u> in a particular "lost" way. Today I said that when she spoke it was as if she did so *from* a position of extreme isolation, as if she has been abandoned and there is no one there. (Other analysands speak as if they do so with company around, in some <u>relation</u> to their inner objects.) I told "X" it was as if some catastrophe had already taken place and she had dealt with it by evolving techniques in self composure.

She corrected me. She said she spoke as from a room where she had to be careful about what she said lest her mother "crashed" into the room in rage. She told me that she had had to "silence the voices of different parts" of herself in order to keep the quiet.

[11/5/84]
"Premature self awareness"

"N" suffered <u>premature</u> self relating. He had to take himself as his own object before he should have. His present state of depression and isolation is sustained by a defensive self-as-companion, which expresses a hostile defiance toward self–other relating. This supplanted a first stage of <u>expectation</u>, in which his passivity expressed a wish for maternal intervention.

Working with him I see that his manic state is intense self-as-object relation at a purely mental level, whereas in the depressive state the body is the object: it is a somatically orientated self-as-object relation. He called it "sucking on my thumb."

When do children become self aware? When does a child speak to himself, as his own object for the first time?

I can recall speaking to my teddy bear and my imaginary companions, so I reckon this stage of play is a precursor to self-as-object relating.

Second, it is probably after acquisition of superego that internal dialogues take place.

In premature self awareness, as with "N", the child must be in his own care. He is too conscious of his sadistic impulses etc. and becomes unspontaneous. He cannot move to DW's "use of an object" stage.

"N"'s anal retention was an effort to form a faecal other, to amass a self. He was left to be at an incorporative-retentive stage.

Incorporation here is a defence against introjection. The child-person tries to take in the other as a concrete object (as food), in order to have it inside him. This is because he cannot introject the object as good, as the only introjects are bad. Anal-retentive holding also indicates a refusal to let go of the good incorporate, and the pleasure here is that if it is let go, it is only as an act of omnipotence.

In considering awareness of self, we must postulate the necessity of a long period of unawareness. During this period (of denial etc.) the child is free to live out instinctual urges aimed at objects, to project self states into objects and the like.

In play, when a child speaks to teddy the way father speaks to him, he is enacting in play a stage immediately prior to the formation of the superego, when he will then objectify himself as an object to be spoken to.

So far as we know, are there people who never speak to themselves as other? The autistic child perhaps.[1] "J"[ii] seems to be, however, a bizarre objectification of self, in that he would only use his name as an object. Never "I want." Does this form of childhood schizophrenia reflect the child's refusal to be in subjective relation to the self as object?

Why would a child not want to be in subjective relation to himself?

In "J"'s case I think it was primarily because his mother's objectification of him—of a "J"—was appallingly unbelievable. He could not be this "J". So by speaking of himself in the third person he refers to someone else's object. Not the "J" of his own subjective perception. He must go through the mother—i.e. "'J' wants"'—in order to speak his need.

[16/5/84]
"The loss of self (in development)"

With "V" his response to his job loss is a déjà vu and I think he was not over losing his mother and father, but he also lost that self that would have continued to develop had things been favourable. This suggests that each child has some sense of an ideal self which he pursues.

In "D"'s case, as he lost his father and further contact with the ordinary ideal self, he could "reach" it only through manic states of mind.

What existed was a depressed child, who took himself as his own object in a nursing relation. The self is split. In this state the subject, aware of the lost selves to be, nurses the self that is left behind.

A masochistic economy can enter the picture and be part of the split. The anger or hate that emerges from loss—and intended to be acted out on the world—is turned inward against the self. The pleasure is that "D" both inflicts and experiences the pain. The pleasure of experiencing the pain is because this person does not believe in his influence to cause the other pain, so in actually feeling damaged he has a vicarious advantage.

[15/5/84]
"Malignant regression"

In "R"'s case, is it possible that her addiction to the analysis is because she did not make reparation to her mother?

[ii] "J" is an autistic child of six.

133

That is, there is true deprivation: the disappearance of her mother and father. Followed by mother's coldness, upon her return much later, which was partly necessary to reject her baby,[iii] partly a feature of her character. But the mother is not around to receive and transform her baby's hate, nor around to receive reparative gestures.

Hate for which there is no possibility in life of reparation is profoundly destructive. It is as if death has been let loose. It comes from nowhere.

In hating in such a way that her destructiveness seems to come from nowhere (it is everywhere) "R" creates death.

The creation of death is her vestigial act of omnipotence. She tries to bring into her control that which is most assuredly out of her control. See Anna Freud's concept of identification with the aggressor.

[undated]
"Hate of one's sane part"

"O"'s hatred of the sane part of himself—projected into me and hated there—is due to his intense disappointment as a child with events around him. That sane part—that tries to understand, consider, and deal with pain and anxiety etc.—was overwhelmed by events. It could not function in a favourable way for the child. The result was flight into schizoid fantasizing, splitting, and projection. And hate of the sane part of the self that had proved in existence to be such a miserable failure. I think this hate is common and helps to explain negative therapeutic reaction and negativity.

[17/5/84]
"Normotic identification"[iv]

The child identifies with and as an object.

Material objects and phenomenon are positively regarded and receive considerable investment. They are esteemed. Being a material object to the parent and to the self—"a good product", "a good guy", "someone people would like to have around"—is the child's aim.

Also, the child identifies with and uses the parental process. Insofar as this process is characterized by a transfer of the self into the object world. When in need, the parents refer the child to a material object or action. The child uses objects to contain and "solve" needs, anxieties, etc.

Material solutions to psychic states suggests that eventually the psychical links to the material, as the child learns to "think" out or "feel" out his inner world through a non-human object. Mental and affective states do not get transformed by the parent. Rituals—or procedures—replace intersubjective transformations, as the child gives up elaborative activity to the concrete object.

[iii] The mother had to put the daughter in foster care.

[iv] The first use of this concept in my writing.

The cumulative effect of this transfer is to move the person from the subjective into the object(ive).

Seemingly self reflective or affectively promising states—indicating continued psychic life—are nonetheless treated by the person as if they were mental equivalents of a material object. They are only objects to themselves. Perhaps pleasure objects, amusement objects, work objects, even personality objects, but still they are in movement away from subjectivity.

The machine—good machine—is an object of identification; maybe a primary metaphor of parental child rearing techniques. And the robot is the self evolved from this condition.

[2/6/84]
"Absence makes the heart grow fonder"

It is interesting to note how with someone like X, when he is actually with a person he cannot be with them and is anxious and phobic. But he does relate affectionately to the object when it is gone.

What is his nostalgia, his intimate relation to the absent object about?

It is because he refuses (destroys?) the presence of an alive other that his recollection of it is suffused with unconscious grief and with conscious sadness.

[12/6/84]
"Extractive introjection"ᵛ

This occurs when a person invades another personality and steals from them, taking the part of the person into themselves by violence.

It takes two forms:

1. The person through curiosity, charm, and aggression asks the other about himself and manages to steal details of his life. Details on the person's history, dream life, sexual desires, etc. This may happen very quietly and some psychiatrists do this when interviewing a patient.

2. That which is stolen is not a content of the mind but a part of the other's mind. An example might be that "B" is working through guilt but "A" states "you should feel guilty!" or "B", trying to work through a complex mental affective process, is met by "A", in a manic state, who "covers" all the psycho-affective ground of "B", drilling "B" into situational silence, as "B" feels that he has been robbed of mental function by "A"'s mind.

3. A variation on 2 is the person who engulfs and steals a person's mind in a more permanent way, such as a parent who is too critical stealing and controlling a child's superego; a marital partner who steals the other's spontaneous self by being hypomanic, etc.

ᵛ First use of this concept.

With "X" it's possible to see how EXTRACTIVE INTROJECTION worked in such a way as to rob me of mental function—to convert this into a nullity we call conversion:

CONVERSION AND EXTRACTIVE INTROJECTION

Bion also writes about the "obstructive object" that refuses to accept projective identifications.

Use Bion's concept of the double nature of the senses to show how

—an analytic interpretation (insight) may be an analyst's expulsion into the patient of an extraction—a taking away which seems to be a giving to.

—the transference interpretation may be an extractive introjection if the analyst continuously steals and converts therapeutic intimacy into the transference interpretation.

—this will interfere with the patient's introjective capacities.

—it will leave the patient feeling frustrated, angry, destructive, and only able to function via projective identification as the patient's projective identifications are attempts to invade the analyst's mind in order to retrieve stolen parts of themselves.

—DW's "Communicating ..." is a crucial article.

Bion "the capacity to introject is transformed by the patient's envy and hate into greed devouring the patient's psyche."[2] This as a result of the mother's failure to receive the child's projective identifications.

[undated]

"The self (mind) at work"

At any moment each of us is at work on some problem of self. It is difficult to conceptualize this, as in fact, that which we work on is more

an element of our mind, and/or personality.

[21/11/84]

"The silent patient, integration, the internal object"

"X"'s silence.

—She relates to "me" as an internal object. To this "me" she speaks freely, frequently, etc.

—It is the preverbal mother; no words; it's integrating & satisfying.

Fantasy takes place, but not analysis.

—In the countertransference I am unconsciously invited to be her twin.

    a. to relate to her as an internal object—as she says nothing.

    b. To wander in my mind—a state of reverie.

As this analysis ends, we do so in a transitional state. She is at the point of discovering the relation between the internal and the external.

She is discovering that I might be of use in enabling her to understand herself.

Her inner life—fantasy life—serves the fundamental purpose of self integration. This is one of the features of fantasy—perhaps its true aim: to integrate the self and its objects.

She has not reached that point—let's say that point defined by the neurotic patient—when her fantasies, as content, are of interest in their own right, an object of understanding & knowing. We might say that this demonstrates the 2 uses of fantasy.

1. As a self experience serving integrative purposes & providing inner gratifications—e.g. reverie.
2. As a mental product which means something, in its own right, having its own structure and history.

"X" is experiencing through inner analysis, fantasy, etc., her male self, female self, me, etc. etc. She is not at the point of seeing a need to objectify these mental contents and express them.

Over the years I have interpreted her silence in different ways:

1. as projective anorexia
2. as sadism
3. as need to control the object
4. as resistance to sexual thoughts
5. as her male self's rivalry with me
6. as her need to triumph over me
7. as a way of proving her own self's independence via secrecy
8. as a wish to get me to beat her.

Now, how can it be that this seems correct and yet incorrect?
—she had to destroy and nullify my presence and expectations as an external object.

[21/11/84]
"Extractive introjection"

It's when someone says something to a person as if, prior to its being spoken, the person will not have experienced the thought.

In the process the person from whom the idea is extracted feels depression or despair or anger.

What is the aim of extractive introjection?

Is it the same thing as introjective identification?

[21/11/84]
"The body of language"

When "X" says that he creates through language a body he means he gives himself presence. Otherwise he is uncertain of his existence. When he speaks he falls in love with his own rhetoric.

[26/11/84]
"Ejection anxiety"

This is that fear characterized by the dread that someone will eject the person from their inner world.

It is not the same as rejection. Because the ejector may simply rid the self of an internal object.

Rejection implies relating.

Ejection suggests unrelating.

[27/11/84]
"Countertransference along with developmental stages"

At any one point—even within a session—the analyst may be—in his countertransference—the:

1. early mother—holding
2. the toddler mother in—presenting
3. the good depressive mother—disillusioning
4. the father—confronting
5. the family
6. the double—playing

That is:

I hold

I play

I confront

I empathize

I refuse

and in accord with my patient's psychic place.

[5/12/84]
"The dread of perception"

"X" has no ability to look either into himself or into the other.

There is a sort of dread of catastrophe over my interpretations.

It seems based on a dread of seeing what is happening. This is due to his need to deny what he observed with his mother and of his own pathological adaptation to her.

Much of this is based on my statement that he is not bringing into analysis simple observations from the content of his mental life.

His association to this is to tell me about how he spends money carelessly. I point out that:

1. he observes his world as an outsider and wants me to do the same.
2. and that the observations he makes are important if we substitute for spending money, the spending of perception. That he wants to empty himself of what he sees.

[undated]
"Introjection"

"X" does not want a woman to introject him. He wakes up this morning with the thought "I can't bear babies" and this leads me to interpret his envy of his mother and the reproductive process. Certain thoughts:

1. He wants to maintain a female self that was broken up by mother's giving birth to sister.
2. Introjection is a female process—an inception. He does not want a woman to "take him in". He has himself as an introject and this self-as-object relation is the mother with the idolized child.
3. His preference for boyish women is really his rejection of the pregnant woman.
4. His urge to fuck the dance girls is really the wish to prematurely push his penis into the vagina, to fill it—to close it up. What he wants to do is to foreclose further cognitive realization that babies are born from the vagina. He confirms this by saying he wondered how big the gap was between the dancer's legs.

[7/12/84]
"The disturbed setting"

Of course we know that some children are reared in a disturbed setting. Often, it is not so much that a parent is ill as much as it is that a parent has a depression, or a phase of uncertainty, or the marriage, or the family may be ill.

So what do we make of the internalization of a disturbed setting?

As the child will internalize an ambience rather than a person, etc.

I think this must be a follow-up on the moods paper.[3]

[7/12/84]
"The implied (sometimes hidden) world"

Certain patient's objects suggest a particular kind of world. In the case of "X" this implied world is so frightful that she has attempted to remove herself from experience and object representation.

[undated]
[untitled]

"X"'s envy of a good relation is determined by her mother's unreliability: the fact that mother interrupts relations. I point out that when we have a good relation some part of her envies this and she (mother) steps in and enviously smashes it: e.g. "Bollas thinks this is a good relation, that he can rely on me etc. Well, I'll show him."

I point out that I never know who she will be or what my status is, and I point out that she always begins sessions walking to the couch, asking a question etc. As I don't answer

139

she can say "Well *this* is an analyst? What do you expect?" Or "Why doesn't the creep answer me?"

In her self-as-object relation I point out that one part of her envies another part that is fending me off and says "What's *become* of you, enjoying this man and trusting him, etc.?"

[undated]
"Time, superego"

"X"'s dread of the superego is the dread of death.

Death and the superego. The superego is that part of the mind to which we are responsible. It calls us to a reckoning. In this it is affiliated with death in that ultimately we die and ultimately we respond to death, i.e. the day of judgment.

Thus the superego is also linked to the <u>passing</u> of time. Unlike the unconscious which is timeless, the superego is the timekeeper. "X" prefers to use free association as it breaks up time or rather breaks up my interpretations which are integrative and involve the patient in some form of self reckoning. He wants to go back to the timeless.

He feels nauseated, like vomiting, when I speak of this and I say that the infant knows time only through the need to eat: this is biological time, which is linked with urge. He tries to vomit this out, to rid the self of the feeding side. To be independent.

"It's time": the analyst's refrain. The <u>end</u> of the session. "X" says he dreads it. He feels a tension in his legs.

Time that passes. The past. What is it? Unconscious timelessness. What is it?

[undated]
"Time and manic illness"

"A" talks about his wish to find some sources of self, some "points" of recurring realization that he knows to be his "me."

I take this up in the following way:

1. In the manic state time and space are infinite
2. In that <u>state</u> he can imagine endless selves in endless places.

The result is, however, no sense of place or time.

It is a spaceless and a timeless world.

"Like always being on the road" I say and he says "Yes, which is exactly what I did when in a manic state & I wandered about." It's possible that manic wandering is a futile attempt to literalize or to realize the timeless and spaceless element, as by wandering and passing through and by people and places the manic tries <u>to</u> be in a certain way.

Yesterday I took up with him the manic's dependence on MIND as alternate to object and reiterate that he cannot depend on the other, but feeds off this MIND-BREAST. (He actually smacks his lips when free associating.)

1985

"Language and incest barrier"

"Y" uses language to create the incest barrier. He <u>talks</u> to the object of desire, rather than acts on it. Talk becomes the only vehicle of desire and in so doing he does what a family does: desire (love) can be verbally expressed, but not actualized.

Indeed, narrative becomes erotics.

NARRATIVE EROTICS

The barrier must contain frustration—<u>be</u> frustration. By moving ecstatic body need into language this person creates the tension barrier.

"Y"'s language barrier is an incest bar. It embodies resistance to intercourse, especially parental copulation.

In his own manic way he diverts erotic desire into the barrier of incest which he controls and represents by platonizing eros into talk … talk … talk.

Gradually, what had been her desire for him becomes their sharing the discourse of desire which becomes the sharing of a barrier to eros.

Why does he construct the incest bar??

[21/1/85]
"Excited denial and perversion"

"A"'s lust for "X" is determined by the eros of denial. It is the lie itself—not the transgression—that excites.

He unconsciously makes love over the corpse, the dead body, of the father.

When "X" says there is nothing between her and "F", she excites "A" by virtue of her denial, her lie.

This negation of truth is somehow linked to murder, to the massacre of the father, upon whose body the fuck takes place.

When "X" tells "A" there is nothing taking place with "F", it is as if at that moment she calls "F" over and pulls out a gun, killing him in cold blood.

"A" enjoys the killing in cold blood. The cold blooded side of "F"'s execution, the superb and finite murder of the truth and of "F" are committed and are very exciting.

Also, she comes on the scene as have the other such ladies when "A" is composing a work of music.

It is as if mother says to "A": "You come from my body. We have prior knowledge (memory) of each other. Your father is no longer on the scene."

Structurally, it is more interesting that negation is eros. Excitement derives from the act of denial which is the murder of truth. Its execution. Its decomposition. "When the cock stands up the brain dies."

[undated]
"Psyche to bulimia"

"L"'s patient who turns her boyfriend into a samosa. Order and transition of the conversion.

1. Psyche (with problems)
2. To affect—cathected as alternate to thinking
3. To sensation (e.g. excitement or depression)
4. To eating

From mind to body.

With the over-eater it is important to analyse the early forms of conversion. For example, they detail events in life for the analyst in order to experience a pretend affect, where affect is now functioning as a defence against thinking.

The patient says she is distressed with her boyfriend and she fears his need of her. This is psyche. Then she says that she teased him at a party and she enjoyed this: it gave her pleasure. She does this in order to feel sensation. To transition from the psychical problems created by the relation.

"Look, yes, men are problems. But I cannot talk to you about him if you turn him into an apple and eat him up and then shit him out."

The bulimic's frustration with interpretation of the analyst is partly disguised to coerce the analyst into giving up interpretation. To get the analyst to experience affects (e.g. anger), then sensations, then ultimately to get the analyst to eat a chocolate!

142

[6/3/85]
"Extractive introjection"

This mechanism takes place when a person appropriates someone else's psychic structure. Thus if "B" is on the verge of guilt, "A" may correctly attack "B" for a misdeed, preventing "A"'s guilt from being an inner experience leading to reparation.

"B" is empty because "X" has her dog in his flat. Rather than tell her that he wants to get rid of it because he is bothered by it—thus shouldering the responsibility for the riddance—he says he thinks it is cruel for animals to be kept in the house. Thus he exploits "X"'s unease and guilt and renders her inner experience the voice from the outside.

It is a reversal of ordinary development: from the inner to the outer.

"J" morally criticizes people at work for wrongdoing. She assumes the answer to their own inner guilt and unconsciously appropriates this by being too harsh. She invites rebellion and this seems to confirm her view that she is the only one who acts responsibly!

This leads to a situation where the "victim" of extractive introjection gives up a part of the self to the other, or does not resist its appropriation. Indeed, they may fulfil the other's extraction.

Extractive introjection differs from ordinary introjection in that a part of the other's psyche is stolen.

When "R" enters the room and says "Does your wife know how you talk to your patients?", as she assaults my capacity to think, herself being the one capable of organized thinking—as she has rehearsed a script which she acts out in my presence—I momentarily lose my mental apparatus to her. She extracts my function (of reflection, analysis, confrontation) and assumes it.

[10/3/85]
"Warsaw"[i]

One of the problems is that Solidarity provided the people, particularly the men, with a good internal object. Then they felt an impotence. Now the failure to survive means there is a depression.

Symbiosis and families: with an external reality that is so difficult the young person finds a necessary on-going dependence on the family. This constitutes a kind of reproductive act as well.

[12/3/85]
"Warsaw: 'here a tomato is a tomato'"

Simple facts—close to the true self—are significant. This has interesting implications for psychoanalytic interpretation. These people have always been interpreted to: told who they

---

[i] This entry took place during a visit to Warsaw with colleague. We were guests of the first "above ground" meeting of Polish analysts, psychologists, psychiatrists and others. It was a very tense visit.

are and what they mean. In their world a tomato has never been a tomato. Thus an analyst must first form a warm relation to the patient in order to enable him to feel trust. Interpretations must be close to the core, otherwise the analyst becomes just another interpreter of the patient, who has already been over-interpreted.

[undated]
"Forepleasure is history"

Freud's scheme is such that in forepleasure the adult relives the stages of pre-genital sexuality.

[undated]
"The need for guilt"

A moment when a person uses guilt to intensify internal object relating as a defence against inter-subjective intimacy.

[undated]
"Sleep as womb/waking = birth"

As Freud says, to sleep is to return to the womb. Some people cannot wake. Does this reflect some difficulty in being born?

[4/4/85]
"Manic depression and mother–child relations (cf.: self-as-object)"

"Q". We know that he is engaged in an intense relation to himself as an object. In his "ordinary" moods—neither manic nor depressed—he is obsessionally preoccupied with the thought of himself. This is not the same as thoughtfulness, as he can be thoughtless and careless in the details of self care.

It is more the mnemic enactment of a rather schizoid mother looking after the baby-infant in a distant if kindly manner. The mother's thoughts reach out to the baby, but nothing else: she is not a good enough mother.

In "Q" I believe there is a regression from the early stage, a regression back to intrauterine states. On the couch this takes the form of guilt sleep, or of long silence.

What occasions the manic state?

In every case I have observed with him, it is when the environment offers itself to him in a favourable way. A new job. A beautiful woman. His level of anxiety increases. What is fascinating, however, is the subtle emergence of the manic mother, of the anxious mother who "steps" in and solicits him with praise, but again distanced and of no help.

Now obviously this takes place as a split in the self. There is the continuing dishevelled baby-self in need of mothering. The manic mother is revealed in the way "Q" whooshes into a room (or out), orders people about, exhibits an extraordinary language capacity, and all the while it is as if he is in a bubble.

He is talking about relating only to himself. He grows his blonde hair very long and braids it. His behaviour is feminized so that a certain bisexual disposition emerges—a bisexuality that is oriented only to the self as an object, with one part of the self the mother (female) and the other a boy (male).

The triumphant, aggressive, denigrating aspect of the manic state is the effort of the child to grasp the promising mother and to vigorously exclude the outside world.

To us, it looks as if this person simply loves himself. To "Q" it's a delusion in which manic euphoria is a state of being loved by a solicitous other—the loving mother.

There is an oedipal triangle, or a kind of one. For the aggressively repudiated outside world is collected together into the person of the father. This is because the father is associated with the function of reality orientation and appraisal. As such the father is perceived as a threat to the delusional relation to the mother.

[4/4/85]
"Birth memories"

THE PATIENT IN THE WAITING ROOM!!
I now know why "M"'s look of shock is to do with my (his) premature birth, or a birth accompanied by anxiety.

[undated]
"The borderline"

As this object is known by its effect on the subject, the effort to find this mother takes the form of the borderline "burrowing" into the other's psyche.

They do this in order to become a particle in an affect world—for re-assembly—but they are not seeking a relationship. Discovery that they are inside a relation (container) may lead to claustrophobic experience, as they on the other hand, free themselves in relation only when they are free to split and live in a fragmented world.

[4/25/85]
"What does the analysand inspire in the analyst?"

Some patients create images in the analyst.
Others create boredom or emptiness or compel the analyst to use his own inner resources.

[4/25/85]
"Self"

Is the experience of the varied particularity of one's being determined by the idiom of a person's character and personal experiences, and dependent on "its" knowability according to a person's subjective capacity: i.e. ability to know from within?

Self is not a mental object, nor indeed, predominately a sense; it is an intrasubjective position, a place for the knowing of one's being, often varied, never settled.

In this "place" self may be "recorded" or "seen" or "known" through feelings, lingual formations (e.g. slips of tongue, etc.), images.

Very often "self" is "encountered" via play with the other, when some previously unknown "portion" of a person is released.

First there is being.

From the capacity to be there is the ability to experience.

From this there is knowing.

My self is that inevitable restriction I place upon infinite possibility. I know this self as I limit my possibilities. I know about this limit because I see the other possibilities lived out by others and because I know of imagined possibilities in my own self.

History of self. I can recall my early 2–3 self very clearly. I know this both via recollection (from without) and from within. I know my oedipal 5–6 self. Then I know my 9-year-old self. Then the 12-year-old. Then the 16. Then 19–20. 22. Then 25. Then 30.

Inevitably, however, something escapes me—eludes my knowing. And if I try to name what that is, I am cheating.

What is inevitable is the position as subject and object—one moment the speaker, the next the spoken to.

It is wonderful to find some one—other—with whom one can be released from one's self relating.

Winnicott emphasizes experiencing. Play.

The Lacanian play of the other is not equivalent to the Winnicottian concept of play. The Freudian slip is not the same as play.

A schizophrenic is full of slips but incapable of play—empty.

[14/5/85]
"Parental omnipotence and oedipal violence"

With "D" the violence toward the mother and father is determined by the fact that they refuse him access to adult identifications through play. He therefore has to kill them in order to identify with them.

[undated]
"Psychoanalysis and group therapy"

Some people prefer to confess themselves in a group: others to only one person.

Sacrificial power vs. true power

Jesus Caeser

[12/7/85]
"Knowing the unspeakable"

In a psychoanalysis we know our patients but much of what we know is both unavailable for ordinary mental representation and unspeakable. Except perhaps for slips of the tongue and the like.
  Elements:

  1. meeting someone after absence
  2. following a conversation asking a question

[undated]
"Pleasure"

Not the same as instinct or libido as it involves the id and ego.
  "What is your pleasure?"
  Any stress on each word in the above suggests a different phenomenon.
  Pleasure in being one's self.
  How many analysands can claim to have achieved this in an analysis? This is not the same phenomenon as knowing or acquiring self knowledge—it's about a capacity.

[undated]
"Knowing the unknowable"

"J" ceases relating because there is something exchanged between people (at the intersubjective level of transference and countertransference which he wishes to know, but never will) and therefore he terminates relating until he does know.
  This factor or element constitutes an enormous part of human psychic life. It is there partly as a result of the projective identifications we receive.

[30/7/85]
"Ego and self"

The ingredients of both are present at birth. Self is originally based on the inherited disposition. It has to do with idiom of being and is first known by the other—the mother—before it is known by the infant.
  Ego is a process of managing the self in relation to id and reality. It is the unconscious mental mechanisms.
  Self is there; ego is the process of self's negotiations.
  Building metaphor: self = the architectural drawings and the building finished. Ego = the process for its total construction.

Self is the character of the personality. The ego is the unconscious operational <u>mental</u> realization of it in a micro-way.

An ego is too shifting to house a personality.

So, what's the difference between internal world & self?

Self is, in part, mentally knowable through object representation. But the genesis of ego operations that go to forming the self representation is from the self.

Self is first a <u>given potential</u>, embedded in the inherited disposition and the true self. It is released into being through object relations. It can further be influenced by the other who mirrors back their recognition of the child's self. But, sometimes—perhaps universally—there is discrepancy between what is experienced as self from outside and self from within.

In other words, what happens if mother mirrors back a self image inconsistent with the infant's self co-ordinates? I think it may be an ego alien introject—quite distinct, even if contributing to the child's sense of self.

Otherwise there is a kind of rapport or match up.

[undated]
"Countertransference and the unknowable"

I am interested in states of mutual being that exist between analyst and analysand that neither is capable of speaking.

It is the analyst's task, however, to ascertain what this is and to try to speak it.

In "Q" the unspoken and unrepresented state <u>prevailed</u> in session after session. It could be described as his mood (cf. chapter on moods). It was a kind of joy. A pleasure taken in being with the analytic object: a pleasure that was always present, even when he was sad, angry, depressed, etc.

"Q" could report on situations and engage in pseudo reflections but not real ones.

He also never dreamed.

But sometimes his descriptions of situations were, if not dream-like, dream-evocative. except *I* dreamed the dream.

The example is the session when he was telling me of being on a movie set and walking into a library to see books on architecture. He created the dream setting and I <u>imagined</u> someone coming into the room and discovering he was an architect.

I said "Let's imagine something. Let's imagine that into this place someone arrives and says …"

The conscious aim of the interpretation was to show him that he was keeping a <u>partly</u> realized talented self hidden, waiting to be discovered.

My thinking or imagining <u>was</u> that discovery. Therefore it was an act in the transference-countertransference.

It also meant that this patient <u>needed</u> my imaginative presence. He needed to be "in on" my imaginings.

This phase of the analysis superseded an unsuccessful one, in which I simply focused on the dreamer and the omnipotence. What he wanted was my participation.

"X" requires similar thought.

This is really <u>play</u>.

Afterwards it must always be commented on.

[undated]
"Extractive introjection"

Is a stealing of <u>functions</u> (Bion) of the personality. As with "K" who walks into the the group saying "You don't know what it's like to feel frustrated. I am very angry." In a violent manner she appropriates the functions of (1) frustration (2) anger, leaving many people in the group feeling (a) inert (b) helpless, etc., as she has <u>momentarily</u> appropriated (extracted) the function of anger.

Only someone who would have <u>prior</u> knowledge of this action of hers could have their wits about them sufficiently to deal with this.

[17/9/85]
"Countertransference and self analysis"

Where in a psychoanalysis is the process for the development of self analysis?"

The analyst's use of the self analytic function is an important part of assessing the counter-transference—or, indeed, of perceiving it in the first place.

In the first place, the question "<u>how</u> do I feel?" could be answered "I feel like a functioning psychoanalyst." So, the function of being a psychoanalyst, to some extent interferes with <u>the range</u> of this question. Indeed, the professional stance—i.e. neutrality—though valuable when listening to the patient, may not be so valuable when it comes to listening to oneself.

This listening to oneself is a continuous dynamic process, taking place in a different part of the mind from the other parts.

In <u>what</u> ways does one listen to oneself?

Through what medium(s) is this listening possible?

    a. introspection
    b. fantasy
    c. object relating
    d. dream

It is important to stress that <u>the analyst's thoughts</u>, what he is thinking about (not so much only what he feels), is an important part of the countertransference.

Do psychoanalyses prepare an individual for self analysis?

In some ways this function is enhanced and enlarged by the practicing analyst. In other words, it is a function that develops through practice.

Therefore the life of a psychoanalyst's analysis comes in two phases: the analysis and then the self analysis which continues after, through practice.

The "mental field": this is one place where we live.

Analysis of self-in-countertransference is a specific type of self analysis, in which the analyst is aware of two patients and listens to both.

This has implications for reading, for surely in reading a novel etc. we are often as much interested in our own wandering thoughts (daydreams etc.) and responses as we are in the novel itself. Why, for example, did I find *Women In Love* so compelling? It must have had to do with my state of mind at the time.

What do some of these questions entail, e.g. about the psychoanalytic state of mind?

1. Am I thinking?
2. Is this thought?
3. If it's not thought, what is it?
4. Where am I?
5. What sort of an object am I to myself at this moment?
    a. a good container
    b. integrator
    a. absent, etc.

When "Z" would describe settings, which came out of prolonged silences—where was I? Was I thinking?

I was in a sleep. I would like to say: pre-dream, or that place prior to the creation of a dream.

Her descriptions were like dream events.

Have I ever been there before?

I think I have.

When?

My associations: afternoon naps as a child with the objects in the room slowly giving up their authority to my dreaming. To my sleep.

I "slept" with "Z" and with drug addicts.

I think that as each of them was with an "absent" mother, that as they slept, and occasionally narrated, I was in on the beginnings of mental life. It is as if I am at the beginning, where words and objects are only partly released.

When I consoled myself, talked to myself, about how these analyses were going—who was I then? Like a mother speaking to an infant. Yet my task was to preserve this state, to present it in myself.

This raises another question.

When a psychoanalyst is in a room with a patient, where is he? A question that assumes significance when we realize we are talking about psychic life.

Where does the hysteric place us?

Where does the borderline send us?

The psychotic?

The pervert?

What are these places and who are we when we live in them, or what are we, or is the concept of "I" or "we" archaic, ever wishful, in this terrain?

Does the concept "madness" apply to the relation between two people? Is this ordinary?

Madness is the experience of a release (in behaviour etc.) of the idiom of the self—in fractures.

In psychoanalysis, we assume we know where we are, what we do. These are false assumptions.

What do our patients tell us? Is what we know of them what they fundamentally tell us? No. It's how they are in us; it's the nature of their being. And this in-forming[ii] takes place in the psychoanalyst.

[5/11/85]
"The lost object"

There is a difference between:
    a. the object lost by virtue of its destruction
    b. the object lost by virtue of its disappearance

[undated]
"Madness versus psychosis"

Some people are mad but not psychotic.

Madness bears relation to the structure of comedy, to a violent rupture & dissembling with some purpose & a conclusion, while psychosis is a more tragic event: the true loss of self.

In madness there is ego fragmentation, violent splitting, resulting often in bizarre acts, but with no loss of self. Perhaps because only the objects are being projected.

In psychosis the self is projected out and lost.

[11/8/85]
"Reagan and the Americans"

Watching TV news tonight Reagan is reported to have changed his mind about the Soviet sailor who jumped ship, etc. Why should the Americans tolerate this man's confusion?

Because he expresses that confusion present in the Americans. In that respect he is their representative!

Nixon was a liar and not so American. Reagan creates untruths out of confusion and is America. From the Lie to Confusion.

[ii] Perhaps the first use of the concept of form in my work.

[13/11/85]
"Where is the self?"

We cannot say that "it" is solely within the individual's possession.

It is also "in" the other, insofar as we experience the person's self.

One task of psychoanalysis is to find a means for the "accurate" registration of experiences of this self and for the interpretation or telling of this to a person.

[13/11/85]
"The unthought known"[iii]

A child is "inside" an "atmosphere" (choreography of moods etc.) created by mother's depression, lets say.

He comes to know this world as it constitutes his life, his existence. But he has been unable to think it through. It is unthought: simply there.

This raises a question—where is that knowledge that is unthought, not by virtue of repression but because the nature of the situation was beyond comprehension?

[13/11/85]
"Madness"

May very well be the person's expressive experience (& memory) of the unthought known.

A person is driven mad not driven psychotic.

The mad person is creating a mad world around him. He somehow holds "it" together. This world is his mnemic creation of the object setting from which he came.

The mad person is afflicted with or by memory. The psychotic has lost parts of the mind and is deficient. The mad person has all parts of mind active and is creating content (material).

In a disturbed person there may be vicissitudes between mad and psychotic states.

The hysteric is the quintessence of madness.

When has an otherwise psychotic person become mad?

When out from de-compensation (absence of mind) he comes into mind and is productive of material and creates a universe that amounts to object usage in the transference, such that the analyst becomes part of something.

Madness implies memory or re-collection and is a progression from the psychotic state.

At the same time as mind and memory come back the person is very vulnerable and suicide is a real possibility.

---

iii This is the first use of the term "unthought known".

[undated]
"Madness and the unthought known"

A person may go mad in order to collect the details of the total situation.
    This means that he must become or portray all the elements of the early environment.
    Acting out or enacting is a feature of this. See *Lear*.

[undated]
"From person to element"

When does a person cease to be a person and become an environment of something else?

[18/11/85]
"Madness"

Has to with acts. There are mad acts and psychotic states.
    Psychosis is a state of mind whereas madness is an act of being.
    Mad people aim to be, to control something, to put "x" into the world as an act in order to control it.

[undated]
"Regression to dependence"

Has something to do with generative disappearance into silence. As the sounds of the world (building, the clock, distant voices, airplanes) take over, one abandons talking. As talking is given up the patient is free to undergo exclusively private experiences.
    Importantly images and daydreams abound. One does not have to speak, so words are not thought. Images come. Often memory comes that way.
    This is the state of the infant—child at rest with M/F assumed (holding).

[26/11/85]
"Extractive introjection"

Example. When "A"'s parents attack his school progress and remove him from the prospect of feeling his own loss and guilt.
    Example: In a meeting when one person arrogates to himself an exclusive function, such as "concern" or "caution."
    The above action in which the subject feels robbed can leave them cynically attacking the other person's "possession" of functions: such as "responsibility" etc. Or if they agree with the robber they feel as if they are not real.
    Moral aggression is often the feature behind the attack. Indeed to get back that which has been lost via moral aggression, a person may respond to this.

[4/12/85]

"Madness and the bizarre object"

The mad person is engaged in an unconscious ordering or sustaining of the bizarre object. The psychotic's bizarre object contains mental functions (mind) and so cannot be "held" or organized.

[5/12/85]

"Madness and the strange"

Some children grow up in a "strange" family. Or they feel odd or strange as children.

In adult life they gradually externalize this strangeness, soliciting partners who may be of like mind.

Strangeness may become madness through an intensity of organization. The mad person is highly organized.

The mad person's object world is complex. The psychotic's is impoverished due to the loss of mind.

I think it is possible to say that manic depression is a form of madness and schizophrenia is a psychosis.

[6/12/85]

"The unthought known"

Is the primary repressed. Secondary repression is the forgotten known.

The unthought known is born in or lives in the structure of the ego, its deep "grammar" or idiom, which develops out of the paradigmatic dialectic of the "it" (inherited disposition) and the maternal process.

This is before consciousness proper and before language. The assumptions and idioms of and in one's being are established then.

Ego memory. See Federn??[iv]

[iv] Paul Federn (1871–1950), an Austrian-American psychologist.

1986

"Self"

Self is a subjective position, determined by or conditional upon the looking at/into the self.

Self is an "object" of contemplation that includes internal and external.

[12/1/86]
"Hiding behind the mother"

To what extent do Klein interpretations about the patient's relation to the mother's body, constitute a screen behind which the analyst hides? As if the mother's body becomes re-used, ironically enough, by the analyst, to process a patient's transference experiencing. This mother's body (living via the analyst's interpretive discourse) is something of the fetish: a protection against that emotional reality aroused through transference and countertransference experiencing.

[12/1/86]
"Projective identification and the transformational process"

When someone talks to me a demand is made on my mind for work. The person introduces ideas, possibly feelings, maybe imagery, and does so in differing degrees of organisation: some people are clear, direct, to the point. They may only be explaining something to me and not demanding much work from my psyche. ("Psyche" here includes mind: i.e specific cognitive and mental processing, affects, inner states.) Or a person may be requesting something of me in an intense and confusing manner. My inner experience (state as subject) and my mental work on that inner experience (transformational process) may shift and alter according to the other's transference usage of me.

Example. "S" calls. He is depressed and vague about why he has called. I feel a request from him to seek him out, an uncertainty in me about what he wants, an irritation that it is taking place at all. Through a series of questions and comments (mental work, process) I discover he is feeling cross with a colleague over a slight. My work gives him some relief. In a few minutes his depressive affect is gone and he is talking about some aspect of his work which I find interesting. As he changes, my inner experience (state of subject) alters and now I find listening to him pleasant. A few minutes later he is curious about a trip of mine and clearly wants news about how I could arrange something for him. As subject I experience his wish for good news and my mind is required to work on how to put to him the good (news) with the disappointing. Later he informs me of not having had a call from someone I said would certainly call, so I feel guilt and my mind must now work on him and on myself as object.

The point is that when the other approaches us for use as an object, a complex set of events ensues, involving projective identification, subjective state experiences, mental work and transformational process.

The process involves handling the other, but also handling the self as object.

Sometimes "my" intervention will have to do with my subjective state, such as feeling "I am not going to help this guy anymore" which leads me to deal with this (transform it) by saying "Come on, he has done a lot for you, and he is a good true pain!"

1. Some use of me as an object
2. My subjective experience & state
3. My mental work done on the state
4. My mental process (transformations) of the state in me/and/or in the other

To some extent one aspect of, say, indigenous countertransference is an autistic core in each of us, the wish not to have such work done on us, compelling us into mental work and transformational process.

Indeed, as a person "works" on us we may fob him off via adaptive agreement, or by not listening closely, or by daydreaming (splitting).

[14/1/86]
[untitled]

It's interesting that Freud's definition of the economic factor of an instinct as a "demand upon the mind for work" is almost exactly what I'm saying about the presence of the object as a demand upon the mind for work.

So, we can say that an instinct (& ego) chooses its object to eliminate stimuli, and the effect of the other invites the object (& ego) to process via mental representation the experience of the other.

[14/1/86]
"Death instinct"

According to Klein the first workings of the death instinct give rise to a fear of annihilation.

This makes sense as a fear of the mind breaking down or being eliminated, thus leaving the self helpless—almost a phylogenetic dread: a fear as a human (without instinct) of being at the mercy of the natural world. Because, according to Freud, the death instinct seeks return to inorganic state and life instinct is binding or linking.

Therefore the mind is an agency of the life instinct.

Is it possible that some schizophrenics imagine animals and beasts because as mind is being destroyed, the self experiences a phylogenetic dread of being at the mercy of the animal world?

[undated]
"Perversion, the transference, and perverse structure"

M's case of a 32-year-old who comes for therapy feeling he is homosexual; expressing anal sensations and feeling vulnerable. In life history mother seduced him into bed as an adolescent, asking him to penetrate her. He would sleep next to her and ejaculate by rubbing against her body, particularly her clothing. Mother may have dressed him as a girl when young. He has 5 sisters.

Problem. M's patient has been in therapy for 2 years, first once every two weeks, then 1 × a week, now the patient wants to make it into 3 × a month and possibly to have supervision.

M comments that the patient is very co-operative, talkative, and reads magazines in the waiting room then "zips" into the consulting room.

Also he describes his sexual encounters with women in graphic detail and M feels the patient is trying to excite him.

Also patient has relations with many women. Fell in love with X 3 years ago: intense involvement but X withdraws and does not have sex even though she is idealised. A woman in Jamaica. Others.

Discussion

The patient's description of sexual imagery (anal sensation, thoughts of penis, etc.) is a pseudo integration: a "collage" of an experience of the object (mother). It functions as a scrum. Not to convey meaning but to arrest it and contain it.

Patient's descriptions of life are immediately acted out and in the transference.

The patient's wish to get the analyst to focus on "homosexuality" or "so-called perverse fantasies" is the perversion (enacted in the transference) in that like the use of mother's clothing as defence against the true (psychotic) experience of the mother, it's a use of a fragment of analysis as defence against surrender to analysis.

The perversion is:

1. A defence against transient psychotic self states
2. A defence against depression

Psychosis

The mother <u>is</u> in her person a bizarre object. The patient cannot integrate the whole object as it is too split. So he integrates "pieces" of the object (anus, penis, breast) as part of a pseudo integration, which organises the object (and self) <u>amidst</u> self-object psychosis.

In a sense, the patient <u>does not want to contact</u> the mad mother, because of a dread of psychotic experience, and in <u>this</u> sense the patient's splitting process <u>colludes</u> with the mother's <u>unintegration</u>.

In the transference–countertransference the patient enacts fragments of the object. One moment the patient is sane and clear, another moved, another sexually over-stimulating etc., and in this sense <u>he creates</u> for the analyst the experience of the maternal object. The mother was in one moment loving, then too seductive, etc., etc. In other words the object is not in itself integrated.

In the transference the patient does not want to get <u>emotionally and psychologically</u> involved. This is why there is all the stuff about spending less time with the analyst and turning it into supervision. At the same time the patient <u>does not want to</u> contact the object and, according to the self-as-object, does not want to contact his own mind and self. His self analysis-supervision is an effort to control the transference.

Further, the pervert defends against depression. The depressive experience is an <u>after-effect of</u> being with the mad mother. I think there is a cycle of:

1. Mother involves child in a psychotic experience that is <u>exciting</u>. Libido is linked up to unconscious processes in mother that breaches reality. It is also <u>manic</u>. (The manic element is part of the pseudo-integration present in perverse thinking. It organises the world in spite of the madness despair.)
2. Mother then <u>drops</u> the child, the excitement being over. In the <u>wake</u> of such self–other experiences the child experiences the true despair over what all this means. Mother is mad and this fact is depressing.

Parenthetically, the depressive experience cannot be accomplished if the object is not integrated enough for splits in the child to come together.

There is therefore a double defence in the pervert: against psychotic self–other states and depression.

[8/2/86]
"The two egos"

Early infancy is a negotiation by two egos: the infant's and the mother's.

This dialectic process takes up the first years. Some of the mother's processes of the self (= ego) are taken in by the child. Others are "refused" and may become introjects, slightly distanced, not to become part of the subject but split off.

Then there is the father and "father's ego". Again negotiation. Dialectics.

158

In the adult there are ego positions, many of them, each constituting a different processing of inner and outer reality.

An adult may process according to:

1. early mother
2. middle mother
3. late mother (adolescence)
4. early, middle, late father
5. early, middle, late child

[12/3/86]
"Beauty and the beast (the hysteric)"[1]

Ah! I think I know what I shall write about next: the hysteric.

About Beauty and the Beast, as the hysteric must deform men and then her kiss restores them. This potency is the reverse of the story of Sleeping Beauty when the man kisses her into life.

Within the countertransference I am the beast. She tells me that I am the violator and she becomes the virgin, who will take this innocent self to the beast. Indeed, I feel this rejection and in my countertransference it is as if I am no longer of use.

The dead object

Hysteric's two objects (bodies)

The living object

Why does she paralyze the other's body in the transference?

What body does she create?

Her projections create the Beast.

As I wait for "B"[i] I find that my ordinary movement and ease at being in my body is not there. I sit in my chair. I refrain from wandering to my desk. I do not want to distress her, but interestingly I construct myself on her behalf.

In the hysteric there is a very harsh element. The critical portion.

[undated]
"Anorexia/hysteria"

The anorectic/bulimic is the hysteric in contemporary garb.

Now the body is not enervated but depleted (of objects) or stuffed.

The conscious control of the body as symptom has usurped its apparently unconscious paralysis.

---

[i] Analysis was in a hospital.

159

[undated]
"Countertransference and the hysteric"

By not coming to sessions <u>she isolates</u> the father, forming a circle with the mother.

She attacks me (father) at level of desire <u>or</u> reproach. By not coming she wants me to say "please come" making it my desire. By telling her "come" I make it an obligation. By saying nothing I convey indifference. In short I (father) am <u>speechless</u>. Why is the father the speechless one?

I am not to speak.

[undated]
[untitled]

"Q": in her touching friendship with "P" (male patient) she has kissed <u>the beast</u>. First she turned him into the beast, or, found the beast and has now transformed him.

Perhaps the above is related to her fantasy of being a <u>heroine</u>, someone who will sing music and lead all the fellow patients into departing the hospital.

The beast is partly the excluded father. Both "L" and the "bad morals" boy of the two previous centers were already "beasts"—the bad father. She somehow transforms this.

[undated]
"M"

Countertransference: again, as an <u>isolate</u>, I am the beast to whom this young virgin is sacrificed. The accusations of my intent to molest her lead me to feel like the beast, a monster. In that respect I carry the projective identification of her impulses, which seem to have congealed in me and manifested themselves in my body/image deformity.

At the same time, as I wait for her in my room I am slightly paralyzed, not wanting to disturb the setting. Who am I in this moment?

[undated]
"B"

By seeking out nurturing from the women at the hospital, she clearly puts me in the role of <u>the man</u>. Indeed, in my conversations with "G" (female nurse, colleague) I related to her on the male/female level. That is, my maleness (the awful man) and "G"'s femaleness (the nice nurse) has been stressed by "B." In <u>this</u> sense the hysteric aims to polarize the sexes in order to get the two elements (male/female) clear. She cannot bear the mother in the father, or the female in the male.

[undated]
"Dream: a cry no voice"

The dream of being unable to speak is a memory in the dream experience of the preverbal self: the child unable to put inner anxieties into words.

If there are people in the dream it is dreamt at the time of language, so it's a sense of frustration. No one is there. It's well before language.

[27/3/86]
"Hysteria/anorexia/bulimia"

The anorectic becomes a psychic innocent. She asks for nothing (literally) and saint-like she refuses sustenance. This anti-incorporate act compels the other into a frantic and helpless effort to save her. Rather than paralyze the body of the other, she attacks the concept of a female body and self and inspires in the analyst agitated affectivity. This is the opposite state from the bulimic who inspires no such agitation in the analyst, but who in her person is an affectively agitated presence.

Thin/fat are 2 techniques for the distribution of "internal economy" (of time/energy devoted to objects.)

[27/3/86]
"Madness and psychosis"

Madness involves the action of the other in the life of the subject. A recognizable discrete action. A cathected action with the subject relation to the object either a complicitous cathexis or a countercathexis. Madness always involves two, often three (or more) people.

Psychosis is the disavowal of the other (and the self in relation to the other). It unites the subject in his disappearance. Freud's emphasis on loss of cathexis is important here.

[undated]
"P"

Perhaps the situation changes after I have consented to her going home. Even though she used the father part of herself to invite me to believe in the totalistic ("If I go home I won't ever return"), I believed she would come back.

In this I say: "I know you can leave the object and come back." Leaving is not equivalent to destruction.

By being away from me for so long she transfers to me the pain of "the left one". My feelings are hurt. But she reversed the passivity of her own state by repudiating me.

[undated]
"Where is mind?"

Extractive introjection and projective identification raise the issue of the location of mind.

If a schizophrenic puts lost circular integration into a record player where is this part of the mind?

Perhaps at all times our "mind" is partly in us (as objectified reflective thought) and partly in others (in projective identification or extractive introjection) and partly in our body as somatic thought.

[undated]
"Expectation: the image of"

As I await something, the <u>image</u> of a person or event comes into prominence.
    --------as an "object" in a potential space
    --------as an organization
Last night I could not sleep, as outside my New York City hotel jackhammers were going all night. The generator, I discovered, had a rhythm and I found that if I waited I could anticipate the rhythm—a sort of breathing. As I did this, instead of fighting the sound I tried to "fit" with it. I then dreamed (a half waking dream) of a surface and as each hammer sounded, an opening, a square, or rectangular gap—with a grid—opened on the surface. I tried in this dream to set the image to the sound: the more abrasive the sound, the larger and more irregular the hole, etc.
    This <u>venture of dreaming</u> failed to ensure my sleep.
    Now to "B". As I waited for her to return to analysis I had several different objects in mind. The structure of anticipation insures the power of the image.

[undated]
"Eris"

Is the brother of Eros. Eris is the god of <u>conflict</u>. Interestingly, this does not seem the true opposite of eros, but rather of Thanatos.
    Conflict brings two or more together in order to confuse, etc.
    Conflict undoes integration.

[4/5/86]
"Interrelation of external and internal (following discussion with friends in Stockbridge)"

How do we illustrate the relation between intrapsychic processes and intersubjective ones?
    Example. A child is 2½ & masturbating. The instinct is being gratified because the child has repressed the idea and a displaced derivative is in its place: i.e. the child is stroking "bunny" or whatever. The parent enters and says "You should not do that; its filthy and disgusting." Now the effect of this intervention is to <u>de-repress</u> the child's repression. So, interestingly the child's instinct comes through full force <u>and</u> the parental act excites the child's superego, which along with the parents condemns the instinctual child. If the parent continues the child will lose the superego to the parent who appropriates it. This is extractive introjection.

Now let's assess the parental act of projective identification. Let's assume that a child's mother or father projects impulsivity or masturbatory impulses into the child. They find the child's instinct and over-condemn it, as they use the child to represent bad or forbidden impulses.

The child grows up. He feels condemned and an idiot. This feeling and self-representation seems "unfair"—a sense of "the unfair" pervades the child in relation to this introject. We know that his introject is also a project—from the parent. It is fuelled (economically) by the child's instincts and parental projective identifications.

What do we call an object that is both an introject from within and a project from without? (new word needed)

Such an internal object will have a different feel than one purely or fundamentally intrapsychic.

Now also, internal intrapsychic objects are not only determined by instinct: from the body or the id. Some intrapsychic objects are derivatives of the kernel of the self, the "plan" of the inherited disposition. Maybe here we can say they are ego derivatives. Thus the ego places a demand on the mind for work; i.e. for thinking.

[4/5/86]
"HOW DOES ONE DIFFERENTIATE BETWEEN THE PROJ. OF AN INTROJECT THAT IS A PARENTAL PROJECTIVE IDENTIFICATION & THE PROJECTION OF AN INTROJECT THAT IS A TRUE PART OF THE SUBJECT'S EGO?"

A person may project an element that is an introject of a projective identification from the parents. But as it is alien and is not an essential part of the intrapsychic workings of the person's ego when it is expelled via projective identification, it no longer has a dynamic relation to the patient's self or the other parts of the self.

[undated]
"Unthought known and countertransference"

When thinking of the nature of the unthought known in our work this is often true of the countertransference. I know something (x) but it is not yet thought. Unconscious processes are at work, but I have not yet thought it.

[5/18/86 Arild]
"Unthought known"

Seeing the Louisiana[ii] catalogue on modern art and primitive masks, it occurs: how does Picasso create faces so similar to those of a New Guinean? Is it possible that this is an "old brain" creation, a "memory" of racial perceptions? Is this not part of the inherited disposition?

[ii] The museum in Denmark.

Perhaps endopsychic perception involves new brain transcriptions of old brain percept traces?

[21/5/86]
"Institution as container"

What is the nature of this "object relation" when differentiated from the patient's relation to the analyst?

Q's patient who goes to the medical centre and evokes contradictory and therefore faulty responsiveness from the container. She was developing ordinary splitting between good/bad, but perhaps as a result of a missed Wednesday session she acted to create a psychotic container.

I think she shows how in the course of splitting and projecting onto the mother, the borderline/psychotic mother increases the splitting and engenders fragmentation. But the question on the mind now is: what is the institution in such a moment?

I think the group = the environment mother. A mother known for her function of processing the infant. This is the moment to moment object—as a process, not a mental imago.

In health a patient gives creative contributions to the group and gets back "relatively" good feelings, etc.

In illness a person sends out destructive elements and disturbs the container. The container retaliates. It becomes the illness.

So, in a therapeutic community the group = the environment mother or the infant's transformational object.

What then is the status, in the transference, of the analyst, particularly if the patient seems fairly coherent and the relation fairly stable?

The patient may be splitting from the transference and projecting this into the group, so it's not metabolised. Who then is the analyst in the transference? The good object, devoid of hate? Or the blank object, no longer bearing any projections?

Or, can one speak of 2 objects: the environment (group) and the object mother?

[undated]
"Unthought known and the true self"

Is it possible that much of psychic life is the unfolding of the inherited disposition, rather than the recreation of early life or the representation of the body (id?).

This means that the course of a life is a developing of a print: an unfolding.

And what is the nature of the revealed: the unfolded? That enigma (the unconscious?) that is like death.

[21/6/86 Budapest]
"The conservative process"[iii]

It is important to distinguish the storage of an experience that is beyond

---

[iii] This idea works its way into the chapter "Moods and the conservative process".

comprehension from unconscious processes.

An experience beyond comprehension (unthought known) will be conserved, and the details of the experience "held" in memory, but in an analysis what had been conserved can be transformed.

[undated]
"Destiny and fate"

The *American College Dictionary* has a good differential definition.

A sense of one's personal destiny is based on an awareness or sense of the positive potential or realisation of the true self.

Fate is based on the opposite, on a compliance and reactive living with the sense of one's future feeling out of one's hands.

The manic personality moves between extremes of fatedness (depressive state) and destiny (manic).

Manic time.

Ahab: Fate.

Huck: Destiny.

[undated]
"Negative and positive space"

A mother who becomes "dead" creates a negative potential space. The child's experience of this space is of a vacuum.

"R" split his personality, with one side emerging as a cynical caretaker, hostile to the mother. It is the creature of negative space.

The image (gargoyle-like) & the sound (AKK!) predominate in psychosis. Language has a different more organizing function.

The image is mad because I think the mother's departure occasioned enraged images of the mother and child. Possibly he was dreaming as a child and unable to differentiate the dream (nightmare) from reality.

[undated]
"The object's demand on mind for work"

Is it possible to trace the nature of different demands on my mind?

e.g.: the patient who narrates clearly versus the one who does not.

e.g.: the patient who uses metaphor & imagery.

e.g.: the patient who frees me to listen creatively: i.e. unconsciously associative.

[undated]

"From mania to schizophrenia"

I will begin with "Z"'s dream.

In the dream he is asleep in his room when a bulldozer ploughs into his room and pushes him into a pit. I take up the dream as reflecting a manic frame of mind, a frame of mind when he does not listen to me. This is supported by the fact that we have been struggling over his manic attempt to exclude me by:

1. seeking therapy with other patients
2. missing sessions
3. hyperactive use of my interpretations to give himself therapy/supervision in my presence

I say that the pit in the dream = another side of himself: a depressed area into which we will crash, moved there by a bulldozing-omnipotent part of himself that is trying to bulldoze its way through life but now feels out of control.

The <u>interpretation</u> of the dream calms him, as he did not know what it truly meant, even though he had many interpretations of it—all self analytic omnipotence.

The above was in a Monday session.

The manic mood, of intense omnipotence, of controlling the sessions continues. He over exaggerates his health, claims he is now cured, says he is in love with "A", will have to follow her to university, can end therapy and become what he wishes. He does not need this anymore.

I <u>create</u> a space with him, which is what I feel I must do because he is so omnipotent & fragile, so near <u>the brink</u> that I say, "You know, 'Z', there are sometimes when I regret being an analyst and right now is one such occasion." He replies with a true smile, "you are going to burst my bubble." "Yes," I say, "I am." I proceed to say that he is in a manic mood and I re-introduce the dream and say he is trying to tell himself something but now is tempted not to listen even to himself.

As I speak, he develops a facial tick to which I say "I know this is difficult to hear and infuriating, no doubt" and I then proceed to say that I think it's essential for me to be frank with him, to tell him what I think, rather than to simply reassure him or "support" him but withdraw by giving him medications etc.

As this session progresses he calms and I say that he is not now manic but was, and I think this indicates my usefulness.

Then he tells me that <u>in</u> the sessions now and then he <u>sees</u> a purple cloud—haze—image some 10 inches away to 2 ½ feet, between us. He then says that he has just seen me as if I were at the end of a long tunnel, far away and small. I have noticed that in the last minutes he looked "day-dreamy". I see this as a schizophrenic process and say I think he <u>has</u> found my interpretation of his omnipotence upsetting because he thinks he should be able to control everything & now if he cannot control the actual world, including the actual me, he can try to control the imaginary me.

166

He says that he has been "controlling" me, by making me small then large & he was amused with this.

I say that this kind of omnipotence creates its own problems as we can say that he did this to the patients in the hospital prior to the dream, making them disappear, and this created an empty pit which metaphorized what he had done. I said that I thought right now he was very anxious and this was the result of moving into a total omnipotence divorced from the actual world.

In the above we can see:

1. how manic omnipotence devolves into schizophrenic omnipotence.
2. in the manic-omnipotence the patient is aiming to control the actual world & to do so through words: fast, free, loose associations weaving a web through & around the object-other.
3. In schizophrenic-omnipotence the patient aims to control the imaginary world, not via words, but via the image (colour purple & me vanishing/returning etc.)…
4. Is the colour purple the visual representation of affect? Purple with rage?
5. The schizophrenic state is more withdrawn from object cathexes.
6. Recall him saying in a public meeting that he would make another patient "smaller".

[9/8/86 Laguna Beach]
"Being carried"

In re-reading my paper on the transformational object I can see that I failed to dwell on certain functions of the mother's transforming of her infant. Her carrying the infant. What a remarkable act! We cannot assume carrying to be uneventful, or, because so common, unremarkable.

We are carried first in the uterus. We are moving inside an object which in turn is inside an object (the mother) that moves about.

It's almost a physical correlate of a mental state: i.e. psyche is inside and yet moves itself within a container (Bion) that in turn is inside something (the body) that moves about.

[undated]
"Absence and the size of God"

The largeness of God is due to his distance.

Distance and idealization.

We make Him by projection so omnipotent because he represents the object that is gone away, out of sight, not present.

[undated]
"Fate and destiny"

If a child's mother is not in touch with him or her external presence compels compliance, then this child will have a sense of fate: of the external fundamentally determining the internal.

If the child has used objects to <u>realize</u> inner reality, thus enriching inner and outer, he will have a sense of destiny which is the sense of one's inner core unfolding in a positive and rewarding way.

Fate is to the False Self

What Destiny is to the True Self

[undated]

"Schizoid phenomena and the introject collectors"

There is a difference between internal objects that reflect the actual object world and the schizoid internal object which reflects a deep bias of the internal.

There is the narrative object solely under control: even the external object.

The schizoid is an <u>introject collector</u>, as compensation for the lack of play between self and other. So the introject collector takes everything "in", but it is kept there, not to be moved into object relating.

This raises the issue of what's different between object representation and object relating in the transference.

C's patient can represent his inner experience, just like Sylvia Plath. But he cannot move such inner representation into intersubjectivity or between self and other. This of course is the split.

Analysis which focuses only on narrative content, even if it is used to make a transference interpretation (linking inner object with actual object) is not equivalent to the patient's use of the object.

A patient who is schizoid can have his experience of the object, but he may not be able to <u>be</u> <u>with</u> or <u>use</u> the object.

This raises the question of how the analyst facilitates interplay or object usage.

The analyst may have to:

1. comment on the physical appearance of the patient (as an actual as opposed to a narrative object) <u>and</u>
2. carefully note and comment on allusions of the patient to the specificity of the analyst's person.

There are <u>many</u> patients who could never bring into their relation to their parents their feelings, thoughts, questions, and so forth.

Thus the analyst must find some way of establishing object usage.

[undated]

"Differentiating aggression from violence"

For DW aggression is the capacity to grasp. Linked with <u>motility</u>, movement, initiative.

Therefore its opposite is passivity.

A violent person may not be at all aggressive; indeed, violence may be due to the inability to initiate, grasp, or move.

Narcissistic rages are not acts of aggression but the opposite. They are <u>expulsions</u>.

[undated. Aboard American Airlines Flight 685 over Texas]
"Fate and Destiny"[2]

From Ágnes Heller's *Renaissance Man:*[3]
"Destiny implies ... immutability ... the ontological function of 'irrevocability'" (363).
"Moira" (fate) meant the inevitable unfolding of destiny with the Greeks.

In the Old Testament, God can elect someone whose qualities he likes to be the executors of His *destiny*. I gather the Epicureans believed destiny to be synonymous with the unfolding of the natural essence of man.

Fate differs from destiny because the inevitable is only one aspect of it. Fate does not denote a predetermined path, but rather a range of possibilities or possible causes. It is social and objective in its point of departure. It cannot be impelled or guided by gods and leaves room for men.

Fate evolves; it is not present at the moment of birth and it is immanent, sensed from within by the person as he moves in life.

According to these definitions I would have to conclude that:

1. Destiny is the idiom of the true self with its own <u>logic of unfolding</u> and
2. Fate is the subject's experience of, relation to, and the social possibilities of destiny.
3. Fortune is that which is circumstantially determined by society etc.

I should focus on the person whose destiny becomes a fate, in the good sense, and when it spells catastrophe.

In health the child/adult feels destiny to be from the core of the self: an unfolding of intrinsic being.

In illness the person feels this is either in the hands of the other, or, if in one's thoughts, managed in a magical, psychotic manner.

[10/9/86 Santa Barbara]
"The borderline"

This person does not have structure producing internal objects. Objects are known by their trace which is through affect, the effect of affect upon the subject.

Objects create affect states which give the object its presence. Or, the emergence of feelings, of pain, is such that it slowly evolves into the mother experience, and this person can exploit a feeling into an affect storm.

The schizoid's mother could not link up his true self with relating and be adapted to the environment.

[18/9/86]
"The narcissistic complex"

What is the transgression here?

It is the usurpation of the mirroring function of the other. The right of the other to mirror one.

Thus one aspect of the embarrassment and anxiety that is present when a person glances in the mirror, is that he usurps the other's position as the one who sees us.

This Narcissus does to Echo, who is pushed away and subordinated.

This cancellation is an act of aggression, a displacement of the mother, just as the Oedipus complex is a displacement of the father.

[undated]
"Projective identification and infantile omnipotence"

It may well be that alongside the infant's primary narcissism is the fact that mothers and others project into the infant idealized parts of themselves. The baby is "wonderful", "gorgeous", "perfect", etc., so in considering the origins of infantile grandiosity we must allow for the fact that we partly make them this way, and by keeping our treasures in our child, we make it difficult for the child to grow up. Growing up, here, would mean being less adorable etc., so such a parent might violently oppose or deny the child's aggressions, differences or naughtiness. The point here is that the parents' projective identifications of ideal parts of themselves into an infant does not mean these are indulgent parents or overly protective. They can be actually quite dismissive and neglecting of the true or actual infant, preferring to dwell on the child as an internal object in his absence. The actual child could be too real and too difficult to be with.

[undated]
"Projective identification/extractive introjection"

Differential. How do we know that the missing part of a person is missing by virtue of its projection or its extraction?

Take the superego. It could be missing because the child or adult cannot bear the guilt associated with destructive urges, so the superego is projected into an object.

Or, the superego could be missing because it has been extracted by an overly critical parent.

In the latter case, the person could feel something like *relief* at inner experience of guilt and preservation of object, as up till then they may only have experienced persecution at recognition of hate, or high anxiety, as a fear of being denuded or emptied of the responsible and loving part of the self.

Some people enjoy the exploration of destructive urges in relation to the analyst because instead of acting punitively the analyst explores where the guilt is in the patient and tries to enable him to experience the relief work of the superego.

The differential here, between projective identification and extractive introjection, is that with the latter there is relief at the arrival of guilt which signals the arrival of love and the possibility of reparation, whereas before there was only anxiety.

[undated]
"The unthought known and the transformational object"

By transforming the infant's being and putting it into language the mother moves the unthought known into thought and speech.

Thus the mother's function here is crucial. It's the talking cure, as the mother's act is so important. This "speaking of being" or "speaking being" is a function she passes on to the infant, enabling him to become a subject.

In my "expressive uses"⁴ paper, when I argue that I put my experiences or being states into language I am arguing for the analyst's transformational function of doing what the mother does. This is simply an extension of Freud's idea of the talking cure, as that referred to secondary repression and this talking refers to moving the unthought known into thought. It's the talking cure of the primary repressed.

[26/9/86]
"Extractive introjection: reflections after meeting of the William Alanson White Institute"

1. The positive value of e.g. when a parent assumes into themselves excess distress or psychic conflict in the child.
2. What is the basis for the perpetrator of extractive introjections? Is this a narcissistic personality who greedily assumes others' minds, to gain power over them, and ultimately to prevent inter relating?
3. Probably for every extractive introjection there is a corresponding projective identification.
4. Extractive introjection takes place at different developmental times. Some are more vulnerable to it than others, depending on how much they have from the mother, etc. Also one should be able to differentiate types and intensities of extractive introjection.
5. What is the intrapsychic usefulness of extractive introjection? What is the alternative? Empathy?
6. The schizoid has received something from the mother but is cut off from object relating.

"Cocooning in the countertransference"

When the analyst along with the patient goes "inside" the mother, using the analytic space-process as an interior locale, where there is no interpretation of unconscious communication, only self object gratification.

In such a state the analyst <u>does not know</u> much and is <u>no longer working</u> or using his mind.

This may be a necessary period in analysis but if it goes on too long can represent a defensive collusion against the distress of conflict. Against birth into conflict.

—the internal breast.

[7/11/86]
"Life and death instincts in psychoanalytic practice"

In his technique the analyst represents these two forces. By integrating and holding he represents the life instincts. By subverting and destroying defences etc. he contains and binds and represents the death instinct.

[undated]
"Patient-analyst 'where are we?'"

This is not clear. Never will be. Bion: what is speaking, to what? Could be amended: "<u>and where?</u>"
   What is this space?
   Two bodies
   Supported/yet <u>very close</u>
   Voices separated from eye sight
   The absent
   The present
   Where does the world come from? This is a Bionian-Lacanian issue.
   Lacan: the subject grows out of absence.
   When I carry a patient "in" my soma, where, what is he/she & who/what am I?

[15/11/86]
"Winnicott, Bion, Lacan"

Lacan's imaginary = Klein's idea (in part) of the internal world. A world of/from the image, first of the infant in the mirror, then from that split between the subject and all other objects.

To some extent <u>this imaginary</u> is DW's false self as it is not <u>true</u> to the core self. Both DW and Lacan have an idea of an original split, but the reasons for this differ. Lacan's is inevitable and emerges from the paradox of seeing oneself.

But DW's true self is richer than the subject prior to the ego (in Lacan's world). Lacan's ego is made out of this split. It is composed of the imaginary. It does not exist before this mirror self.

Lacan cannot account for the other forms of representation. Somatic, for example. And Bion's idea of beta to alpha if linked to the true self is interesting because we could say the true self is at the beginning beta but only comes to alpha through object relating. In other words, thoughts can only develop if there is an idea of a container: an other.

[undated]
"A symptom"

"S"'s first symptom is an obsession with vacuuming the rug in the living room, so as to keep all the weave clean, etc. No one is to walk on it.

This symptom emerges soon after a move. And she has moved many times as a child, adolescent, and in marriage, and every time she says she likes it.

Let's imagine that the symptom expresses other feelings: she hoovers up the imaginary dust, she cleans up her feelings to create a vacuum. By vacuuming up she takes part of the self back in.

[undated]
"Lacan/Freud's ego"

For Freud the Ego is "a precipitate of abandoned object cathexes" and "contains the history of those object-cathexes" while Lacan's ego is a narcissistic projection. It is built out of the image of the body and through the other images. Freud's ego is history.

[undated]
"DW/Bion/Lacan"

DW's transitional object might fill the gap in Lacan's theory. For Lacan, the image constitutes the ego which splits the subject. For DW the transitional object is an actual object which bears the imaginative uses of the child. If we say it's both subject and ego; or, that the split subject uses it, then this object also heals the rupture, the *béance*.

Also, Lacan's idea that the infant alone confronts the image is not true. The infant and the mother do. Both. And the mother all along has sustained the illusion of the unified infant through the illusion of omnipotence. This gives a sense of unity to the infant, of psychic unity which is part of the sense of self.

The Symbolic (and unconscious) do subvert this sense but only successfully in psychosis. Because this sense (of omnipotence, of unity, of centrality) is that which forms the core of being.

But Lacan's idea of the unconscious as subversion is good. One problem though. In the mother/child relation there is never just one unconscious, there are at least 2. And mother and child are in an intersubjective dialogue with each other. Thus, there is a companion object for the unconscious with which it does fit. This mitigates the sense of division created by the image.

[undated]
"Self"

I have uncovered an old lecture I gave, or prepared but did not give, in which I said that the idea of self referred to "an absent presence to which we are in indirect relation." I have been dwelling on Hillis Miller[iv] and the idea of there being no self. It's an illusion, etc., etc. Could "it" be not a content, a trace of memories etc., but the point of the gaze, the object of the question that poses it, that addresses it? An active presence. No, the presence of absence. Into which we imagine. The mother leaves the room. We imagine her. Then we imagine anything we wish.

If the self is a present absence, a space, not a content, then it functions partly as a transitional area. It does not entirely exist. Nor is it entirely non-existent.

[19/11/86]
"Nina Coltart's paper at the Boston Psychoanalytic Society"[v]

The transvestite "B" takes to analysis quickly and uses Nina as a mirror for reflecting himself. When "B" gets inside his mother's clothing he demonstrates that this is as far as he can get. The question is, how to get inside the mother, and the mother's body when she does not introject him, does not do so because she clearly demonstrates that she will project her unconscious organization around (not into) the child. Around, because she will enlist the child into something, a something that defines the use of potential space.

After a while Nina and the patient become more deeply involved in a kind of struggle. At this point the patient is pushing to get inside the psyche-soma of the analyst and the analyst allows and enjoys this and this undoes the mother's damage. It is a symbolizing in the transference of the problematics of projection/introjection with the mother. It does not mean the patient could never project or introject, but that he needs to re-experience such basic processes with the mother.

Finally she becomes the "cupboard": she feels he stores things "in" her as he goes on his way and this countertransference metaphor indicates the final psychic change: that he can entrust parts of the self to the mother and she will store them for memory and dream use: i.e. alpha. Thus in considering the theory of psychic change the analyst facilitates the use of illusion (which is the transference) to re-present (and that's what it is, a representation) the origins of trauma.

Thus, because it is fundamentally a symbolic process the ego's need to experience a re-structuring via object relating, it should not require so much work or have to go on and on. Those patients who are, perhaps, interminable, are those for whom the illusion is not, as such, and who seek out continuously a fairly literal re-experiencing.

And the person who cannot make use of illusion may create a sense of overwhelming burden in the psychoanalyst for whom illusion no longer functions. Such an analyst will not feel the benefits of the psychoanalytic process but will feel that he and he alone must cure the patient.

[iv] J. Hillis Miller, English Department, Yale.
[v] Nina Coltart, senior member of the Independent Group in the UK. Her talk in Boston was part of an East Coast tour where she spent a week at the Austen Riggs Center.

Perhaps the analyst must not function analytically with such a person but refuse them analysis until they are ready.

[21/11/86]
"Projecting around"

Following previous entry about "B", we may consider that some people project <u>around</u> the object but not onto or into it. Thus the mother who selects female clothing for her boy projects around him (in the articles around him).

The mother projects into the objects surrounding the child (or herself) such as <u>clothing</u>. By wearing the female garb the transvestite <u>enters</u> the mother's symbolic field. He gets inside her projective space.

[23/11/86]
"Hysteric's orgasm"

"B"'s escalation of feelings, from irritation into rage and then into power is a kind of ego foreplay until the final collapse which is like an ego-decompensation-as-orgasm which then becomes a depression. Or "reality" seems to pop up and she comes out of it.

[undated]
"True self"

Is <u>organised difference</u>, or better:
   inherited organised difference
   or
   inherited difference

[undated]
"Object usage"

We need to analyse not what the content of a dream means but why the dreamer dreams this dream. What is he seeking to find here? What does he potentialize in the dream? Make available to himself?

In turn, in a session what is he doing to create for himself?

[28/11/86]
"Unthought known"

If the unthought known is an inherited core then some persons live this out (elaborate it) more successfully than others. My father could be more successful at such articulation than Mark[vi]

[vi] My second brother, two and a half years younger.

175

or I. Who could be further elaborating it? We can wonder who in a series of generations elaborates a genetic code.

[undated]
"Fate & destiny & unthought known"

Much is written about self realisation. There would be ancestral realisation through object usage: choice of vocation, partner, even country. Destiny bears on ordinary ruthlessness whilst fate is the art of compliance in which the subject is at the whim of the other.

As in false self. (But also, it could be a part of the self that is split off and seems to be in the other.)

Where does one put the Other: the parole of the subject? Can we say that it is necessary for the subject to be free to associate. Indeed, isn't the concept of free association a form of ruthlessness in which the patient is encouraged to report all without fear of censure.

Does a psychoanalysis fulfil fate or destiny?

Certainly many patients come to an analysis "stuck". They may be in a dreadful marriage which is harming their articulation of love. It may be that X establishes his sense of core self, his essence, through a particular kind of loving: say, a sort of generosity. Further, X's grandfather, to whom he was quite close, is of similar "character".

To be able to "destroy" the object (in Hegel & DW's sense) is a sign of health. Think of Martin Cooperman's[vii] jokes which are loving and not cruel. This form of destructiveness allows expression & establishment of true self. Also, Stuart[viii] to some extent, and one of the accomplishments of the Lacan short session might be that the master dismisses the analysand, establishing a good destruction.

Those for whom destruction is not possible may, as with perverts, be involved in (1) dissociated & parodic "violent" sex (2) premature reparation. Sometimes the reparation may precede the act of sex, may even usurp it. Possibly they have been the victims of one or both parent's cruelty. It is cruelty in the parent (malignant destructiveness) that prevents a child from establishing generative destructiveness. Is it possible that the hate some perverts have is the transfer of cruelty, to be always diminishing and devaluing? Which is, in turn, split off from their intimate ordinary sexual life, & vigorously "kept" there.

[20/11/86]
"Endearment & the true self"

In work with "R" he is developing mannerisms which are endearing. This endearment has something to do with idiom, with a knowable personal idiom. Nowadays he has a habit of saying "YCap" (yes, captain) and looking suddenly earnest and thoughtful. This is usually a response to

---

[vii] A psychoanalyst working at the Austen Riggs Center.
[viii] Stuart Schneiderman, a close friend, and analysand of Lacan.

something I say. There is a naturalness to "taking" (introjection) in of my comments and his way of using them. Such endearment has to do with the mother's love of her baby's identifiable and unique gestures. In working with the severely disturbed patient the arrival of a term of endearment, a gesture, is perhaps quite important. It is a manifestation of the true self, a sign of difference.

[undated]
"The Mirror"

Lacan does not include in his mirror theory the fact that the child who looks into the mirror sees

1. an image differing from inner self
2. an image that differs from mother and from all others

What the infant sees, via the gaze, is therefore a potential. He sees his imaginary difference. Will this difference be accomplished?

Do infant researchers tell us whether or not an infant recognizes a picture of himself out of pictures of other babies before object constancy? Is there an innate knowledge of this image?

[1/12/86]
"The blank slate and nuclear war"

Much of the controversy in psychoanalytic discussions focuses on how unthinkable a nuclear war is. I am not so sure. People think it all the time. In fact, this is partly the problem: it is only thought. At some point people want to see it. And the disregard even in psychoanalysis for the value of memory acts too in this sphere. Did an A-bomb drop on Hiroshima/Nagasaki or, is this merely a form of reconstructive interpretation? This devaluation of memory is part of the problem and is partly why everything must be in the here and now. And what more important here-and-now event could there be than nuclear war?

I had intended, as my title suggests, to address the topic of the clean slate. I intended to make the following point. It is odd that we cannot think it, it is that we are only guided by an unconscious fantasy to wipe the slate clean. This has a corollary in the theory of the second coming, etc., and the more complex and seemingly evil is the world, the more tempting is this phantasy. Ultimately the idea of being innocent, & surrounded by evil, which feeds the wish for a clean slate, may be the worst threat to mankind.

[undated]
[untitled]

There is an interesting relation between the economic plundering of the whale and Ahab's psychological projections. That is, as something is being stolen, something is put in.

Is there a relation between plundering and projection? Such that taking from is compensated by projecting: putting in.

[6/12/86]
"Memories/futures"[ix]

If we have memories, do we have <u>futures</u>? Memory is investment in the past, future is investment in tomorrow. Futures could be based on destiny, the unconscious, <u>intrinsic knowledge</u> and its future. Visions may be phantasies of the future determined by the potential of the true self. We then could dream of the future. Instead of this being the shadow of the object, it's the shadow of the subject.

[undated]
"Destiny"

DW's example of "the electricity" that seems to generate in meaningful or intimate contact, that is a feature, for instance, when two people are in love (PR 98)[5] is a good example of that X factor that typifies a <u>sense</u> of destiny, that <u>at the moment</u> there is no doubt about the choice. Only <u>that</u> woman (object) will do and only then can the true self find elaboration. Easy to contrast this with a <u>forced choice</u> etc. which allies to fate & the false self.

Also, there is an electricity when one discovers an idea, either in reading, writing, scientific work. Or in discovering an author. There is an excitement and a sense of fulfilling one's destiny by following this through. Fate would be in following an idea, or project etc., for the other.

DW also says that every infant has his own favourable or unfavourable experience & that potential space happens in relation to a feeling of confidence (PR 100). Therefore destiny, or the sense of confidence, links up or evolves from the construction of potential space. Indeed, we may say that potential space is an early idea of destiny, one which is realized by the mother's function as transformational object. Indeed, a person with a sense of destiny is partly living out an object relation, in that he has a memory (now as a sense) of mother transforming the world to fulfil his needs. Thus each person with this sense of feeling is <u>guided</u> by his destiny where destiny is now = to mother, but <u>should</u> have some correlate of gratitude, in that the child recognizes that his existence is a cultural act: mother, father, family and society act together in making things work for the infant. If the mother and father do not familiarize the <u>child</u> with the social effort or context that facilitated him then something like a <u>delusion</u> of significance will prevail and this may sponsor a kind of fascistic person. While the introduction of society may facilitate a sense of destiny within society, for society, and via <u>participation</u> & the joys of participation, which probably has something to do with the parent's enabling the child to identify with the processes that supported him.

In some ways this has to do with identifying with transformational processes.

[undated]
"Language & true self"

DW's idea is that language is used by the infant as part of the subjective phenomenon. Its use as subjective (i.e. as an indirect communication) would be the infant's freedom—and the

---

[ix] First use of the concept of "futures". Will find its way into *Forces of Destiny*.

sense of feeling or being real has to do with subjective use of the language. Language is part of the non-communicating of the child. This differs from Lacan's notion of language splitting the subject and causing a permanent rift. For DW the subject is already split between the 2 mothers: environment and object that creates a split in self between a non-communicating and a communicating part. The Lacan idea that parole speaks the subject could be true for DW as well insofar as the true self is a core that is not knowable but effective. For DW this surprise, this unknowability, is the source of pleasure (& play) rather than alienation. By using the true self, or unconscious, or core, we "play it out", not into comprehensibility but into being and relating.

Perhaps it's more like this.

Communicating emerges from silence.

The true self "speaks" and parole is a detour, as the gesture is the Other.

[undated]
"The unthought known"

The recollection of memories, the return of the repressed, in the system ucs/pcs/cs is based on an idea that it is cs or pcs being put down into the ucs.

But that which is known but not thought could be e.g. a foetal defence: when a foetus is habituated to sound. If a foetus "knows" this, how is it known? Not through secondary processes or object representation or abstractions. It is operationally determined or existentially negotiated. It is the stuff of existence. Or existence making. Existence making. Or idiom forming. Or form. The logic of form. The point is, this would be in the system of the primary repressed in that it has never been conscious, but is repeated in the transference.

If we ask, "what is the mental status of operational paradigms—existential 'laws'—negotiated between foetus and uterus, neonate and environment mother, infant and mother, prior to the establishment of a mental apparatus capable of secondary repression?", what are the possibilities?

To begin with, there must be crude forms of memory based on primitive learning that enable the foetus-infant to alter his mood or behaviour in response to stimuli. Habituation is one such response. Thus the foetus "knows" something without our stating that he has thought what he knows.

Here it is useful to state that an accomplishment of the brain is not equivalent to thinking a thought, which is the work of mind. If we stick to the brain, the limbic system could process stimuli and decide on a response without ever involving the cortex. So even in terms of the brain something can be known but not thought.

This of course is also true of the genetically transmitted.

In other words, the topographic and structural models are not adequate to specify the nature and effect of this unthought known.

Even the theory of primary repression does not address it.

Freud: "The content of the *Ucs.* may be compared with an aboriginal population in the mind. If inherited mental formations exist in the human being—something analogous to instinct in animals—these constitute the nucleus of the *Ucs.*" "The unconscious" (1915), SE14, 195.

[undated]
"Counter countertransference"

This is a response in the analyst to analytical reflection on his frame of mind etc. in relation to the patient. Could be a form of acting out, of course, but equally it could be a way of aiming to preserve or facilitate a state of reverie or free floating attention.

[undated]
"Unthought known and its transitions"

Is it possible to talk about a transition of the unthought known to its knowing? Because we cannot speak of a knowing or the knowing, but only of its knowing.
    First, it is relevant to isolate the multiple sources of the unthought known.

1. the genetic/inherited
2. the "core" and the intrauterine
3. the logic of the mother
4. experiences beyond comprehension

—the genetic involves use of the other's creativity.
—in response to DW's phrase "where do we live?" & "where are we when listening to a symphony?" we may be there where we cannot speak because we are not in sufficient contact.

[13/12/86]
"'Conversation', Alitalia, NYC"

"I got to say this to you in person. They say phone him. I got to tell him: You are fucked. I know everything you did, I know it all. G is a nice guy, but I've no respect for him. Do you think I need your failures? What do you think? I have to get up and shave in the mornings. I have to get up and look in my face in the morning. I'm telling you this and looking you in the eye. And I can be like this, look others in the eye, because I've nothing to hide. You understand me? You see, I know everything. Those failures you wanted: the samples, you sent. (Yes). You sent them to M, didn't you? (Yes, I could have told you that). You have to be straight with me because whether you tell me or not I know. They never got beyond M."

[25/12/86]
"Unthought known, transformation, representation"

If we begin with an inherited core (true self) then psyche = an evolving representational, internal world in which aspects of the core are represented. In Lacan this is the Imaginary.

But Bion shows that some elements never get alpha and are not represented. They are expelled or concretised.

I think we can now say that there are different fates for different parts of the true self. Some are transformed to be phantasy, dream = internal world. Some are to be in play (DWW). But some of the unthought known will never achieve such representation. Some will be somatically carried and represented. Some will be projected and stored in objects. Some will be extracted by the other.

Question is: what and how much is made psychical?

Certain idioms of the true self are simply encoded into character and become the person's way (form, idiom) of processing life. This is structure. Perhaps the Kleinian effort to see defence as phantasy determined is okay up to a point, as I am saying processes reflect a logic, an idea. But most of this will not have been thought, and in analysis, in the transference countertransference process, the way the patient processes existence, the way the analyst is guided to process this particular patient: this is a form of knowledge.

Therefore, how much of any one person is "in" psyche; "in" soma; "in" the other; "in" language? People vary, in other words, in the balance, the distribution of the true self. The knowledge that is the true self is the unthought known. It is also the primary repressed unconscious.

Endopsychic perception is unconscious and preconscious insight into the core of the self: into one's psychic structure, and perhaps in to the "history" of one's ancestry. Ancestral knowledge?

I suppose I am considering the different pathways of representation. Psyche, soma, character, etc. Is it possible that literature, painting, music, maths, and dance, represent completely different modes of representing the true self? That is, may we say that elements of the true self (of the unthought known) become "known" through different modes of representation, such as above?

Can I link destiny to the above, in that perhaps using as many modes as possible realises more of the core?

What does it mean to choose music versus literature?

[29/12/86]
"Love and insight"

When I say that Sacha has my father's ears, my mother's eyes, my wife's mouth, I can only make this statement because I love him. Such love allows me to notice the small details and to wonder about them. This is a loving perception or the understanding that love gives.

181

1987

[14/1/87 Newport Beach]
"Reflectors"

Lacan's ego, composed of the image of the body (out there) which radically splits or alienates the self, is a special internal object in the psyche. It is a reflector object or reflector introject that does embody the difference between, as Lacan sees it, the subject and the ego. Such reflectors are introjections of the images of self and will proceed along with similar ones: the images the other gives to the self. But there are other internal objects: from instincts, from affects, etc.

Example: We may have an introject of self which is a bad object based on destructive feelings. This will exist alongside the reflector introject in total contradiction, as it is composed from a different order of reality.

Then there are "objects" evolving out of neuropsychological evolution enabling the inherited core to print itself more completely in the psyche. This is the true self.

[14/1/87]
"Ghostline object"[i]

I don't know exactly what I mean by this as the concept occurred in a dream last night. I was dreaming about a conference on the borderline and finding the concept so overused that in fancy the idea of ghostline came up. In the dream I tried to figure out what I meant and I thought it meant the border between the psychic and the real, the corporeal and the spiritual. Then I thought of a ghostline personality, along lines of the schizoid, but someone who is

---

[i] "The ghostline personality" became a chapter in *Forces of Destiny*.

living a completely different, organised, and ghostly life in total phantasm. I think now of my patient who has a TV character with her all the time. The ghostline personality then is someone who lives the essence of their life in fantasy.

The ghostline personality relates to "inner objects" as if they were real.

—and grief (e.g. seeing the departed)

—and imaginary companion

[21/3/87]

Reading the above now, I can see that in dreaming this up I was on the ghostline. The dream came out of this.

[undated]

"Unthought known"

Anything that informs. This is a response to a question put to me by Michael Russel.[ii] How can I call these phenomena "known" etc.? In the end I say "anything that informs our existence is knowledge." I should qualify this of course to mean anything that does so from within the psyche-soma.

Therefore knowledge is anything from psyche-soma that informs our existence. That conveys information, whether such knowledge is conscious, unconscious, or not even thought per se.

[undated]

"Reincarnation"

Reincarnation as previous selves (conservative process). This comes from a session with "R" talking about it.

Re-incarnation, or, the idea in a person that he has been previous selves, prior existences. I think this is psychoanalytically true if we understand these selves to be the different individuals we have been during our existence. Such as the foetus, the self at birth, with the 1st mother, in the body as motor phenomenon, in the mother's arms, being carried by the father. Is it possible that each of these self states is conserved as a separate self phenomenon before habituation "sets in" and the experience in being yields to psychic structure?

So, we have been many selves.

However, those people who do think qualitatively and with deep re-assurance that for sure they have been someone from the past, etc., they introduce another factor. What is it? Is it a lost self? Is there some very particular need to re-contact lost selves? Is there something for the analyst to learn from this person's search and the séance?

In what way does this idea link to concepts of fate and destiny?

[ii] A philosophy professor at Fullerton State College in Orange California and a psychoanalyst.

Déjà vu: the conviction held in a moment that it has happened before
Premonition: related to above
Reincarnation: the idea that one has been one before
Ghosts?

[undated]
"The alternate object"[iii]

This comes to me because the concept of transitional object is being overused. A transitional object signifies the infant's and child's creative forging of a play space that allows inner and outer reality to mingle, to influence one another.

The alternate object is very different. It will be a thing in the beginning, but it will signify thingness not creative use (alteration) and the alternative process will become split off from the object, entirely in an internal world.

Now some imaginary companions are the surfacing of a purely internal relation and this kind of companion should not be confused with one that expresses transitional object use. In other words, use determines the nature of the phenomenon, whether it is an alternative object or a transitional object.

The transitional object and phenomenon express true self life and is part of the cultural diffusion of the inherited core. Inherited core is not discoverable in contents per se but in usages of objects, in discoveries and creations, in processes.

The alternative object is an internally created self-other, split off, cultured and sustained in private because it cannot be transformed into life. It is alter. It is also the fate of the alternative process, which now operates only in the internal world. Or, the alternative process is really a transformational process that is entirely internal.

The concept of the "alternative object" links to:

1. autistic objects
2. alter, alterity
3. alter ego
4. ghostline personality
5. organising personality
6. symbolic equations
7. pseudo epistemophilia
8. premature objective objects, or the subjective objective object
9. not a fetish

Anxiety occurs in this person when an actual person makes a claim on them. Either that the actual person loves them or hates them, or worse, that they fall in love or hate. They have no room for actual ongoing relation. And—self/as/object/—the self is a clear narrative other, even

---

[iii] The concept of the "alternative object" did not find its way into print.

with a different name or identity. "F" was The Princess. "K" the Co-Ordinator. (What relation does this have to Tausk's[iv] "the influencing machine"?)

—the séance transference. A conjuring of objects.

—alternates are objects never meant to be communicated, to be given cultural or social space.

—alternate objects become ghostlike, having their own personalities.

Does the ghostline object reflect the psychic processes of cathecting and then de-cathecting an object? Of doing this to a mother? After all, a ghost is something that has at one time lived, been alive. So the ghosts of this person's inner world represent the objects that are cathected/decathected.

And these mothers tried to relate to the child as if he were only an internal object. As if the true corporeality, true passion, was "in" her.

[undated]
"intrapsychification"

Refers to a process of making psychic. Close to Bion's beta to alpha. This is a capacity. To make psychic. It's different from internalization as that assumes the object representation is there. This process would also have to do with the undoing of projections.

[undated]
"Alternate object"

Stern[v] writes of the fact that during infancy 3–4, 8–9 months, there are quantum leaps and we are dealing with "an altered person". This is the transformation of self, but if the child just feels altered—as in different or alter (as in alter ego) due to lack of connection to the transformational object—then the infant may turn to alternative objects.

[25/1/87]
"Fate/destiny"

Virgil writes of Aeneas:[1] "They wandered as their destiny drove them on" (p. 4, line 47).

Of Juno: "The fates forbid me, am I to suppose?" (p. 4, line 59).

Interestingly destiny cannot forbid. Fate can. Fate has an interventionist quality. Virgil represents destiny as owned by Aeneas, "their destiny" and destiny is associated with drive.

Michel Small[vi] tells me that destiny as a concept may have to do with the rise of the middle class, which fits with my idea of it being in the 17th century.

Aeneas at one point talks of "weighing out one fate against another in the scales" (p. 12, lines 324–325) and this reminds me: there can be several fates. (The 3 fates, etc.) But only 1 destiny. There are not "destinies".

---

iv Victor Tausk, pioneer psychoanalyst and neurologist, a student and colleague of Sigmund Freud.

v Daniel Stern, American psychoanalyst and prolific author who was a pioneer in infant studies.

vi A friend from undergraduate days and a professor of English at Reading in Northern California.

[undated]

"Asthma as signal presence"

Letting mother know (by sound) where one is.

[undated]

"Contextualisation"

This is contrary to deconstructionism. I think of this because of the articles in Poe's "Purloined Letter" and the failure to grasp the contexts (other texts?), layered or overlapped texts.

A structural analysis—as Kleinian—fails to grasp the history, the contexts of the self. Part of an analysis is a contextualisation which is a feature of reconstruction and of elaboration.

[undated]

"The recipient of projective identifications (as child)"

Borderline: the self containing too much of the projective identifications of the mother.

Narcissist: the self refusing containment of the other.

Schizophrenic: has de-aggressivized his relation to the actual world. There is a de-libidinalization & this gives way to destructive processes & violent splitting.

The narcissist defends against the object's encroachment by refusing to introject but reverses the procedure by aggressively incorporating (greedily) what is available.

Projective identification and the death drive: the violent placing of internal life into the other, or the body.

[30/1/87]

"The patient who creates the good environment"

"Q" had a mum who spied on him and whom he felt persecuted by. And in his life the figure of the spying other is prominent but he does not transfer it, in that I do not feel persecuted by his spying etc. He is in some respects extraordinarily determined to give me my space whilst disagreeing with me etc. on many things.

I take this to mean that he wants to give me a space in which to be, i.e. to give me what he did not have.

Am I the alter self?

[undated]

"Precursor and alternate object"

The transitional, the alternate, and the conservative objects all emerge from the precursor object, although one needs to see if the autistic object holds here too.

The alternate object is accompanied by an alter ego. With this object comes a self. Alternative to the mother, father and world.

The precursor object and dolls and toys simply enable the construction of a fundamentally alternative world and self, which is not in relation to the living world. It is a fictionalizing of existence and a move toward fictional rather than intersubjective organization.

The conservative object is different. It's a conserved self state linked up to life details (as a memory with a dream screen) that simply stores the states of being and relating character-istic of a moment or relation. The aim is to have this state perceived and transformed into understanding or language.

[31/1/87]
"The haunted mind"

The idea of a haunted house is a metaphor of the haunted mind. The same fears apply. Someone is dead or killed. The dead one haunts the place like a ghost. This = the deadened parts of the self which live on as deadened parts. As this is split off the person lives in some fear of these now split off parts. It is a form of memory as the deadened parts are the independent ghosties.

Links to the conservative object process which preserves former selves. Are all former self states the haunting objects? No. But for those people who have "lost" former self states, the person feels that he contains haunted elements like the house that is haunted. This does indeed describe the schizophrenic's dread of containing anything. See "Z"'s painting of ghost figures: the deadened parts of the self.

So! A musical hallucination is a haunting, a moment when the subject is haunted. And it is like seeing a ghost or the ghostly.

Title: "The Haunted Mind".

"Z"'s memorial de-repression was like a séance. He heard from former selves. He held himself very still. It was a séance transference.

Fate links to being haunted. The figures of fate link to the dead selves whereas destiny is the future of the alive parts.

Destiny and life (and life instincts)

Fate and death (and death instincts)

Destiny-use-elaboration-completion

Fate, being used by, foreclosures & bits—incomplete

[undated]
"The good parent analyst"

Of many patients it is incorrect to say that they treat the analyst as if the analyst were their particular mother or father. It's more that they use the analyst to be the good mother or father that they did not have, to talk to this figure about their hurts. They know the analyst is not their mother, but they use the illusion of psychoanalysis and the psychoanalytic space to speak to the good mother and father about themselves, a conversation they did not have with their own mother and father. Importantly, the analyst as mother–father is built up on all the positive features of the actual mother and father and the illusion is that now the mother and father are ready to repair damage done. This is one of the strangest transference features of psychoanalysis: that now the parents are ready. And children, who conserve damaged self states etc., hope for a parent to be ready to reflect, to go over injuries to the self, so they need not be stuck or lodged in the patient.

Of course the patient brings distressed former self states to the parent-analyst, and speaks to the crazy mother or father, insisting the analyst be this person, but it is known that the analyst is good.

[undated]
"Alter ego"

There is an alter ego therapy where a person speaks for the subject. I do this for "Q", as I imagine him, thus speaking for him. In a sense I am the alter ego, and indeed I contain many of his projective identifications. This has implications for technique. Use of counter-transference and …

Alter egos:

1. imaginary companion
2. the transvestite's female self
3. in adolescence: the chum

Note, that with "L" I function first as an alter then eventually he owns himself.[2]

[undated]
"Countertransference experience"

It is our experience as the patient's object that gives us the information we need as to their mental processes, their laws, their object relating, and so forth.

And some patients while putting us through the process nonetheless have a sense of humour or gain perspective on themselves, and we are relieved. What does it mean to gain relief?

[undated]
"Autoscopy"

Seeing an image of oneself as a double.

[13/2/87]
"Fate/destiny/etc."

A patient whose sense of self is fated will aim to fate the analyst (& himself) to a pre-ordained conclusion, while the sense of destiny (use) of analyst as an object of intelligence, of knowing, is open. Destiny seeks the analyst's use as an <u>analyst</u>, while fate is the revelation of the imaginary.

"J" is abandoned by his mother at 6 months in an orphanage. 6 years later she abandons her other children to the same place. His <u>scene</u>-making is a showing of a self as he has lost the context of his idiom and tries to put, or create a new environment for idiom presentation. Scene-making is a <u>conservation</u> of idiom. He <u>creates</u> a look in the eye of the other. Hence he visualises, acts out, or is verbally provocative to see himself reflected in the face of the other.

Face and counterface.

"I want to go to your apartment!"—a <u>behavioural force</u>. Behavioural force and destiny. The forcing of the object to give in. The need to make a destiny not to have a fate.

   I. Fate (false self) compliance
  II. Destiny (true self) ruthlessness

   I. REPETITION (conservation) of early environment
  II. ELABORATION (transformation)

   I. PROJECTION/INTROJECTION (collecting)
  II. EVOCATION (ridding)

   I. FALSE REPARATION (alternative object and alter ego)
  II. DESTRUCTION OF OBJECT (transitional object and spontaneous (dialectics of argument) (thoughtlessness)

   I. ANALYST'S INTERPRETATION
  II. ANALYST'S UNINTERPRETATION

[undated]
"Alter ego/ alter object"

Is it possible that imaginary companions etc. become or derive from first a splitting of the object:
Actual
Fantasied
Such that there is now a fantastical self: an alter ego?

[undated]
"Freud and female sexuality"

Freud's idea that the woman does not have a superego because she has no fear of castration and wishes to have a penis/child etc., all of this can be seen as the female (read the female side of

189

Freud, or Freud using the female) continues his (Freud's) failed strategy. He must accept superego or be castrated, so how does he sustain the challenge of the father? He uses the woman.

Interestingly the superego for the man is hardly that at all: it's more of an intimidation introject. Klein's theory of the depressive position is a much better theory of the origins of superego.

[undated]
"Free association, true self, elaboration, destiny"

Given the generative and complex paradigms of analysis, the patient's free associations are articulations/elaborations of the true self moving through (using) mental objects. Some mental objects (ideas, memories, dreams) are to be discarded (not thought out), others are to be thought out (reflected upon). The choice of reflecting (which is elaborating) is ruthless. It does not follow the laws of concern, empathy, sympathy. A patient may consider many issues in a session having just come from a scene of destruction, etc. and not consider that. Or he may not mention his wife and children. Or do so and yet pass them by without considering them fully. Patient and analyst must not dwell out of sympathy but both follow the flow of moods and ideas etc.

Lacan's sole emphasis on *Associazion* and not *Einfall* means that he probably misses the moments when objects are being used to elaborate, or in the first place to establish self states and to situate new object formations and object relations.

What is the destiny of a session? What would be a fated session? Destiny has to do with the patient setting the pace of a session, fate with the analyst's need to organize the material into an overriding frame of reference or model. The concept of evolution from paranoid/schizoid to depressive is an idea of fate. It evokes a medieval psychomachia. The patient knows what he is meant to achieve. The self is on a fated journey to become everyman.

[23/2/87]
"Other in Lacan"

By having the subject subordinate to the Other, such that the conscious subject knows nothing of himself, Lacan simply finds another category of entrapment for this feeble subject. The Other complements the ego's capture in the Imaginary. And, what are we to make of the originating interpreter behind the final logic of the symbolic? Who is this? It seems to me that Lacan simply moves the sense of captivity: from the Imaginary to the Symbolic, from mother to father.

[undated]
"Conservation & transformation"

The 2 processes:

Conservation: the true self, inherited core, repetition, unthought known, death instinct, isolate, analytic silence, holding process, being.

Transformation: true self into gesture, transformational object, elaboration/articulation, the self and others, facilitating environment.

Conservation:	Transformation
Repetition	Symbolic diversity
Death instinct	Life instinct
Silence	Interpretation
Being	Aliveness
Aloneness	Self and others

[undated]
"Psychic change"

Freud: Free association, mental economy, symbolic richness.

Klein: Interpretation of internal objects and mental processes in the transference. Allegory. Binding of life instincts.

DWW: Object relating (use of), use of potential space.

Bollas: Free association in analyst. Being shaped.

The analyst's reflections over time give the patient a field for the placement of ideas (cs/ucs.), feelings, etc. The analyst's reflections over time imply and establish a processing medium, in that his containers are revealed as well as his handling of psychic contents. I think analysts must reveal the imagination, as this becomes container for, and therefore potential space for, the patient's imaginings. The patient needs to witness the analyst's psychic work, workings, as it can be used.

Psychicalization: what I make as an analyst.

The intersubjective: evolving.

Evolution comes through the articulation and elaboration of the unthought known.

Dialectics of difference.[vii] I believe in differing with the patient. This is accomplished (1) by openly correcting myself (2) sensing when the patient disagrees, to say "You disagree."

Where does interpretation or insight come from? The point of the above is to indicate the established unconsciousness of it. It is inspired.

Bion conveys the analytic in his writing. So does Lacan. That curious place where all analysts live.

Idiom: interpretation is to establish the idiom of thought.

What about the patient who does not repress? The thing presentation versus word presentation.

Q: Where does Winnicott come from (as an analyst)? Also, where does Bion come from?

Q: When we practice psychoanalysis where have we been?

Point. I want to talk about my life (as an analyst). Where do I live? Where am I? What (not who) am I?

---

vii First use of the concept of the dialectics of difference.

Point. The provision of a psychical [...] by the analyst may be a loss. Each analyst partly prepares for his unknowing of the patient, who is "off" on an unspeakable journey.

Q: How does the analyst prepare the patient for this?

Q: How does he prepare himself for this?

[undated]
"Unknowing"

What is unknowing? Or analytic unknowing? I realise that one of the most difficult resistances in the analyst is his organisation of the patient into knowledge. How do we unknow? So that the patient and I can freely associate? This is a kind of deconstruction.

An unbinding.

A loosening.

A return to reception.

With "Q" my analysis of his superego activity meant that he selected out that which fulfilled this.

All the above is what Bion means by no memory/no desire.

But the unknowing is a process that complements knowing. In this respect Lacan's no self and DW's self are both correct.

The patient realises this paradox is essential to the function of analysis and it becomes part of his way of proceeding.

Therefore interpretation can itself be a resistance to free association.

[undated]
"Ego, self, subject"

The ego is composed of genetically transcripted rules (or operations), or biases in processing and the thousands of rules (operational paradigms) that infant, mother, father, negotiate.

These are unconscious. Indeed the unconscious is formed out of this set, or these infinite sets. The infinite possible combinations of the unconscious are determined from the rules and principles of combination (signifiers, meaning) determined operationally. The sense of the depth of the unconscious is historically apt. Also it is a complex structure and its functioning can (as the ego) be likened to the brain and its organization. Genetically funded, operationally "set", it structures internal life.

Self is the emerging of an invariant experience in being obviously based on ego organization. It is a kind of meta event, or "higher" sense, as it does come out of the matrix of ego.

Subject is one invariant (as a speaker) self experience, in which the person finds an unconscious (repressed) other voice that obeys the symbolic and that has the power of language to authorize it. Basing an analysis on the language of the absent may be an analytic recapitulation of ontogenesis, in that special status is given by the analyst to the subject who is born again in the hands of the father (according to his laws etc.) out of the matrices of the mother. In a way it's an act of undoing, then doing.

[9/3/87]
"Secrets of analytical life"

Jean Baudrillard says psychoanalysis buries the unconscious and sexuality in theory, which is partly true. But I do not speak everything. And we should discuss "untalking" or the "not talking cure". The silent uses (gratifications) of the analyst. 2 ways. Pleasure. Unspoken. How the transference destroys meaning/analysis, in order to use the analyst, for pleasure (love, hate, knowledge). This is part of the dialectics of difference in which the use also differs from the reflection. Use/reflection/silence/use/reflection/silence follow use/reflection……. Both destroy (use/analysis) each other.

[undated]
"Destiny, etc."

—The dream and destiny: it determines the course of a session. Associations come forth. The word/dream are fate: oracle. Subject is held up to reflect. "It" determines. And is different from transference usage. Use = destiny: making, forming, securing. It is wordless. A force of destiny. Force & object relations.
    —Parents & superego. A sense of their guiding presence. A fate.
    —As projection. Destiny serves as location of projection. Of one's own impulses. Use fate for this function: container of projections.
    —Perhaps each person has a destiny but it remains for the person's personal qualities to see if they achieve their destiny or carry it through to victory. It is a way of saying loss of it is destined to be an infant, an oedipal child, in mid life, etc.
    There is a Freudian/Kleininan/Lacanian idea of destiny. And DW suggests a line. I like the use of the object.

[undated]
"Oedipus"

When Oedipus says of Laius "I will fight for him as if he were my father", Sophocles captures the ego split of the oedipal complex, as the child does feel this loyalty to the father. He is unconsciously unaware that it is himself who poses the threat. Thus the child renounces father murder out of love and loyalty, not out of anxiety, as Freud would have it. Call it a new depressive position, or "the law of the son", or "the love of the son". And this actually is the foundation of the superego in Freud. Love. Taking in father out of a wish to be like him. The taking in and out of anxiety is a paranoid/schizoid creation of the superego. It is harsh and punitive. There is as yet no contact with love or life instincts. Oedipus before the plague.

There are therefore two superegos. One that like Freud's is born of fear of castration: a paranoid/schizoid superego. The one that Sophocles envisions. Love. But in Oedipus the paranoid/schizoid superego is still there, obviously, as Oedipus is savaged by the wish to know.

Why does knowing lead to self destruction?

Is it because the original crime is perpetuated by Oedipus' preservation of ignorance? Still unclear about L's murder. To see or to hear is to discover from others: outside. No in-sight. No looking in.

The plague is a metaphor of that communication. A disease spread from one to another and eating up from inside.

The Sphinx which holds everything inside is the opposite.

Teiresias, blind, is the representation of the Sphinx: now in the father's domain. If we imagine that the first Sphinx = mother, both what she conceals and what the child projects into her of that which he knows and wishes to be unconscious, then Teiresias = father's knowledge, so that the play involves a son's breaking out of the mother's secrets.

Parenthesis. Much of what occurs in the New Testament, in terms of Jesus' actions, are efforts to cure the damage (to the minds of men) committed by God in the Old Testament. In this sense one could see here a story of a father and his son (a myth we are as deeply involved in as the Greeks) and compare it to Oedipus and Laius. A son who follows the father.

Oedipus realises that first he killed Laius and then that this must have been his father. But why, if he genuinely believed Polybus?

Jocasta implores Oedipus not to think. So his thoughtlessness comes from the mother. The laws of his ego are based on thoughtlessness.

Interestingly the entire tragedy begins with Laius paying attention to the original oracle.

Oedipus' effort to interpret his way out of the destiny, to cling to hope, is similar to the dreamer's effort to emerge from the acts committed in the dream. Is it possible that the experience of an interpretation of the dream is the very basis of drama and literature? It is very hard these days to find that weight that the dream must have had. Before TV, radio, written, literature, it was then man's only theatre. Most common theatre.

Oedipal thoughtlessness

It was Jocasta who gave the baby Oedipus away. In his solving the riddle of the Sphinx "… and the Sphinx came crashing down, the virgin, claws hooked" a matricide? Has Oedipus' crime been not against the father but the mother?

[12/3/87]

"Play"

The analyst becomes a different object when he is humorous etc. An object of play, for use, true self elaboration. Also in aggressive confrontation for patient's differentiated articulation. The patient resists the analyst: with such resistance a positive factor.

In *Learning from Experience*[3] Bion says that only on the replacement of one emotion by the next emotion "does the capacity for re-formation and therefore receptivity, of Q depend" (94). By extension, when A is an object to be destroyed, only such destruction and recreation elicits the receptivity of the patient to <u>new</u> experiences, generated by the true self in the transference. In other words, true self experience enables further true self experience and strengthens this factor in the person.

[17/3/87]
"The ghostline personality"

This is a kind of schizoid person who established an <u>alternative</u> world, with an alter ego (a fictional self) involved with imaginary characters. It is intact and secret. Sometimes the self is present as with my patient who sees his TV hero in the room with him.

These people cannot use objects. They cannot be ruthless and therefore live through a false self. There is intense bitter anger (though secret) with the external world and some of this is lived out.

Is it possible to say the person <u>contains</u> ghosts? And how does this differ from an internal object?

Well, it's the containment of <u>a presence</u> and I think it's the containment of <u>a future</u>. A future is a vision, an imagination of the self and its others. They come alive as ghosts. So these ghosts are the embodiment of futures: investments in the self and objects along favourable lines.

Ghosts that haunt, then, or that become part of the fate constitute a loss of <u>containment</u>.

Some patients who <u>contain</u> ghosts are like houses: the haunted mind. They wish to be inhabited or haunted.

This is the loss of the future or mourning the future.

The question is when and how does the patient transfer a ghost into the session or onto the analyst? With "P" there was a very strange atmosphere, almost a séance. As she talked to me (as her internal object) and of her feelings toward me it was like a séance. The patient is extremely cautious about bringing this to life.

Unfortunately these people have no experience of live objects. It's as if they are without knowledge and dreadfully confused.

Autoscopy etc. etc. are means to put the ghosts into the actual world as <u>alternates</u> to live objects. As such they are more akin to autistic objects.

The transitional object allows the child to use the actual world because it is invested/created out of the child's subjective idiom.

The ghostline person chooses an object that is alternate. If it is real it's only used as a means for alternative use, alternative to <u>matriculation</u> into the world of subject's using objects with other subjects (i.e. play).

The perversions (fetishes, etc.) are in-between because the actual object is essential.

During the course of evolution in childhood these children feel <u>altered</u> but not progressively integrated. The alterations in being are disturbing. They are not "in" themselves, so each

195

alteration gives rise to a new alternative self, which is a ghost. Thus these people have internal selves that are separate and different beings, not connected to one another, and they can report the differing selves of life in this way.

To some extent this is true because the child was the mother's alternative object, as mother imagined and related to the different imagined children through the person of the child. "Q" and "C" both had intense dislikes of the mother's imagining of them. They felt alter to her creation.

This is not an object relationship, it is the projection of internal object relations into external reality.

Thus the ghostline person transforms a purely internal object into a ghost by silently, invisibly, passing it through (as invisible projection) the external object in order to come back inside as a figuration, a figment of the imaginary and the real. It has to be given a sense of actuality which can only be done through silent invisible projection.

Thus they try to keep a house/mind. They contain and look after and try to nurture these ghosts.

Both "Y" and "D" came to analysis because they could not cope with actual people. They were terrifically confused and terrified by actual persons.

The aim of containment is to provide some alternative to integration.

This procedure is part of the conservative process.

[21/3/87]
"Fate"

Think of "S" who was at Stanford and on the verge of success and then failed. She watched others pass her by. This sequence—failure & watching the others pass by—is an important aspect of the idea of fate. Of the child who was on track until something happened to put them off track and this arrest is recreated in failure.

Complication with others does not evoke envy the likes of Klein. They are angry because it objectifies a loss, the loss of a future, of the self's movement forward.

Think of the young Polish men.[4]

So this "sibling rivalry" is not inspired by envy. They mourn by being preoccupied with the other's success.

In analysis they feel compelled to prematurely terminate thus arresting the course of analysis.

[1/4/87]
"Ghostline"

The reverse séance. In analysis the patient uses the actual object [other] to transport material to the alternate world. Instead of the patient bringing the internal objects "into" the analysis there is a reversal of this transference. The patient "takes" the analyst into his world. But does not "put back" (project) into actual objects. No 2-way process. The person who creates the alternate world does so in order to keep the true self (and its objects) safe. The ghosts, however, somewhat accurately register the deaths of potential selves & possible actions with conceivable others. The belief in re-incarnation probably [derives from] this, as it's some memory of having lived another, prior life.

Some people nurture their ghosts; others are victims of them. What's the difference?

1. Some of the ghosts are deadened by the person. They are killed off self (feelings) and others. These deadened parts have been psychologically harmed. They therefore have an "intent" to harm back. The person lives in fear of them.
2. Some of these ghosts are deadened by the parent. They are therefore lost objects which the person tries to recover.
3. Some ghosts are alternate objects. They are the creations of self and others and may reflect 1 & 2.

In (1) the person tries to keep the ghosts away and they may haunt the person through hallucination. They may order the death (execution) of the person as punishment for their death. (2) is different. The subject may mourn them, nurture them etc. Some like "R" feel such rage over the killing of the self that they have an alternate world composed not of objects but of destructions: gaps, holes, annihilations. They may keep this world of listening to music that violates the senses. It is the music of the tear, the roar, the emptied, the frustrated, the broken, the pieces. Music of the pieces. Or art of the pieces. The vortex, gap, shred, etc.

We could say that when the object says "use me" the person cannot. The ghostline says "no" and turns to the alternate world. The writer creates fiction and publishes the book. This publication seems to be the opposite of the secret. It is a disclosure. But, if the other upon seeing the book, says "ah, here you are!", the writer more often than not says "the book is not me." This license suggests that some fiction writing must be certified as not meaning of the inner world. Thus the writer by changing characters may be less aware of himself than the person who keeps his alternate world going in fantasy. This might explain why some who are quite profound writers are surprisingly shallow persons.

[2/4/87]
"Music and mother/child relationship"

A poetic syllable has stress, pitch, duration etc., and infants and mothers do, as well. A question. Our effort to understand the person through language—as the vehicle in which the person is framed—does not address what is articulated through personality. One of the means of personality communications is closer to music than language. Language (wording) is of course important but not the exclusive means of representing the person(ality).

Is it possible to say that some of the elements of personality follow the laws of music? Is musical choice proper a selection of personalities in/through the object (musical object). Why on one day do I wish to listen to a Bach cantata and not Liszt? And yet another day to

Liszt and not Bach. (Although I think I am always in the mood for Bach's partitas, Corelli's concerti grossi. What does that mean?) Is music the proper discourse of feelings? Of moods? Is it an artistic realisation of the music of the infant–mother? Is it, and our use of it as an object, an elaboration, an articulating expansion, of the basic elements of the particular idioms of the mother/child relation?

If the inherited disposition is really an organized set of process assumptions—such as iambic pentameter is a process convention for conveying meaning—then is it not possible for the personality to evolve along poetic/musical/mimetic lines?

The theory of projective identification is closer to musical communication than to semantics. Music creates an internal state inside the other. This creation is then worked on by the container. It then may move into language, into counter projective identification.

Let us take Bion and the idea that there is a thought which needs thinking. One person may think this thought by speaking (free association), another by writing a poem, another by painting, by dancing, by music, by projective identification involving another personality. The thought being represented will have a different fate and significance through this choice. Therefore some people are incapable of poetic, musical, painting thought. Each of these techniques is a different element of personality, a different kind of object relation.

What does it mean if I say that I cannot paint[viii] or "do" algebra? These are personality difficulties, meaning that there are some thoughts I cannot think, some objects I cannot use, potentials that shall not achieve a destiny.

Is there a registered loss, a mourning, for an unfulfilled function? I think there must be. My not knowing time (am/pm) is my protest over math loss. Then there is music loss, painting loss, bicycle repair, science loss, and so on.

[undated]
"Ghostline"

The transitional object has died in the child's hands. It is the ghost of the transitional object.

They have experienced its death.

They repeat this creation/death/ghost sequence

Is the child's ghostline figure an early out of body experience? Do they have dissociation which then gives them a self experience, an a-real place, a locus for putting themselves subsequently?

Do they have sudden experiences of intense self observation, knowing something is wrong with them, leading them to stand (where the parent is) to look at themselves. Is this an early prototype for OBEs (out of body experience)?

Are OBEs powerful waking dreams? Is there a special repression, one that allows the subject to believe he has had a non-dream experience? For, the dream provides a common OBE experience. In the dream we commonly are OBE.

[viii] I did not "turn" to painting until 1998.

If OBEs are common then this could be understood as a wish to leave the body in order to escape corporeal annihilation. Is it possible that some children feel psychologically near to physical extinction and they leave their body because the pain is too great?

Is my concept of ordinary regression to dependence a form of OBE? Is the person viewing the self? The life?

Is the ghostline world a projective identification of the transitional object experience into an alter ego and alter objects? For safe keeping?

If there is an OBE? Might there be an IBE: inner body experience? Where you go into the self and there "see" the world of the introjects etc.: the imaginary. If so, it's an IBE following on a depersonalization, or OBE.

It is an inner projection (not out onto/into other, but to an inner object) to characters that are traces of the body ego and perhaps projective identifications in objects now re-introjected. There is a phantom corporeality to them. They can be sensed, like the phantom limb is sensed. This is because they have once had body, been embodied, either in the self (body) or other-body-containing-a-self-body.

This sense of their being a body gives them a different feel.

I believe there is a deep space or special inner space, or select inner space. It's beyond the ghostline. To cross this inner boundary is to paradoxically kill off an inner object at the moment that it is given a life after death in a select inner space, a life after death that is perhaps more enlivened than the inner objects relation to actual objects.

But the internal space reserved for ghosts is also a phantom mirror, or shadow, of the child's experiences of reality. The internal character relations are either reflective of the child's relation to mother, father, or strictly alternate.

An inner character relation is a form of projective identification which denudes the subject of life. The technical sophistication of the internal world is depleted by the transfer of energy and psychic contents to this inner space.

There is a sense of the transfer of power as the person shifts the life of the inner world beyond the ghostline. The ultimate beyond is to see the ghosts in reality, to push this inner mental space in such a way that it envelopes the actual, usurps it, and is extraordinarily powerful.

Clinically, only by intense confrontation can the analyst get to these factors.

Marginality. The ghostline person has been pushed there by the mother/father or life. Pushed into ghostliness. Across the barrier.

[undated]
"Death in life"

In a certain kind of way it can be said that we
    do not exist
    or, we contain our non-existence

This is the structure of death which is present in life. In our discourse, the hesitation, blank, absence.

We have a foreshadowing,

A structural knowledge of it.

This is not the death instinct.

It is our non-existence.

Our non-existence gives counterpoint to our "self". And may explain why post structuralists are infuriated by the concept of self.

[undated]

"Nonexistence"

… of psyche is not equivalent to death, as death refers to an act, a process-of dying, which is not what I'm talking about.

Non-existence and areas of no meaning.

The symbolic suggests our personal non-existence as our unconscious language is the structure of infinity.

Nonsense is organized meaning and does not apply here.

Is non-existence an intrapsychic state? Is it a knowledge that exits alongside the creation of meaning?

As we come out of non-existence (to which we return) is there any clinical evidence of this fact? What is the voice of non-existence, the nature of it? It does not mean the absence of thought, or the absence of anything. It's more dynamic than that. "It" is alongside us all the time.

Is it related to our body? Does this knowledge come more from the body? Is the empty tooth a non-existence? The loss of hair?

How does it dialect (as in dialectic) with the presence of me? Does the superego (the observing part) owe something to the facts of non-existence?

What is non-existence? I think of it as friendly. The backdrop?

DW talks of a transition from non-being to being. The great changeover.

I suppose I know "more" about non-existence by virtue of the utter disappearance of loved ones. It is insufficient to say that of course we maintain these lost objects as internal etc. I do. But I also internalize the present of their present status as non-existents. Non-existents. A non-existent is a former being now utterly gone.

In life we are born with some trace of our origins out of non-existence and as we move through life we come back to this through the deaths and then presence of non-existents.

In the fort/da the child not only registers the absent object but under the bar of the signifier, the fact of the mother's instruction in non-existence.

So, where is this clinically?

With "B" the loss of his sister is not a catastrophe because of the loss of the sister, the person, but because of a premature or excessive experience of non-existence in his inner world. This creates an imbalance. Otherwise we have a balance, a way of dealing with this factor.

What is the nature of this balance? Is it not the mother's wonderful seduction into object relating? If the mother does not do this, does she leave the child to feel the non-existence of being? Does this situate the child in a particular way toward life?

Non-existence is a factor then that needs repression. We repress it assisted by the mother, but the superego somehow inherits knowledge of it. The idea "the world can live with or without you" is out of this.

As a child when I didn't go to school I would ask my brother "did anyone ask about me at school?" I think this is a recognition of the fact of non-existence, along with existence. It has a parallel in death or reaction to our eventual non-existence: will anyone ask after me, remember me?

Endopsychic perception and non-existence. There is a limit, a boundary to the psyche. There is a border where psyche faces the machinery of the brain. Indeed, is psyche's body the brain? This knowing of that which is beyond psyche is also the knowing of non-existence.

Non-existence is a factor of existence. We know that prior to being as our non-existence which I give a quality, a status, rather than not mention it because my thesis is that it has a status in the psyche. Further, we have thoughts, imaginings, possibly visions of our eventual return to non-existence. Sometimes in a session when analyst and patient are unable to find meaning, or to feel that a silence is a resistance to something, or a condition for facilitative renewal etc., there is the presence of non-existence, as if the background of our being, non-existence 1 and non-existence 2 (i.e. 1st non-existence, 2nd non-existence) was itself represented in being. We are an interval in non-existence, or from non-existence. We relate to the dead as remembered figures but also to their status as a non-existent.

Mythology and religion are efforts to give continued life to non-existents.

[undated]
"**THE** history as object & space"

We each possess our own history. It is both an object to consider/analyze and also an experience we can re-enter: a certain type of mental space.

When I think of my past (as object & space) I am reluctant to understand it as a metaphor of a present state of mind. This is so because I have had continuous points of reference and invariant recollections. These are like sets in time that are established as history, as the historic. The historic is not established in the present; it is not laid down as the historic in the present. I am not to know the history until long after, when the historic (as object/space) is established. When did I first establish a set in my self? This is difficult to say because it involves a double act: I must think back to the past when I then first thought back.

My first historic act was I think when as a boy I recollected:

1. Walking with my grandfather to the drug store.
2. Listening to the mail train at bed time with my grandmother.
3. Playing with red ants.

4. Punching a hole in the oranges.[ix]
5. Playing with the toy train.
6. Eating tinned spaghetti.
7. Sitting on the front porch listening to the church chimes.
8. Wondering what Methodist was.

But already I can see that I am missing the point, as I am simply remembering my past which is different from history as object, or the historic place, which is preserved through sets of time. What are mine?

1. Early Glendora (set Glendora)
2. Neighbourhood South Pasadena
3. Glendale (set Glendale)
4. Laguna Beach

No this [Glendale] is <u>not</u> a set and I should try to think why. It is not a place of <u>historic life</u>, except for "Sally" with pigtails and the classroom, and God. So what kind of historic set is this? What does "it" hold?

1. Early Laguna: the motel
2. Wave Street: conflict with my father
3. Alexander Road: when my parents divorce
4. The Antique House: where we lived with mother
5. Glomstad
6. University of Virginia

Each of these sets[5] corresponds to a move/house/significant persons.

They are memories but also moments of evolution. Each set has been invariant for me. They do not change. But <u>my relation</u> to the sets of experience does change.

An historic set is a matrix of experience in a defined unit of time.

My task should be to consider each set, to contemplate the logic of each, the "essence" of each, to consider how I relate to and use each set. Which sets have I referred back to more frequently than others? Why? What is the relation between this and screen memories?

Then there is my <u>loyalty</u> to my past. I am fiercely loyal to all the persons and places. Sally with the pigtails. What is the nature of such loyalty? It has something to do with my father?

I think each set is determined by the period of its creation and this doesn't change. The train memory is the set created by a 7-year-old me. The Wave Street by the 9-year-old. As a 43-year-old I use each set via the child who created it at the time. As such I can still <u>get inside</u> the experience of being these different ages and selves.

Discuss the images of the objects (in detail) pertinent to each set and the **body** experiences. Such as a <u>sidewalk</u> in Paris. It was warm. I walked and felt my foot: etc.

[ix] My grandparents' house was next to a large orange grove.

202

Historical sets are the mental objects for the true self. They are its history: of use/elaboration/ emotional reality. It was here or is here that we can live or record our being, and its transformations.

Does the self get transferred? I don't think so. Each set is organised by a typical me, as is the film making idiom typical of the film maker. My body objects/libido objects are typical.

An historic set is something to which I can refer, or gather, when I relate to a set I relate to an entire time/space object. A period of time and a defined space with objects is set, or held in one unit, that does not change over time.

[undated]
"The historical set and reverie"

When I form a set it occurs through reverie, an internal containing of historical fact. It is not phantasy determined. There is plenty of material for that. It's a marking. The elements of a set are psychical facts. They do not change.

The person stores the emotional reality in a set. The 8-year-old's creation of the 5-year-old's set is to store the prevailing emotional realities of the previous period. It is this emotional reality that is conserved over a 3-year period which is then set in invariant images.

[21/4/87]
"Direct expression of the countertransference"

This is only appropriate if it is clear that the analyst is struggling and does not want to make a direct countertransference interpretation. If this were easy, or, if the analyst had contrived a technique for disclosing direct countertransference then it would be profoundly wrong. Instead, the direct disclosure should be an intensely meaningful moment, made so because of the analyst's struggle with his own psychic pain and the breakdown of the analysis, which can only be recuperated by the disclosure.

[undated]
"Memory"

Each of us has a mnemonic part, a part of us whose task is to remember. Thus the work of creating an historical set is accomplished by the mnemonic part of the personality responsible for storing self experience "in" images or events from life. This part must be a reflecting part of the personality.

[undated—Winnicott Conference]
"Informative object relating"

AP's[x] point is important: that DW differs from Klein in that the subject's not driven by guilt in reparation to the internal object but by the use of a surviving object (which points to the object's contribution).

But there has been a confusion about the use in that:

1. The internal object changes through object usage.
2. As the child introjects the quality of the surviving object or the survivable object.

Indeed, I maintain that the object (mother or analyst) enjoys the infant's use, so the child internalizes the pleasure of the other in the subject's use. This is not simply an imaginary scenario, but a principle, mentally an element of psyche, as the child sets up an area (or internal object) constituted out of the object's pleasure in the subject.

Thus one can "struggle with" or "grapple with" oneself such that the receiving end of this is pleasurable; or, another way, there is an

aggressive internal dialectic.

[undated]
"DW: father/mother etc."

DW concentrates (almost as in a primary maternal preoccupation) on the mother/child relation. Also he saw mothers and babies together, not so much the father.

When the infant establishes the transitional object, which eventually he gives up, he finds in this emblem of separation a secret connection to the mother, or, more accurately, to the maternal element. This mother (internal element) will always be his.

Thus the infant possesses the mother literally then psychically before the father, that is, according to his experiences. The father's possession of the mother is sexual and it is the child's sexual objectification of the mother brought on by his genital stage that establishes a new mother: the woman. The man is the father not the boy.

This recognition of the mother now as woman, and father now as the man (whereas before he supported the mother) creates an oedipal complex, which in part implies a sequel to the secret affair.

Sexualisation of the mother is the principle of separation of the two objects.

The infant's creation of the transitional object is his separation from the mother, separation that does not occur through the intervention of the father.

The law of the name of the father is almost just that: that this law defines the father as man and mother as woman and child as child: a law of generations, of biological capability (as the child cannot procreate).

Through the jouissance of the transitional object the child discovers the right to create pleasure or to have access [to objects].

Perhaps this area (1) mother/child (2) child/transitional object, excludes the father, just as the law of the father excludes the child.

1. The mother/child area does not involve the father in his function.
2. The oedipal area does not allow the child (his laws).

There is a mutual bar (exclusion) in the boy-mother relation to the mother/woman. This split shows up in the division each sees upon marriage: is she 1 or 2? Am I 1 or 2?

The father is the outsider.

[15/6/87]
"DW & father. Where is the (F)?⁶

I think F is to be found in the paper "The use of an object". DW quotes the following:

1. subject relates to object.
2. object is in the process of being found instead of placed by the subject in the world.
3. subject *destroys* object.
4. object survives destruction.
5. subject can *use* object.

I think the (F) is 2: the object being found at the moment of placement outside. The (F) is discovered through this destruction, a destruction that takes place in relation to the (M), but (M) who introduces the child to the (F) in herself. Thus the Oedipus complex is in part a continuation of this destruction.

Also, the transitional object is the use of the (M): it *is* the (M).

The destruction of the objective object, of the internal object linked to the actual is the destruction of the (M) in the moment of finding the father. The internal object (of omnipotence and illusion) is the world of the mother, which gets destroyed through discovery of the actual object = (F).

This is why the child of age two likes to *crash into* the body of the (F).

Also, remember the child must himself be an internal object. When inside the (M) there is some sense of having been the (M)'s internal object, and this is sustained by the child who puts her in him. Being inside or the inside being is the world of (M/C), while the child was never inside the (F) and the father comes from the outside.

1. as the penis entering the (M).
2. and the child is the outsider too in that the semen he once was the outside penetrating an inside to which he/semen went for dwelling.
3. the (F) is outside the labour.
4. the (F) is outside the primary maternal place.

[16/6/87]
"Fusion of instincts"

Freud's theory leaves out the (M) and (F). Instincts of sex and aggression fuse in accordance with the object's facilitation of this maturation.

The father, here, is very important in that he becomes the aggressed against sexual object—the one who enjoys a tumble-about—and the (M) is the sexually desired object who pushes the child away. One has to speak of the whole family.

[20/6/87 Torino[x]]
"Projective Identification and the Unthought Known"

Some people project an aspect of the self (or introjected phenomenon) into the analyst because they do not know what it is. The projecting is not to get rid of something or to store a valued part of the self, it is to have a part of the self processed by the other. This view follows DW & Bion: the other as a container and we can say that the subject who had part of the true self or unthought known refused by the (M) (as in refused expressions and knowing) brings this part to the analyst-(M).

The child who experiences the early withdrawal of a parent (for whatever reasons) may not know what it is that causes suffering.

[22/6/87]
"Unthought known"

In the first year, and probably till 3/4 or more, the (M) instructs the infant
in complex rules for being and relating. She communicates this operationally to the infant, who can be said to learn from this. This is, then, a form of knowledge, but it has not been thought. It is there, available for thinking, upon the arrival of language and the symbolic. This body of knowledge is the unthought known.

It occurs to me that this development corresponds to a theory of trauma. The events occur; it is the memory of events that is traumatic.

Equally, when a child and adult comes *to think* (dreams, insights, analysis) the unthought known, this may be very disturbing as the (M)'s communications may be a madness.

This is the matrix of the unconscious in a way. To think it could be terrifying.

[30/6/87 Catania]
"(M) as introducer to the baby"

The mother by no means *only* introduces the outside world to the (B); she also introduces the (B) to the outside world. She must interpret the true self to the others, in a wide ranging explication of her child's idiom: "John is a little bull and he never says sorry, so you must forgive him for …"; or "Bill is frightfully shy …"

Is it possible that this narrative function is important to the child's survival? Does something of the world's reception of the child depend here on the (M)'s interceptive narrative: her mediation?

---

[x] Visiting Parthenope Bion.

"Mind-fucking and empty mindedness"

Unrecovery. The person who forces themself to keep in mind a disturbing event. As if peace of mind, is broken by the penetration of an idea. Or, more to the point, of "B", as if the preservation of a disturbing idea (the death of a baby for example) exemplifies the unbearability of having a psyche. Exemplified by the preservation of unbearable content. There is a *hate* of psychic reality. What is the alternative? A psyche that is meant to rid the self of all conflict. This is empty mindedness.

With "B" the disturbing internal object = a mind-fuck, as the occurrence of such = the penetration of the phallus: to create confusion. ("B" is often dizzy and nauseous.)

Some internal objects are experienced as efforts to drive one crazy. This is overcome by 1. denial 2. somatisation 3. suicide.

The analyst must not do too much holding. The patient must be in a fix. He or she needs to experience mental conflict, to endure the problematics of conflict.

[1/9/87]
"Neutralization of self"

A certain narcissistic/schizoid character develops a minimalized style, to be neutral in response, but not offensive. The aim of neutrality is to avoid offending the other, an other, in this case who is constantly attacking.

cf: false self

cf: psychopath

Above all, the psychopath is not apparently troubled by events.

[undated]
"Extinction and death"

Death is a conversion: from life to extinction.

The extinct refers to the status of the dead. The mental status in the minds of the living. That is, the living have not died. They do not know death, but they do know non-existence, they do "know" of a transformation from non-existence *to* existence.

In the foetus, what are the earliest (by date) brain waves?

Do we know this?

If we think of nuclear war, we think of the wish in people to return to the non-existence which in itself is a positive.

[undated]
"Historical sets"

The internal mirror/other. As each of us is solitary, as our experience of self cannot be conveyed, we search for this knowing within our self. The resource for this is memory: we store experience—a library—where we can research our self, we have this inner companionship of images that store prior selves. So I have these prior self states as my internal companions. And over a life this village of selves is of immense solace.

Narrative representation to an other about these selves is a failed moment.

Except that two people can each store a mutual experience together—with of course different internal make up—and this mutual storage brings the two closer together, even though not through mutual recollection, but through mutual storage.

[undated]
"The inspiring person"

What is it that makes one person inspiring? Such as when we meet someone who gives enough of themselves to inspire our own personal creativity.

This occurs to me when reading Anzieu,[xi] who says Freud's dreams were ones where the voice of desire can be heard.[7] This brings to my mind a correlate: the voice of desire in personal relations. Such a representation (personality and being).

Who has achieved this?

[undated]
"Countertransference and inspiration"

While the patient free associates he provides a field of meaning which the analyst uses as a source for a sudden insight or affect which is a counter to the free association.

Thus what the analyst does is part of the total process.

The patient free associates so that the analyst may be inspired.

The analyst's stance is one of holding, storage, and visualisation of the patient [guided] by the patient's narrative.

This bridge between the two *is* the therapeutic alliance.

[undated]
"Freud/Fliess"

Interestingly, the nose is a bisexual object. If we take Fliess' view that the nose reflects the genitals. It is phallic and vaginal. Thus when Fliess operates on Freud they engage in bisexual intercourse. He vaginalises Freud and leaves him to bleed. If so, are Fliess' migraines a male pregnancy as his head hurts?

Bear in mind that Fliess suggested to Freud the universality of bisexuality.

[xi] Didier Anzieu, French psychoanalyst.

"The split (M)/(F) in the transference"

With my patient "Q", he contests my interpreting like a competitive boy, puckishly batting away the (F). I respond by sustaining my position and utilising the essence of (F) to stay with it. At this point he insists upon what appears to be narcissistic wounds—I don't understand him etc.: in effect calling for (M). The patient demands this of me. This sets up an internal rivalry within me: do I stick with it, is it right to be the (F)? or have I expected too much, does he truly deserve an empathic other, do I become the (M)?

The patient knows of these elements in the other and experiences the presence of such elements oedipally: that is, he elicits the (F) in order to denounce him and to call up the (M). He only in part wants to do this: to create only a (M) for himself. He is actually afraid of killing off the (F) in the analyst, of losing the toughness of the (F), and of being overwhelmed by the (M). Still, he needs the analyst to hold these two parts, as he will try to destroy them.

I should begin this by considering how each of us is composed of elements of (M) and (F) that forms an internal partnership. Perhaps for lack of a better conceptualisation we may say (M)-(F) or maternal, paternal. I think, however, this is so because elements in us become more significant in relation to the (M) than the (F): i.e.

(M) nurturance, unconditional support, softness, allowable confusion.

(F) support, crisis management, confrontation, aggression.

[undated]
"Primary aloneness"

If it's difficult to imagine a foetus recalling the transition from non-existence to aliveness. There is another transition: from the aloneness of preverbality to speech. This perhaps revives the earlier changeover.

[16/10/87]
"Cutting: reflections on Otto Will Jr's talk at ARC"

At ARC there have been competitions between cutting female patients that I think is a form of exhibitionism in which the cut = the bleeding vagina. The woman feels attacked by menstruation which she puts in an attacking form.

First, *what* is the vagina?

—a cut

—an opening

—a mouth (with teeth)

—opens to the deep inside

—opens to an inside that can be penetrated

—it is excitable

—it receives the penis

—it is covered over with hair and is a secret (sewing up)

—it has a complex interior: a series of passages

—it delivers babies

—it is the route back inside the mother

Therefore in a way the vagina is the most psychologically complex human organ. Cutting seems to:

—follow in a microcosm the evolution of being a woman: a cut *followed* by bleeding.

—a sense that the vagina (cut) is a wound. The conviction of being damaged.

—the dissociation from the pain, a frequently cited example of identification with the superego etc., may be identification with the male as the cut body = the repudiated cast-off self.

—as menstruation rids the ovaries of eggs etc., it becomes a paradigm: cutting = riddance of the contained. It is an evacuation into the world of infantile elements.

—it arrogates a pseudo power to a woman, as now they feel they can control the flow of blood.

—showing the cut is an important moment, which follows the secret of cutting, as the woman shocks the other with the vagina.

Suturing fulfils the unconscious wish that the vagina be sewn up, to stop the bleeding, to close the opening.

There is a wish *to smear* the blood, perhaps to have the other process, the anal fantasy that menstruation is defecation, that the discharge is horrifying.

Indeed, the cut and the blood *compete* with one another. This is the silent question put by the cutter. Do we recoil because of the cut or the blood? The cut separate from the blood signifies the girl-self prior to womanhood. Do we recoil at this cut, the vagina in the first place? Or, is it the bleeder, the woman who repels us?

—How does one know a woman is menstruating? She is less active, moody, may isolate herself, may be bloated, is tender. That is, if we know the woman well, we intuitively know when she is enduring this.

Therefore for the other to know constitutes an act of empathy, which is conveyed to the woman who need not bleed to prove her self state.

Thus the bleeding patient may be complaining that she is not yet being known intuitively, or, that there has been a breakdown of intuition which causes this rupture.

—the bleeding woman says "No, I'm no good. I'm a woman. Can't you see I'm damaged"?

—Menstruation is a violation from within, a gender betrayal, as a girl may not feel ready for this public announcement of her maturity.

She may not feel ready, yet she is at the whim of the body. Men do not face this fate, of affliction by the body. A cutter suffers this sense of being the victim of the body. The body is the enemy.

[19/10/87]
"Oedipus"

Interesting that when the oracle of Apollo is handed down, Laius cannot overcome it. He gives in to the (F): the oracle.

[25/10/87]
"The anti-narcissist"

This person hates and dismantles his narcissism. Excessively idolized by the (M) he experiences her as saying: "you are wonderful, you have no need of me". He assumes her to say: "you are the breast. Isn't it wonderful to feed off yourself"!

This infuriates him and he begins by being destructive towards his own talent, trying to dismantle himself. Partly *to spite* the (M), partly because he experiences his talent as depriving him of the right to ordinary dependence.

In the transference the patient aims to punish the (M)—as the analyst's idea of being good, a good analyst giving the patient a good analysis—by undoing himself in the presence of the analyst.

1988

[9/1/88]
"The homosexual'"

He creates interesting responses in the heterosexual:

—The sense that the homosexual is not "one of us". This is a form of thinking, an exploitation of thought, such as when one says "x is lower middle class and not for us". What do we *do* when we think this? Don't we alter the person, situate them *away* from us, refusing human elements?

The homosexual acts sufficiently differently *precisely to* effect this thinking. To split himself off, to become the "not us".

Perhaps this transference/countertransference recreates the
homosexual child's experience of feeling not part of the human
situation.

[21/1/88]
[untitled]

Discussing soul, Aristotle argues that it may be made up of elements. Is true self made up of elements? Can we say that the movement of the true self is the movement of elements acting on other elements? Is it possible to de-construct a human relation in terms of elements interacting?

Force and counterforce.

The elements of a true self, or more, each idiom of personality (true self) expresses itself through elements. Some personalities have idiom of elements, others do not.

[undated]
"True self"

This movement through objects is, in some respects, meaningless. It is not, per se, a narrative unfolding. The choice of object (inevitably including the destruction of other objects), the use of the object, then the inevitable movement to/through the next object is more a force. In analysis, the analyst may need to give room to this unconscious. Perhaps it is implicit in (a) the right of free association (b) the equal right of evenly hovering attentiveness. That is, this feature of ourselves is allowed its destiny within the analytic process.

[2/2/88]
"Extractive introjection"

"X" talks about the inability to remember what children of 4 or 5 are like. This loss of memory is due to extractive introjection as the internal cathexes have been taken away. Here the 4/5-year-old is her child self taken by the parents.

She then says that she feels she has no direction.

There is, then, a relation between loss (of parts of the self), therefore an impaired remembering and a loss of elaboration.

With this patient and others who are passive there is an absence of projective intensity. Except that they imagine being taken over or sucked in by something, which is based on experience and they are relieved the analyst does not do this.

She comments on the long gap between sessions, that it feels like a week. This is due to inability to elaborate, to evolve.

This person does not feel a sense of destiny, a sense of elaboration.

As they have been assumed and something taken from them, they are prone to submit themselves to people or causes. Including the establishment of a false or rigid ideal self which they submit to and feel robbed of their life and identity.

[undated]
"Countertransference as philosophy"

It seems that in *this* theory psychoanalysts have created a very new vision of human life. The theory of projective identification in effect claims that in a two person relation, of "A" to "B", that "B" knows "A" in terms of the effect "A" has upon "B". To this I add extractive introjection, but also I want to say that "B"'s "true knowledge" is through his imagination. He imagines "A". Now, what is the psychology of *imagination*? What if we say that "B" decides to entirely invent fictions about "A"? That is, he aims to conjure wild stores about "A". Are such wild stories not—as elaborations countertransference—articulations of some unthought known in "B" about "A"? So that *imagination functions as the elaboration of dream.*

[undated]
"Mind/body"

In my papers I have focused on the infant's true self negotiation with the mother, while in different though equally complex ways the infant's psyche negotiates with its body: hunger, elimination, grasping, moving around, etc.

Another way is to take Descartes in the 6th Meditation and say that the soul/mind which is limitless in its extension (a thinking non-extended thing) and his body—an unthinking extended thing—must negotiate.

I think of Miller's[i] writings and his position that the body is functional immediacy. Is this another way of saying it puts a demand on the mind for work? He says that our knowledge of this object—our body—is different from our knowledge of any other object and that is true.

[9/2/88]
"Hate and dissociation"

"X"'s hate of her husband (denigration of him, contempt, etc.) is so powerful that "it" dissociates her from the object. That is, rather than removing herself from the object, she feels removed from her hate. She recoils from her contempt. These factors give her a sense of isolation and worry.

[undated]
"The here-&-now transference interpretation"

I do not think it corresponds to the Freudian unconscious as this is a reading between the lines *to find* an object: the analyst, the projected parts of the self. To listen unconsciously or for the ucs. requires evenly hovering attentiveness and most specifically not a looking for.

The repeating of such interpretations conveys to the patient that he speaks in tongues, or, that his true meaning always resides in a reflexive act: he is always referring to himself and the analyst.

The Kleinians introduce a mythology of breasts, penises, inside the mummy (etc.) which of course is certainly not a here and now but a there and then.

There are two transference interpretations:

1. The conversion of any narrative object to the analytic couple.
2. The emphasis on what the patient is *doing to* the analyst at any precise moment.

In compensation for this paranoid squeeze, which eliminates the subject, the analysand is placed inside a favoured English fiction: travel literature. He can travel to the land of the persecutors, the omnipotents, the manias, the depressions; he can be eaten by the bad breast,

---

[i] Henry Miller, American novelist.

214

lost in the uterus looking for the penis. As he loses his own culture and its analysis, he gains access to a fairy tale world with the Kleinian analyst as the Hobbit figure who holds the key to this universe.

Analysands think of having a Kleinian analysis because it means a special entry into the psychotic, the unknown: to the upper Nile or the Amazon of the mind.

Another compensation for abandoning one's own culture is the partnership that evolves. After a while the analysand senses just how his manifest text is actually his secret voice to the analyst and the analyst shares this secret. Like two travellers inside the mother's womb (with father's dangerous penis lurking about) they speak in a knowing hushed voice. Analysand enlightenment means delivery from this incarcerated world into the light of day.

There are those, of course, who do not take to this Orient Express and who ...

[24/2/88]
"Homosexuality"

Let me assume there is an

(1) ACT which erases. That is step one in the process of symbolizing *that* which the homosexual faces. Then:

(2) What is it?

Who is it?

What am I?

Who shall I be?

All questions that emerge at the pub or bar, while cruising, are derivative of the act: the erasure of self.

Therefore:

(3) Sex as re-assembly

The homosexual fuck = a kind of erotic fixture: a re-assembling of the body (particularly the genitals). The body is reassembled powerfully and by male transmission, as the act is the trace of the woman.

Foucault says that the pub is the location of the surreptitious wink, or glance etc., because the homosexual historically had to do it quick on the fly. To what extent, then, is the impersonal pub the re-presentation of cultural erasure? This point must be addressed.

The homosexual carries inside the element of "riddance". They rid themselves of each other. This lies inside each. The pub is an area where the impersonality of riddance congregates into a semi erotics. The choice of partner is an act of riddance: as surely as each will not see each other after.

At the pub the subject is an "object self" (see Baldwin).[1] Each homosexual aims to be an object. As he has been de-subjectified by humiliations (outside the self looking at it as an object) he now masters this by being the object.

What Baldwin teaches me is that every homosexual carries inside himself the trauma of the act and his depersonalisation. There is a terrible loneliness. To enter the bar as an "it" to be

215

with other "its" in a parody of the human world is to reconstitute the scene of erasure. Sucking off impersonal lovers is a failed attempt at recovery from this, while homosexual relations are somewhat successful cures.

But the man's body is sought as the ever present mirror of one's own body, always reassuring because it means the homosexual's body is still there: he suffers no erasure. The woman's body is the not-me body and its difference creates alarm about one's safety. In a sense the boy thinks that his masturbations are violations of the mother's proprietorial relation to him: he is her object. He must be her virgin: clean of his possession of his own body. Homosexual fucks are often masturbations in which the homosexual struggles to retain guiltless possession of his own body.

Homosexual empathy is a sincere and deep care for the damage caused to the other (often lover) by the ACT of erasure which is always a potential. And the manic states are efforts to transcend utter lonesomeness.

Because he has lived in the space of eradication, the homosexual finds spaces which he decorates, which he enlivens, humanises, and fits to the precise need of the subject. Against this unique care is the terror of its opposite: a holocaust, genocide, in which the subject is de-personalised, sent into the chambers of "it", standing outside the self, feeling excremental and damned.

[11/3/88]
"Excitement & psychic economy"

"M" maintains a level of excitement, by keeping erotic objects around, so that when he feels guilt about his need to betray his former girl friend (due to phobic dread) he can say to the imaginary reproaching other: "You expect me to give up my pleasures, my erect cock, just like that! Well screw you!" So the economy of excitement is used to nullify guilt. A fear is of having no excitement, thus nothing in the psychic economy to get rid of or deal with the guilt.

[undated]
"A self without a lifestyle"

A problem for "M" is to find a lifestyle for the self. In a way, the true self-in-her is okay, but she has not found a lifestyle for it.

One problem is that she transforms excitement into relational complexity. She moves from a body-self need to her mind. From body self need and orgasm to mental coverage. There is a competition between her body/self and mind.

She begins (in the transference) with emergence of excitement in relation to myself. She re-presents this with "J". She does not surrender internal reality to him—and the actual—by retaining her orgasm. She then re-transfers this (a further displacement) to "K", crossing an incest barrier of sorts to further complicate things. Now it is a problem of/for *mind*. Mind is "pleased" to cover this. Indeed, the idea achieves an intensity as almost the body of ideas, or ideas as body. She then practices them. Congregates them.

[undated]
"Differentiating objects in the internal world"

"L"'s splitting allows her to love "O" and hate "Z" but in such a way as to neutralise each. She lives a passionless life. Hate of "Z" is private, seething, preoccupying. On the surface— still addressing internal objects—she is very busy, occupied with many things. What is the status of *these* internal objects? I find they screen or obscure her more essential object relations. But these surface objects are closer to the fields of inter-relating. Superficial objects are held inside and she acts on her pleasures or displeasures in relation to the other. But on a deeper level, of passions, all is kept inside. There is no movement from the true self. She is depressed (privately) in such a way as to be a kind of conversion to affect of passion: passion transferred to depression. She suffers, also, an over-containment, that is, putting too much into the mind as container and not acting (true self) enough.

She persistently refused to accept my comment that she hated "Z". This after innumerable examples of how loathsome he is. She says that she does get angry with him and I say anger and hate are not the same. What's the difference, she asks. Imagine "Z" asking you to make love. You say "no, not now. Your timing is typically awful". That is anger. Saying "Making love to you is like trying to screw a monkey covered in shit", that's hate. And hate is what you feel toward him but have never expressed.

[undated]
"Regression to independence"

I am thinking of P's patient who comes from a mad world. Her interpersonal relations carry this madness while curiously, it is in the dream that she integrates herself. This suggests that when reality is mad there is a reversal of function for the dream which then becomes more integrative than reality. Also with P, the patient puts the analytic session to remarkable use. They seemingly regress very quickly. Instinctual life is very present (in the transference) as are affects, as are symbolic presentations, condensations, and so forth. But the therapist does not feel burdened even though they may wonder if something is split off. Indeed they find themselves to be in real intuitive rapport with the patient who uses interpretation to great effect.

I think this is because they lend their use of the dream to sessions. A maximum use of illusion in order to live, to be safe—with the instincts, etc.

[undated]
"The dream and regression to independence"

Is it not possible that in more ancient times the dream collected the details of a life into one place—a kind of inner temple—linking up parts of the subject who, in his consciousness, is quite split. Is so much weight given to oracles and hallucinations because the dream seems more collected/real than the mad world? Insofar as irreversible catastrophes in life (deaths, etc.) are workable in a dream without catastrophic effect. In the dream space the paradigm, then, of the temple, the place of worship, where *reversals* take place: the theatre of the gods.

In the *mad* family lives of the 2 parents, parents enact dramas of traumatic consequentionality (*consequence*) where impulse + act = a mad world. The disturbance of the day gives way to the place of the night and dream space is a place of *no consequence*. No victims. Instincts, affects, self states, etc., are representable. Such a place may be profoundly re-assuring for some. (This may also be true during adolescent conflict so I should see if there is a literature on adolescence and the dream.)

The patient and analyst try to bring the beneficial non-traumatic nature of a dream into object relations in the transference. It therefore has a curious dream-like quality with the patient regressing and using the analysis as dream. From here they test the actual object world to see if need, desire, self, etc., can be represented in the presence of the other without dire consequence. The skill (transformational) of the other is then felt and appreciated. Then more destructive (potentially consequential) states are brought in to the clinic. Again there is profound gratitude in this patient with the other's tolerance and absence of a mad world. Then, finally, this patient will warn the analyst of a world of mad actions: often lived out by the patient outside the analysis. This patient does not tend to act in, but to act out. However, the analyst brings mad actions into sessions via transference speech, and this profoundly reassures the patient who will use this. The "mad world" then becomes an object of scrutiny; the world of (m) & (f) and of present external enactments. In other words, the world becomes an object like a dream content. The condensations, displacements, symbolisations acted by the parents is regarded like the dream-it-could-not-be. The mad world then moves toward the dream world. The dream space then becomes increasingly the scene of mad enactments and life itself is less crazy.

These patients have all along been striving for independence from mad parents. But instincts, affects, object needs etc. tend to be abreacted in mad scenes with others and the rest of the time they are in a state of alarm: a kind of manic alertness. Grief, depression, etc., seem not on the scene.

The alarm is over the consequence to the self & other of mad scenes. But the clinical space has immediate affinity to the dream as safe, and this inspires regression to dependence that is a move to independence.

In their lives the families sound like houses of Atreus and are lived remarkably like a Greek tragedy. That which should be dreamed is lived. Or, when the world goes mad it seems like a dream (nightmare) and the characters in life assume the subjective part (i.e. passive) of the dream.

What, then, is the *sacrifice* to the gods? (In Iphigenia?) A hallucination comes into reality via an oracular person which demands the death of an actual person. Is this to be the sacrifice of the actual to the imaginary (dream/hallucination) as a pre-emptive act, of hope, that not all of actuality will be victim of a dream-like structure? As such these people know that life can become nightmarish with each need, instinct, fear, creating annihilation. The sacrifice of the actual (real) to the imaginary is to placate the forces that move the person into mad scenes.

[undated]
"Freud and the id idiom and convention"

Freud sees the conflict between instinct and society, whereas slightly differently I see it between idiom and convention. The first such conflict—(M) and (C), between two idioms, with one the convention. However the child also likes his novelty, so this is a factor.

[13/4/88]
"The hysteric's body"

What does the hysteric do when she presents the body as idea? For this is what she does when she paralysed her *idea* of the hand rather than, of course, to experience a true paralysis. What, then, are the ideas of the body (the imaginary body)? By enervating a part of the actual body she asserts an omnipotence, she transgresses the laws of neurophysiology, by overriding disorder to *create her own body,* laws that follow her own omnipotence.

Does she, in fact, have a dread of the workings of the soma? Is there something about containing an inside that follows its laws, disturbing? Indeed, by transferring an idea to the body, she insists on keeping matters on the surface. If she had felt sexually excited she moves this inner state to an external actual part of her body.

Why this not wanting to know the inside?

[21/4/88]
"Emotional turbulence"

As analysts now we are not only analysts who analyse the contents of the unconscious and the transference, but we undertake to see them through a period of emotional turbulence. In this state they need us as a container to process the turbulence.

[undated]
"Between the me and the I"

"Q" says that he is continually surprised and troubled by the schism—difference—between what he thinks, feels, and imagines while with me and what emerges when he speaks. Indeed his voice seems not true to his inner state. To some extent this is what Lacan must mean by the difference between the Imaginary and the Symbolic, as when the subject speaks (or is there in speech) he is a surprise to himself. Indeed there may be a feeling that the subject subverts the imaginary, or spectral me. Not to speak is to silence the subject and to eradicate the problem.

[June. New York]
"The hysteric"

Wanting to be the father's boy. If a man desires her, she feels he is dislodging her as the male. Yet, at the same time she is a woman and needs to have a vagina confirmed, so if he does not seek her as the woman he insults her. She passes on this dilemma.

[undated]
"Legends of cultural immersion/recovery"

When we write or speak of the culture prevailing in the various decades of our life—the 50s, 60s, 70s etc—what:

   a. are the different sets of cultural objects in each era?
   b. the differences of or between cultures per decade?
   c. are the terms of this order? For example what does it mean to be part of this?

Why is it that for an adult the 80s is nothing like *a formative culture*? Is it possible to define the generationally defining first decades as a formative culture? Can one define the 80s, 60s, 70s?
What place, if any, does peer pressure place on the cultural formations?
If we look at the 60s and 80s, what do we see in:

1. the macro culture: politics, etc.
2. micro culture (i.e. the first 10 years).

In what way does the micro culture reflect or interpret? The macro?
What are the intermediate objects (held jointly by the generation)?
e.g. film, TV.

[undated]
"Milieu"[ii]

OED [F. milieu, middle, medium. L. Medius (see medium) and lieu, place]
   A medium, environment, "surroundings".
   Webster. "Social or cultural setting".
   So it's a *medium*, a middle place, for the patient. A social or cultural setting.
   —Mother as an internal object.
   —Mother as derivative of family.
   —As container.
   —The milieu is *created* and sustained by the team (which is a category denoting a quality and so forth). For the psychotic it means going into the holding environment.

[ii] Notes assembled prior to a lecture on "milieu therapy" at Capistrano by the Sea residential treatment center in California.

[21/8/88]
"Violent innocence"

Thinking of "L" and "M" the patient who does not know and who therefore compels the analyst to be all knowing and therefore persecuting. In the countertransference to know is to feel isolated in knowing, to feel one is equipped with knowledge that is damaging because the patient has no idea. What does it mean to have a bad experience of knowing? Part of this situation is the fact that the innocent says "you will have to try to force this into me".

[undated]
"Boredom"

In the clinical setting may be a transitional moment, suggesting a change of use.

[undated]
"Psychical genera"[iii]

The opposite of trauma. It's some profoundly ego enhancing internal experience that only becomes useful later, upon a remembering. The lag time may, however, be short.

[4/10/88]
"Oedipal complex/motherfucker"

There is an important failure of understanding in the oedipal theory. At a point (age 4/5) the boy (also the girl) understands that he/she originated inside the mother. He was totally within the mother. The father never was. Then that maternal love and introjection is a very powerful process which also distinguishes him from the father, but eventually the father's access does indeed supplant him. But the boy has been "inside" the mother and the heterosexual "complex" rests on this "triumph" of origins.

[undated]
"Internal world"

Some inner experiences (or objects) are the outcome of the others' active projective identifications into the subject. The person has been shaped into something. This forms part of the subject's internal world.

The transference–countertransference experience is one form of unconscious life being thought. It can only be thought on its own terms, in and through relationship, although its status in the internal world will have its own property (i.e. interpersonal imaginings).

Another level (or type) of unconscious life is Lacan's Symbolic. But the mother conveys the speech. It is part of a relation and this therefore must be part of the Symbolic order.

[iii] First use of this concept.

Then there are the instincts, seemingly endogenous, but we can agree that all instincts originate or are part of a link to an actual other, so this unconscious is a feature of interaction. But this is not so clear and requires more thought.

So, each of us is possessed of an "inner life" of several types of unconscious organisation (symbolic, imaginary, projective identification), or levels (Matte Blanco[iv]), each of which processes human experiencing differently.

Perhaps music, dance, painting, fiction writing, are also different orders of unconscious presentation. In my internal world I may be objectifying "X" in an image (or succession of floating images), in a reminiscence, in the abstract idea, in talking to myself, in wording a parapraxis, in being "inside" a conserved self state, in working on a set of received projective identifications or extractive introjections.

Each of these levels, orders, categories of the unconscious is a totally distinct area of self experiencing. Each occurs in the self. In each I am in some relation to myself
—when I "play" music to myself.
—when I present a memory to myself.
—when I concentrate on a projective identification for myself.
—when I word slip to myself.

Are these domains of separate unconscious areas not akin to different orders of experience in life? Involving perhaps different senses: sight, sound, touch, speech and so forth? And each is a relation?

Compare the unconscious work of a dream, daydream, symptom, their practice, and unconscious fantasy.

[undated]
"Transference interpreting etc."

The object relations theorist sees "things" more clearly than the other schools, or, this perspective is a view into the patient early on. The problem is that interpretations are repetitive as a result and the patient's material is organised into a point of view that ironically may stall the associative process. So, then, although the analyst may collect things into a deep sense, this can be an overly binding sense.

[14/10/88]
"Violent innocence"

Harry provokes James who is disturbed by this. Turning angrily to Harry he finds Harry innocent of any apparent knowledge of James' distress. Indeed Harry suggests the distress is unreasonable and so forth.

[iv] Ignacio Matte Blanco, Chilean psychoanalyst who moved to Rome and wrote several enigmatic but compelling books on unconscious thinking. We "corresponded" by phone on a few occasions. Very decent and thoughtful man.

"M" suggests to me that she will no longer contribute to her analysis. Sorry, but a blankness descends. I am distressed by this. But she is innocent.

[undated]
"Internal objects and interpersonal processes"

There are many kinds of internal object, besides those characterised by self and object representations.

1. When a patient projectively identifies an unwanted part of themselves into a child this creates an unprocessed inner state inside the child. This "area" of self experiencing is conserved. It arose out of a two person interaction and the subject will store it until an occasion for its externalisation in another two person relation.
2. When a parent extractively introjects qualities of personality the child is left with negated internal objects. During intrapsychic or intersubjective experiencing there will be islands of hollowness, of narcissistic wounds, occasioning affects (tears or rage) without ideation.
3. Internal objects the result of violent innocence, in which "A" provokes "B", then insists that "B"'s state is endogenous and that "B"'s fury with the object is purely imaginary. If the victim is a child, the child will be provoked by the other but feel that what was a two-person action is purely intrapsychic. The internal status of this event maybe a retrospective attention as the child believes he is imagining everything and causing the world undue harm.

[undated]
"The unconscious"

Is there a fundamental difference between:

1. the unconscious that is endogenous, that prints the purely internal.
—secondary repression.
2. the unconscious that processes the effect on the subject of the actual world:
—the unconscious ego or primarily repressed.
Is the work and the nature of these two systems different?

[undated]
"Internal object/ internal subject"

What is missing in the concept of internal objects is a notion of the internal subject or subjects. Positions. Positions that process elements of life. Positions essential to thinking even the "true subject" or the "true object" are never represented—or at least in any moment—in the internal representations.

[undated]
"Unconsciousness"

For unconscious work to take place, the subject must be unconscious of it! Unconsciousness then, is a factor in the success of symbolic representation. And in the here-and-now transference interpretation too much of the unconscious is *rendered* into consciousness thus demanding unconscious processes of a deeper integration.

Transference and countertransference interpreting is hypertrophied reflexivity.

The argument that the self fragments with an over objectification misses only the source: the mother is ill at ease with her object (the infant) and passes on this ill at ease-ness (dis-ease) to the child in his self as object relation. He will scrutinise himself as he was scrutinised.

Possibly the dreamer is dreaming all the time, but only "aware" of it when he comes into a dream experience in a certain sort of way. The same is true of self experience. We are "having" self experiences all the time, but only aware of it when "entering" the experience *with consciousness.*

[15/10/88]
"Actual/ phantastical"

Let us assume that a patient complains of a father as a harsh person. Imagine we do not possess any sure indication whether this is a neurotic claim or a character's certainty. Has the father failed the patient or does the father carry the patient's split off violence, etc.?

1. If it is, say, oedipal, then in the transference the patient should come to experience the analyst as violent or angry, and this should be proportional to the patient's competition and so forth.
2. If the father *was* violently damaging, then the patient may set things up to imply the analyst is harsh or disapproving, but this role evocation will not have a force proportional to unconscious competitiveness.
3. There will be even relief, although an oedipal conflict *may* emerge out of this.

Then consider that as analysts we make much of how patients put projected self states into us. Imagine that they put us into an enraged state. How do we differentiate this from rage that does not occur that way?

Perhaps it cannot be relieved. We cannot be relieved of it. In a character state we would project it out and be relieved, but when you receive a projective identification we have no place to put it?

We are under pressure from the outside (not inside) to be in this state. Relief is sought through intrapsychic work aimed at *objectification.* The analyst seeks to objectify his state, to contextualise and to see his mood in terms of intersubjective action. Such an aim—to objectify in order to perceive—(a kind of naming) is a different type of self as object relation to the one where the subject is enraged by virtue of his own aggressive drives and so forth.

The recipient of a projective identification is in some confusion. Unconsciously he knows of a miscarriage of intersubjectivity and aims to see things clearly. (Even when he cannot.)

A patient who transfers their state of confusion into us does so in order to help us sort out the containment of a pathological [parent?] act, whereas the patient who uses the parent imago to bear a split off portion of the self works very hard to get the analyst *to stay* stuck with the projections.

What is the status of a child with the current victim-recipient of parental projective identifications?

[16/10/88]
"The terms of generation"

The psychoanalysis of generation.
Generational consciousness (and historical context).
—To parental past.
To children's future.
—Generational effects (like personal effects). The toys of parents, one's generation, one's children.
—Generational presence as custodian.
—The place of the novel in generational identity. For example,
a) Hemingway b) Mailer c) ?
—role of friends and friendship.
a) loss of friends.
b) waning of friendships.
—Concept of era or epoch. The 60s, the 70s, the 80s, the 90s.
—Loss (first deaths: of parents and friends).
—Solitude.
—Is there such a thing as a generational pathology? (Have a look at the yuppies).
—What makes for a creative generation?
—Objective correlatives of a generation (a popular novel like *The Great Gatsby*).
What does an objective correlative metaphorise? What is the function of an O.C.? Are they myth generators?
—The love of evolution. (Link to the concept of the true self and the use of an object.) We can love to generate, to watch the other's evolution, which is to truly *identify with generativity*. Men who leave their wives in midlife may be breaking their affiliation with generativity. Even if they go to a young woman and have more children. Such a *procreativity* would be different from a generativity; indeed the defence against it.
—"Turning out"; how things turn out.
—"Personal history". Take Berkeley, a part of my history. It means something to me. But this is *an object* of subsequent generational interpretation. What then is the fate of ones generational objects? They are changed in the "internal world" of one's country. Thus I become a separate interpreter of Berkeley inside a larger vision of it that differs from me.
—The media and generation. Note how media does not mediate for a generation, but presents myths of a situation (or historical era) that displaces actual generational experience.

—"Generational difference". What is the basis of the common generational hostility, of one era to/with the next? And the effect of denigrations?

—Is there a loss of generational cohesion in midlife when those in their 20s and 30s generate new sets of generational effects and generational myths? One's generation is now no longer the procreative act it seemed.

[undated]
"Cutting"

When "S" cuts herself she creates the vagina that wounds. Wounded by it, she creates true somatic pain whereas she thinks of it as psychic pain. "My vagina is a wound and a curse. I am awful because of it. My sexual ideas are evil. So I cut, cut, and cut myself and I feel relief, because I turn this wound into true pain against myself. I am cursed by it, so I repeat it. I am cursed by my sexuality, so if I cut myself I am the agent of this punishment. I cut myself. I vaginalise my body. Pure punishment vaginas. Pure pain vaginas. Pure blood."

[26/10/88]
"Innocence"

"L" has a dream that she goes downstairs to a breakfast room full of colleagues. She sits down and forces three packs of cereal into a ball, but each pack proves empty and then she finds a big heap of cereal on the floor and her colleagues leave without her. I interpret this as her pouring emptiness in to herself and analyse how another part of her, not part of that consciousness represented in what the dreamer knows, cut the packs so they would empty. (Note that the dreaming subject is innocent of the motivations connected by the ego to create the dream settings and the actions.) She cannot understand what I mean by the packs being split and so forth, she did not see that, nor did she do it. Then who dreamt the dream? "Did someone else and not you dream the dream?" I queried (exasperated).

We went back and forth on this and it was a struggle but finally she got it. Then she told me that yesterday she met a colleague from whom she had great respect. This woman came to see her, ostensibly to be helped by her with her marriage and despair but said she did not have any more nurturing in her. She began the session by saying she suffered after yesterday's session, knew I was right that she did not nurture me by bringing other material, but wanted to continue the analysis. Though interestingly I did not know when she told me of this colleague that it is the same moment she described to me yesterday as irritating. There was no link!

Eventually she says this woman told her that she was very angry with her because she felt she was undermining her work with the group through her profound passivity. As if she just went dead. I was surprised to hear this and had to repeat it. She said that? This was an interesting moment because I could hardly believe my ears. What good luck, I thought, that this other person said very much what I had said. So my feeling horrible derived from my countertransference writing that I was feeling lonely. As if I knew I felt subtly persecuted but thought perhaps

I was crazy. At the same time, as "L" told me this detail it was her life instinct contribution to the analysis. I told her this and we celebrated her candour.

Then however she said that she did not understand her co-worker's feelings as she, "L", simply felt that the co-worker (very pretty, bright and self-confident) just simply took over the group so "L" simply shut down. What was so surprising about this comment was how obvious it was that she didn't just shut down, but was furious and so forth and shut down to punish her colleague. "Now Mrs "L", you say that you just shut down, but tell me what are you feeling?" A long silence and then she says that she felt jealous. Yes, I say, a new punisher refusing to relate. As you do with me when you announce your blackness, with your husband by refusing to relate to him and self. She replies with her husband she is if anything locally critical. She does not shut down. I say that when she verbally criticises it is true, she is not shut down. But this is a very different phenomenon from what I'm describing. When she won't touch him, won't sleep with him this is the shutdown: a self full of hate.

Eventually she says that she does not want to say anything critical of her colleagues because something awful derived from jealousy would come out and then she outlines the steps of innocence:

1. you are furious but express hate by totally withdrawing from the other (colleague, me) by blankness.
2. colleague. "What is wrong?" "L". "Oh nothing, just not with it today."
3. the other feels kicked in the guts when asking about this meets with no reply, or rather no recognition.
4. the subject is innocent. But all the stirred up feelings are inside the other.
5. the other is invited to feel crazy (perceiving wrongly) and to feel guilty for pushing "this" onto the subject.
6. I link to transference by adding that as she is innocent of this process it forces me to be the one who to know, who is inflated with knowledge, while "poor she" is not in the know.

[undated]
"Anger"

Anger is an expression of feeling.
  What causes the anger?
  —the sadness of anger.
  —precedes violence. A warning function to the other?
  —shrinking with anger. Mr. Hyde shrinks. Anger simplifies.
  —a person has a fit or spell of anger just as they have a dream. "I'm sorry, I was just angry", which is an allowed-for dissociation. It means that in Western culture we are allowed this happening, in which a person may say what they do think in part but it will subsequently be treated as if this event, this dream, is not representative. And, indeed the part expression may be true.

Does the outburst of anger then serve as a relief? Like the sneeze (which also distorts the face and progressively comes over one) the type of anger expels and feels good. Does it serve them a feeling or somatic relief function?

Stevenson's *The Strange Case of Dr. Jekyll and Mr. Hyde* suggest that some outbursts of anger are based on predispositions, to internal issues or fissures of personality. Thus what are the underlying faults that validate the eruption?

Jekyll & Hyde suggest that to be angry is to create or to become another person. Indeed, a person looks different when angry and thus facilitates the idea in the other, "oh, but that's not him."

Jekyll wonders if he has lost his identity to Hyde.

Jekyll says of Hyde he felt his faculties were sharpened by anger. Does anger function to sharpen the self?

—Seething anger, being consumed or eaten up by anger. Make a distinction between expressed and unexpressed anger.

—Jekyll speaks of Hyde's being like an ape when angry. Is anger the ape in us?

—Is violence beyond anger? As in *A Clockwork Orange*, the cold ritualistic violence?

—There is warm anger (burning with fire) and cold anger (violent).

—Swearing (the signs of anger). Wagging the finger.

—Ahab.

—*Clockwork Orange*: Alex is a split character.

[undated]
"Essentialism"

Spinoza says objects have both an essence and an existence. I think objects gain essence through human endowment. We turn an object into an object with essence. And our world is replete with essences. Is this a definition of a cultural object as opposed to an object not cultural? Does cathexis-investment mean the giving of essence?

The mother's handling of objects, investment of them with her love in her play with the infant, is a core transfer. She shows how objects can serve one's love. It is the foundation of essentialism. Which a depressed mother cannot do. Indeed objects feel to her like objective correlatives of her inner despair. They are therefore not longed for, not there to receive or give. Infants will not transfer love of the object, or need of the self or some such thing.

The use of God in Spinoza brings to mind that God must be the mother. Is this a primary projection? Do we transfer the enormity of our birth and helplessness to the concept, God? Thus we are born from nothing, yet contained in mother: again God. Our ideas seem to be determined by this God.

"H"'s erotic life is an autoerotic enactment. These women are only instinct objects. He is foreskin man. He has his hand on his cock all the time, creating erotic sensations which preoccupy him. I say he stimulates himself and this is what he did as a child as he went into autoerotic existence. As if he experienced true pleasure only in the dream, whereas actuality was fraught. He says that last night he awoke and was briefly attracted to "M" but thinks it was because from the moment he thought she was a translator. Then he says that "M" wanted him to bring her back a bikini from Corfu, which he did and found that in the act of giving it to her that he was excited. I think this is his effort to take from the dream experiencing (and fantasy) to give to the actual object.

—Dreams rely upon day residue, in part. Or, may we distinguish between dreamers who use immediate life experience. from those whose actual recent life is so diminished that they must dream the part up, or, use universal cultural objects.

—True self experiencing is encoded, available for psychical life the same way trauma works, as the effect of memory of the actual. We have experiences, they are encoded, then over time we have subsequent experiences which make it possible to use the earlier.

Anger.

The simplification provided by anger is a pleasure. Or, hate/rage is a pleasure.

fear/anxiety; anger/rage. Often both are nonspecific and diffuse.

—Anger as a manipulation, to affect the other, to alter the course of events.

—What is the advantage of anger?

—What do we see when we look upon the angry person?

—"Anger is close to the surface." Does this suggest that anger comes from "deep down?"

—Deep wounds and anger.

—The function of anger as a necessary stimulus to creativity.

—To express or not to.

—Expressed anger and correction. If you speak.

—The acceleration created.

—Affirmative anger (and closure): Othello.

—dismantling anger (and terror): Hamlet.

—Expression as experience. It is put out "into" the world.

—Hate and projection: the Northern Irish project their violence into the object which in turn is therefore seen as aiming to harm them.

—Hate and the survival of the object. The ability to "destroy" the other and pleasure in seeing them survive.

—Adolescent anger!

—If the parents do not retaliate, the child does not feel that his hate destroys the integrity of the object. If they do, then there is a fear of hate.

—So, who is the implicit other of the hating person?

—When is anger or hate life enhancing? (Freud's life instincts). When is it destructive? (death instincts).

Life = confronting

Death = elimination of the object

—The *OED* has anger as an affliction or pain (of anguish or despair). Anger then could be a form of mental pain which the person then tries to deal with by expressing (and getting relief) or containing and not getting relief. If it "hardens" it leads to hate.

—*Webster* on anger, distress, sorrow:

angh = constricted

angustus = narrow, tight

angustia = tightness, distress, anguish

see angina.

The above suggests a physiological source or a form of mental pain that is physiologically effective as in a tightening.

—Temper. Latin

A temper is a mixture, to temper something is to add, to balance; hence, to keep temper or to lose temper.

So a bad temper is a state of the loss of mixture.

In the Middle Ages a temperament (L. *temperamentum,* proper mixing, temperamental and proper mixing), was composed of four parts of the body and mind. The 1) sanguine 2) phlegmatic 3) choleric or bilious 4) melancholic. Each linked to one of four humours.

—An outcome of internalised anger can be a violent splitting into internal objects: see schizo-phrenia. Terror is the outcome.

[undated]

"God and man"

God does not want man to have a mind of his own. Having a mind of one's own, anyway, is problematic. Even dangerous. When they eat from the Tree of Knowledge (of good and evil) they have this mind of their own. They are now informed.

[undated]

"Daytime or 'a day'"

A "day" is an object. It is its own potential. The factors that determine it are to an extent not of our making. It starts on its time, progresses in its own way, and in a sense has its own history.

What do we make of our day? What do I do?

I have tasks. Intervals. Objects from which to choose.

To our day we may bring our dream.

We may bring instincts.

What do we do with it?

In fact, what is it?

Isn't our creation of it like a dream-event?

[undated]

"Dream space and inner space"

I think there must be a day residue of the dream space.

A space into which new experiences of the self arrive. Perhaps this is what is meant by evocation. Maybe certain memories or daydreams.

Can we speak of the Day Space? The subjects experience of the day as an object? Where what to be, to do, to use, depends on intersecting factors?

Is the dream space a condensation of day space? Is the day space the other location of self experiencing?

[undated]
[untitled]

The day space has a different content per person: I see my patients while a factory worker has his objects. The "contents" of our lives (cultural objects??) vary, but the overall structure of the day: morning, lunch, afternoon, evening, etc., are all different.

[undated]
"Mnemic objects"

Things which are significant as containers of memory. They are of the past, specific memories linked to them, and surround us in the present, in locations.
—what function?
—visibility?
—the private village of each of us.
—the anthropology of self.
—my grandfather's watch. Pipe. Pipe bowl.

[2/12/88]
"Generational consciousness"

Each of us lives "within" our own generation which itself bears (contains) its own history.
There are points of varying entrance to generational existing:
A) is popular music
B) sports
C) political events, etc. There are also exits (as each entrance can be left) into universals (or transgenerational phenomena).
Languages (clichés) of one's generation.
Clothing. " " " "
Values. " " " "
What do we make of people who do not join their generation? What to make of those who achieve no transgenerational effect?
Each generation, or era, has its wars: ennobling? Not so? The guilt of the generation.
History-making:

Violence or violating and the entrance into history. Berkeley.[v] When is a generation formed?

—a generation

—to generate

—genera .... What is the Greek?

A group of the generated (i.e. the born together).

The transgenerational universals (birth, illness, death, marriage etc.) are lived by us in/or from a type of solitude. But to be in a generation is to feel part of something, one's culture, that collectively objectifies the laws (rules) and unconscious phantasies of our existence.

Indeed, our generating—or a generation—elaborates the prior generations phantasies, while at the same time violating them. Isn't adolescence a violation of the phantasies conveyed by the parents: a collective violation? And in a country like the United States where each generation develops powerful phantasies of itself, the adolescent may feel compelled to even more powerfully violate the norm.

See Freud's *Totem and Taboo* as the adolescent peer group: probably the primal horde.

So, does generation begin with violence, with violation? Is "Berkeley" the signifier of this process? Were the 60s generation successful because we violated the corruptions not the ideals, and hence launched our generation as a positive ideal? Is it possible that certain generations launch along negatives?

Do we know of a time when generations did not form? What of the youths who go off to war?

Can we say that one generation gives birth to another? Do we prepare to be usurped or displaced?

As soon as a new generation is ignorant of the prior generations mnemic objects, the generation feels its boundaries: made by the next generations defining ignorance. Where is this cut off?

Generational genocide and the destruction of generational objects. History taking (and reading) as care, as love.

My father's autobiography.[vi]

[3/12/1988]

"Passing through one's time"

Do we not, each of us, pass through our own time? A generation has its time, filtered by its culture. At what points in our lifetime do we sense ourselves passing through our time? As a generation that uses time?

Is there a generational time?

[8/12/88]

"Self experiencing" (Guild lecture[vii])

Question: What is the nature of the development of the person through self experiencing?

---

[v] Refers to the political activities at UC-Berkeley in the mid-1960s.

[vi] My father, Sacha Lucien Bollas, wrote a long autobiography when he was in his sixties.

[vii] The Guild of Psychotherapists is a psychotherapy training institute in London.

Question: What about trauma? Does it hold up self experiencing?

Question what about the person who does not have a self?

—We may use the model of the dream for self experiencing. The Freudian view is to see the dream as a manifest text; indeed to see the visual order (thing presentation) as pure veil to conceal the word order. But the dream is also a self experience. Indeed those elements, condensation, displacement, etc., that go into the dream work to make units of meeting also go into the making of self experiencing, which, then, is "composed" of different factors—instinct, day residue, memory etc.—which collect together resonating experiences (endogenous, exogenous). The dream is, par excellence, an experience of self, and self is the outcome of psychic activity.

As dreaming is self experiencing, where to dream is to have a self experience (insofar as it occurs only in these moments of psychic assembly). Some people, those who dream, have these experiences, whilst others have a diminished capacity for this.

—I suggest those factors that go into the making of a dream—condensation/displacement/substitution/symbolisation—go into the making of a day experience, which, in turn is the place of self experiencing. During each day we collect together "possibilities of self" through memory, percept, out of interaction with our own world, and have significant units of self experiencing. Perhaps we need to look anew at the role and function of imagining, of the daydream. Or of aesthetic experience. Or of our creativities.

In any event, the day is a potential space, as is the dream. What do we do with our day space? What do we make of it? It is a thing in itself; it is also a psychic object. It has a morning, an afternoon, it's evening. It has a biological, earthly order, as well as its symbolic order. We work in it. We play. We recreate (what is really-creation, recreation?). Some make love during it.

—Self experiencing involves the selection and use of objects. The range of choices is important in terms of multiple routings of the true self. Expression (or is it also representation?) is a key idea here. Indeed nosology, the division of people into borderlines, schizoid, narcissistic, does not necessarily apply. Beethoven, who was borderline, no doubt selected and used objects to facilitate the true self. So, too, we have borderline parents who are mad. But some of these mad parents are rich in cultural objects and make objects available to their children, so that the children can grow or express themselves even if acquiring parental madness. It's one thing for such a parent to go into the object then get claustrophobic and leave, if say it's a rich object.

Self experiencing involves at least three categories or levels

—being

—using

—relating

To take this, relating releases self to experiences latent or potentialized through the other. This is important as some schizoid people who unrelate could have true self experiencing only through cultural objects. Indeed, do I differentiate between articulations along these

233

lines? Well, surely in relating, certain ego processes are evoked (i.e. erotic life, creative life, affective life)—including being provoked by the actions of the other (where we are "played" by the other). The other has access to us, surprises us, provokes us, responds to our idiom in an idiom response which is different than, say, our response to a work of music, literature, or the like.

—The power of the object to evoke self experiencing. It is 7:30 at night. I could be (1) on the phone discussing group policies (2) at a concert (3) playing with Sacha (4) talking to Suzanne (5) reading, etc. Now each of these "objects" promises different types of self experiencing. Thus when we look at any persons experiencing we need to note their field of self. If someone only reads he is deficient in other potential experiences.

[8/12/88]
"Boys"

The myth of Jesus, immaculately conceived, relating to God (and the betrayal). What does this tell us about boys and their fathers? And why do we so identify with it?

[8/12/88]
"Family photos"

A patient tells me that he thinks many of his memories derive from his relation to photos. Indeed. What object is this? How does it function? As capturing space and time for a child. Screen memories? Remember a photo of a child and family kept for the eventual adult is a very different object than any photo of an event. But metapsychologically, what is the mental status of the memory of a photo?

And, as they are the parents' objects (they take the photos), what does it say about the child in relation to himself, through the parent?

[9/12/88]
"Each of the psychoanalytical schools of thought generates theory that reflects fantasy"

1. British: the digestive
2. French: gap/phallus
3. American: ego machine
4. Stern: wired-up infant.

The parts of the body—and of the mother's and father's bodies—are divided up around the world. Breast in England, infant in US, vagina and phallus in France. Schools form around parts of the spoils reflecting the primal horde that follows on upon the death of the father.

Not transmission or generation but death and dissemination.

How each group cannot make use of parts of the body, which cannot be collected.

"Representation"

1. "The two worlds" of dreaming life, of waking life. The Merleau Ponty quote in Pontalis—"the prose of the world:"[2] how also day life is a dream like composition. A nice point. So at night there is a more pure (or is it a more displaced?) concentration of dream.
2. "systems of representation." There are different symbolic representations: e.g. painting, music, narrative, prose, poetry.
—How do they differ?
—What is the psychic function, i.e. the capability and the task of each of these different categories? And what part of the body ego is behind each?
3. What does it mean when a patient dreams and creates a space and is more available to be understood there? Is there a primary need to convey? Of human need? A need for understanding? Does understanding not bind the ego?

[15/12/88]
"Characterization"

We may speak of a patient's capacity to characterize being, like that of a novelist if we inquire into the quality of representation of the other. Further, as parts of the self are projected into the other, characterization may be a form of elaboration of parts of the self.

A transference interpretation which collapses the characters into the constant figure of the analyst is, to some extent, unnecessary destruction of characterization. If done all the time it forestalls that elaborate process available to the subject through characterization.

[15/12/88]
"The ironic sense of life"

Giannotti[viii] asks what is the eventual outcome of the creation of the third area between analyst and patient. In addition to facilitating this object I think it can have an intrapsychic equivalent, when the patient develops intrasubjective playfulness. When he can receive the dream, the associations, the movement of ideas, the moods, there are parapraxes with <u>amusement</u>. I mean this is a profound sense, of taking pleasure in the unconscious. This pleasure in one's bewilderment to oneself: an ironic position, part of the ironic sense of life.

[15/12/88]
"The play is the thing"

Pontalis believes that the unthinkable produces thought and yet the factors that determine the functioning of the apparatus are beyond its grasp. Therefore the lacunae, gaps, etc. are more real than the words, memories, or fantasies.

[viii] Adriano Giannotti, psychoanalyst, and Director of the Program in Psychoanalysis at the Istituto di Neuropsichiatria Infantile of the University of Rome.

But when patient and analyst "play", they create in André Green's sense the analytic object, which is a form of analytic psyche—a form that processes the contribution of the participants. Indeed playing is rather like a representation of the unthinkable as a process. We can see the unthinkable. We can see its derivative: this ghost that informs us, that runs us.

Therefore play is mind. The play is the thing. What cannot be given to meaning can be given life.

When patient and analyst work well they create a psychic structure together, which permits each to know by this metaphoric act—this transfer of the deeply internal into or onto an indeterminate space—the nature of one's psychic idiom. It will be there as part of the analytical object, along with the analyst's psychic idiom.

Play invites the nature of one's mind (self, soul, idiom) into this space.

"The unthinkable makes what is thought", but in the "making" of play we can witness the movements of the unthinkable. Or can we? Can we see the thinker of the thought? Perhaps not.

Playing/free associating, allows both patient and analyst to witness the idiom of the patient's mind/self/soul. Its nature.

[undated]
"Irony, the third area, intrasubjectivity"

Winnicott, André Green, and others write of the third area. This can become an internal area, between the completely unconscious and the fully conscious. Indeed in this area, contributed to by both, we are between knowing and not knowing, or, "we know but we do not know what we know". This knowing that is a not knowing is a position. It never changes and is an essential part of self experiencing. It can never be resolved. But we emerge with an ironic sense of place, of amusement in being the thought of an unconscious thinker. The joke is "on" us, as is the dream. The amusement comes from this impossible position.

[22/12/88]
"Self experience and the dream"

In the interpretation of dreams Freud reports his "sandstone figures dream".[3] He has this dream which represents "a specific spatial relation to myself, on my left hand side, I saw a dark space out of which there glimmered a number of grotesque sandstone figures." This is a self experience, and, he comes to understand this dream when he travels to Padua some years later and sees the sight that had been represented in his dreams. Thus some of our life experiences have been dreamed, i.e.: a dream confers upon life objects (places, people etc.) its precise psychical reality, so that when we walk amidst the real we also travel in a special dream space.

[undated]
"The internal world"

Perhaps it should be the internal theater.

I think this concept surely comes from the dream. Where is the dream of space? This must be the internal world.

Freud, considering Fechner's[ix] distinction between waking and the dream reality says of Fechner that Freud "suspects, rather, that *the scene of action of dreams is different from that of waking ideational life*" (SE4, 48).

So the internal world is a different scene of action. Thus whenever this internal world is externalized through the transference, there is a transfer of place (as well as content) from the place of the dream to the space of the real.

Does this occur because of the analytic illusion: that its reality is psychical?

[undated]
"Self experience and the dream"

Dreams, says Freud, transfer thoughts into hallucination so that "we appear not to *think* but to *experience*" (SE4, 50). This total submission differentiates the dream from the daydream. Inevitably therefore we are betrayed by the dream space which proves not to be real. What can be made of this daily betrayal? Is there a link here to paranoia, to the person who feels he is being fooled?

The dream is also the first "contact" we have with our own madness. Freud: "the mental disorder made its first appearance in dream-life, that it first broke through in a dream" (SE4, 89).

"As you know, the instigation to a dream is always to be found in the events of the previous day" (SE4, 147). So, that self experiencing provided for by and in the dream space is always sponsored by a day event. Therefore as we live, we unconsciously reflect. Events possess potential psychic value and they link to our instinctual urges, histories etc. In short, to our idiom. Therefore the psychic potential of objects and events depends on this "fit" between the existent and the essence, between the event and the idiom of the subject. Therefore we are sponsored by cultural, social, events. Self experiencing is through the object, which sponsors a dream. As I "move" through objects some of them have dream potential. Do I know this? Freud knew if he had sardines he would dream of water. So do we know if we go to X, see Y, etc. that we will have a certain self experience? For example I know if I see a film I always have a rich dream. I know that sometimes I choose not to go to a film for this reason.

Objects therefore have psychic specificity to release idiom elaboration. As we know this, we can choose either to follow our destiny (to release idiom through selection of objects) or not to.

[undated]
"Paranoid honesty and internal denial"

"X" teaches me this afternoon why some people are obsessed with revealing the truth to the other. When I say I think he is particularly intent upon confronting others with their

---

[ix] Gustav Theodor Fechner, German physicist, philosopher, and experimental psychologist.

dishonesty he says it's because his mother always denied her actions and his truth telling was his fury with her denial. This nicely illustrates the relation between a character trait and an object relation.

When the boss says they are running at a loss, he reveals to him the £10,000 profit. I say he corners the boss and others with the truth that hits home and he searches out their Achilles heel. However, I think there is an anguish here, not a wish to punish or to destroy. It is as if he can confront the bad mother and change her and she will then be good. He agrees.

[undated]
"Humiliation"

"W" seeks to expose the Achilles heel in the other because there is a fear of this being done to him.

In humiliation the subject is forced to stand outside the self—which is a frozen object of the gaze—and look at the self through the eye of the other.

I say I think he seeks to humiliate because he dreads it. He tells me his mother dressed him as a girl and he was endlessly teased at school.

Now humiliation I think is a psychotic experience, specifically a schizophrenic one, where an element of oneself (or one's actions) is so condemned that one is objectified as a dead object.

[undated]
"Self experiencing"

"… we only bother to dream of things which have given us cause for reflection in the daytime" (Freud, SE4, 174).

Self experience is here firmly linked to reflecting. The dream is a form of resubmission of the self to its day experience, a "once again".

[27/12/88]
"Characterization"

Broadly this should mean any person's ability to represent life. The ability to note, organize, and give fictive unity to life experience. A form of mirroring. Thus we ask the patient how his life has been and he tells us. How well does he characterize himself, his others, his experiences? This is characterization—a form of mirroring.

[30/12/88]
"Nostalgia and generational consciousness"

Friends and generational consciousness. What is the function of the friend? Of friendship? Is there such a thing as generational partnerships? Isn't that what a marriage is, in some ways?

Time and generational consciousness. I did not know World War Two except as it was reflected in the passing of time in my parents. I lived the 60s, but it was before the time of present youth. Such time marks generations. But generational procreativity (or transmission) has to do with one generation overcoming such gaps to inform the next generation about their own time. This is history making or transmitting. Why can't some generations do it? See Germany and the gap where generations of World War 2 does not transmit.

If one transmits one's generation to the next—and takes in turn from the previous generations—one has been, as a generation, procreative. How does politics figure in this? No doubt Aristotle/Plato thought of the role of parents etc. in this. But is politics at times a poor delegation of a larger collective responsibility?

[undated]
"The dream and the new place"

Borges "The Waiting": "The man thought that these things (now arbitrary and accidental and in no special order, like the things one sees in dreams) would in time, if God willed, become invariable, necessary and familiar"[4] (165).

Lovely.

In a way the dream presents us with the new, the previously unseen place. Even when it recapitulates the day.

Do we need to dwell in the new place?

In life do we provide new experiences: new novels, paintings, cities, for that precise, dream-like event of the new?

1989

[10/1/89]
"Repulsion"

The object or part of the woman's body that is the focus of repulsion is like the opposite of a fetish. The fetish is not a part of the body and is brought to it to have intercourse. The repulsive part of the woman's body is the object of intense preoccupation and prevents excitement.

The person notices the object as mildly objectionable at first: a largish bottom, mole on the cheek etc. Thus the prominence of the object widens.

[11/1/89]
"Jesus/Oedipus"

Mary is with the child by the Holy Spirit before wed to Joseph, so, unlike Laius, this is not his son. Note too the difference of the oracles: Joseph has a dream (contains it) which urges him to marry Mary and keep the child, whilst the Oracle in Oedipus urges Laius to get rid of the child. The dream is <u>inside</u> the father (Joseph) so already he <u>contains</u> the anxiety, whilst the Oracle comes outside of Laius whose worries are "beyond him". Herod is the father who fears the newborn child; who is already the object of the <u>search</u> by the wise men: not searching to kill him as in Oedipus, but to worship him. Interestingly the wise men betray their promise to Herod—to return after seeing the newborn Jesus—because they are warned not to in a dream. So the prophetic—if that's what it is—leads to a disobedience of the word to the political leader. Therefore they are already fathering the dream, which act usurps the authority of Hesiod, while Laius and Oedipus insist upon controlling and obeying the oracular. Joseph's second dream leads him to escape with Jesus and Mary, so Herod is outwitted. He has all infants of two years and under executed, so the infanticide continues.

[undated]
"Violent innocence"

The innocent insists upon a paranoid return of his violence. By provoking the other, the innocent is victim of his own aggression, but retains the purity of innocence, now increasingly defined by the attacks against the innocent. For the innocent must suffer. By provoking the environment into aggressive response the innocent suffers.

In *Radical Innocence,* Ihab Hassan writes: "The disparity between the innocence of the hero and the destructive character of his experience defines his concrete, or existential, situation" (7).

[undated]
"Generations"

Ihab Hassan writes "the old fashioned war of generations rooted in different climes of childhood—the war of the generations and the battle of the sexes are perhaps the only wars we can still afford" (66).[1]

Hassan is observing the novels written by the new generation. This illustrates an important point of the total issue: one generation—the older ones—watched the new generation's formations of itself. We do this mainly by noting their use of cultural objects, particularly film music and literature.

Does not each generation transfer its childhood culture into a generational culture? That is, each generation has its childhood. Theories of child-rearing, material and cultural objects (toys etc.). How and in what ways does this group of children transform itself into a generation? It happens in adolescence, which is perhaps the first and most important experience of group awareness, of one's age as simultaneous with and at power with others: able to form a mass culture.

What are the terms of this transformation?

The older generations "bear witness".

When the child is "in" adolescence—this rite of passage—he is initiated into adult life. His passions, identities, have been lived in the defined forms of the family, but now he is in a culture of the group—the mass. His isolation is severe. A family can no longer hold the self. Mass culture, then, is formed in an abyss between generations. Between the family of origin and the new family. How does the child group cope with this intermediate age? What do they see from there?

The adolescent cult film is probably a good genre to look at. The house that one moves into kills one. The child who is victorious over adults and so on. Are there disparaging terms for one's effort to be part of one's generational form? A "trendy" and trendiness were terms used in my day. I think now it's a "beck".

241

The rock group. A microcosm of the group searching for its identity as a group (a new family of 3/4? = the peer group?).

At what point does a parent regard his teenager as a generational specimen: a critique of culture that is valid? A beginning of a critique that must be heard.

In a way generational consciousness may be a new discovery. A new phenomenon, as adolescence is a recent event.

Poirier[2] has argued that the youth movement destroyed forever the older generation's idea of youth as pastoral: an ideal. But is it not possible that this is the dynamic: each generation feels the next generation to desecrate an idealized era: their own adolescence? And why is adolescence romanticized this way? Partly it's due to the collective transformations of selves from childhood to adulthood, when heroic acts of violation are recalled with fondness, partly as the anger etc. is forgotten. The ideal is "youth" itself. The most powerful pressure group that vaporizes, but resides in mnemic objects of the adults who carry it. It is my youth: "self, you are trampling under foot", screams the middle generation over the very fact that youth occupied that space.

In mid generation, when looking back now at the new emerging generations one sees a ghost of one's own generation in formation, which allows for something of a critique.

Hughes[3] shows how in the early 20th century, philosophers, writers, sociologists, artists, musicians etc. differed in their acceptances or rejections of themes: some advanced, other forms can serve. So each generation has its forms, some "conservative" in presentation, others radical. Therefore most of the total views of a culture are represented and held by a generation.

Hughes writes of the intellectual community of the time. What is that? What objects does a community create? Isn't popular culture also a community? And each form—comics, novels, music, painting, etc.—is a community and people may join. And of course there are professional communities and we are part of that: psychology etc.

A generation, then, uses its forms and their communities to process and transform its habitual circumstances. It is like a symphonic movement held together by generational consciousness which is simply a sense of collective experiencing and transforming one's society. So although I know nothing of say skiing, Kidd is the figure of my generation because "those" of my generation who ski chose him. I am shaped then by stories of others of my generation, whether I like it or not. There is a kind of pluralist dialogue to a generation: to being in an era. Which raises the fact that I may not like it: that I might be distressed by some of my generation.

Those objects that define the generation are "generational objects".

Perhaps one must consider what a generation's relation to the decades is.

There is a period in adolescence of pre generational "rooting around". In my stepdaughter's generation I ask about music and she names the Doors and the groups and it's clear they are experimenting. On her wall—part of teenage culture—was James Dean, Sid Vicious, Sex Pistols, Marilyn Monroe. These are gone now (her age 15–16). The culture of her room has changed but this room is displaying, or has also displayed, objects gone through by her generation, so the room is an invitation to her generation and repudiation of the family—or at least we are not specifically invited to it. Also her room has letters, postcards, photos of friends, of herself, souvenirs of occasions etc. on the walls. She and her friends are on display. As time passes this may change, and the wall may display non-generational objects—a Picasso print etc.—but for now, it is externally crafted: a "cinema screen" with idols and so forth being displayed upon it.

My 10-year-old son put 20 karate posters up in his room. This joined objects his mother and I had put up before: Indian tombstones, art portfolios. Now he—and all his male friends—are "Beano" freaks, and the karate posters are somewhat passé.

"Beano" has been around since the 1930s and virtually all English boys get into "Beano". This culture has been created by the adult community for the child. Gradually children take over the provision of collective passion.

Passion in being. As a generational phenomenon. Values. Beliefs. Ideals. "A child's room" reflects the creation of cultures from that created by the parent to that eventually created by the child. It is an historical cinema scene of this child's generation-in-the-making.

Generational consciousness emerges when a generation begins to create its own primary art. First perhaps in adolescence: sports figures then in music and pop groups, then in other forms. Or as consumers, when its payment for objects in the free market determines adult provision. And in the consumer sense, in terms of choice of object, generations start early. There may be a generational sense, like a sense of self before generational consciousness. They shape themselves as consumers before they become creators. Consumer creation continues of course through life and is another aspect of a generational sense.

Generational consciousness is an act (acts) of reflection over time.

German youth after World War One had contempt for the old liberal values esteemed by their parents. Hardened by the atrocities of a war they were in a different mood. Although Vietnam profoundly engulfed the generation of the 1960s, the war was a TV war period. Reagan, the man of television, was the ultimate healer of it: Walter Cronkite became president. In Bush, America had a new Anchorman and it's interesting that Bush's finest hour, his truest victory, was his defeat of the other Anchorman Dan Rather.

[undated]
"Self experiencing"

Each person creates their own environment or culture in which it can be said that they live. It is made up of actuals and internals and really is in that third area.

However, do people provide transformational objects that catalyze self experience? As potting (ceramics), or a film would? Or is the self left to inertness and underdevelopment?

[11/1/89]
"Violent innocence"

When A uses a mood or self state to convey their fury (though silent) or X [any nonverbal expression], they provoke B into concern, worry, anger or whatever. "What is it?" asks B.

"Nothing at all," says A, appearing innocent. B feels disturbed. B searches about for probable cause of the mood. "Did I upset you when …?" met with a "no". In extreme cases B is meant to suffer. But what is this suffering?

A difficult question. Some speculations.

In a way A indicates his survey, affirms that our internal worlds are only ever truly known to our self. The other can be locked out. B is to be excluded from knowing.

This is one of the several positional functions of innocence. There are others.

As "B" asks, queries, wonders, struggles, "A" uses denial or innocence to witness the ability (or not) of these efforts to read. This can be a pleasure. But if "B" is meant to have no reply or recognition then he may be in that strange place of the child who is affected by the mother's moods, but who is excluded from knowing. What is there is useless projecting or mentation with no effect and the ultimate registration of the event by the mood's effect.

A problem. In some cases the object that is the response in the subject defines the borderline personality, who unfortunately is to know the object only through disturbed self states precipitated by the actions and moods of the other.

But in other cases—the more sadistic ones—the "A" figure witnesses the confusion of "B" as a form of pleasure.

It is possible then that this "A" is a falsely resolved borderline patient who has found some way to occupy the power of the mother by controlling the process of putting the other through hell.

"X" used the father to organize the infant–child disturbed by the mother, perhaps because the father structured the mother, or the father was simply different.

The borderline is the child who cannot ever "know" the object because the object is beyond minimal recognition, will not let the child know it. The child is only stirred up. But "B" is put into this position: of being stirred up by an object that assumes no knowledge or link, between its actions and "B"'s state.

"Y" also organized the chaotic child by identifying with a father that she sadized [was sadistic toward]. The sadistic abuse by "A" of "B" is to be in the father's place watching as the mother (a part of "A") stirs up the infant "B".

A person may have an anal view of this: the mother who shits or farts but is not there to accept the responsibility, even to acknowledge.

To ACKNOWLEDGE. This is what is missing.

The source, for the child, of the object's intention—the child's idea of the mother who stirs up and is gone—will often be associated with anal functioning, with the backside, the unseen that causes stink and nausea, but is gone.

Sometimes, as with "X", I think she intends for me to know all, to sadistically push it all into her, and we enact this the father-child relation in which the child uses the father's authority to know and structure everything, just because the mother/child relation was so chaotic and unknowable. Such a child could be the daughter of a hysterical mother and a narcissistic father. Such a child could use pseudo stupidity with the father to elicit from him all the answers.

[undated]
"The internalist"

Someone who lives inordinately <u>within</u> the internal world, who eschews interrelating, who converts possible engagements with the other into internal scenarios.

[19/1/89]
"<u>Making a scene</u>"

The person who seems to need to do this and whose sessions are taken up describing "scenes" of life.

[undated]
"Psychosis: to think is to experience."

"Z" often told me that she was afraid of thinking about something because she would then experience what she thought. For example, she would think that the girls at the gym did not like her. As this thought occurred, she would then feel the full effect of the idea: in that moment she was no longer liked.

The process is similar to Freud's theory of the dream, that we experience our thoughts rather than simply thinking them.

Indeed, with "Z", whose hallucinations were auditory, visual and olfactory, her sensational state preceded her ideas or announced a moment of transformation into the dreaming machine that also dreamed her. Her perceptual transformations foretold the metamorphosis of self into the dream, where she would be the "experienced".

The psychotic hysteric is a scene-maker who transforms self into the event, into an event that is larger than self and in which the subject is only a part of the whole.

"Z" would create mad scenes.

By forcing the staff out of their roles she brought dream reality into the world of actuals. She becomes a nightmare and the inevitable period of recovery a kind of extended association: an elaboration.

The analyst (hospital) is the container.

Interestingly, the patient <u>tests</u> whether the analyst or hospital responds violently to the scene, as this then reflects her effort to stamp out dream experiences. But through holding and interpretation the dream event can be put back.

Vivid experience. The screen. Memory. To recall risks going into dream. Recollection is linked to reflection. She cannot do this. Remembered events already augured the dream. If "Z"'s wish to be a heroine is seen as a wish to create scenes, then my first scene with her—in which I feel myself to be Beast and she Beauty—is interesting. As if the psychotic hysteric puts the other into a scene which he must assemble into narrative. By working on my countertransference I transform my condition into an image—Beauty or Beast. (Read Cocteau's play.) Elaboration: the feel of being set up. The analyst <u>transforms</u> self experiences: finally analyzing.

By being childlike the hysteric goes into the child's world of dreams. When being only a subject, with events larger than one, is the ordinary child's state.

Each child is managed by parents, dreams a lot, and such a sense resonates with the dream experience. Childish omnipotence can be seen as a defense against childish impotence.

Anyway, for "Z" to be a child who was to give in to childhood experiencing (of being inside a scene)—see Joyce's *Portrait of an Artist* etc.—that is a dynamic where one is a figure in a group play.

"Z" regards her smells as either good or bad. ("Z" smells her world openly and rather loudly, walking the hallways, in the dining room, etc.) Her mind rewards her or punishes her days after. So she is the object of her mind, which is a higher intelligence treating her as a mother or father treats a child.

Is it possible that the schizophrenic lives as a minimalized presence in a vast dream order, silencing the self, in order to hide?

The hysteric tries to make the scene, to capture the actuals in the theater.

[23/1/89]
"Generational consciousness"

—contemporaries. Who or what are one's contemporaries? A synchronous period of the same era.

—generational phases. Psycho developmental synchronicity. Or, epigenetic synchronicity.

—generational transmission. We have our time. We have a sense of "our time" in history. Three generations contribute to an era: youth, midlife, old age. What do we make? How do we signify ourselves in our time? Our artists speak us. Historical acts.

—when a child becomes a generational specimen. When my stepdaughter's friends ask questions or borrow particular books.

[undated]
"Decontextualization"

When a patient removes the context to isolate and thus render senseless an interpretation.

Children remember what the parents said or did but eliminate the context (i.e. why they did/said).

It is a defense.

[25/1/89]
"The dream to which the analyst has no associations"

Ordinarily when I hear a dream from a patient I have associations. Indeed, the dream evokes ideas in me, etc. But sometimes there are no evocations.

"Q" begins sessions describing the previous day with me when she felt inside a womb, how different it was: how difficult it was to leave, how the outside world seemed abrupt. Interestingly it had been a session when I made no interpretations. Then she reports anger with "R", how "R" opened a letter addressed to her and how she had been unable to be angry. Then she reports a dream. She is in a greengrocers with a toddler of two who seems left with her. She goes up to buy broccoli. The shopkeeper is very slow. She is handed a plant which the woman says is broccoli but it isn't and has flowers growing out of it. The patient protests, the shopkeeper says that it's the only broccoli she has left. Then the toddler disappears and "Q" goes to look for "her". (First time the sex of the child is identified.) Panic, but finds her. The articulate child says she was playing. "Q" tries to queue up to get potatoes, but gives up. Back home she opens her bag to discover potatoes and a cake with a cake knife which leads her to think "Oh no, now I'll have to take these back." She has no idea how this happened.

Now I have no associations to this dream, which I find vivid, clear, even interesting. After some 10 minutes I think that she wants this dream to be hers, to be private. I am not to open this letter before she does.

Indeed after a while I note the dream as a communication about itself, rather than any evocation. I see that the child goes off, unknown to the mother, to get the potatoes and cake, a secret to the dreamer, just as the previous contents (why broccoli, why flower, why green etc.) is not available.

[26/1/89]
"Scene-making: the play's the thing"

Some patients have lived with an impossible scene that drives them crazy. It is this totality that the subject takes in.

The mother and father do not internalize. They evacuate and affect the object. This patient evacuates into the object.

The patient creates scenes. If the analyst asks for associations the patient says "don't be silly. It's meaningless", and goes on to create another scene. The analyst who perhaps has <u>seen</u> <u>something</u> enacted by the patient and does not understand, asks what it means. He is there where the patient was as a child <u>who sees</u> the sight, asks what it means and is batted away.

[29/1/89]
"Generational consciousness"

We could argue that each age aims to comprehend it's historical circumstance. There are "facts" (events like elections, earthquakes etc.) and the views of the period which seek to capture it: to create an internal sense of collective existence. And of course the views do effect historical movement, but accident is evocative and plays upon the internal reality.

[2/2/89]
"Composition as communication"

Composers transmit their message to the next generation.

[2/2/89]
"Self experience in psychoanalysis"

In Freud's metaphor of free association—the passenger on the train—he gives the patient an impossible task, as we cannot report our self in that way. Indeed the train's movement is the unconscious. (Not the sights) and the passenger is, in some respects, surrendered to it. It would be interesting to see if Freud's travel phobia—dread of trains—is partly to do with surrender to unconscious processes, perhaps an offshoot of his not reporting his relation to his mother.

In analysis the patient surrenders to self experiencing and it is the analyst who observes the sights.

So the intrasubjective split in the self, of being subject then reflected upon object—is a split that needs time. The reflected upon is always the past. Yet in analysis, there is simultaneity accomplished in the split, where both patient and analyst experience together. Therefore, there must be a kind of creative interplay of assignments.

Lacan's technique allows for the surprise intrinsic to being a subject and Winnicott's squiggle game also does the same thing.

Freud did not know that the train (of thought) was the important factor, not the sights.

[undated]
"Internal world and transference"

There is a process of transformation and a selection of transference modes for each patient and for perhaps the same person at different times in a session.

There is an inner world of thought which, in speaking it, must be transformed into speech. How did different persons do this? Indeed, may we not argue that if the transformation from thought to language is not good, then the world of thought will suffer as there is no expressive possibility.

Many people think visually and this involves transference to words or paintings etc. What if a person cannot hold an internal image? The borderline probably fragments images and therefore cannot represent the self.

Stravinsky wrote that wherever he was in life the instrument (piano) was the center of his life. For a writer it is the page, for a painter the canvas or studio. I think I am shifting from the consulting room to the writing room. The above suggests that there are windows, objects we choose through which to process our inner life. And we are different, we choose, for example, fundamentally different modes. Each of these modes must be a more important person category then the psychiatrist's nosology. With patients, can it be said that each chooses a different transference window? For example, X is highly visual, Y abstract, Z wordy. Each of these people seems to choose a different transference medium and my countertransference is different: I visualize X's world, have an inner thought association to Y's world, and follow Z's word presentations. Sometimes a patient shifts representational modes. What are the implications of different modes for the transference?

Also they use me—and the analytic object—as different objects: of reverie (when quiet), of analysis. They may do so to gain access to the different parts of the mind which in turn reveal different modes of representation.

Different schools of psychoanalysis may <u>imagine</u> the internal world differently. For example, structural people see the image Freud provided through which they process the patient's communications. Others see a <u>theater of people</u> (Joyce McDougall and the Independents). Kleinians may see the paranoid/schizoid world and the depressive position, or see the breast, the nipple and the infant sucking, or shitting. They possess this internal world. Others see the words as transcripts to be edited (Lacan). Others see the patient's full history, imagine the patient in terms of their past and their stages. Others see the patient-analyst relation, imagining the patient as always representing his relation to the analyst.

Now ideally, these analytic internal worlds are many internal frames of mind, each processing the patient in a different way.

Vera John-Steiner[i] (henceforth VJS) writes "Composing thus emerges as a process which demands—as do other forms of creative endeavor—an ability to synthesize germinal ideas with elaborative structures. The transformation of inner, frequently vague notions, into orchestrated works is powerfully evoked by these composers" (157).[4]

This is a good summary of the evolving of self. We are born with inherited idiom (ideas) which link with elaborating structures. The elaborating structure <u>is</u> the mother, who transforms the infant. There are modes of elaboration:

1. <u>Visual</u>: Through the mother's face and expressive capacity the infant sees himself pictured there. May link up to the autistic, visual element.
2. <u>Auditory</u>: she transforms or elaborates the infant through sound.
3. <u>Kinaesthetic</u>: feeling: a complex act of physically holding and kinesthetically processing so that a total body sense is there. This may link to music, where musical composition moves the whole body (tingling of spine, etc.).
4. <u>Feelings</u>: Conveying of an affective attunement.

Patients seek out the analyst in these modes, they are elaborated by him, they represent the <u>unthought known</u> this way.

It may be that each of us registers internal objects which are endopsychic representations of the form and content of our idiom. If we evolve in person(ality) like we do physically, deriving from a genetic code that directs the body to its articulation, then we may from time to time sense some figuration from within. Some ideas, visual thoughts, etc. may be the first representation of an idiom element. Although I can't see here how this can be distinguished from the mental registration of an ego process.

—an internal object is a pre-representational nucleus of a self state composed of unthought known feelings, somatic sensations, abstract thoughts and so forth. Or, it is also the core

---

[i] Vera John-Steiner, linguist.

of the subject, the source which feels like inner areas or objects that make up one's self. An internal object may move to representation (in affects, fantasies, thoughts, enactments, etc.) or it may not.

Perhaps the visual images in the mind that are essential to creative thought are like the images of/in the dream, in that they become experiences. Or, think of how when I go off to sleep I imagine something. I am looking for something pleasant to enable me to go off to sleep. So it's the search for an image, into which I fall into the loss of consciousness, into a dream event.

Now the images in that moment are phenomenologically different from the images I conjure, searching around beforehand. Likewise a creative idea or image is a total experience: I am inside it as a participant, being told something, a thinking participant. I then try to write my experience as quickly as I can in my notebook, from within the experience, before it is "gone" and seen as only an objectified object.

—the idiom we are evolves through dialectic with actual objects. The ego is the result of this dialectic and is that system of internal organization made up of idiom and the logic of mother and father and other actual objects.

No idiom element can be unless there is an object to release it : to trigger it. There are trigger objects that evoke idiom elements. In our internal world there is a continuous rendezvous between internal trigger objects and idiom potentials. We can feel the birth of a realization, coming about through the ongoing dialectics between an idiom feature and its trigger objects.

That inner process is itself mentally represented through an internal object that is a composite of sensation, image, abstract thought, motor inclination etc. It is the working area of inner transformation of unthought knowledge to representation, a representation of an inner transformational area.

Perhaps the inner image-object will be more verbal, visual, kinaesthetic etc. according to the predominant movement of the idiom potential into speech, visualization, or movement etc.

—When I work on a paper, a topic, I feel that the paper, or the core ideas of the paper, are inside me. I have an iconographic sense of the idea, or its cluster, and I have an inner sense of its status. It can be in early stages and I let it be for long stretches of time, as ideas and observations occur to me and join in with or to the core. Then a period of reading and more adding on and the sense of the idea changes or I feel it is more developed. Ideas, views, seem to spring from some inner core and then I have an even better feel of where I am. Then I feel it is time to write and I know I should be surprised by what emerges even though I know I have it inside me all ready. Now in some ways isn't this an internal object? And isn't its development the nature of thinking itself?

—Internal objects and the Eucharist. The belief that one is taking in the body of Christ (the symbolic body).

[6/2/89]

"Where is the dance?"

We may ask where is the dance of which each of us is capable? When we hear music and dance, we each of us move differently. In a way this captures something of my theory of idiom. If we ask where is the dance we cannot say. It is the true self, which is a potential. Were we to film the complex choreography of infant movements, then film at age four when the child is free dancing, again at 15, then at 25, I think we would see something of a characteristic idiom to a person's dance.

In turn, however, each person will, to some extent, dance differently to each piece of music. Or, some will. They allow themselves to be worked by the object, to be moved into their differences. This is a true self capacity, to be played by the object, which in turn allows the subject to articulate and elaborate the core.

[undated]
"Generational consciousness"

The new generation must do something or create something which the preceding generations do not understand and are offended by.

—How much "play" does a generation have? Is history too close? With no room for play?

[23/2/89 Laguna Beach]
"Categories of experience and representation"

If or when I sit on a surfboard in the sea, and move with the waves, I am not just inside a different experience from when, say, I am reading a novel. I am in a different category of experience, different neurologically (in that a different part of my brain is evoked) and psychically. In the world of re-presentation the category of representation that processes this is probably dance, as it is true as an elaboration of the category, whereas if you write about it, it doesn't exactly stay true to it. Perhaps a good writer can describe surfing in such a way as to evoke self states in the reader that are akin to the surfer's self state. The difference here is that dance represents the process essential to the category experience (of surfing) and writing represents the memory of the self state inside the process.

In any event, there are probably thousands of distinct categories of experience, each with its own laws of effect—or logical effect, or process idiom and each with some analogue of self-representation.

As we meet up with an object, the category paradigm of the unconscious ego—the part of us that will engage the object-process—is evoked. These are therefore different areas of the unconscious ego, each as it were primed to respond to the different categories of experience provided by the object world. (These categories are activated, rehearsed and given technique by the mother's paradigmatic teachings to the child. She goes over things with him and elicits the areas.)

So if I ride in a plane, read a novel, make love, talk to a friend, give a paper, walk on a beach, I am inside experiences that are categories of the mind/self, each of which elicits ego categorical processes as a response. Different parts of the mind/psyche are involved.

To represent each category there are probably quite a few representational categories—

1. gestural: frown, wave of the hands
2. somatic: internal, respiratory
3. verbal, language

4. visual, image
5. dance, body
6. music, sound
7. abstract thinking
8. hands on
9. maths

But each of the above categories can be broken down.
Verbal:

1. prose
2. polemic
3. poetry
4. oral

Therefore the different arts or representational genres process different categories of experience and in an ideal world, each person should be capable of representation of each. Each of us should be a dancer, musician, mathematician etc., because these are different representational systems for processing the inevitable categories of experience.

Now, if we do not have a representational ability then the ego-category elicited by the experience-category will not really function so well and we will close down this part of the self.

We are therefore being elicited all the time by objects, that are categorically different (in a phenomenological way), that have different though distinct and reliable neurological profiles and that have distinct representational genres.

We are, then, more often played by the object, but we are also the player.

Idiom is the basic musical idea of the true self, ego is the conductor who interprets the work, orchestra is the object world that is there to be used in the service of the idea.

[27/2/89 Del Capri Hotel, Los Angeles]
"True self use of the analyst"

A presents a patient who is ruthless in her use of her. In the previous week A thinks of the image of an eraser and tells the patient it's like she is an eraser. This week the patient uses the metaphor.

This can be seen as a true self use of the analyst. The patient evokes an image inside the analyst (force of idiom acting upon the analyst) who thinks it (from unthought known to thought) and presents this as an interpretive object which the patient can use to move: to articulate the self.

[undated]
"Ruthlessness and the nonverbal"

Thank God infants can't talk. Otherwise the mother couldn't possibly love them. It would be like giving birth to an adolescent.

[undated]
"The environment"

There is a subtle hostile reaction to the environment, as the infant comes from within the mother who disappears: to leave him there, in the environment, with no links to it, especially no links from the inside world to the outside (the environment) linking up the true self to the object world.

[18/3/89]
"Thought provocation"

Some people are thought provoking. Or an object is. As in an evocative object. What does it mean if someone provokes others to thought? When do the mother and father do this?

Something (a paper, say) is thought provoking. It moves someone to think.

This can be a positive function period. How can the analyst be thought provoking? Interpretation does this if it frees the analysand to think. The best interpretations are those that are incomplete, or half formed, or half thought out, as the patient can then complete it associatively.

I seek people who are thought provoking. André Green is. Sometimes this provocation is unsettling (un-settling/to settle (word?)).

Sometimes it compels me to ideationally free fall out of linear paths. Which is thinking.

Freud was thought provoking. His whole method was aimed to do this, although he used a moral imperative (speak don't resist) which raised its own resistances. Winnicott used play. What do I use? Each psychoanalyst has a technique designed to provoke the patient to … to what?

[23/3/89]
"Sandler, discussion"

There are internal object relations racial relationships which heed the laws of the internal world and which are constituted out of the process of internalization.

But, to take this internal world (or part of it) and transfer it onto the analyst (not just as an introject, but in person) is to bring this "internal" object into "play" with an "actual" object (or other). Here there will be a <u>mixed experience</u>, as no transference totally appropriates the actual by the internal.

DW called it an "intermediate space".

Further, what is the category or the transfer and its mode? Is an introject transferred more easily (?) than an ego identification?

We <u>convey</u> ourselves. A term better used than to say we transfer ourselves. In transferring internal objects we also convey our self. Thus we do so in language (partly): is the word an object of the transference? What is the function of speech?

There is a poetics of the transference, as each person uses us differently. Cadence. Rhyme. We are the object of this.

[undated]
"Poetics of analysand's free association"

Breaking down of units—paragraphs, sentences, words into:
—Time (duration)
—Stress (relative emphasis)
—Pitch (rising and falling of voice in spoken language and silent reading)
—Tempo (including pauses)
The countertransference as Echo (to Narcissus, the patient).

When the patient chooses a narrative voice to tell us a story, he/she addresses the narrative content as an object to be conveyed as an organized unit to us. When the structure of the session is more of a poetics, we are moved as an object "inside" a content, part of a process.

Is language inclined to become metrical? ("There is this natural tendency of language to assume metrical patterns."[5]) This implies that each analysand will have a poetic idiom: a particular way of speaking. We are moved by such speech, as its used object, but also as the spoken to.

Rhetoric is "the art of persuasion, in the narrow sense the studied ornament of speech, or eloquence" and poetics is "the theory of making and judging poetry" (Princeton, 702).

In his Notebooks Rilke[6] writes: "verses are not, as people imagine, simply feelings (those one has early enough),—they are experiences" (26). And in a way our patients provide us with experiences (not just transferences).

Again Rilke, on the conversion of memories into something else: "For it is not yet the memories themselves. Not till they have turned to blood within us, to glance and gesture, nameless and no longer to be distinguished from ourselves—not till then can it happen that in a most rare hour the first word of a verse arises in their midst and goes forth from them" (27).

So what is this factor that converts the memory to the verse? Unconscious organization.

[27/3/89 Essex, Connecticut]
"The analyst's relation to the analytical method"

Each analyst learns what we might call the method, a body of theory that lies outside the personal creation of the therapist, one to which he has willingly submitted, a theory of method which he conveys to the patient who learns it.

So the method as object is a crucial hidden factor, like two people who meet to discuss music, and for whom the laws of musical composition and structures are an assumed presence.

When the analyst learns the method it is there for him as his object, with its laws, and against which boundary and structure he is free to be subjective: to imagine, invent, play. Subjective invention in analysis, on the analyst's part, that is cut free from the method is valueless subjectivity.

Of course, the method is continuously predictable by patient and analyst. Some interpretations seem to come naturally out of the method—such as transference interpretations—and

254

patients will complain: "I just knew you would say that." But this complaint is essential affective relief at the continual presence of the analyst and the method. It is the presence of the ordinary, indeed even the limited (as the psychological method has clear limits) but this factor checks and supports the freedom of unconscious thought which otherwise by virtue of its nature knows no limit.

[undated]
"Patients create environments"

Is not fiction a good example of an internal world? With people represented, but also with certain structures that generate types and with atmosphere as well.

Patients create environments.

They transfer objects, act on us, but also there is the transfer of rhetoric, of soma, of the imaginary, the symbolic, and so forth.

Betty Joseph does not convey these particular categories of transfer: rhetoric, visions, ways of hearing, somatics, and so on. Theory is important but she is too content to process these patients according to the Klein model.

I'm not sure that the internal world is only a world of represented objects and selves: a ghost world. Or that the unconscious phantasies are the only forms of thought. There is an unconscious form of thinking that never gets to the level of representation, but perhaps to the level of implication, of implied selves, others etc.

—The analyst through transference interpretation links patient to analyst, moves the discourse from the patient's relation to narrative objects to the actual other, opening a pathway to or into the other. Kind of paving the avenue of projective identification.

[undated]
"Psychical genera"

If I think of experiences in my life that assumed their true value later—upon remembering—then I can list the following:

1. Farming in Wiliamsburg,[ii] the setting, cottage, as a place I chose for myself at the time that was fortuitous and uncannily accurate. Living this experience amounted to the <u>construction</u> of a generative psychic structure, which in later years in life, would nourish me.
2. Erikson's[iii] comment: "well young man, it's a long life and you take your chances."[7]
3. Solnit[iv] interview when I tried to describe my life.[8] The interview became a session and I "confessed" to thinking I could not do child psychoanalysis because of my hate or imagined hate of a 6-to 8-year-old boy. This scene, so powerful, recurred for years as

---

[ii] A small town in Massachusetts where I farmed in 1971–1972.
[iii] Erik Erikson, German-American psychoanalyst.
[iv] Albert J. Solnit, American psychiatrist.

I gradually realized the boy was the loathed part of myself, that speaking it to the father whilst in a strained relation to my wife (mother) was amazingly akin to a potential moment <u>nearly</u> lived out with my father, but never so. A screen memory in the making.

4. The Hindemith Viola Sonata or Mahler Symphony Two, which I would hear again and again and play on record.
5. The birth of my son which generated, on reflection, an entire new way of thinking of life.
6. Of Sue's running down the stairs at Roger's house to greet me, with an exuberance, athleticism, joy, love, that was deeply nourishing.
7. The dream of the blood stained coat:[9] somewhere between a trauma and a genera, though ultimately generative.
8. The yoga session[v] and the other's handling of my body as the object of care and skin—ego <u>knowing</u>. Of pressure applied and somatic response; of pain discovered; of absences of pain and thus preserves of potential for body movement: all unknown to me. And the memory of this, as a general.

And of course in analysis, there are moments equivalent to the above, but perhaps many remain unconscious.

Genera are internal sources of psychic nourishment, as trauma is a source of psychic pain.

Webster: "genera" is the plural of "genus" which broadly means to be beget: genera Latin, birth, origin, race, (G) for genos: race; to be born.

So psychical genera are origins, moments out of which we create, produce, or give birth to our own meaning.

[undated]
"Representation"

Vygotsky says of inner speech that "a single word is so saturated with sense that many words would be required to explain it in external speech."[10] "Inner speech" is given to "heavy predication" and "semantic shorthand". Consider this in terms of transference: how to transfer the nature of internal speech to external speech? An impossible transfer? Is inner speech close to poetics? Must be. Poetry is an effort to put the nature of inner speech into external representation and free association is Freud's effort to externalize his self analysis.

[1/5/89]
"Cutting"

Monique Wittig "… J/e is the symbol of the lived, rending experience which is *m/y* writing, of this cutting in two which throughout literature is the exercise of a language which does not constitute **m/e** as subject."[11]

—is cutting a rending? A dividing? To divide oneself on the surfaces of the body?

---

[v] First yoga session, in Stockbridge Ma., when instructor had us lie on our backs and "love your body".

—Who cuts? Whose hand makes the cut?

—Who is watching the cutting of the body? A division of the subject who does and the subject who watches.

Wittig: "The desire to bring the real body violently to life in the words of the book …" (10).

—Is it not possible that this is also an aim of cutting, to bring the woman's body to violent light, as violated, further violated as a displacement, this opening, vagina, that never gets talked about? The blood that flows secretly, the underground rivers of blood, emptied in secrecy and silence.

Wittig "'m/y' skin bristles and becomes covered with stains" (16).

—to stain, to paint. Entomology of stain?

Wittig page 21:

—drop of blood

—red: primary color, coming from inside

—turning black in drying stains: here to dry on the surface of the body.

—"your most precious blood": i.e. what is precious?

Wittig (see page 28). Woman sees self as container of fluids. (Ferenczi: the lost sea?).

Wittig (p. 30): vagina as walls, as entrance. And entering into the cut: the forbidden entrance. Entrance flowing with blood/death. Entrance that shocks men, that covers the eyes. Cuts as eyes.

—there is something about being the physical container, of having to hold, of holding con-fusion.

Wittig (p. 37) odor: the cut is odorless. Olfactorily inoffensive. To be sutured. For the hospital. For the doctor. Not for the man.

—playing with the depths on the surface. A cut is on the surface. A sign. (Signifier?) It speaks this refusal to get to the depths. It does not admit to the interior. It is a cul de sac. A false vagina.

—a woman can't see her own vagina. She would have to use a mirror to do so. A lot therefore never see it. A new mirror stage. The cut is invisible. The inside of this skin is a different color inside.

See: virginity and hymen.

—referring back to the entry of October 87: the patient cuts partly because she does not believe the therapist knows, although he is meant to know. There is a question posed here at the level of heterosexual intimacy. "Do you know I am bleeding?" i.e.: "also do you know me well enough to know I am bleeding?" This question will be answered in the affirmative by a lover or husband who knows by the early signs of pain, of change of skin color (more pale), of puffiness, of breast tenderness: all before the blood. So, do you know me before the blood, or only after, when I bleed, smell, soil, etc: i.e. "do you leave intimacy up to the negative?"

The patient who cuts does not believe she is known. But she does share her secret with the analyst.

Who or how can bleeding be stopped? If we stay with intimacy, it can be stopped by impregnation, to allow the woman to form an internal object (fetus) which she can deliver whole—not as desiccated menstrual fluid—to the world. "If you analysts love me, you will know to penetrate me, to give me the seeds of form."

If the analyst does not know, or interprets it only as relief, (i.e. superego), then he does not know, and the patient assumes he is shocked, unable to bear the sight of the vagina.

Question. How does the psychoanalyst mirror the vagina? The Lacanian baby—(*le corps morcelé*)—looks into the mirror and there finds unity, but the other mirror stage, where the woman does not wish to look, returns her to the *le corps morcelé*, not a mirror reflecting integration, but the opposite. The cut therefore is a virginal blood, a pure/purifying vagina, that does not mirror the other cut.

Question. What goes wrong when a woman cuts? Specifically, what sets it off? Who is properly prepared for the period?

[undated]
"The psychic status of the body politic"

How do we, historically, "psychicalize" our political structures?

Beirut, a permanently divided terroristic small group conflict. This scene, is internalized by the modern man, as was the scene of mass nuclear annihilation. See for example those who saw World War One as soccer. So, what were the psychic scenes for each major historic period? particularly the Greeks, Romans, Medievals (i.e. feudal structure). See Freud's world, Anna Freud, Hartmann etc.

But how <u>do</u> we psychically work the body politic? What do we <u>do</u> with this? As these scenes organize violence for us, what do the structures imply about psychic life?

[29/5/89]
"The evocative object, orders of experience, categories of representation"

After my "self experiencing" chapter, what should follow is a second chapter in which I identify different types of evocative objects (a poem, painting, sonata) each of which involves a different sense (sight, sound, touch) or combination of senses. Then the question is, if I decide to represent such evocative experiences, how do I represent these orders? I can visualize, dance (move my body), sing (musicalize), poeticize, narrate, eroticize.

1. I can hear sounds and make sounds
2. I can be excited erotically and I can represent erotic states
3. I can read poetry and I can write it

Is it possible to say that I can (in response to an object) have an evoked abstraction; that is a thought brought about by an object? If so, if I wish to represent this how do I do it?

Also, some evoked states will not be represented in the same mode of evocation. That is, I may choose to describe in language what I have heard rather than sing it and so forth. But think of Beethoven. He heard the 9th but he could never have sung it. What he could do was to write it down in musical language, which is <u>sound evoking</u>, rather than linguistic (word evoking).

So there are pleasures, there are phenomena which are:

1. visually evocative
2. sound evocative
3. language evocative
4. body evocative

So, in the clinical situation, specifically in the transference–countertransference, we may ask in what (through what) categories of representation does a patient convey himself and in what categories does an analyst experience him?

Bear in mind cross modality. A patient speaks, but I experience them somatically (instinctually), bodily (I look at myself or them), I associate (words), I hear the poetics of speech (poetics), I follow the meaning (abstraction), I have feelings evoked, etc.

What is the specific order? How do we convey affects? Bring them about? What are the affective evocative objects? I think music is, so is poetry. Perhaps all orders have affective potential.

Now, how do I receive, transform (modally) and communicate back to the patient?

1. Evocation (patient affects me)
2. Reception
3. Transformation
4. Communication
   A. The patient plays upon the psychoanalyst.
   B. Some patients are multiply and richly evocative: others are not.
   C. Psychoanalyst's communication must be multi-modal, or at least will be, although the "word mode" is the sought for. Others: metaphor, affective resonance, identificational empathy etc.
   D. Psychoanalysis and the psychoanalyst should be evocative. How is this accomplished? Why should an analyst aim to do this? What is the purpose of this? Pitfalls?
   E. The word order (symbolic?), somatic order (is there something like instinctual evocation: i.e. oral, anal, genital representation?), visual order (metaphor, picturing, dreams).
   F. We should aim for some multi modal dialectic, a movement of orders, each processing what it can of phenomena in its own way (the unconscious, unthought known), and giving over to or collaborating with other orders, as indeed, the psychoanalyst must work in different orders, move from one to another (in his receptive capacity) and assist the patient's categorical dialectic: the movement of self experiencing.

[undated]
"Representation"

Just as each of us lives within traditional forms (of speech, gesture, manner) do we not also aim to create new forms for ourselves? New manners. New speech idioms. If I create words do I not do so in order to speak something new?

So, do not our patients also seek new forms, or the means to new forms?

A turn of phrase, and affect, a gesture, a description may be new, a new form, or evidence of a new form.

John Russell on Matisse. "He tested the possible modes of painting, one by one, against his own needs and his own potentialities"[12] (p. 51). This could be said of all of us, that in our lives we test out the form potential of an object, its potential to serve our expressive needs. So too with patients, who test us out to see what in us, at any moment, is of use. Do we notice this?

Of Matisse, Russell says "each of his paintings … was … a 'condensation' of experience, not an imitation of it" (56). How interesting, because our patients certainly also condense experience into the hour. It is a representational place for the conveyance of self, a condensation.

Russell says that before Friedrich's "The frozen sea", paintings etc. were allegories, they told a familiar story, but with this symbol no story is told. The Klein group's repeated story of the mother/child, transferred to the here and now, is allegory: it will tell the analysand a familiar story. Freud's view, at least of free association, is different. It is a theory of the symbolic: of the true moment of here and now in which the words refer to no other place than the moment. The analyst, who thematizes the patient's session (into the allegory of Klein or reconstruction etc.) works against the symbolic and against what Freud set free in the Freudian method.

[undated]
"Representation"

Think of the polyvalence of forms, in personal being and in uses of cultural objects, of layerings, or echoings, or intersectionings that make some lived lives more complex, rich, etc. than others. Psychic works.

We work on our realities. If we are formally receptive we render our object world, we are part of a polyvalent morphogenic movement through culture and history.

See Russell (p. 117) on differences between Picasso and Gris: that Picasso layers in a more complex way. It's akin to condensation theory of Freud, but to which we might add that such a capacity for greater complexity of condensation reflects an ego ability.

Russell says of Picasso's "Guitar" (1913) (p. 117) that it is "a storehouse of allusions". Now this is a strength. Perhaps the dream suggests this strength: to amplify life by containing a multitude of allusions, but to this I would add that such ability probably rests on the person's range of experiential categories and its usefulness in terms of formal representations.

Freud's hysterics were "storehouses of allusions" in contrast to narcissistic characters many of whom are minimalists.

Yet each person dreams and it is the source of allusion etc.

Russell (p. 118) calls P's paintings "a play-structure as subtle and as complex as can be found in art".

So too is an analysis. Patients speak to us in a kind of cubist synthesis of notional representations. Parts of reality are represented. Parts of body gestures (suggestive of a larger act), parts of feelings, of poetry, of music, of dreams etc., and this storehouse of allusion moves us as we mediate and are moved to occasional interpretation. But aren't we part of a <u>morphogenesis à</u> <u>deux</u>? In which we move together?

[10/6/89]
[untitled]

In *The Interpretation of Dreams* Freud says dreams think in images, sounds, ideas, thoughts, words etc., and I suppose free association is also a distinguishable movement: ideas, images, auditory images etc. Now how do these forms of differing free associations move in the interpersonal field? And, in dream or interpretation, what is the unconscious reason for modal choice or categorical choice (visual, ideational etc.)? I think each mode is a psychic area open to a different category of experience and available to a different logic of expressive representation.

Psychic life is "composed" of formal categorical possibilities. Health is the maintenance and enhancement of psychic categories.

What does the analyst do (categorically) to meet (or mediate) the orders? I think if I speak in visual metaphor, auditory metaphor, or if I represent somatic states (in metaphor a "yuck") or body movement "I think you want to run away" I give categorical representation to psychic areas of experiencing.

[12/6/89]
"—continued"

Let's imagine a patient is resisting something: anything. Call it X. I can use metaphors, each of which expresses a different form of self experience and which also may serve as an open door for further expression. So to the metaphors:

1. "You feel like running away"
   —refers to movement of the self: motoric.
2. "You cannot stomach it?"
   —refers to somatic processing.
3. "It is hard to swallow"
   —again to somatic, but not even inside yet.
4. "You can't bear it"
   —refers to bodily caring.
5. "you don't want to hear about it"
   —auditory.
6. "You can't imagine it"
   —visual.
7. "You don't want to think about it"
   —abstract.
8. "You don't know what to say about it"
   —verbal/speech.

9. "You seem uncomfortable or distressed by it"
—affective.

Consider the relation here. If I say it is hard to hear, this implies the patient is blocking at that level. If I say it's hard to imagine I accept they have heard it. If I say it's hard to speak, I accept they have heard and have imagined.

What does it mean if my metaphors are somatic?

Each of us has experiences that differ intrinsically according to the evocative object. To hear Bruckner's 8th symphony is a different experience from hearing a popular song. So even at the level of the senses—in this case hearing—there are differences between types of experience. It's a different self experience to hear a fire alarm, the sound of an audience applauding, the sound of a child crying.

How do such differing self experiences get represented (re-presented)? Speech is the obvious mediation: "I heard Bruckner's 8th, my child cried, etc." And each type of experience may evoke a type of empathy in the other.

Assuming the analyst speaks up, what he says may be categorically essential. For example:

Patient: "I heard Bruckner's 8th."

Analyst: "Um … inspiring?"

Patient: "Yes!"

Patient: "My child was crying."

Analyst: "Distressing?"

Patient: " Yes."

"Inspiring" or "distressing" are categorically resonant with and re-presentationally expressive of the patient's self state. Perhaps all of the above is a form of empathy, a putting of oneself into true place, via category resonance.

In theory the use of metaphor or categorical residence is a door opening for idiom articulation. It allows continued movement. It is the means, or one means, of assisting with free association.

[18/6/89 Arild, Sweden]
"Analytical sensing"

The different orders of representation: musical (auditory, sound), written, motoric, etc. If a poet visits Arild he writes it. The musician composes it, the dancer choreographs it, the painter paints it, but only the poet could name it and therefore identify it.

Music re-presents feelings. Choreography: the body's movements.

As a psychoanalyst I can see the body and sense pain. This sensing has to do with my receptive capacity. So, for orders of representation there must be capacities of reception and categories of re-presentation.

I must be able to hear and see, but also sense. What does it mean to sense?

This links up to intuition. The etymology of in-tuit.

262

So, if the above people visit Arild, and represent Arild, each does it in his own order. Really, only writing can directly identify it although the visual could. Musical and dance could not.

But if we know the artists and we ask who painted, wrote, composed, choreographed this, the represeneters could be identified.

Psychoanalysts are metaphorists. If I <u>sense</u> (or know) a patient is speaking from a certain category, I will speak from the terms of that order, or use them, which I presume evokes ego memories true of the person's psychic content. So if I say "you wish to jump from that" I speak to body movements and body experience (and memory); if I say "you cannot hear of such a thing" I speak to the order of hearing and sound.

[19/6/89 Arild]
"Sense of humor"

What is this sense?

This is a psychic capacity. Some people have it. Others do not.

Why is it linked to the senses?

Senses relate to the reception, transmission (organically), and re-presentation (motorically, thoughtfully) of external reality, but psychic senses refer to the processing of internally derived formations of representation, of course, often in response to reality, but often <u>removed</u> from any interpersonal occasion, such as with the dream.

The sense of humour enables one to laugh, to joke. Psychic senses are probably enablers.

Related to the above is <u>a sense of play</u>.

Sense of pleasure. He or she has a sense of pleasure.

Insight. He or she is insightful. Sense of perception. Aren't these psychical senses?

The analyst works to develop these senses (among others) and does so through production of generatives; paradigms that open up increased sense capacity.

[6/7/89]
"Intensity and the formation of a 'generative'"

If I think of that set of interpretations worked on with a patient then we are in a period of intense interpretive work of basic evolved strategies, like paradigms that each person lives by. Each analysis has moments of intense effectiveness, like a screen memory, except its opposite: when all the essential factors (in material, transference, words, affects, etc.) are involved. My interpreting is like a dialectical encounter, a paradigm synthesis not intended to effect immediate change but to create <u>a generative</u>, a seed that will be effective when released through subsequent experience.

I think analysts know when they are forming a generative. There is a particular intensity to it. Then the generative goes to the system unconscious, where it shall—as a structure—stay until called into consciousness by experience.

[undated]
"The therapeutic effectiveness of the false self"

M's patient puts a stinky toy hippopotamus on her lap each session. She finds this offensive and her true response is repulsion. I say, however, that often we must be false with patients. She must appear to accept it. The paradox is that false self allows time to pass, creates a potential space for the hated object to become an object of affection and no longer repellent. The patient is presenting her infant self and seeking maternal instinctive love. All mothers love the smell of their babies and small children, including the shit. But we do not feel the same about someone else's child. M's patient's mother rejected her body self and she seeks the analyst's rejection (by testing her) but hopes to find an experience symbolically equivalent to maternal instinctual love, which means the absence of repulsion. The use of false self by analysts allows for an illusion of maternal love, out of which paradoxically enough something like the absence of repulsion (which equals instinctual love) does emerge.

[7/7/ 89]
"Cutting"

X told me that when she cut herself she found it was wonderful, because she enjoyed looking after the wound: running it under water, putting cream on it, bandaging it. It was a kind of body love. This she did not get from her mother, and she does not allow for the self to be "healed" by dependent relation upon the other.

[7/7/89]
"Anorexia"

G's anorexia:

1. reduces the body's energy so depressive decathexis ensues.
2. removes him from the gender issue: he is no longer mother/father but neither.
3. pits the mind against the body, as mind says "do this" but body is too weak to follow orders.
4. this follows on from his fury over the mother and father who say "what can we do to interest you?" He walks London, trying to find an object of interest, but he is "bored" by it all. This boredom is his rebellious reply to the part of him that says "now let's go see a bookstore": so he defeats himself.
5. To eat or not to eat, to vomit up food, is to return to a pure self, which is the self with nothing in it: no internalised representations of the outside world. It is a way of saying "go to hell". I shall deal with all of you by purifying myself.

[10/7/89]
"From reality to imagination"

Infants and children process reality thoughtlessly, but in their imaginative life (play, daydream, creations) begin to think their reality. In the adult to imagine may well be to think one's prior realities.

Indeed it may well be that imagining the womb, or birth (cf. Gestalt etc.) is indeed as valid a subjective way of remembering it or thinking it as can be.

[10/7/89]
"From internal reality to unreality"

X's affairs (for example J): he says it was all "a bit unreal". I suggest that for him to matriculate his internal world of wish and need and so forth he must find an actuality that is unreal, because it is here—in an unreality—that he can enact his internal world. Such a person, then, seeks places and events that are fundamentally outside their ordinary life (i.e. reality). The unreal place has a higher structural evocative effect, as it were, the arrival of the screen with a projector. For X he is "in and out" of the unreal before the effects of grief and depression and other affects. It is to be pure dream life "in" everyday life. The loss must be carried by the other.

[19/07/89 TWA 761]
"Orders of representation"

Differentiate between the dynamics of verbal and visual thought.
 —What are the differences?
 —How did the "dynamics vary"?
 Einstein did not think in words.
 —What is an "element" in thought?
 —This raises the question: what is thought?
 —there are different orders of transformation
 —there is an individual skill to each mind
 —in the re-presentation of experience
 —what is a movement idea?
 The body thinks
 —children
 —Some recall past events by body cue: such as posture.
 —How does one think through the body?
 "Visual"
 —An image is a construction.
 Poet and sense impressions he never forgets.
 —what is a sense impression?
 —is there a sensory representation as in a physical feeling state?
 —such a physical feeling state would differ from a feeling state unaccompanied by physical sensation.
 Einstein's "clear images" are the "constituent forms of his thought" according to Vera John-Steiner (VJS, 28) who claims that "at a certain stage of his work were expanded and verified through the use of mathematics".

—So what are the <u>constituent forms</u>?

—how do they get transformed into a representational order, such as math?

—do the patient/analyst work on the creating of such a form, through associations, which then bursts or explodes into multiple representational categories? For example X and I are constructing, over a long period of time, a constituent form of meaning, which then gets transformed into meanings.

—what are the dynamics of internal verbalization?

—what is its mediative function in the here and now of experiencing? For example, could it be an alpha process, <u>wording experience into psychic reality</u>, first/or second stage of transformation?

—images also last longer than words. There is a sort of time lag. One can fruitfully dwell upon a single image (it is worth a thousand words) but one cannot dwell on a word or sentence like this.

—what does it mean when I "fundamentally" cease to speak to myself about a patient: to imagine something?

—then there are <u>silent blanknesses</u> or "blank silences" of no verbalization or imagination, when I am nowhere. Such no "wheres" are part of this process.

There are preferred modes of thought for each person, to be found from prevalent activities in childhood.

—where? What are my preferred modes of thought?

—what activities in my childhood were a part of it?

—how do my patients vary?

—how do different psychoanalytical theories reflect this, insofar as they may be operating from different modes of thought: for example Klein the visual, Lacan the verbal?

The visual: Images are *fast*, ephemeral, displaceable.

—this is crucial!

—pictures are highly variable: easily changed, much more internally mutable than words.

—therefore some unconscious thoughts are more quickly represented than others in words.

—the fact is, words can be spoken, while pictures cannot be! Words like violins can be carried around by us and played to the other image. Images are pianos!

If a patient is in a visual mode of self experiencing and the analyst asks what is on his mind, it can be very difficult to speak this. But if a patient is talking to himself, or wording experience, and the analyst asks what he is thinking, it is not so difficult.

Visual grammar (of film)

Films fragment time—in or through the inherent things in our mind.

—interestingly, this "fracturing of time" as the documentary film maker George Stoney[13] put it, is a function of visual memory, of inner "clippings".

—where is this appreciation of the visual in Freud? In the dream book he ultimately converted visual to verbal, thus crossing modes, or erasing one mode entirely.

—what are the differences between inner and external speech?

Music:

Aaron Copland calls it "the language of emotion".[14]

So we have:

1. images
2. words
3. emotions

To which we may add

4. sensation memories
5. thoughts. A musical idea arrives before it has been thought.

—a good metaphor for my idea of ourselves as idiom, in that we do not really know ourselves until we take form through experiences, and then we "see" ourselves for a moment.

　　—This seems to me an entirely different order of representation than words or images.

　　—what are the forms of representation?

　　—images

　　—words

　　—musical sounds

　　—body gesture or movement

　　—what about a building, or a toaster or a sculpture? Aren't they realized thoughts? Or plans?

Music: Transformations are an important part of music. As Bernstein claims, that musical motives correspond to noun phrases, chords to

signifiers, verbs akin to rhythm.

　　—To sing or make music, one must transfer sound so it performs certain differing functions.

　　—Where in analysis (or life) can one be said to be sounding off according to the laws of music, where ... if one is not composing or singing. Poetry may be an intermediate form between words and music, and at the same time with an affinity to images, and to sensation creation.

　　Choreography.

　　—Movement is thinking. Dancers often try out differing moves and assemble a work together.

　　—Interestingly this form of representation depends on the use of the other's alive body, and the effort to convey one's idea to the other's body. It seems like a kind of maternal knowledge, like the mother's arrangements with her infant, moving against, with, and in negotiation with one another.

　　—Vera John-Steiner cites John Martin on movement: "Movement, then, in and of itself is a medium of transference of an aesthetic and emotional concept from the consciousness of one individual to another" (VJS, 159).

　　—so, it uses an unthought knowledge we all have within ourselves, both of our movements and "dancing" with the other!

　　—in analytical hours, patients do move. They gesture. Change posture. And within the choreograph ritual dance—we could call it "on the couch in silence, in speech, with feeling and meaning" the patient speaks to us! Of course he also walks into the room and departs. How about a dance sequence called: from sitting in the waiting room to the analyst's greeting, walking to the consulting room together, taking separate places together,—"having" a session, getting up off the couch and out of the chair together and parting. This is the dance that each analyst and patient dance differently. It is a form of representation.

—dancers often dance to music and create an image. They move well between modes, a bit like poets.

—emotional images do the evoking. So movement is evoked by an internal emotional image. The intellectual process is a kind of secondary elaboration.

Dance movements are "evocative symbols" that leave part of the interpretation to the audience. So.

There are representations and evocations. Some forms re-present; others seem to evoke.

Intuition (etymology)?

Vera John-Steiner cites the physicist John Howarth: "Intuitive solution of problems is important. Essentially it is finding the answer to a problem before you have solved it" (VJS, 183).

Now.

Intuition functions in psychoanalysis. We suddenly see something <u>before</u> working it through or solving it.

[24/7/89 Big Sur]
"Representation"

The visual object world is already set up for the perceiver, whereas the verbal is not. If I look at a room of people, it is visually already in front of me, organized. The verbal elements are not there; or, if all the people "spoke" themselves it would be difficult.

Private world of verbalization and the public of visual.

Representational jump to the verbal.

Images are more memorable than words. Is the storage different?

Do different sensory inputs (other than cognitive/representational) have different mnemic strategies?

Visual thinking is less mediated than verbal thinking.

Visual representation always suggests a point of view

—the subject is looking, but the verbal world does not immediately locate the speaker's relation to the object.

Auditory: the crucial function of being able to hear behind you. Deaf people are more paranoid.

Olfactory mode: an angry father who evokes his child's olfactory sense through the father's anger.

Communication. Commune.

To hear voices, the hallucinate is "inside" or closer. Whereas the visual is not so close.

Fetuses response to the sound of the mother. After birth they will respond to the pre-birth sound.

Fetus hears sound but does not know how or where the sound is coming from. In auditory hallucination one does not know where the voice is coming from. But if you see a lion or tarantula you see it and you have a location. If someone calls your name in a crowd and you look, there is no evidence of speech, whereas if you look after someone has <u>waved</u>, there is a kind of gestural aftermath.

Auditory hallucination: hard to know the location of the speaker. Where from and who from?

If a patient is speaking to you in abstract terms (verbal) patient and analyst are more likely to lose their place vis-à-vis one another, whereas the patient who visualizes creates a scene that we "see" and they differentiate themselves more clearly.

We can follow a patient who uses images.

Proprioceptive.

Somaesthetic.[vi] Somatize

Kinesthetic

Think of the above from a countertransference perspective:

I feel

I hear

I imagine

I word

I idea (ideation)

I proprioceive

I somatize

I smell

I see

[28/7/89 Comstock Hotel LA]
"The structure of interpretation"

It is not the <u>content</u> of an interpretation which is so effective, but its <u>structure</u>. That is, it bears a psychic structure that will process mental life differently. "You are depressed because your esteem is low due to your unconscious hate of your father" is an interpretation, but it is also a factor in the formation of a psychic structure: the subject's "use" of the internal and actual father. Analysts use interpretation to work and work on the patient's psychic structures.

[15/8/89 LA]
"The oddity of the analytic relation"

We do not consider the strangeness of the relationship; also, how though strange, is also so easy and familiar. One person, prone, talking at length to the other who listens with the profound intent of understanding. It is more like the attempted externalization of an interesting internalized intrapsychic dialogue than the realization of a relationship. When the patient feels

---

[vi] Neologism: the soma as aesthetic organizer.

understood is this so pleasing because <u>one</u> of his voices (places, narrative positions) is confirmed; only to be displaced by other voices.

The fundamental privacy of intrapsychic selvings[vii] is given <u>audience</u>.

[undated]
"The parts of the self"

Poets feel the multiplicity of self. What do we mean by <u>the parts</u> of the self? By what authority do we usually feel <u>one</u>? (i.e. instead of many?)

"Introjection" suggests we contain many others.

Perhaps the new interest in "multiple personalities" simply expresses the interest in the fragmented self.

[15/9/89 TWA 760]
"Representation"

"For many years poetry has been becoming more a vehicle of consciousness than of representation": Eugenio Montale (in Gibbons, p. 67).[15]

—A fascinating quote which suggests that some modes of expression are used to promote (elicit) the unconscious contents. They are not, so much, used to represent something already thought out.

—Hence, in terms of considering the unthought known, there are perhaps modes of representation (or should I say expression) that are selected for differing unconscious contents.

—the above raises the question of what is doing the representing? Think of unconscious representation for example.

[16/9/89]
"Representation"

Thiher[16] writes of the iconicity of language, to de-pict, scenes, and of Flaubert's MB: "the rhetoric of presentation turns on a constant attempt to add indices of explicit visualization to the description" (Thiher, 3). There is a "constant act of viewing" as if there were a "third person of objective consciousness" (3).

—with any given patient, what is the rhetoric of presentation? Where do they situate us, the viewer?

—what place are we given in the seeing of the object?

Thiher says Joseph Frank writes of a "spatialized form" and T says Flaubert's text is crissed-crossed "with a network of observation posts from which 'one' looks at characters looking at characters who in turn become observation points from which the world is viewed" (TH, 4).

—patients present "characters": i.e. describe events in which other people served as new or different ways of seeing.

[vii] Neologism: the creation of different self states.

270

—when I read a book and there are different characters, do I give each of these persons a different internal (to me) voice? When I have heard someone speak, like Bob Hass, when I read his poetry, I often hear it through him. This is a form of re-presentation. What could it be called?

—Thiher on Wittgenstein says that W in *On Certainty* argued that we live by many presuppositions taken as known in order to live (see, for example, CB on illusion of the understanding) and further that our language games are precognitive, we may only "know" them by use, although we never truly know them. This may well accord with my unthought known, which perhaps can be linked to Lacan's subject who "knows" but doesn't know. The Symbolic out of which he is constituted.

—Thiher on Heidegger: "the past would have being as tradition when it is thought as a past in the present; as *presence*, it would be" (38). Thus, the <u>presence</u> of the past period or, the past as its presence in the subject. It has a presence. It exists in the present. So any patient, at times, conveys the presence of the past. This is very different from speaking about the past, because what is important is the <u>past's structure as a presence</u>.

—Heidegger does not think we can communicate authentically with the other. I agree. Our truest profession is what we do, or, who—in our characters—we are, not what we say. Yet how do we assess this clinically? Isn't it through the use of the analyst object? It is <u>there</u> that we are participant in the essence of the subject's idiom, not as a result, per se, of what he says to us.

—The freedom of countertransference, its "play", rests within the laws of analytic practice. I can play freely because I am ultimately constrained by my obligation to collect meaning toward the making of an interpretation in which I believe and to be given to the patient in a form that will be of psychic use.

—How do we assess an acoustically delivered visual image, such as "the boat sank"? An image of a sinking boat comes to mind. Or could do. But the image potential may be displaced in time (very short time) by what is uttered next. "The boat sank, or so it seemed to the bank manager, after the run on his bank's deposits."

The subsequent signifiers link quickly as space displaces picturings, indeed, the pictures become metaphors on the way to concepts. Time and context seem to be conditions necessary, then, for the survival of an acoustic image.

—I think that when we speak, write, paint, we intend (intention versus delivery) to save something, but the act and mode of expression changes in and through <u>itself</u> what we intended. We shall always misspeak ourselves. What we say and what we intend are always different. Lacan would, I suppose, argue that this is due to the unconscious which becomes knowable only through utterance.

[19/8/89]
"The evocative field"

Each of us lives life using objects. In turn we are played upon by them. An evocative field is an area of engagement with a type or class of objects. For example, if I am with Sacha, I am with a child. Being with a child is an evocative field.

Other evocative fields might be work in the garden, listening to music, reading, etc.

The above are classes of experiences, biased by the specific nature of experience to be had between the subject and the object. But there are no formal properties to an evocative field, as each subject's idiom will engage the field differently (and therefore define it), and each field, in turn will play the subject differently.

Evocatives.

[19/8/89]
"Representation"

Assume for a moment that our accounts of our past have nothing to do with it; they are only inventions. The past, however, is still an object of reflective discourse. We seek to embody it in language. We may fail, giving it many bodies. The point is not whether we capture it, represent it as a whole, because we cannot do this with the present. Indeed at any moment, or if we take a day, it is "composed" of many different states. Tomorrow, if I recollect today, I may link to a part of it that is not totally accurate (because this is an impossibility), but one self state will probably link with a previous self state in a synchrony of memory.

—Secondly, to think of the past (to re-collect) is a different mental act from when I:

—imagine

—foretell

—account for the present

So, the past, the present and the future, are mental areas or domains (epistemological catalysts) that sponsor mental work specific to that domain. Mental work of a kind is activated in relation to the mental area. So it is psychically essential to think of the past, the present, the future.

[undated]
"Genera"

There must be a certain intrapsychic openness to the experience of objects (or to experience) so that experience can become generative. By generative I mean elaborative.

In Berkeley I see the art exhibit of candles against the wall. In distinction from my other experiences I "know" this is important, or of a different weight from other experiences. But it is not an epiphanic moment, it does not release me into immediate association. It is a potential generative, and must wait for time to pass, until later something triggers it to return to consciousness now linked to many associations. It would then join the class of genera.

—some people have plenty of experiences, but no genera.

—to become a generative an experience must be psychically acted upon to release elaboratives.

—Or, if there is preconscious receptiveness, allowing the work of evocation to take place, then experiencings of evocative objects (actuals that evoke internals) will generate further elaboration of the analyst's capacity for experiencing. That is, the subject will elaborate the initial experience with after experiencings that are psychologically elaborative.

—What is elaborated? Both an understanding or grasp of the integrity of the object and the personality experience potential of the subject, or the idiom of the subject.

—Our idiom comes into being by being released to being through experiencings, when such experiencings are out of generatives.

[19/8/89]
"Inner speech"

It is possible that inner speech is more infantile than spoken speech. In that like the infant or child we talk to ourselves in cryptic part sentences, not aiming to communicate and not needing a reply. Piaget would call it egocentric.

So, the analysand who free associates may be able to represent inner speech precisely because the analyst is quiet, thus supporting the analysand's need not to have the free associations taken as communication, but instead as expressed samples of inner life.

Also how the child uses (and desires) entirely different modes of representation: verbal, relational, ideational, hallucinatory, etc.

Inner speech is similar. We do not only think to ourselves, we search for expressive categories, moving in an endless sliding of differing signifiers: auditory, visual, verbal, ideational etc. Perhaps each of these units (and some may be coterminous) <u>processes</u> some form of knowledge that cannot be processed otherwise.

As I speak (think) to myself I may (1) have an idea (2) remember what someone has said (3) stop over a word, or a or phrase and repeat it (4) have a daydream (5) form an incomplete sentence etc., moving in a series of coterminous but not homologous structures of representation.

Is poetry an attempt at the representation of inner speech?

Is a poet searching for the right category of expression, moving about or, more to the point, <u>realizing the movements about</u>, demonstrating the characters of inner expression?

A patient's free associations are to some extent poesis, and the analyst's response should not be prose like, but closer to the category movement of the patient. So, ironically, the "um" or fragment of thought, or association is more <u>dialogical</u> than an organized interpretation, although Kleinian speech may be closer to attunement as it is more an allegory than an interpretive narrative.

The analyst's countertransference is also an inner speech, and that dialogue between the two (patient's free associations, analyst's inner speech) may be the most important communicating, which takes place, often, in silence.

Analysts who, in a session, can move via <u>metaphor</u> through different expressive modalities are more capable of being in touch with their patients, but they need not be wordy. A French classicist, who only rarely lifts a patient's word from the text could, over time, lift many categories suggested by the word.

[20/8/89]

"Within the narrative"

Writing of Nabokov's character Hermann, Thiher says that:

—the narrator of the novel believes he is the narrator of the world, but by making the reader aware of events of which Hermann is ignorant Nabokov displaces Hermann.

In a sense, analysts wait for their main character's discourse and then, through their mastery of the unconscious discourse, illustrate how they—the analyst—are in narrative control. Sad but often true.

However, such supplementary contextuality is a feature of thinking, as we displace what we knew (5 minutes ago, 5 years ago) with what we know now. There is, then, a kind of tyranny of narrative point of view.

[20/8/89]

"Self representation"

—and countertransference as ...

—all representation of "reality" is anyway only ever a representation of the subject's relation to reality. It is a simultaneous representation of the subject and his objects. Thus when we hear from anyone who describes "the world" we're always hearing of a description of the subject, and sometimes, as in analysis, of the subject's unconscious experience of ourselves being transferred into their discourse on the world.

[20/8/89]

"The pleasure of illusion"

Thiher writes of contemporary writers' reluctance to use pronouns as these are illusions disguising X. I think we should embrace these nominal locations. It is from such positions, including the "I", that we create ourself and our others. It is from such positions, as receptive-evocative spaces, that the true self can move into being (becoming).

Beckets "unnameable" (Thiher, 134) is true of us, but it must be the primordial (i.e. fetal) pre-subjective voice, a voice with no self, that only enunciates unmediated psychosomatic states, like the fetus and neonate speaking "itself". "Mothereze". "So how am I feeling today?" Where "I" is spoken to and for the baby—which the baby "takes" in some way—is perhaps the first manifestation of an "I" which of course is an illusion created by the mother, and not truly speaking the baby. Perhaps this is one of the foundations of language, of illusion.

In a good enough illusion we leap into the prearranged spaces. It is useful. We can articulate ourselves there.

But it is probably the case that the voice of silence remains a different order.

[20/8/89]
"Presences/presents"

The analyst listens to an unending sequence of presences/presents, as the patient speaks the "I", shifting, creating new places, etc. At some point, the analyst speaks. To whom? To which of the "I"s? Perhaps to a special "I", to the ideal "I" who listens to analytic interpretation, who comes awake for that purpose. What then? It comes to exist, although what has been said, or, more accurately, what has been heard is stored in the unconscious.

[20/8/89]
"The dissemination of meaning in psychoanalysis"

Derrida's term to mean the decentering of meaning into meanings.

I think meaning must be disseminated in psychoanalysis by decentering the interpreter from the place of the analyst to at least two places (patient and analysts) but perhaps to many: to the associations of patient and analyst, speaking many voices.

[20/8/89]
"True self and chaos"

Is the true self chaos? Does it work according to the laws of chaos? Is this the way it (the true self) moves (chaotically) through objects? Working on chance.

[22/8/89]
"Solitary intimacy"
This is the phrase by Roland Barthes[17] in *The Responsibility of Forms* (p. 293): "Schumann is truly the musician of solitary intimacy, of the amorous and imprisoned soul that speaks to itself ..." The phrase "solitary intimacy" captures the nature of that relation we have to the self as an object, and it's better than my term which ("self as object") creates the illusion of great distance—the self over there as object—and suggests a great split (the subject and itself as others) when in fact our dialogues etc. are very intimate and close.

[undated]
"Play forms"

Thiher says the modern writer believing in ludic consciousness believes he should create new play forms.

To me, this is exactly what we seek: to articulate the true self by finding objects that allow us to play into a new form, which evokes us.

Categories of representation, as a theory, should perhaps give way to a theory of play forms, of expressive forms.

[22/8/89]
"Music"

"Each piece of music can be said to possess a particular emotional quality"[18] so in a way when we listen to music our emotions are played. We are affected. And perhaps we move from emotion to thought, to whatever thought will be created (evoked) by that emotion aroused in us on that occasion within that context of our lives.

Budd says also that a person need not feel the emotion behind the emotion in the music composed or played, which could be at times an interesting form of splitting, as emotion is created but split off.

—Budd (p. 28) suggests that a listener must submit to the emotional structure of a musical work, to really listen. It cannot be background. Just as a person must truly gaze at the total painting (rather than glance) or read the text to grasp what is conveyed in language. A musical work, then, is a structure over time that plays the listener into feelings.

—Budd writing about Edmund Gurney's work *The Power of Sound*: "for Gurney the cardinal units of music were melodic forms: short series of musical sounds of different pitch that are heard as unities" (53). It seems to me this is also a good description of the nature of a self state, where "bits" of image, sound, abstraction, conception etc. achieve a temporary unity allowing us to experience "self" which is that "harmonic form": not the sum of its parts, but achieved through the congregating of past experiences.

[22/8/89]
"Evenly hovering attentiveness vs. object relations listening"

Freud says evenly hovering attentiveness is the effort to be calm and to avoid deliberate attentiveness: "for as soon as attention is deliberately concentrated in a certain degree, one begins to select from the material before one."

—note how those who look for the transference interpretation cannot be evenly hovering.

[22/8/89]
"Music displaces the intrasubjective dialogue"

I have just turned off the radio—a piece of music I found distracting and irritating while trying to read—and it was followed by silence, the sounds of the outside world (birdsong, a ladder smacking against a wall, a lorry passing by) and then by my internal voice. I thought to myself "oh, that's a relief … much better. It's quiet now. The birds are better … what has happened?" and on I continued to this point. Intriguingly, music displaces this intrasubjective state, perhaps forcing me into self-object dialectics, much as the mother's voice brings the infant to her. Also I think that my inner voice is non-distractive. That is, I can still

276

hear the birdsong etc. while talking to myself. There is an acoustic background and a voiced foreground to my life.

Sometimes, however, I go deep into myself. My cathexis of external reality diminishes and I have a daydream or hatch an idea, having many thoughts. This is an intrapsychic phenomenology.

[22.8.89]
"The necessity of conflict"

Roland Barthes in *The Responsibility of Forms* says of Schumann that he was mad because he lacked a "conflictual … structure of the world: his music is based on no simple and, one might say, no 'natural' (naturalized by anonymous culture) confrontation" (p. 297).

—this idea of "natural conflict", or a natural conflictual structure is important. It is why I think "the dialectics of difference" is a term technically important as it allows a model of conflict to come into the intersubjective place, first through intrasubjective conflict. Freud's model was a purely intrapsychic model of conflict. Indeed the symptom—product of such intrapsychic conflict—may actually come into being—as with Dora—when the intrapsychic is barred from being represented in the intersubjective: that is, when the subject feels arrested by the wish to or need to externalize.

Thus the symptom, ironically enough, signifies the end of conflict. It suggests the failure of purely intrapsychic means to process mental life, or the problematics thereof.

[undated]
"The 60s radical"

Berkeley, through a comparatively minor action (Strong's agreement with Knowland about off campus representation)[19] erupted. The *Herald Examiner* doctored the picture of radicals going through Sather Gate. Over the next 10 years the radicals drew out into the open the corruption within the establishment. But this was not an act of intelligence, but of unconscious provocation. The right so hated the radicals that it could not conceal its corruption; indeed, it resorted to more and more and more corrupt means to try to stop radical existence. From newspapers to the police, to university officials, to parents etc. We drew out the poison. Through hate. And to accomplish this, we were hateable. We were shabby, arrogant, sexually promiscuous etc.: we provoked hate that revealed the structure of hate in the other: specifically in the right wing.

In becoming a scapegoat, we extracted or elicited hate. It concentrated around us and our political consciousness led us to identify it. We in turn disarmed the right as their credibility and effectiveness depended on their ability to hate us effectively, but their own corruption was used against them.

And of course, it was <u>hate</u> that motivated the United States in Vietnam.

Innocence and hate in Vietnam, the US as innocents (defending the United States against the evil Vietcong) bringing out of the Vietcong <u>latent hate</u> or the structure of hate.

Bush's innocence (of flag-waving) brought out the hate in Dukakis.

Why does the emergence of hate—or hate revealed—defeat the hater?

It is as if there is a kind of primordial shock of the innocent: "my God, look at that hate!" The world draws back. All the platforms or positions previously held by the hater disappear or are invalidated.

The reason there is no effective opposition to Bush and the right in America is that there is no political group for Bushism to hate, thus to reveal the structures of hate and to be hoisted on their own petard. Perhaps they will come to hate women who abort.

[22/8/89]
"The fascist substructure"

Any institution, or group, which deals with internal or external opposition to it by the attempt to eliminate the opposition is fascist. Its opposite is non-genocidal discourse: discourse engaged with or against the opposition, but not aiming to eliminate it.

In the 1960s the radicals discovered the fascist substructure to American monopoly capital structure, and by being hateful provoked the fascist substructure into disclosure, unwittingly disclosure driven by hate. They then revealed it to itself (and the public) whereupon the eye of innocence—almost an erotic presence in America—was forced to see and repudiate the substructure.

American radicals began as idealistic identifiers (identifying with liberal parents) in civil rights and so forth and were not hateful, but they discovered the fascist substructures. And then by growing longer hair, and so forth, became provocative, outing the fascist's hate: revealing the nature of their structure.

Recall Sproul Hall and the police beating the Orange County girls. Politicization was "the word". Being politicized.[20]

Now there is also an intrapsychic equivalent to fascist structure: indeed we could call it the fascist part of the personality, to designate our dealings with opposition by the mental elimination of the other. Refusing discourse by mental elimination is a form of denial, but it is more pernicious as it aims to eliminate the other.

There is a spectrum as intellectual genocide is the class and fascist substructure the area. In intellectual genocide the spectrum is:

1. denigration of the opposition
2. elimination of the integrity of the opponent's positions

[22/8/89]
"The depths of thought"

Wittgenstein: "Virtually in the same way as there is a difference between *deep* and shallow sleep, there are thoughts which occur deep down and thoughts which bustle about on the surface" (Wittgenstein, *Culture And Value*[21] (42)).

—Today in the garden I was thinking just that and tonight I read it in Wittgenstein. After I turned off the radio and heard the silence and my interiority, I thought of Mary Sue Moore's[viii] talk in Los Angeles on the four stages of sleep and wondered indeed if there aren't <u>stages of wakefulness</u>: from surface to depth.

—what would these be?

—how do the different forms of self experiencing lie on the vertical axis of depths?

Sometimes I am "lost" in my thoughts. I feel "deeper" in myself, a process closer to the dream experience, when I am, more a simple self "inside" a complexity. At other times I think <u>to</u> myself, as a complex self.

[22/8/89]

"Self experiencing"

The thought occurs to me that now that Masud[ix] is dead I am no longer periodically possessed by the feeling: "I must go to see Masud." It is too simplistic to say this is guilt, or was guilt. It was a feeling of my own, but one linked to Masud: to the object of the feeling. It is no more because he is gone.

I think such feelings, or experiences, are very important in our life. As if experiencings shift and go away.

The object evokes a self experience in us, that becomes an idiom—background of feeling, image, body state, gesture etc.: that collage of categories that make up self experiencing.

[23/8/89]

"Self encounter"

Hegel argues that in each experience we encounter an object which then becomes the means of encountering the self. There is a self state for each experience of the object.

I can link to evocation

1. experience
2. evocation of a self
3. structuralization or not

When does a new self experience become assimilated or simply introjected? When do we make it part of us? Perhaps when it accords with the true self? Do identification and structuralization proceed according to whether experience is syntonic with the true self?

—Secondly what does it mean for an experience to become part of a structure? Why should it?

viii A gifted American psychologist who lectured frequently at the Tavistock Clinic.

ix Masud Khan who died of a prolonged and painful cancer that precipitated a mental breakdown. After his breakdown I would visit him even though these were painful encounters.

Is a mental structure a particular act of identification or assimilation whereby the subject commits to "memory" the concepts latent to experience? That is, each experience which evokes a distinct self state, expresses a paradigm (law, concept) which can be taken into the psyche as an assumption, to become part of the subject's assumptive idiom. Assumptive idiom is the complex structure that processes the subject's pre-dispositional relation to reality. It is what the subject "carries" inside him as he lives his life. The assumptive predispositional—or is it dispositional, i.e. the assumptive-dispositional—is modifiable through experience, in that new experiences can change one's assumptions (see Bion on basic assumptions) and therefore influence structure. However it must also be through care that the true self is relatively uninfluenceable: it is a core. But its idiom is a set of theories, the outcome of which can be infinitely varied and definitely influenced at the operational-process level by experience and new assumptions.

The evocation of new self states (brought on by the discreet integrity of an object) may yield a new assumption when it is assimilated into the deep grammar of the true self. Otherwise, if not, it shall remain a distinct experience, an object of memory, possibly an introject.

[undated]
"True & false self: a dialectic?"

Is there a dialectic between the true and false self? There is not in Winnicott. But the false self is a form of intermediate action which adapts to the other in order to preserve the true self. One problem with this is the assumption that a correct division has been made (by what, the ego?) to hide the true self and construct the false self in relation to an impinging object. But what if the object is not in fact impinging? What if this is a wrong idea on the part of, say, the child?

In any event, some false self adaptations create an opposite set of views to true self views and in some cases, over time, true self and false self assimilate. Initially I may not like someone, but I conceal my true feelings—or should I say real feelings? I construct a false self, that is I do not use them as objects or as experiences according to the nature of true self use (pleasure, jouissance, ruthlessness) but according to the nature of false self (suspension of pleasure, use, jouissance and construction of a false response to the object).

I suppose we could say that my true self or false self is elicited according to the experience of a first encounter.

Now, imagine that I do not initially like a person. I recoil from him. I am not myself (although I am my recoiling self). I cannot engage him from the true self. Imagine, however, that as part of my false self I decide to discuss films with him or airplane travel, or the politics of Columbia. We discuss matters. Time passes. To my surprise, I find him more likeable. I still, perhaps, dislike something of the essence of him, but through false self I have found something worth (for the true self) engaging. In this respect the true self benefits from false self work or labour. Indeed the false self can be seen as a kind of scout or forager about for potential true self movements. A true self movement is the finding of an experience with an object that enhances (elaborates or activates) the selfness of the true self.

Is false self a function of the true self, a "no" function, that refuses the object through false adaptations? Thus we could in a sense do away with the distinction, except to say that the false self is a particular functioning of the true self, its negation of reality through personality construction.

[23/8/89]
"The narcissistic character and pure being"

The pure being self is the narcissistic character (his entitlement). But to live from such pure being may be essential in order to avoid the pain of judgments or the judgmental faculty, especially as it may have been experienced in the other.

[23/8/89]
"Knowing or thinking the unthought known"

How do we know? In a sense by expressing the self in and through experience. Living is knowing. Much of our self is unthought. We think ourselves through experience, but we do not know this as such; we do not know this is us thinking, insofar as we assume it is us simply living or experiencing. However, insofar as experience articulates us, it is one of our forms of thinking the self (in the experience) but it is not thought aware of itself. It is not reflective thought.

What is the aim of such unreflective thinking? It is the destiny drive at work: the urge to elaborate selves and their experiences through the course of time. It does not add up to anything, although memory will store such self experiences and history (historic consciousness) will render it later.

But the nature of such thinkings is ineffable.

[undated]
"Anorexia as remembering former selves"

I learned this from my diet. I am 192, trying to get down to 180–85. One month ago I was 210. Now, however, I feel fat and I look at myself from the vantage of my 175 pound self: a good 25 years ago. A former self state looking at my present self!

[24/8/89]
"The firing of the mind"

Neuronal firing may serve as a physiological base of a mental metaphor: that we have experiences fired by the mental homologue of a brain area, that we receive firings all the time. The firing of the mind. But psychoanalysis teaches us that we fire more than we are fired upon. Psychic conceptualizing is the absolute reverse of neuronal firing, although the brain's responsive action to external stimuli, to fire toward parts of the body and other areas of the brain (mnemic storage), maybe likened to the psyche's firing of the imaginary (the equivalent of actions) and the mnemonic.

"Primary representation and unconscious as cognitive unconscious"

Can the infant's negotiations with the mother and its storage be internal to the cognitive unconscious (equally the primary representational unconscious) and the secondary repressed unconscious to the psychological unconscious? This way an infant constructs the psyche out of the cognitive unconscious which is not representable.

A metaphor.

The infant's mental work is like that work that goes into the building of a cinema which when completed will be open for screenings. The logic of such construction, building the buildings, take years, and this cinema's architecture—its rooms etc.—mirrors the nature of its construction. Theoretically, not until it is completed, with projector in place, does it screen the films: which is the secondary repressed unconscious. Imagine, however, that with the first bricks laid, a fragment of a screen and a fragment of a projector and a fragment of film is "projected". Months pass and the screen gets larger etc. and the projections more sophisticated.

In the course of the showing of the films we must imagine that in times of duress a film is interrupted due to a problem with the cinema theater itself.

Let's say people are watching *Parenthood* and the film is interrupted by an "endopsychic screening!" The word "loo" shows up lit in red on the left side of the screen. Imagine further that such projections do not use pictures of the loo but sign-symbols such as a sign with the word "loo" in it. As the sign lights up, a sign for the manager also flashes, and a map of the inner workings of the cinema comes onto the screen to illustrate the problem.

This would amount to the "firing" of an endopsychic receptor driven by an anxiety over function or survival etc. (psychotic anxieties).

Now imagine that there is a <u>dialectical</u> cross modality between the two systems. They are not equivalent to one another but they do affect each other.

For example, the film *Parenthood* has a scene of the child talking about shitting which resonates with the shitting area of the cinema eliciting (akin now to receptiveness, etc.) endopsychic data.

Imagine further that "content" can fire "structure" into content and the structure now fired is new content, so the audience (the ego?) will <u>recall</u> the content and fired structure, such that both are now part of the film experience.

Imagine that as the child develops new experiences of a particular type (generas?) that the cinema complex grows a new structure. We might even say that certain films affect the cinema house, so a new room designed out of the experience of *Parenthood* is built. How about a family recreation room?

Indeed, the cinema never stops adding structure. Only one screen though! To create a more accurate picture, let us imagine the cinema to be the size of a small city (a mall city!) with sections, houses, buildings, each somehow supporting the screen and the audience.

It grows from the center outward.

The aim of such a complex is to support the cinema's projection of the city's experience of its internal existence and its relation to the outside world.

As a new experience comes its way the city adds houses to hold the experience and such houses join the structure supporting the life of the cinema and the single screen.

The projections onto the screen are coherent (usually) because the director of films lives within an illusion of identification with the city. He can represent its parts. But we know he hires out this private privilege to others who show their films in his name.

Sometimes the city people (psychic structures) take over from the film director and screen their protests (psychosis).

Or is it neurosis? Because such takeovers are probably contents (not structures) or at least contents active inside structure: memories, introjects? When the structure represents itself (endopsychic representation) it does so by a sign system that is profoundly disturbing and different.

The inherited potential (true self) is the blueprint for the cinema—city and its construction (hinges, workers, outcome) is the work of the mother child relation.

—use Anna Freud and Hartmann's works on the city as metaphor of the ego.

[24/8/89]
"Self representation"

In psychoanalysis I am affected by the other in my self presentations. That is, the nature of my relation to myself (or Hegel, self-identity) will change according to the analysand's effect upon me.

The question analysts ask is: "Is this sometimes a reflection of the patient's self identity?"

[25/8/89]
"Intuition, figure and propositional forms"

Howard Gardiner's[22] discussion of how a young musician must move from "figural intuition" in the grasp of music (sense of the melodies, forms) to understanding the structure and laws of music (propositional) is useful in countertransference theory.

Intuition could be defined as a "feeling for the forms" of any phenomenon. Or of a feeling for forms that are only findable through the exercise of feeling, where feeling here may mean a relaxed submission to the structural properties of the phenomenon engaged.

In any countertransference I submit to the patient's structure: the flow of a session, the nature of being with the patient. I feel him. I am felt by him. But I also have a highly systematic coterminous ability: the analytical structure. What I do is wait until there are points of convergence between intuitions and analyses before embarking on interpretations.

However my comments to a patient—often my associations—will reflect one or the other of these two positions. I will comment from the intuitive me (feeling about for forms) and the analytical me (deconstructing, re-assembling, objectifying).

[undated]
"Intuition and empathy"

Intuition links to my theory of genera in that as we apply the areas of our mind to X (a phenomenon or the unthought known) there is a complex unconscious evolutional work being performed.

Our sense of the effects of such unconscious work is in part our sense of intuition, as we process X. We therefore have senses of X, where these psychic senses (humor, play, etc.) "group" the net effect (network) of the work done so far.

At some point (if ever!) there is a moment of recognition—an epiphany—when we objectify the work through some form of knowledge (of the self or of the object).

"Genera" refers to the unconscious work applied sensationally to an X, to "thinking" (through the different categories of experiencing) the unthought known. The place of the subject in these successive moments is in the place of intuition: he looks through feeling or psychic senses which yield unconscious data for contribution to the eventual conscious thinking (or objectification) of X.

Take my walk back home from Dresden Rd.

On the way I saw:

1. a police van and wondered why they were there. Thought about safety of the place, averted the cop's gaze, looked at the house to my right and noticed how neat it was.
2. thought about safety and children and Sacha playing on streets. Berkeley and New York City came to mind.
3. noticed how unclear the street was.
4. walked along Hornsey Lane and felt the toxic fumes in me.
5. along footpath reflected on the upward angle of the sidewalk, for some reason saying to myself it was European, then thinking it reminded me of my early childhood and the sidewalks where I walked with my grandfather.
6. saw woman with black hair returning from town, wondered if she was attractive, couldn't decide.
7. crossed road, thought of traffic and Sacha getting to Crouch End: safe or not. Replied it was.
8. walking and wondered about reviews of my book.
9. turning corner thought about the death of R.D. Laing and whether I would be asked to write an obit, imagining a scenario: being asked, accepting, being criticized by Laingians: "he didn't even know him", replying in the abstract that one doesn't have to know someone well in order to write an obit.
10. Noticing sign, cafe, it's "an area" of psychic interest, a kind of *déjà vu* or screen memory area that I find curious—a sort of special place—but no imagining out of it. (Is it the screen's place and the abandoned railway and the soda fountain cafe?)
    —grandfather? I think so.
11. Haslemere Rd/Union building/recent book party.

12. time thus far spent on the walk.
13. workers constructing and my mixed feelings.
14. Shostokovich's 5th Symphony "plays" in my mind.

An examination of the above internal free associations is the psychic movement of the self. I am in some respects at work, although it is non-purpose, relaxed work. I am at work on my life: living it.

Such work is unconscious although its derivatives are these associations and it will be seen that such work is dialectical between me and the actual world, although not exclusively, and that it is multimodal: perception, memory, music, etc.

(recall body states. etc.).

The above constitutes the

1. areas of experiencing
   —their categories.
2. modes of thinking

Experiencing and thinking
Experiencing:

1. see police
2. see sidewalk
3. memories

To backtrack a moment, maybe such free associations are my way of thinking through the problematics of another move?
   —how this is the opposite of false self relating and knowing?
   —intuition: the psychic sense of the work of the true self? Rummaging, moving, growing through elaboration.

[undated]
"Self experience and representation"

Can it be said that when a patient "chooses" to represent something inside the dream space— or in dream as a category of self experience—he does so because the dream is a good place for that content? As opposed to thinking it abstractly, or by walking, or by painting it or writing it?

And is it possible to separate a category of experiencing from a mode of representation? I think not. For whatever X I take to the dream, or for a walk, or to the opera, or to writing, it will be released according to the nature of that mode. And it's not necessarily a question of active representation (such as writing or walking or painting) because I could listen to music or some one could call me and X would come up. But sometimes I choose and sometimes it just happens.

Films are experiences that are generative: they sponsor a lot of thought. Is the film a good example of how all the orders and categories (or many at least) converge?

285

Often what proves to be a trauma, an event that in memory/recollection brings up psychic pain even greater than at the time of occurrence, is an untransformed genera: a cluster (see screen memory) of phenomena that are collected into a trauma (i.e. linked to an event) that could have become a genera, thus sponsoring further elaborative work period. A trauma just sits inside the subject causing pain. It is not elaborated. Just recurrent. But it may be recurrence with pain that is the trauma. If trauma were non-recurrent and elaborative then it would cease to be a trauma and become a genera.

Do we pick objects through which we simply recur (recurrencies) or do we pick objects through which we elaborate? A good example is Sacha's space games: simply recurrent although he achieves a certain kind of mastery. But is this mastery, of which ego psychology speaks so much, a false mastery? Does not mastery support trauma in that it yields the same feelings constantly repeated, while genera open the self to previously unknown selves, self states and so forth.

Think of the boy he played with last night whose parents provided them with a jigsaw. He made objects. Each day he makes a new one and we can say he makes himself as well. Elaborates the self. Sacha made a Prince Charles, a catapult etc. Via this action he came with the making self into an elaborative corridor rather than into repetition.

Ironically, is mastery the foundation of trauma? Is it the urge to mastery that sets us up to be deeply unsettled by events that signify the loss of such mastery? Thus it is not the ingredients of the event, per se, which are awful but the loss of mastery.

The alternative to mastery is play. If one plays with the object rather than trying to master it, the object can give more.

Genera: Vera John-Steiner in *Notebooks of the Mind* argues that composers and other creative people are able to link seminal ideas with elaborative structures. I would change that: a genera is a germinal idea replete with elaborative structures. Or, it is a germinal idea equipped with multi dialectical elaborative structures?

My view: "A genera is a germinal idea derived from the multi dialectics of self experiencing which comes equipped with elaborative structures partly derived from the separate but homologous categories of self experiencing and suggestive of multiple means of expressive representation."

The above is partly modeled out of the mother child relation as:

We are born as a set of potential ideas, we come into contact with objects and experiences that evoke this potential, and we are born also into the elaborative structure that is the mother's processing of the infant.

The object in the first place elaborates us: auditorially, visually, kinaesthetically, affectively etc.

This is the muse. We are partly called into expression.

I have tried to give to genera a character: as visuals, as words, as auditories. But I think genera are intrapsychically featureless, although I do think we have a "sense" of them. To be sure, we have derivatives. Or firings from the categories. Otherwise we only have senses that we are unconsciously at work-play on genera: complexes nucleating around "key" issues in our life at the moment.

Genera: complexes nucleating around key issues in our life at the moment.

A generative experience (an experience typical of genera) is the birth of a realization. Birth of realization versus morbidity or repetition. And such realizations are not so much content producing as they are psychic releasings.

[undated]
"Paradigmatics"

The conveying of a logos by example. Teaching the other (mother teaching child) through the actual handling of the other.

[undated]

There are many ideas or workings that never reach the level of representation and yet have existed. Perhaps this is the unthought known.

In our intrasubjective states, we:

1. are conscious of many things and continue to think about them.
2. are unconscious of genera but conscious of working on many issues without knowing quite what is happening and without knowing the result.
3. experience non-existences, absolute blanks, which are the mental recognitions of non-existing.

[undated]
"Genera (continued)"

Are genera those multi dialectical phenomena that constitute, as they evolve, the emergence of new psychic structures?

A psychic structure, here, would be the development of an ego ability, born out of the individual's multi dialectical processing of objects and their evocative effects. So certain experiences give birth to new structures if there is that X Factor present to generate. This must be the elaborative factor: the moving of the true self.

What is the aim or motivation behind the generative? Why seek to play with life? Is it simply pleasurable, even if some of the experiences are painful?

Perhaps there is a pleasure specific to each of us when we are elaborating our idiom through life experience. How could this pleasure be defined? Is there a word for it?

Is the movement of orders (the multimodal dialectic) a logos?

A genera is a condensation of the multimodal dialectic, just like the dream. The true dream is not part of the representation. The representation is simply the place of the many condensations. Indeed a genera is very much like a dream and works like it. Dreams bring together many dimensions in response to the day and are memorable.

[undated]
"Representation"

Neither internal speech or imagining bears much relation at all to their external counterparts. In both case the speech or image is represented to the self as other and is "saturated" with other contributing categories.

[undated]
"Genera/generative"

Take the Art Museum in Berkeley. The experience there. This is a genera: my transformation of an experience into unconscious significance. It is also the result of coming into contact with (and seeking out) an evocative object. It will join some internal object in formation that might eventuate into a generative: a realization (an insight) that becomes recurrently reproductive of meaning. A generative is the nucleation of genera: after-experiencings that are personally elaborative. Such phenomena constitute the release of our being into idiom articulations.

[undated]
"Trauma/genera"

A person can be contributing to the formation of a trauma—to the self—via defenses, destructive actions, or through genera: to a generative.

[undated]
"The illusion of presence"

According to Thiher, Jacques Derrida with his notion of "trace" proposes an alternative to the simple notion of presence. With trace he has found a way to show "that nothing in language, neither individual elements nor the system, is ever fully present—or fully absent." Thiher goes on: "Language exists only as the text, the tissue of movement of differing traces. This play of movement of the present-absent traces, in the play of *différance*, can [according to Derrida] be called spacing (*espacement*)" (Thier, 88).

I do not conceive of the true self either as presence or unity. Indeed, it is more absent. And it is more a set of theories. Of "handlings".

[undated]
"Voice and saying"

Thiher writes "I would propose that contemporary questions about who speaks and from where correspond to a shift in the practice and theory of fiction that was largely initiated in the thirties. This shift leads from the modernist conception of fiction as vision, and language as iconic plenitude, to postmodern interrogations of literature as saying and voice. This change in viewpoint parallels the breakdown in belief in an iconic or representational function of language" (120).

It is interesting that Paula Heimann raised this issue: "who speaks?"[23] (etc) as if the narrative theory of psychoanalysis—looking for the meaning—gave way. Heimann's is a post modern vision, of sorts.

[undated]
"Dissemination"

The distribution or scattering of the seed, as in sewing.

The true self (idiom) settles in and through varied and disconnected objects, the culture of which does not add up, or tell a story, except as the trace of that particular subject's <u>choice</u>.

[undated]
"Genera and the group of ideas"

Freud's theory of condensation, in which "a group of ideas attached " itself to a person or event, etc, is a good example of how a genera is formed. Layers and layerings until X is formed.

Now in analysis the epiphany may seem—just like a dream—rather simple. But it will serve as a "point" of generation, and in time, as the subject returns to the event, it will yield more of its latent elements.

[11/9/89]
"The mind of fascism/the fascist state of mind"

I read a few days ago that in Germany one of the strengths of fascism was the crowd, how in the crowd they became powerful. This reminds me of the comment about X, and how individually they are fine, but in a group they are nasty (use the John Birch society). Indeed this transformation from decent person to genocidal self is the moment of elimination. It is <u>witnessing</u> this; indeed being part of it—as the illuminated—that is the effect of the fascist act. What is this? What is being transformed?

There is a split between these two selves: one (singular) good enough; the other (in group) that is monstrous.

As the fascist joins the group for solidarity he simultaneously slaughters a group in intellectual genocide.

Is fascism part of the psychology (in all of us) of joining-in-with-a group? An act of identification with the corporate (the institution) as "love" that can only exist as an act of elimination of the other elements: such as critique, doubt, hate of the institution.

So the fascist has come to be an extremist to cathect the corporate and to be a member of the group: the mass.

Therefore that which is split off in relation to the group is always directed toward another group.

But how is it that the corporate endures?

The fascist destroys his humanity (the processing of the human) in order to join the mass. Humanity creates genera of ambiguity: doubt, question, elaborative need, temporal requirements. The fascist destroys ambiguity and simplifies life through ideology and hate.

The fascist processes a dialectic solely between the self and other whereby the other becomes the genocidally vanquished. Humanity depends upon multi dialectical categories within the self which are transferred into group structures, as in democratic states.

Violence against opposition (its elimination) is a feature of fascism. My patient who had violent daydreams of shooting people: this is the fascist state of mind: the personification of parts of the self put into the other who is shot.

"The officers sympathize with fascism because it represents a prolongation of the state of war internally and a possibility of war externally ..." Giovanni Zibordi in Beetham.[24]

—the fascist state of mind cultivates hate toward the opposition.

—it is the expression of self doubt (or group doubt) that keeps the self and group open to other views—and the views of others. Doubt is the hallmark of the multi dialectical mind that processes as much as possible.

Is exclusivity a part of fascism? Excluding others?

[11/9/89]
"Warlikeness"

Is there a mental equivalent to waging war? Is there something such as a warlike frame of mind, or war likeness?

Do people internalize the assumptions of a nation and personify them, as it were? For example, war is now systematic. Is there therefore a systematic warlike area of the mind and self?

[undated]
"The fascist state of mind"

It is likely that fascism is ordinary, or any psychological movement that begins by

1. the crippling of internal representations of the object.
2. the loss therefore of parts of the self.

As the internal "mass" of selves and objects is condensed and narrowed, the fascist mind seeks nourishment through the idealization of what remains in the mind (the remaining parts) but almost as a grim irony of its endogenous fate the fascist enacts the internal scene in external reality by eliminating opposition to it. The mass destruction of opposition is equivalent to the mass destruction of the psyche.

In psychoanalysis we write of the "parts" of the self, suggesting a parliamentary internal order, as these parts represent instinctual, memorial, situational, needful, wishful constituencies. Such a democratic order—a well-integrated one—rests upon plurality.

When the "democratic mind" meets with opposition, it gives it parliamentary representation. There would always be a place in the mind for the representative consideration of the objectionable.

Even something like the P.L.O. or the I.R.A. etc. would require adequate psychic representation and we could say the failure to do so is less democratic or psychically safe.

When the many parts of the psyche are involved, opposition to an objectionable phenomenon is indeed possible, based on full consideration as in South Africa, the Medellin cartels and so forth.

But it is easy to see if a representative process has been in effect because there will be traces of the psychic work of consideration: the South African, Medellin cartel groups (etc.) will have been thought about.

Recall the man on the San Francisco street responding to Bush's action against Iran and my/our fascist response (simplification). This was genocide in me.

(See Freud *Civilization & its Discontents* and Wilhelm Reich on fascism.)

The problem is not that to become part of civil (group) one must renounce one's instincts, but that one will not find there a representative place, a correspondence—representationally—between the internal world (of selves and objects) and actuality. It is a place of personal foreclosures and the false self, which can become inspiring if broken off from as an object of desire. One must not desire the group or wish to find desire in the group. Unless that place has a democratic order.

Extremism: the movement to a mental state that eliminates other considerations. Too far to the left, or too far to the right etc,.

Is political history (theory) an effort of continued attempted internalization? Are we trying to be Greek? Is the theory of democracy a psychological ideal, a metaphor of the effort of mind to achieve a position?

The view that fascism is the effort to act upon a vision that excludes the law brings to mind Bush's devotion to the American flag. This is an extraconstitutional movement and is part of the Reagan Bush fascism, but it is now brought to the legislative democratic process and it will be slowed down. In a way the Bush flag issue is his way of representing fascism (simplified eliminatory extremism) and in this sense is good. Probably all American presidents have represented their fascism in this or like manner.

A key issue is what happens to the opposition. Is opposition represented?

Movements that aim to revolutionize bear a fascistic element. Certainly the movements in psychoanalysis came to eliminate (or revolutionize) the build up of psychoanalytic theory and in this sense are fascistic.

Genera, however, are multidialectical contributions—movements, not a movement.

Parapraxis as mutilation; i.e. the "dual correspondence theory" rather than "dual track".

I think one has to temper even the idealism inherent in the notion of psychic representation and democracy—which could become a utopian vision—with a further idea of "the incomplete"; that we are to be incomplete, that there will be no integration, that any picture is only ever a fragment, and this is a kind of postmodern philosophy of democracy.

On revolutionaries killing off of the parts of the self as precursive to violence.

[undated]
"Dare I eat a peach?"

The extreme notion of evil which must be gotten rid of, is now in the food chain, as death comes to poison us. Hence, dare we eat a peach? Our professional lives lived in this way, a testimony to our age.

[undated]
"Freud's surgical metaphor"

When Freud says the analyst must assume a dispassionate position isn't he talking about the killing off of the parts of the self (in the countertransference) that was only revived in object relations theory?

Bakunin says of the profession of the revolutionary, who aspires to an ideal state rid of opposition, that the revolutionary must kill off his love of home, children, wife, etc. But in his own way, after his own ideal, does Freud advocate a nobility of killing off?

[undated]
"The fascist state of mind"

Is there a special fascist process of binding? There are the physical signs of loyalty—i.e. uniforms, flags, insignias etc.—but what would be a less concrete psychic equivalent? Would it not be any idea or group that recurs in order to bind, to simplify? A process of de-semiosity. (Semious as in multiple meaning.) A restriction of meaning. To simplify is to create ideas that bind by arresting associations other than to themselves: sign systems. Psychoanalytical language—for example the true self, core self, etc.—could suffer the same fault.

Binding creates what Sullivan calls a "martial sense" and we may wonder if the martial sense isn't a quality that features in genocide: the binding of forces to create a sense capable of murder. It eliminates symbolic polysemousness as the slide of signifiers dissipates a bound meaning and subverts ideology by the plays of unconscious affiliation.

In *The Future of an Illusion* Freud writes:

"An inquiry which precedes like a monologue, without interruption, is not altogether free from danger. One is too easily tempted into pushing aside thoughts which threaten to break into it, and in exchange one is left with a feeling of uncertainty which in the end one tries to keep down by over-decisiveness" (SE21).

Interestingly, then, as the fascist mind pushes out the other it feels weakened, and it tries to compensate for this by intense certainty. So <u>certainty</u> is a function of anxiety!

[undated]
"Freud's self analysis"

In his style of writing, particularly the Socratic type found in *The Future of an Illusion*—where he creates a dialogue with himself—I think Freud continues the terms of his self analysis, which proceeded in this manner.

Now where in psychoanalysis is there room for such a Socratic order? Perhaps in the free associations—dialogues—the patient has with himself. Indeed, by trying to get the analyst to be a dialogical partner the patient corrupts the representation of their own freely associated inner dialogue.

[14/10/89 Rio de Janeiro]
"Representation"

An experiment in imagination. Let us imagine a five times a week analysis in which the patient lies on the couch on Monday and Friday and the analyst lies on the couch Tuesday through Thursday. The analyst would freely associate to the patients material etc., and the patient would assume analytical silence. "There" the patient would look for echoes of himself, notifying the analyst when the analyst's associations elaborated the patient's associations etc. The patient's countertransference could be transferred to their own transfer now being processed by the analyst.

The point is, the true value of free association is its intrapsychic value; its interior movement.

Each analyst "internally processes" the patient: in a very special, we could say, psychoanalytical way. But still this is the place of the patient: in the analyst. It is from within the analyst's subjectivity that the patient will be analyzed.

[undated]
"Evil"

Evil is the act of destruction accomplished through the appearance of good.

A person is evil when they represent themselves as good in order to destroy the other.

Or, when they act in a good way, rousing hope, affection and love in the other, in order for it to be destroyed.

The adolescent, in pathological process, does this to the parent, appearing good, then arousing hope, love, affection, belief in order to destroy it.

The person being evil enjoys this process of arousal and its destruction as it is pleasing to see the destruction of belief in the good.

X did this but as a comic procedure, in that he destroyed the fabric of good in a session, shattering our mutual hopes.

[undated]
"Fascism"

Stuart Hampshire[25] claims that the Nazi aim was a nihilistic movement which aimed to destroy the moral landscape, to leave "a dizzying sense in German minds that all things are possible and that nothing is forbidden … and that there is an infinite moral space now open for natural violence and domination." He writes of "a great vacancy … a moral void."

I think this is the effect of intellectual genocide. It is to destroy the prior culture of ideas, to sever links, and to create a "moral void" into which and from which a "new" philosophy, with no links to previous generations is created.

"Revenge was to be substituted for justice in relation to enemies, loyalty to party and to race was to replace impartiality, and favor and maltreatment were to depend on a person's origins rather than on his character" (Hampshire, 69).

In terms of group dynamics, look at:

1. revenge
2. loyalty
3. favor

[undated]
"To visit the dying"

When we visit those who are dying we stay awhile with our own death to be.
It is practice, of sorts, in the art of dying.

[undated]
"Fascism"

Hampshire argues that when the Nazis used force, or the threat of force, in place of negotiation with groups, they knew they were creating a compliant population.

—what is the equivalent in psychology? It is the threat of force: the threat of the use of forces at hand, such as the power to fire an employee, to exclude a member, to pass on gossip: i.e. to cripple the object representation. This is the threat of a "crippling" force.

Perhaps it is also the abuse of interpretation: "X is this way or takes position Y because of …" removing X's position from the field of discourse to another place. This is a power of removal of sorts.

The hatred of complexity.

"Character assassination"

And gossip. What does it mean to assassinate character? Character is mark, signature. If I gossip about X to assassinate his character I change his mark, his signature. I eliminate him as an object represented in the mind of the other, or, as a signifier which now signifies something else. Character assassination often takes the form of caricaturization, an altering of the mark of the other by falsifying the complexity of a self.

[undated]
"Genera/concepts"

Is it possible that a genera is a concept? Or, that it bears relation to condensations of concepts married up to or by a purpose (or a theory employing them)?

[undated]
"Fascist state ..."

See Eric Brenman on "narrow mindedness".[26]
   —how can one define human understanding? (Brenman)
   —what is evil?
   —What is the nature or genesis of the <u>movement</u> in personality or group from the elements of fascism to a fascist state of mind?
   —the Function of Doubt.
   —Fear of "the good" in the other and its establishment.
   —There is a fascist state of mind. State of mind. The concept of a state of mind.
   —There are positive and negative representations: i.e. the presence of denigration and the absence of reference to points of opposition or difference. One must look as much to see what is not present as to see what is present.
   —There is a relation between the destruction of the parts of the self—and the power—and <u>perversion</u>.
   Patient X:

1. lives in a Daydream fantasy world (on stage with ballet) projecting the good parts of the self into a therefore overloaded idealized drama.
2. leaving the actual self denuded of its values. This denuded self is then projected into a victim who is regarded with contempt.
3. There is a marriage (of sorts) between the two splits: the idealized–ideological self and the destruction of the other.

I am interested in thinking about what it feels like to <u>witness</u> someone decent cross a boundary into a group or ideology (or both) in which they become insane (insofar as the fascist state of mind is an insanity). It is:

1. shocking
2. dissociating—as one feels separated out by their madness, or excluded as one is sane.
3. saddening—the loss.
4. deadening

This process in the witness is the first act of victimization. It is the witness who suffers this first.
   Upon X's re-entry into one-to-one intimacy (the rally is over, the ideological fascist state of mind is superseded) the friend-victim often says to others: "but you know, <u>away</u> from their group ideology, they really are awfully nice and decent and available." This is the victim's pleasure and relief at the recovery of their own humanity following upon its elimination. However comforting this description is, it is ultimately as dangerous as X's move to fascism because it constitutes an acceptance of a split and refusal to challenge the insane parts of the personality. It is precisely at this point of re-humanization of X that his fascism must be challenged.
   What are the processes?

1. the eradication of self doubt (parts of self).
2. the defining of an opponent who will contain the projectively identified doubting parts of the self.
3. the distortion of the opponent's view.
4. the decontextualization of the opponent's views (isolating from his true culture).
5. the caricaturization of the other.
6. the denigration of the other.
7. character assassination.

The above constitutes <u>intellectual genocide</u>, or its precursors. We could call these the visible factors of genocide, in that we can see how the attack is working. The negative genocide is the representation of annihilation which is demonstrated through negative hallucination. The views, person, culture, or history of the other are then never referred to. It is as if the other does not exist.

Bruno Bettelheim says that to survive in a camp one must live for the other who will survive. I think the me that does value and love the person who has now become fascist is akin to this. I know that I keep the love or affection, I am its keeper, as they are in a state of self eradication.

Bettelheim says the individual must elaborate the self. Institutions naturally work against this. The life instinct must <u>confront</u> death.

The "crime" of intellectual genocide results in an immediate loss of one's humanity. This loss is projectively identified into the exterminated who is considered worthless (without humanity) setting up a <u>vicious movement</u> that constitutes the fascist state of mind.

Kuper[27] (pp. 24–25) leads me to think that focus on Nazi genocide of the Jew, and the relative failure to be horrified by the Stalin genocide, comes out of Russian lobbying of the United Nations to exclude political views as the basis of opposition, which is interesting as in the United States an intellectual genocide against people with the political view (communism) was also being launched. The exclusive focus on the Jew is an irony: used to stand in here in a reverse scapegoatism, to be used as an object of focus in order to act out further genocides.

The <u>victim</u> of intellectual genocide feels belittled, diminished, impotent, dehumanized, but also, like Bettelheim, struggles to preserve his humanity.

<u>Ethnocide</u>: Kuper (p. 31).

Ethnocide is the aim to destroy the culture, ideas, etc., of a group, but if this is accomplished via the denigration of the holders of the cultural view then this is intellectual genocide which is precursive to fascism.

Ignominy.

Bettelheim suggests to me that the victim who by <u>thinking</u> about the actions committed against him (thinking even divorced from feeling, which is suppressed) somehow preserves his humanity, not in heroic acts, not in compassions, but in a very private effort—in the last resort— to think. <u>This</u> cannot be denied to him! Feelings, compassions, they can be.

See Kuper (pp. 40–41): intellectual genocide may develop when one group advances its ideas or organizations further than others, thus empowering them and leading to the destruction of the "less knowledgeable."

Kuper's elements of genocide (p. 43):

1. stereotyping
2. vilifying propaganda
3. dehumanizing: target group.

What is the nature of the victim in the group situation? The fear of speaking, of being a ghost of oneself?

The change of name: Jew to Kike, Irish to Paddy, communist to pinko. See Kripke:[x] once the name is changed it is "the other" who is being killed.

Colonization and psychoanalysis: intellectual movements and denigration.

As Kuper believes that pluralism is the ground for domestic genocide, then polytheism is a move to stop the annihilation of the other.

Intellectual genocide:

1. Categorisation
2. Aggregation

Also it unifies the persecutors.

Idealism (and self idealization)

And genocide

I think there is a link between genocide and perversion (pornography) at least, in which the fascist plays with a dehumanized victim.

[12/11/89]
"Intuition"

Works the same way as the knowledge of language or of music: it is derived from the constant interplay between the in-born and the symbolic.

[undated]
"The hostage crisis"

It is curious that so much is made of this issue, whilst no attention is paid, say, to the boat people or to genocide.

Who is the hostage? It is Western individual man held in Eastern captivity, a metaphor of our fear that the West shall be hostage to the non-Western world.

And of the idealism of our effort to strain entire countries to return them? Isn't it that the hostage (captive) is the ideal: the Western ideal, captured, tortured by the Eastern mind.

---

[x] Saul Kripke, American philosopher.

Meanwhile in our ideal of the individual man, with which we are preoccupied, we turn our back to the slaughter of non-Western peoples.

Is the hostage crisis then a perverse politics in which we fill the texts of history with our nobility, our defense of freedom and virtue, whilst we participate in genocide?

What is the name for an object that functions as a screen for an act of negative hallucination, by which, say, "hostage" blinds us to the killings of the Cambodians? It blocks the vision.

[undated]
"Consciousness"

In some ways this is a transformation of the multitude of factors operating at any one time in that unit of presence we may then term a state of being. Such "states" are also self states, and the self that one is, is in part the history of such units of being. But in time we may ask what is the present status of a self succeeding so many prior states of being? Are they stored up, so to speak, each in its temporal corner marked: e.g. "state of being, 20th November 1989, 4:30 to 4:45 am"? Indeed, do all such states of being—each certainly a point of convergence of the psychic, the aleatory, the conventional—become self states, or may we reserve this state for a higher level? Is it a question, even of containment (i.e. the self contains being-states), or is it possible that the self is that idiom of organization (originally just true self, then the internalised paradigms negotiated with the mother and the father) that moves through states of being?

But this seems contradictory. Where would a state of being come from if not from the self?

I wonder, however, if by self we do not mean something like an internal active concept, abstracted from units of experience, generating uses of objects and giving a matrix to experience: to being states. The self might be a vantage point, a point of perspective, derived from its categorical difference: it is a different form of thinking. Abstract thinking.

[22/11/89]
"Transference early on"

It may well be that the patient's earliest communications to the analyst

(and back again) are efforts to construct a shared "mental structure", a joint analytical mind, that can process the patient.

Culture, as Jerome Bruner[xi] argues, may be "a prosthetic device"—that negotiates between our genes and our culture.[28] This is an establishment when mother is the transformational object and in analysis it works too.

Infant observers all believe the infant enters the world with concepts and comes to language with these concepts. (So can we say patient and analyst mentally conceive of one another before speech?) Such stores of concepts are then categorized and organized. The child organizes

---

[xi] Jerome Bruner, American psychologist.

knowledge around what he can accomplish and again the patient probably searches out the analysis and the analyst for what can be done with it.

Patients create many scripts which only then allow for sentence forming representation. In other words, some things must be lived out first. And that something is the discrete complex of transference and countertransference.

By remaining quiet and taking in, the analyst allows this patient to establish the core scenarios (paradigms) first, because speech, as it were, comes out of this. It is partly a question of category orders, as the symbolic may not function quite like this. But isn't it possible that the other speaks to the true experience of place (of scene), of location in the imaginary; that is, the "word" states the true place of the subject in the order of things, in that "real" [cf. Lacan], that is determined in part by the fate of inherent concepts and their organization into desire?

[22/11/89]
"When the other speaks back"

In the Freudian place the subject speaks to himself in, say, a narrative structure. A story begins. But then the spoken-to "speaks" back, via a "breakaway" into memory, into desire, into "X". Thus the narrative is always broken and the structure of this phenomenon comes back to the collision of narrative and psyche or consciousness an unconsciousness. Freud knew where to place himself, between narrative and poetic structure/expression, where he situated himself in that somewhat intermediate space in which all of us live: between our narratives, our speeches, and the reply of the other.

Psychoanalysis makes it optimally possible to narrate the self: history, events etc. But what one finds in the breakdown of this narrative, and in the genre of free association, is a place which admits of a narrative without a narrator—except the unconscious.

Psychoanalysis is autobiography in search of its form. Its human form. From the two in one, to the one in two.

[23/11/89]
"Self analysis"

I think I may be wrong about assigning a significance to self analysis as is. Indeed, at least for me it was through psychoanalysis that my self-analytical place could truly be enriched. As if the quiet place of analysis became my place, as if the patience of the analyst became my internal patience, as if the gentle "to and fro" became a generative dialectic.

I had always had, of course, the capacity for self reflection. I thought about my actions. But meaning now came out of an "inner play" that I think I lacked before. This inner play is the work of analysis and I think each analytical patient is also listening to the free associations spoken to the analyst, and in this way the analyst—or rather patient—benefits from listening in.

"Categories/modes/forms"

Modes of reception. This might pertain to the reception to reality. Form capacity (expressive abilities) have their own receptors (a musical person receives some actuals musically). There are senses: touch, taste, etc. Then there are the meta-sensual capacities derived from psychic integration, innate ability, or ego ability. Modal ability.

Categories of self experiencing. Refers to those internal psychic human abilities (to dream, symptomatise, daydream, imagine, inner speech, musicalize, abstract-conceptualize) to process the interaction between prior internal states an present units of reality. A category can be made up of several different modes.

Forms of self expression refers to any form of expressing the self, which of course means a transformation of the internally processed to the externally expressed. But the act of expression also evokes, indeed creates itself. How can this be conceptualized?

—some patients cannot use form, or form freedom, and cannot transform from categories of self experiencing (or self experience) to self expression.

—perhaps I should take out the word "self" from experiencing and expression as both (indeed all three) involve self. So:
—modes of reception
—categories of experiencing
—forms of expression
Sensual orders: taste, touch, etc.
Metasensual capacities: humor, play
Psychic categories: image, abstraction, inner speech, dream, daydream.

[15/12/89]
"Genera"

What would the psychic representation of a genera be? It is as unintelligible as a dream. It is a protean form, and its representational nucleating may be a simple cluster of associated images, feelings, memories and so forth.

Freud has the dreamer focus attention on the separate elements of the dream, to associate to them, and from this nucleus emerges an associative stream. Meaning is latently condensed in a dream object. A genera is that condensation: something meaningful is formed. Epiphanic revelation—or should it be epistemic stimulation—is the releasing of the genera into its knowledge. Each genera is a theory of knowledge, or a knowledge, so at some point "it" occurs or is released. The sense of it, or the use of it prior to consciousness is intuition. There is an epiphanic moment when the genera is freed into associating. In life this may be hours, days, or weeks of psycho affective associations, so that the person feels freed into new, previously uninhabited self states.

So genera are condensations of things, nucleating to form new self experiencings derived from the genera.

But what would that be? I think it's a new sense of self freed partly into consciousness, but probably revealed through the turning to new objects and therefore new uses, yielding new experiences (qualia). Or also new abilities in being and in relating with and to the other.

Psychoanalytically, it may mean transformation of the internal representational world with new objects formed.

But genera are more meta sensation releasings. The self knows more, yes, but it also feels some intense pleasure in being open (alive) due to the epiphanic moment and the new use or different use of objects, and the new direction of self movement.

Genera release people to take up new interests, to look at their life differently, to feel the "I" differently (or more enriched in its capacity—not content).

Genera do not create new information, although their effect could be this.

It's as if genera is the way in which true self collects material through which to transform the total self into new visions, new uses, and new senses of life.

Why do we form genera? There is a hermeneutical drive, a need to know, an urge to understand (epistemological impulse) an epistemic urge, to collect the experiences of our life into genera (nucleated forms for new vision). It works just like the dream.

A genera reaching epiphanic revelation throws light on one's life. This throwing is pleasing because one now knows consciously what one has felt (unthought known.) Intuitively we act on genera by choosing objects (novels, books, people, landscapes) that seem releasers (epistemic stimulants) of the genera. In other words genera (the "work" of true self collection?) selects out objects which (or the experiences of: memories and rules …) form nuclei that as genera seek objects and experience intuitively. Then at a concert, with a friend, working, alone, suddenly one sees life differently, or knows something new.

In the destiny drive the true self chooses objects through which to articulate and elaborate its core. There is an urge to do this. Along the way such experiencings nucleate into protean forms (genera) that yield senses: a sense of intuition about searching for objects that are sought for their meaning value. This is still part of the destiny drive, but it is an epistemic urge, as the subject is now choosing (only at times) objects that are intuitively known to be the core of an emerging epiphany. Music, book, friend, are now selected because of a need to experience them as evocative, as containers (releasers really, as evocative releasers) of a nucleated genera. These new experiencings are the equivalent of free association to the dream: they arise, indeed seem urgently essential as tellings, but their meaning is not known. For Freud the latent thoughts are still latent and open up to interpretation at some point, but for Freud—no, for me—the release of genera opens new self positions: some new information, new relations to perhaps new internal objects, or to one's life.

Indeed this cannot be stressed enough as it is a new relation to one's life.

Freud maintains that free associations to a dream make it intelligible.

Doesn't this suggest, then, that genera released shed light on the prior movement of one's life? Isn't this therefore a kind of life analysis? Life analysis is a subset of psychoanalysis, but it means that a person who has had an epiphany can then look back upon the past and fill in the gaps—of choice of object, of questions, inquiries, actions, etc.—and that this is <u>an</u> <u>analysis of life.</u>

So there is a psychoanalysis and then there is a life-analysis, when the person's intuitive choices elaborate himself through life experiences and then, suddenly, many things in his life seem clear. Awareness of this process is life analysis.

Steps:

1. a genera is a protean form that nucleates out of the varieties of experience, from which certain "senses" of one's potential meaningfulness emerge.
2. over time, as it forms, it becomes a psychic structure which searches for experiences essential to its search for meaning.
3. this is an epistemic drive.
4. objects sought provide a genera with its quality, contributing into it.
5. then at a certain point an inner experience occurs which is epiphanic, when there is a sudden dramatic sense of viewing oneself and one's life differently.
6. this may actually yield a new perspective even if only temporarily.

Is it possible that there is a Darwinian feature to this? Of genetic change?

Now suppose that the true self seeks to "improve" itself upon the stimulation of events and objects in the environment. Let's say, as a child my true self chooses objects to speak my self, and then <u>an</u> <u>event occurs</u> in which <u>I am moved</u> in the true self, and this core of me, in time, collects to it further such genera, generating a psychic structure, that will sponsor <u>a new natural ability</u> to experience life in an enhanced way. The true self then has an intelligence to its search for objects to elaborate it, and in life—according to the life instincts—if we endure an experience which evocatively suggests that this true self can generate new potentials (alongside its inherited potentials) then it will search for the experiences, and generate the psychic structures that will enhance it.

Is this a structural urge? Is there a true self urge, not simply to elaborate what is but to generate new true self potentials? I think there must be. The search for genera, in response to suggestive stimuli in the environment, is an urge to develop core potentials that will be with one throughout life as new capacities for experience.

Some say that there is an endless struggle to reproduce, a contest for progeny and the only criteria is "fecundity". Perhaps then this <u>species urge</u> is built into us at an individual level—indeed, this is the life instinct. So there is an urge to be fecund, to re-produce the core self, a ruthless scene.

See the life instincts and Freud's ego instincts. I think however this need to enhance is complex. Because genera are a psychic accomplishment and structure, which I suppose increases true self movement. Like discovery of a wheel improves transport or binoculars improve vision, the play-work leading to a genera, or the genera, is/provides new ability which, in turn, allows for more enhanced and articulated elaborations of the true self.

So if the true self is person theory then genera are abstractions enabling more enhanced person formation; or, they add to the theory of this person's personality, therefore and thereby leading to new forms of or in being and relating.

This is the struggle to reproduce or produce newness to the self, or to be new unto oneself, to survive (depression, death instinct) by the struggle to be fecund.

[22/12/89]
"1st read through of genera"

Are there or is there actually any difference between modes of reception and categories of experience?

There is a problem with experiencing and representing. Imagining is a self experience, but it's also a form of representation. But it is purely internal. Perhaps forms of representation should, in my schema, stand for all internal forms, while modes of expression should stand for all means of expressing.

1990

[2/1/90]

"Genera"

"I've been trying to get away from the idea, in sculpture," said Eduardo Paolozzi in 1965,[1] "of trying to make a Thing—in a way, going beyond the Thing—and trying to make some kind of presence" (Chipp,[2] 617–618).

"In collage," continues Paolozzi, "… one is able to manipulate, to move, and use certain laws which are in a way blocked off if you try to do a pencil drawing, say, and then fill in the colored areas" (Chipp, 618).

—so he discovers a form that allows for a new type of representation, or vision, or expression.

Francis Bacon (1952): "[art is a] method of opening up areas of feeling rather than merely an illustration of an object (Chipp, 616).

Bacon: "Real imagination is technical imagination … The object is the technique and the technique is the object. Art lies in the continual struggle to come nearer to the sensory side of objects" (620).

—so a genera could be a technique for the grasping of one state of affairs, which has a sensory base or side to it.

Bacon (1955): "I would like my pictures to look as if a human being had passed between them, like a snail, leaving a trail of the human presence and memory trace of past events, as the snail leaves it slime" (Chipp, 621).

—Bacon's vision is like that of the destiny drive: as we use objects we leave personal effects, imprints of our idiom upon our life. The painter has his paint. But with all of us there is an unrecorded shadow of all those places, events, experiences we have had. Memory may be their only place. Where else?

Note the form sense that Henry Moore notes of the sculptor.

"He gets the solid shape, as it were, inside his head—he thinks of it, whatever its size, as if he were holding it completely enclosed in the hollow of his hand … And the sensitive observer of sculpture must also learn to feel shape simply as shape, not as description or reminiscence" (Chipp, 595).

—the above is interesting insofar as the internal representation of the outside world is concerned, and then, the relation to the objects of/in the world.

[2/1/90]
"Anti-love"

This is not hate. It is the eradication of love, or its foreclosure: i.e. not allowing it to develop.

[undated]
"Art forms as areas of mind"

See Valery. "Other images make me see quite different conditions"; and, "on several different levels of ideas … you have images of various *orders*" and sometimes "the germ is no more than a word."[3]

—now what this teaches me is about the mind. That we are processing orders of experience (which are part of the units of experience). Each order, so to speak, evokes its own level of ideation (of thinking it) and out of this pops a word, or an image that is the nucleus of response. It will almost always be unconscious.

—Dylan Thomas raises the question of why any one poem works for him or anyone else. "You can tear it apart, examine its craft, its words, and say 'Yes, this is it. This is why the poem moves me so' but you have discovered nothing. And each poem affects the other differently" (Gibbons, 190).

—Odilon Redon, 1909: "suggestive art is like an illumination of things for dreams, toward which thought also is directed" (Chipp, 117).

—how this suggests that when we choose an object we "illuminate" it. It is on its way to the dream experience.

[7/1/90]
[untitled]

In self experiencing I have argued that objects contain parts of the self and therefore we move through a signifying universe. I also say that self is a meta sense, an abstraction that is derived from its constituents.

But!

There are symbolic fragments (icons) of self experience, like condensations in a dream, embedded in actual objects. These objects, like my swing,[4] are abstract conventional objects (or self objects—not in Kohut's sense, but objects of the self, that mark it). Diachronic. Versus metonymic objects. Synecdoche. A part that stands for the whole. Or a metaphor. In any event the object represents the work of condensation (of self) rather than itself.

[undated]
"Oedipus"

When Oedipus leaves Corinth (because of an oracle which says that he will kill his father etc., whom he believes, of course, to be Polybus) and kills Laius, whom he does not know to be his father, this confusion (ignorance) plays with the actual and the fantastical. It also plays with the power of words, their priority over actions etc. The internal world versus the external world.

The ennoblements of accident, injury, ultimately death. I wonder if the Greek self was struggling to give life meaning as it seemed to be meaningless. Their deaths were not moments of greatness, but in their mythologies they tried to make it so.

Critics comment on Antigone's seemingly spurious thought that Hymon has been infantilized etc., but this "oedipal action" seems to me to be a principle of <u>actions</u> committed, without thought (which is split off as the bizarre—omens, oracles) so that everyone is acting or reacting with no core to them: that is no seeming sense of self.

Bowra[5] argues that the Greek character came to very rapid decisions (being vigilant etc). Are these very necessary traits at the same time the ruin of interpersonal situations? How do we assess cultural values vis-à-vis their transmission into nuclear family terms?

Bowra maintains that Greece geographically lent itself to piecemeal penetration. Groups could gather and take over. Would this juxtaposition of havens, created by mountains (mother's breast etc.) also be grounds for penetration, sedition, and overthrow? [Would they] not <u>also</u> transmit to the nuclear family? It is safe, yet it is also the haven that can be penetrated unless one listens out—to the foreign voice, the out of place gesture, the shepherds etc. who may have seen something. (Can I find an example in real terms of this? It's in Oedipus.)

The idea here is in the transmission of laws of existence into psychic terms (and then family enactments).

1. The laws of existence. Terms.
2. Their transmission into psychic facts.
3. Their enactment in family life.

Intriguingly, the Greek city state (or village) isolated as an island or in a valley shielded by mountains—this city is a kind of <u>collateral structure</u> homologous to the nuclear family, which is also isolated.

—where the home and the law of the father separate it out.

Indeed Bowra argues that Greek light affected the clarity of Greek philosophy.

Bowra claims that there are essential elements to a culture that shapes its character, and he says the moods of the era reflected themselves in the moods of man.

[undated]
"Oedipus: the play"

The opening invocation by the priest is filled with madness and mixed feelings towards Oedipus. "Look around you", "see with your own eyes", links with O's first comment that they are there because he wants to see them with his own eyes, not through a messenger.

—however, if a messenger is the hallucinate, then to see with one's own eyes is very important.

What is the psychic function of the Sphinx who stops the investigation of Laius' murder? In oedipal terms it's the mad mother (the castrating one) supporting the son's patricide.

Oedipus says he will search for Laius as if he were his father: after saying he sleeps with his wife and they share seed. Now if we imagine this to be the statement of a son exiled by the father (I shall find him!), then sleeping with Jocasta would be as the infant who has had her. The discovery that he <u>has</u> found the father, indeed that he killed him, and must now be exiled: who, now, is the dead (already killed) father?

Tiresias says of Oedipus that he has gone too far in action. This is a human fault. We all know what it's like to go too far in anything and when we think our actions are justified. Perhaps to an extreme position (as with Oedipus) but what happens then is that there is a trauma to the true self that is revealed to be mad.

By blaming Creon, at first, Oedipus' blame is understandable. He sees this in terms of politics. One must wonder about Tiresias <u>remaining</u> silent all those years. There is a gloating quality to his dispensation of knowledge. Why not tell O what in fact he had done?

Creon's defense to Oedipus, namely why would he ever want to be King, is a form of lying. So Sophocles shows how <u>complex</u> it is for one character to determine what his character has done (or is doing) given that other characters are participating in the dynamic. There is no pure insight.

But Creon's plea "natures like yours are hardest on themselves" is correct. This is Sophocles speaking, but to some extent the message may also be: 1. each of us is damaged by early events 2. we have been abandoned; 3. we have murdered; 4. we must not let these blows become the continuing source of paranoid grudge, etc.

Given that it is "the oracles" which cause man such horror, and that O to some extent challenges the oracles, is Sophocles questioning the place of faith in the oracular?

What does it mean, analytically, if Oedipus kills the father, solves the virgin sphinx's riddle and sleeps with his mother? What does the death of the sphinx mean then?

[undated]
"Defenses/releases"

As each of us constructs a defense against an inner excitement or anxiety (and so forth), so too do we choose "releasers" that free us up from conflicts. The search for releasers is an important part of life.

[undated]
"The re-creation of an object"

Winnicott recreated all objects he read or encountered. How does one recreate an object? Is it given a new identity? A new content? Even if some of its original form is present. Are recreated objects intermediate ones?

[undated]
"Private speech in a public space"

In answer to the question, "why is the ruthless person allowed to go to the top?" Because in western culture (I should not think in all cultures) we do not have a verbal convention that allows for the early on verbalization of opposition to a ruthless person. And in the beginning, we may only have a sense of this in a person, and be hard pressed to prove it. How does one proceed? In part this valuable inner knowledge, checked out with and by other people, still does not allow the use of it to oppose the ruthless one. It is therefore a first casualty of the ruthless person's character: the destruction of free speech in the other!

I think ultimately these people become loved. I do not think they were at all loved in their "youths" when coming to power. But the difficulty for anyone who should feel like opposing such a person is quite how to do so, if we keep in mind the fact that the vicious person is ruthless and organized.

What can one say, even if oneself along with many others knows full well they are dealing with a vicious person? There is, perhaps, a fantasy of justice displaced there, an idea that somehow the vicious person will be so clearly unacceptable as to lose power.

[6/2/90 Grammercy Park Hotel, NYC]
"The internal object"

Each internal object is, in fact, a concept. Not an image or picture, but a concept that does give use to a condensation: part visual, part verbal, etc. But not entirely any of these. It is like an idea, but a concept is a conception of the object, an internal birth, that is a condensation of many different elements. It is partly memory (derived visually, physically, sexually, etc.), partly a working model, partly an internal correlate to the many prior processings of the actual object. It is sufficiently dense, or overdetermined, as to be voicing its many different features at any one moment, subject to the state of desire, need, anxiety etc. but it is a structure.

To change "it", it needs a deconstruction of its constituents, which takes place in analysis as an object through its representation. It is deconstructed, also in the transference, where it is also represented. In other words, an internal object is a concept, very overdetermined.

[undated. Rodin Museum, Philadelphia]
"The internal object (genera)"

In "Saint John the Baptist Preaching" Rodin had both feet on the ground, suggesting a succession of movements. At this same time he encouraged his models to walk freely about the room and he would catch them in spontaneous moments. He was able to bring this into his work.

Thus his work conceives the other: no—it condensed many movements (and moods and counter moods and states) in the same object.

He was also always sketching and redoing the same project right up to its completion. His significant works reflected long periods of studying his subject. I think this is the "contributing in" process until a genera is formed. This ultimately is a dynamic internal object which sponsors its own derivatives. It is much like the birth of an idea that sponsors many new ideas (perspectives). It differs from other inner objects (or mental representations) which do not have this dynamic effect.

A genera is formed out of multitudes: the many contributings into its nuclear space.

Analyst and the patient form this together.

[undated]
"E-vaporative interpretation"

This is an interpretation that makes sense of the patient's internal world but removes the truth, because the interpretation is false. When the false self works interpretively upon the true self (or psychic reality, or whatever) it evaporates the "truth" of the moment, substituting it with a false interpretation and false reality. False reality then leaves the objects of the interpretation with an unprocessed self state, if the evaporative interpretation has been used to remove the heart of the matter.

Link to "here-and-now transference interpretation", insofar as evaporative interpretation falsely launders psychic reality by placement in an object relational script, which, untrue (though logical) eradicates the subject's speech and articulation.

Furthermore, this process is couched under the idea that anyway, any thought on the analyst's part must be true. In part, it is argued, it must be evidence of something split off. A psychopathic sleight of hand enters the scene as the analyst can always recuperate through this cynicism: this interpretivism.

[21/2/90]
"Association versus symbolization"

I think symbolic conversion is what I mean by interpretation, when I transpose terms. Usually I associate; namely, I may metonymize the patient's discourse to or with my own, but there has been no move to the symbolic.

There are countless associative "contributings-in", which eventually lead to a symbolic event, or an event of the symbolic when such associations now <u>mean</u> something; when they are part of a structure. This is also a genera.

[undated]
"Devil's advocate"

What does it mean when someone says they're being a devil's advocate? The lawyer of the devil? Paid for this? And who decides the merit? Who judges? The problem of the individual who insists he is only the devil's advocate is that he forces the other into being God's solicitor!

[24/2/90]
"The interject"

"Let me interject." This is the object created in the other by the self's projective identifications. For the recipient it is an interject: something that has interjected the self, as a result of the mother's actions or father's actions.

So each of us incorporates, introjects, identifies, but the <u>interject</u> is an internal object shaped by the other's actions towards our self.

[undated]
"The family dog"

Time sense: i.e. how old is she? Each time we are unable to answer. One year after Sacha's birth? Two years? Her function as a signifier of time not counted, as we know her life expectancy is 10 to 14 years and she is now coming up to 10.

Counting her "human age". Ten times the year or 14 plus years. Our Swedish friend's calculation. Fact is, she has been born in our house and has now passed her middle age achieving a point of wisdom. I think she knows this. When she passed our age she stopped slavish obedience.

Her instinctual life. Like a collage of senses. We joke about her shits, farts, eating, pissing, etc.

Her nicknames: Wood Piles, Pylons, Woods, Woody.

Her habits: Chasing squirrels, cats etc.

Her landmarks: the burglaries. [We had five: she hosted the burglars.] The day the cat stood her down.

America. Our day's mirror of our kids. Roving. Going into other houses. The loss of one nice English companion.

"She". The problem of her gender. A boxer for people is so butch it's always a he. For us she is definitely a she, as she is the ultimate animated domestic object. She turned wild once: a model of the romantic conversion of the wild woman to domestic companion.

Loyalty. Running back and forth.

Poppy and Z:[i] the returning to the Wilds. Z's bite on the basketball court. "You are not Poppy!"

The dog: our move? A patient: "you couldn't possibly move to somewhere. You couldn't do that to your dog!", which is true. We couldn't say it. But we all knew it. We had imagined pooper scoopers and walking along with her. But she cannot shit on a lead! We were done in by her idiom.

Talking through her squeaky. The times (alone of course) when I guess I would do this when I think she is capable of human communication. "Come on Poppy, one squeak if you know what I mean: just one squeak." <u>Almost human</u>. The status of being almost human. The face. Being repeatedly fooled into the crossover fantasy. She is about to change over. It's being human. First there will be an inarticulate hello; a gruff sound, made in passing. "Did you hear that? It sounds as if she said hello! Hahaha!" The sound is repeated. We pause. The room is suddenly silent. We are on the verge of an extraordinary moment. The day our dog will bridge the gap to human speech. We <u>knew</u> she could do it!

How a dog is or would have be seen as a self object or transitional object, but how such anaesthetized objects are not real. A dog is instinct.

The dog's tongue.

The dog dreaming. What does she see?

Dog in quarantine: became instantly insulated for six months. Never a mess again.

David Malan telling me (1976) he preferred dogs to humans.

[26/2/90]
"The perverse community"

Or the community of the perverse, or, community as perversion. A group of people who usually cluster around a destructive-charismatic person. The perversion is that his destruction of people etc. becomes the basis of the group's libido: i.e. their investment in each other is based on a conversion of the "leader's" destructiveness into "gossip". What he does, or how he behaves is what binds them. They may be part of a common task (i.e. publication) but they would not be working together were it not for the need to parasitically be near *destrudo*, using it for the "life" of the group-party, i.e. for juicy gossip.

[undated]
"Genera"

Turning to my theory of the senses, it is possible to argue that sensations affect the body-mind, but do not necessarily have a psychical status, unless they coincide or converge: a sensation affects a body area that becomes psychically significant through symbolization.

Freud's theory of "fresh memories", of concentration: the patient's attention on scenes, events, people (evocative objects) refers to the work of objects upon the subject.

---

[i] Another boxer puppy we brought home who was violent and had to be returned to the breeder.

Is the "swing", "red street car", smells, voices: are they part of my hysterical field? Does the hysteric's body spread to the object world? Why not?

I invest objects with psychic content. From then on, they are receptor-organizers for associations (other, subsequent experiences) and yet they symbolize something specific. For example, the swing. It was also the era of swing (in music). Later I was terrified on the roller coaster (at 5 thinking I would fall out). This was also a swing of sorts. As a child I used to love to swing very high and jump out to land far away (age 5 through 9). Perhaps swing, slide, kickball diamond are so evocative as they represent what I have had to give up.

[undated]
"Word presentation and the auditory"

In *Interfaces of the Word* Walter Ong[6] argues that western civilization is the development from an auditory to a visual scene.

I realize that in considering the dream, Freud's question about word presentation forces us from the visual (a briefcase) to the auditory: a brief case. Do we not sound it out?

The word or the sound "her" is in many words, but only auditorily.

[undated]
"Senses"

Each of the senses has its psychic correlate. The body's way in the mind. Or the body's correlate in self experiencing.

If I am "touched" by something, I mean psychically that my psyche-body is touched. If I say "I see" I mean I see. If I say "I am moved" then this registers my kinesthetic-motoric sense. Therefore the body is always present in discourse. It is always a part of self experience. And it is a form of conversion: from body to self discourse. Or body to self experience.

Therefore there are selves rich in body experience, and those poor in it. Further, analyses may direct themselves continuously to only a part of a person's body (visual, auditory etc.) without the remainder being addressed.

[26/2/90]
"Motherline and fatherline"

I wonder if these terms may substitute for masculine and feminine. For the male, in part, derives from each sex's relation to the father and therefore a girl will have a different relation to the father and a different fatherline feature than the boy will. That is, a woman's sense of masculinity will be different from a man's sense of it. Equally, a boy's relation to the mother, the motherline in him, is different from the girl's relation.

Each sex forms its masculine-feminine senses through the characteristics of the body in relation to the body of the opposite sex. So the boy's fatherline sense is based on his body's affiliation to the father and his sense of identity vis-à-vis the mother, while the girl's sense of fatherline is based on her body in relation to her father.

[28/2/90]
"Genera"

There is a sense in which a person <u>can</u> represent the self through the many different modes, but each person is restricted, to begin with, by the foreclosures of the psyche.

Or by something else.

Imagine that I characterized my mother or father in a particular way. I say "mother never understood" or "father was standoffish". Now this characterization either sets up or reflects in the first place a simplifying of the internal world. My inner objects in this example (mother and father) are shallow, caricatures. I cannot therefore use the concepts of mother or father. Such a personification of the process (what the mother or father <u>did</u> in their mothering and fathering) shuts down the person's continual use of such inner correlates of a prior process. They cannot therefore refer the child's parts to these internal objects for correlative inner processing, because of what they have done to their objects.

Mental conflict is often due to the caricaturing of a process through personifications.

I would like to say that <u>representing</u> is curative. Because, in fact, it subverts the pseudo organization of the internal world (and its objects).

However, each of us interprets our body-self in the world. Our body is connected in a way: it means something. The bodies of objects also bear our private inscription. Our body and our actuals are inscribed like tablets with our renderings. We are interpreters, each of us.

[22/3/90]
"True self"

The true self is not a content, it is a <u>principle</u> of aliveness—of the life instincts. It is the principle of coming alive, articulating and elaborating one's core through experience.

[26/3/90]
"The illusion of understanding"

The illusion of understanding does not mean that all understandings are illusory. Just that this illusion, created by the mother, is part of early life.

The illusion of understanding does <u>ironically</u> authorize true understandings, as it allows people to create each other and thus to transform the experience of the other into some true understanding of the other, a continuous process of "finding" the other, then losing the other (most of the time) but not knowing this, due to the assumption that one is understanding the other when in fact one is not.

An irony. The more one conveys, the less one understands. This is why free perspectives legitimate reasons. Psychoanalysis must be reductionist. Each school of psychoanalysis reduces the experience to a model, to make limited sense of the material. But this reduction should be openly acknowledged. And students should study from the different schools of reduction, to know how to organize the material into potential analytical genera: structures that will generate new analytical perspectives.

[28/3/90]

"Transference and countertransference in treatment of a psychotic child"

Harold's case of Charles (12) who as a small child collapsed into a psychotic fright: "look out, the robot with the red eyes!" he cried out in his sleep. As C entered psychotherapy with Harold at age 6 he drooled and played with his saliva. He repeated what H said as in an echolalia. H felt murderous with him at times. He could only ever enter into a meager play of sorts, as when C had Harold sit between water and matches, rubbing himself with water, and Harold was meant to hold the match.

Recently he wandered into another room and found H's pipe and used it. He recently upset his father as he went into a panic and looked incredibly frightened.

Formulation

1. He slaps himself, bites inside his mouth to use the body against the mind. It does partly work. By playing with saliva he uses the body to blunt out the passing thoughts of the mind. He bites the self or slaps the self when it cannot be controlled.

2. The catastrophes occur when he is unable to eradicate a thought (memory, dream recollections, instinctual fantasy) by using the body. Then he is victim of the mind and panics.

3. As he has refused his mind, refused to tolerate, elaborate—and hence process mental contents—he now has no means of ultimately dealing with the mind's breakdown of his defenses.

4. He has successfully managed to create in a transference and in the other's countertransference a human world that unknowingly colludes with his theory. How?

   i. He acts bizarrely now and then, creating horror in the other, who backs off, shocked at the awful spectacle.

   ii. This is his transfer of an intrapsychic event to an interpersonal one. He forces the other to be horrified as he is horrified by his mental contents. His bizarre actions are the presence of disturbing mental contents.

   iii. In the past his father became enraged by his actions and now and then would beat him. Therefore he forced parents into collusion: they, like him, beat the body, expressed rage against the body, to stop the mind.

   iv. In psychoanalysis he has gotten the father to hold him, and to move his arms about; he imitates his father's speech. In effect he tries to climb inside the other's body: a kind of thoughtless transfer of one psyche-soma into the other psyche-soma.

   v. He has not found useful objects but tries instead to resolve his conflicts only within the space of his own body: especially in the mouth.

Recommendations

1. The father must interpret the transference and the countertransference.
   a. "You are showing me how you try to dull your mind by emphasizing the body as the most important—your spittle is so valued."
   b. "I see how in some ways it has been good for you to seek comfort from your thoughts inside your body but now, however, you have regarded your mind as an enemy and you don't know how to live with it, when it refuses to be quiet."
   c. "When you act like this—so strangely—I think you want to present me with a shocking picture before my eyes, to bring me to horror and panic, to make me feel what you feel when you have a dream, a sexy thought, or a murderous image passes in your mind and shocks you!"
2. The father must tell Charles that these dreams, thoughts, images are ordinary and can be lived with if thought through and spoken about with father.
3. When C acts bizarrely the father or the mother must say "look, you have just thought something which has upset you. You need not panic. It is human to have disturbing thoughts. When you like, you may even tell me."
4. "Environmental prescription". This patient, like a few, does need more than just psychotherapy. The father told me in his report that C's uncle takes C camping and C really enjoys this. C now comes only two times because when the mother brought him he was very disturbed. So being outside the mother–child space is helpful. Father should meet with uncle to discover what is therapeutic in the uncle's technique. He should prescribe more time spent with the uncle and with the father: camping, etc.
5. Intermediate objects must be found to serve instinctual representations, otherwise the body itself does so, creating enormous problems.

The saliva. I recommend the therapist "play" in this, perhaps calling it C's holy water which he uses to feel safe, praying with it even. Then however, this object (saliva) should disseminate to other objects. The analyst must help the child to use other objects, eliciting a symbolic pathway. I suggested father and uncles build a small pond to make waterfalls: with a pump and so forth. Out of this perhaps can develop interest in fish, frogs and so forth. The object world is now a lexicon. C should pour the drinks at the family meal. He should be in charge of the selling of drinks in the store. The father or someone should take him to the other towns where they buy and test the water.

Match. He plays with it. He should make the fires in the home: cut wood, stack wood, perhaps carve wood. Again this is building a lexicon of objects.

"C" is stuck inside the body with therapists and others urging abstract solutions (for example "do you want to grow up?") or forcing behavioral patterns ("act like this" etc). He must be allowed to discover objects beyond his narcissistic shell.

Countertransference dreams. The father had a daydream of solving these problems and being heralded in the press for it. I wonder, is this day dreaming about the patient a move into fantasy—to the same place as the child? Is this a projective identification? If so then the child's horrors are only when he is attacked by his daydreaming.

I recall "Y" at EBAC (an autistic child who never uttered a sound and all members of staff had a dream in which he spoke). The "Y" dream. A sign that it will never happen, except in the dream. An autistic transfer! Where we only ever meet or act in the deep autistic interior of the dream. The dream in which the child speaks.

Perhaps such a dream—or the father's daydreams—are signs of a widening split between therapeutic actuality and therapeutic wish. Of a rift. But perhaps something has occurred in the session with the patient that triggers the wish. Therefore one needs to look at the day residue to see if one can find the instigation of the dream.

I postulate that if there is a link between the dream and the day, then the analyst is elaborating some psychic movement of the patient. If there is no such link, then the dream or daydream may be only a narcissistic support for the analyst who increasingly comes to the idea: only in my dreams!

Biting and sensorial. Is there a sensorial defense? The child who slaps himself or bites himself (outside-inside) announces a sensorial medium of self processing, as these attacks on the sensorium announce its continuous boundary. Perhaps the attacks aimed to establish or continually emphasize the existence of the body.

Instincts and. "C" is now coming into adolescence. He could, in the past, eradicate body urges but now the body is too powerfully driven and mental representations of instincts are breaking the sensorial defense. He can't obliterate memory, as something in the environment might evoke memory. But he can nullify memory. But instincts are too powerful. However, if objects can be found (a lexicon) for the representation of the body's urges and aims, then the sense of conflicts can move away from the theater of the body.

[undated]
"Sensibility"

(*Webster*)
   LL sensibilitas
   L sensibilis

1. The capacity for physical sensation; power of responding to stimuli; ability to feel.
2. (a) The capacity for being affected emotionally or intellectually, whether pleasantly or unpleasantly; receptiveness to impression.
   (b) The capacity to respond perceptively to intellectual, moral, or aesthetic values; delicate, sensitive awareness or responsiveness.

—Note emphasis on capacity. Note emphasis on responsiveness.

   —So it is a manifestation of a person's idiom: the capacities to receive and respond to the object.

   Oxford English Dictionary

"1(a) plural. Sensible species; the emanations from bodies, which were supposed to be the cause of sensation (b) Capability of being perceived by the senses."

—this really is "qualia" in some ways or shows how it is originally something in the object capable of being perceived.

"(2) power of sensation or perception; and the specific function of an organ or tissue to respond to sensory stimuli; sensitiveness."

—sensitiveness!

—the usages given refer to the power of the person's senses; to too much sensibility for example.

[undated]
"Dialectic"

In a way the dialectic of which I write proceeds in the following way: answer to question. That is, the true self is the answer to the authority of self that moves its being which meets up with the world that questions it. The reply (synthesis) is psychic life.

[undated]
"Therapeutic alliance"

The dreamer inside the dream is "in" a therapeutic alliance. He uses and is used by the dream space, as is the patient, who uses and is used by the analytical process.

The therapeutic alliance is the notion that this is "the relatively nonneurotic, rational relationship between patient and analyst which makes it possible for the patient to work purposely in the analytic situation." In Ralph Greenson,[7] (46).

"The working alliance is that part of the relationship to the analyst which makes it possible for the patient to cooperate in the analytic hour" (Greenson, 47).

How does the analyst cooperate in the therapeutic alliance and in the hour? Particularly given the countertransference, the immersion in material etc., and the incorrect interpretation. The analyst continually returns to the rules of the analysis, to its procedure, from deep immersion in the material. Silence. Upholding.

The analyst and patient need to return to the task.

What task? Where? For whom?

The notion of work is important, for both.

The sense of the place, the occasion is important. Of where one is: again, the wakeful dream.

The patients need to tolerate this other, strange voice, who works elsewhere: from the unconscious. This is part of the therapeutic alliance.

And the transference. The transference is the personal commitment of the analysand to throw himself into the madness. In a way this transfer is the therapeutic alliance as it is what the patient is unconsciously meant to do. Go to a doctor and you show him your cut. Go to the analyst and you show him the psychic wound.

Is the transference part of the therapeutic alliance? Is it independent? As in non-neurotic? When the patient "steps outside" the transference to address the analyst or to cooperate is he there, sane?

What are the origins of this? What is this mental act? Is it akin to the dreamer awakening, to say "ah ha! It's only a dream"!

[undated]
"The act of freedom"

Nina's and Neville's[ii] papers are not expressions of freedom from the patient, but from the suffocating structures of analytical orthodoxy.

[undated]
"Lexical elements"

Each object is an atomic thing-in-itself which when used evokes a self experience. When I use objects, one after the other sequentially, I provide self experiences. Also each object is part of the symbolic order

(a word for each) and a collateral meaning may apply (unconscious fantasy) to these uses (for example child's play), but nonetheless the use of the thing-in-itself yields units of experience, so to choose a specific object is to select what it can provide.

[23/4/90 New York]
"Illusion of understanding"

We understand as best we can. That's the point. And it is not much.

[undated]
"Why does the id choose a different object?"

If we have a wonderful partner—an other who is sexually, emotionally, personally fulfilling— why, in our dreams, do we choose an other? If the id's only aim is to relieve itself of an instinct, well I've no problem with that. But why should there be another object? Why? Why is it about this specificity? What is it ? Novelty? À la Daniel Stern?

Perhaps. No. It is evolution. The need to elaborate, to articulate, through new objects. In life—love and marriage—we feel guilt for this. Quite rightly so. But it is a fact, a human fact, that we need the specificity of a different object through whom to find, to question the object, our self, our idiom and so forth. This is ruthless. It is usually lived out in fantasy or in dream life, but sometimes in reality. The point is, it is there, although quite what each of us does is a problematic. It tends to make liars of us all. It is however the secret province, another country.

ii Nina Coltart and Neville Symington, who gave talks on the analyst's act of freedom in the clinical hour.

The other (object) through whom one turns. Finds. It is a horrible betrayal of the contract with the other, as the <u>essential</u> need, is to turn, to turn, to turn, move, use, experience. Hence we must oppose the self—rightly so. In that, each of us is heroic.

Yet the value of the single other, through whom one <u>is</u>, is that such singularity invites turnings within the same space, in which we put more of ourself into one another and, also, discover the many different moments with the other. Suzanne is different for me each time. This is what is so amazing.

[undated]
"Overhearing"

"Well, I'm <u>different</u>. And you are different. I mean, I get into things in my own way. I get into things." (Conversation at the Museum cafe in New York.)

[undated]
"Friends of desire"

I think of how here I am in New York City. One week. I would like to see S. But there is no time. How do I tell him that? It would not be believed and yet, in life, we fail many people. Why? We desire. We choose. We meet. We fail. In what? In sustaining it all. Were I to choose only a few: no problem. But I find I do love too many. I am fascinated by them, but more, I just like them. But I fail. I cannot—in one week—do more than is possible. And yet, S is hurt, as are others and this is my fault. As I <u>cause</u> it.

[27/4/90 New York]
"True self and instincts"

Mental life is the place of interpretation.

But in self experiencing we process states of affairs according to the integrative order (idiom) of the unconscious ego. Therefore <u>this</u> unconscious is descriptive, but not dynamic. It is part of the unthought known.

Mental life is the subject's interpretation of such experience and is always only a derivative of self experiencing and furthermore altered by the intrapsychic dynamics concerned.

The true self and idiom are not the same. The true self describes a type of aliveness and object use. It does not describe an organization.

Idiom describes an organization (in being and relating) but it is not necessarily the case that the idiom will evolve as true self or not.

True self describes a state.

Idiom describes an organization.

One can have an idiom movement through the false self. Idiom does not move through true self alone.

[4/5/90]
"Or-gasm"

A patient of "R'"s came to analysis complaining she had never had an orgasm.

It became clear that in fact she was preoccupied with either/ors : stuck in a world of "mights" etc.

The possible interpretation to this patient is that she cannot stop having or-gasms, or mental masturbations.

[4/5/90]
"Working alliance"

In the course of enduring a state of affairs we do so at differing levels of thought, from the unthought known—a knowing which never achieves representation except by affinities in reality (déjà vu) and possibly derivatives—to deep thought, reflective thought, representational thought, rhetorical thought.

Thus we render a state of affairs through the different orders of thought—and categories—and yet, all is done according to a "working alliance", an internal (intrapsychic) working alliance between the simple self (the self immersed in an order of thought) and the complex self making links as they occur and upon reflection.

[undated]
"'O' and the true self use of the object"

"O does not fall in the domain of knowledge or learning save incidentally; it can be 'become', but it cannot be 'known!'" (Bion, *Attention and Interpretation*, p. 26).

In a way this is true of the idiom's true self use of the object. Or, idiom is psychic "O" which only becomes in and through use of the object. Object use is its experiential lexicon. Different objects allow for different types of thinking (transformations of O).

Op = O of psychic reality

Or = O of reality reality

I shall have to say why I do not think the true self use of an object is a beta experience. Because such use can release the idiom into its articulated experiencing, which lies "in" the object-experience.

[undated]
"Working alliance"

"But it is also true," writes Helen Vendler,[8] "that the poet is often opaque to himself, and senses in his bafflement an obscure need for the critic, a dependency only sporadically acknowledged which by reaction-formation is itself a hidden cause of the barrier between the poet and the critic" (17).

This comes I think from the original split between the two types of thought mentioned before in these notebooks.

Bion's theory of the analyst as container is only partly true as the analyst is also deeply associative. At moments the analyst relies upon the formal rhetoric of the analysand as container! That is another side of the working alliance: the analysand's exercise of <u>negative capability</u> in relation to the analyst's interpretations.

The working alliance as a transference. It is the transfer of a subject-object polarity, of two categories, of mother and child, etc. How is it transferred (received)? When is it not? How and why does it break down?

[undated]
"Reflexivity of idiom"

Vendler paraphrasing Wordsworth writes "the artist must create the taste by which he is enjoyed"[9] (19), in referring to taste in the reader.

But. In choosing objects we taste ourselves through the objects! We are tasted by the object. As in touched. Perceived. Known as well.

Of Keats, Vendler writes:[10] "he sees the work of the artist as the transformation of nature into culture, the transmutation of the teeming fields into garnered grain" (125).

This is true of idiom and life as well. (I am intentionally changing the meaning of Vendler and Keats.) Idiom is nature and the work (aesthetics) of life is <u>to transform our nature into our culture!</u>

In meeting, using, and therefore creating (as in Winnicott's "finding") objects, we transform our nature into our culture (personal effects) which does have its form.

What we create are "the hieroglyphs" of our life (Vendler, 125).

[undated]
"Working alliance"

I shall take the position that the working alliance is a transference:

1. from that intrapsychic polarity between two different states of mind.
2. from the mother/child, mother/father, mother/father/child alliances that are transferred.

[undated]
"The unconscious knows no sense of time"

How can this be so if, for example, the anniversary of an event can be so traumatic? Indeed, if its symbolic significance (age 9, 1979, 1989) is so terribly important. It is like a profoundly accurate unconscious sense of time.

But perhaps Freud meant to say (or said) that first the unconscious knows no time but second events in time are unconsciously signified and remembered as such. Thus my age 9 is there again in 1979/1989, as if no time had passed, giving it both meanings: of no time but a time sense.

[undated]
[untitled]

To what extent do differing analytical theories of intervention constitute simply different rhetorical strategies or stances or positions? What is the illocutionary act of Kleinian interpretation, of Winnicottian interpretation, of Kohutian interpretation?

[31/5/90]
"Working alliance"

Does the analytic working alliance have an intrapsychic precursor, something which the patient as it were knows about?

In life:

1. therapeutic alliance is intrapsychic dialogue. Two positions: simple self/ complex self.
2. transference proper is unconscious enactment: movement against the other. Intrapsychically equivalent to a dream, or simple self immersion.

How does the therapeutic alliance, as a relation of two equal unconsciouses, contribute to the cure?

Mother/child: the infant's "sense" through the mother's care that there is (or is not!) a system of love (care) beyond him (outside his knowing) to which he can entrust himself even when furious with the specific object mother. Over time his ego development allies with the auxiliary ego to form an ongoing area inside the self, a belief, that one can "give in" to intense states of mind etc. and yet there will remain a part of the self available for confrontation, scrutiny, processing. The relation to the dream uncannily emphasizes this, as we are "in" it and yet emerge from it to think about it.

Is there an intrapsychic contract?

—biological contract?

—mother–child contract?

The therapeutic alliance is a transfer: from mother/child, oedipal, [etc.] to the working alliance. Depending on what freedom there was or is to think about or to be participant in it, this will be brought to the working alliance.

Part of the working alliance is knowing how to use the holding environment in which to transfer, i.e. to go mad!

1. Also what point might any patient be making by temporarily creating a breakdown in the working alliance? In which they seem to have lost their willingness to collaborate?
2. Further, to what extent is the here-and-now transference interpretation (aimed at showing the patient what he is doing) unconsciously assaultive of the working alliance: the notion of collaboration?

Part of analysis maybe the flirtation with the <u>real</u>, the noumenon, the thing in itself, to discover the place from which the analyst originates.

Use "X" who reminded me in a session—as an effort to break me down—to observe a zero point of being from which any thought would originate. In other words some patients break it down in order to see if "the real analyst" and "the real person" can be found beyond the realms of illusion—the "for real".

If we return to that unconscious knowledge of the infant, we were <u>in care.</u> Then each of us has been held in an intelligence beyond our knowing (consciousness) and therefore some of us break down the collaboration to see if the ultimate intelligence in the systems of care—the real person—can be found. This occurs usually in a certain type of paranoid person, in which the intelligence of the mother (the "real" world beyond (i.e. projection) was disturbed. This person may then aim to test the analyst's "realness".

Bear in mind the working alliance of two unconscious minds!

But even in a non-borderline patient there may seem to be a puzzling impetuous undoing of the working alliance. Again however, it may be ironically out of appreciation and envy of the analyst's intelligent caretaking, which evokes a memory of early infantile care and a curiosity to find the <u>place</u> of such care.

There is, then, an experience in each of us of being transformed by an intelligent and loving environment, so the patient's search to break the figure of the analyst by refusing to cooperate may reflect a secret wish to discover the nature of an imprint and truth. And indeed the <u>analysis</u> (as opposed to the analyst) does survive this destruction, as the hour is kept, couch is there, space and freedom, all the terms of that intelligence of care that has contributed to the analytical generative movement are still there.

[31/5/90]
"Hate"

Hate is the binding force of civilizations: it holds groups together. Religions are the prime movers of such a binding. Feelings—which analysts value so much—actually threaten the binding force of civilization.

[undated]
"Oedipus"

Fagles[11] on Oedipus (p. 277): "That Oedipus has become a protective hero of the Athenian land, with power over his enemies, is perhaps some kind of recognition on the part of the gods that they had used him, to his cost, for a tremendous demonstration of the fact that human knowledge at its greatest is ignorance compared with theirs."

This really is the Oedipus complex. It is this moment in a child's life when the child is aware that <u>what it "all" means</u> is beyond him, even though he's caught up in the logic of events generated by the differing sources of influence: primary intersubjectivity.

Sophocles does this to us because the play has so many "contributive actions" that its meaning is labyrinthine. And it would be very difficult to remember what links to what in each play. Indeed why did Sophocles write the plays in this order, with the last play first, the first play second, and the second play last? By choosing this order he scrambles our time/space sense. And even if we read them in proper order we find it is still hard to keep it all in mind.

Who shall repress what?

We shall argue over the meaning of the plays.

Is there to be a court of justice? No, but we seek one.

[undated]

"Oedipus complex"

The Oedipus complex is complexity.

The Court of Justice is the place where one can take ones psychic reality for validation.

The oedipal child learns he is among highly difficult subjectivities, including his own.

Oedipus at Colonus:[12] "So that,/you see, is the spirit of the place, old stranger,/not much honored in legends, more in the hearts/of us who live here, love it well" (p. 287) spoken by citizen (lines 74–77).

This is oedipal justice: the place of contest which Oedipus brings to Colonus when he has a dispute with the citizens. But it is a good place for competing psychic claims because this place of justice is based upon "the spirit of the place" (for example the law) which entirely depends upon what is in the hearts of men. Thus the conflicts of the mind and between minds—in the family—can be met with, considered, if there is a spirit of place (in the family) born out of a love (?) or reverence for the sacred.

In Oedipus the name of the founding father lives on in the people: it is the heritage, so oedipal justice depends partly on carrying this person inside. Therefore in a family, who was the father's father? And the mother's father? Were they just men? Do they live in the hearts of their sons and daughters or not?

Is it possible that Oedipus can only find a place of justice after he has killed Laius and broken the paternal lineages? When he kills the father, weds the mother, who gives birth to his sons (now his brothers), in his psycho-logic hasn't he become therefore a new son, born of his impregnation of the mother?

Oedipus at Colonus

Leader:

"What is your lineage, stranger?"

"Tell us—who was your father?"

(lines 228–229)

Lineage as a psychic phenomenon. In a way "does your father remember his father?" O's resting place (of quiet) is on a buried site, a sacred place of the Eumenides. Justice (i.e. in family) depends on memory; on that memory that is the internalization of fairness, of goodness. So in the family, a sense of justice depends partly on a sense of history—as with common law or precedence (pre-cedence) on what the fathers did in the past.

As the women bury the dead, is it possible that if the fathers are the law the women contain the memory: or transmit it?

"You, you're *that* man—?" (line 237)

The moment of the internal object and the actual object (other). The Leader knows of O by grapevine and before him stands the actual O. Is O to be the captive of the leader's "O" (internal object)? This is a feature of the problem of oedipal justice. The oedipal child has an internal object—father—who is vengeful: but when he meets up with the actual father this is not so. The child discovers at the "complex" the <u>difference</u> between the two fathers. This suggests the profound difference between worlds: internal and actual.

"Oh my children—sisters" to me is the most repellent remark. Is O's <u>true</u> crime not the murder of the actual father but of the FATHER, as he makes his children into his brothers and sisters? To sleep with the mother <u>in order to become her child</u> is paternal abnegation, and it is the true crime of the father who displaces the true children to place himself in in the position of the child.

Conflicts of the oedipal space:

1. The father with son
2. Siblings with siblings
3. Mother with daughter

The prayer to <u>kindness</u>. What is "kindness"? One's kind …

This is a different crossroad, with a new father. What then is human fate? It is the fate of all of us to be born into a particular group of people: a specific mother, a specific father. We cannot alter this fate. Furthermore, we are genetically destined to be like them: physically and in some ways psychologically. So a question here, of justice, has to do with O fate, which the O child only begins to realize at about five or six when he can see a bit who this mother and father are.

Through his death O saves Theseus and Athens and therefore fulfills the desire of the father, Laius, who needed him dead to be saved.

Was Sophocles aware of this? The shattered body of Oedipus equals the mutilated, dying body of the son: dying because of the father's murderousness, but handing himself over now as a gift to the father to die in order to save the father.

To what extent do sons die for their fathers? To what extent do they feel they must do this? Perhaps to have wed mum, killed father, been omnipotent, "ruined by discovery of the truth", these shocks and tribulations are the "deaths" of the child demanded by the father who must secure the future of the city. So the son knows the father must demand his "deaths" which eventually become his gifts to the father.

O: "Wait till you hear me out, then criticize me …"

T: "Tell me more … I must not judge you, not without more to go on."

Justice—judgment—depends upon time. On the fathers giving time: to think, to allow opposition. No single internal object will be acted upon, but many objects will be allowed to come into this picture. This is democracy. Time allows for succession of internal states which increases representation. Therefore democracy and justice.

When Oedipus says he wishes to stay in the arcadian Grove of Colonus after Theseus has invited him to go to Athens, Oedipus goes back to his original place of remove from the father, of exile, but now a good exile, as he is not persecuted by this father, but Creon will aim to do so.

Sophocles shows how from moment to moment or context to context a person changes: sometimes acting from what is good, other times from what is bad. This too is part of the O dilemma: knowing that one's self changes according to one's urges and so forth and therefore that the other too is capable of such a change. This dynamic makes life so very much more complex as now the simple mother (of goodness and simple badness) is simple no more.

The mythologizing of sex. How O lives by the prophecies, legends and so forth and becomes a heroic demon at the end. X (patient) also goes over and over the events of his early life, to the point where mythological reality usurps everyday life. Is this the structure of trauma as opposed to genera?

The trauma/myth blocks lived life in the present which seems banal by contrast. The investment is entirely in the internal objects which utterly displace investment in reality.

A trauma like with X simply repeats and collects to it pain. It is the legend of suffering.

The absurd person is the tragic hero, floored by what was done to him or her; denuded now by the power of personal legend to usurp life, as the internal objects displace use of actual objects (which has to do with formation of genera).

[2/6/90]
"Oedipus complex"

One of the reasons for the child's (both genders) ambivalence to the father is that:

1. the father is complexity, i.e. he stands for it, as the third object.
2. such complexity is due to father taking the child away from the mother, i.e. from simplicity.

[undated]
"Modes of representation"

The fact that there are different modes of representation does not equate to the idea that there are therefore different types of unconscious, as the unconscious idea—whatever it is—can simply be represented in many different ways, unless I am prepared to argue that each such pathway (affects, visuals, verbals, somatics, intersubjectivities) is itself a distinctly different form of unconscious. As, for example, akin to a logos of forms.

Perhaps the object lexicon is an affect lexicon: that at least mnemic objects bear affects which are called up.

[8/6/90]
"Oedipus the King"

In order for O to say of Laius "I know—or so I've heard. I never saw the man myself" (p. 164, line 119) it must be assumed that (1) he and Jocasta have never talked about it and (2) he never asked Jocasta. If we reverse this, we can say that the existence and the memory of the father is denied and that he has not entered speech.

Michael Grant terms O's realization "The unendurable moment of truth"[13]—in which O knows who he is and what he has done. What does this moment in the play capture of our life? It seems to reverse the nightmare experience. We dream, we are inside events, but then we wake and we are relieved. In Oedipus, he wakes to a nightmare; he wakes to the dream. He is told he has unconsciously done something. But the unconscious here is different from Freud's, as this unconscious would be as if a figure approached Freud to say that Vienna was in plague until they discovered who had tried to kill Emma Ekstein.

To what extent is O the play and the Oedipus complex a sense of the unfolding of the subject before his own gaze? In which part of his destiny is the fate of parental interjection (of holding interjects) which the Greeks did partly understand because it was the action of the other upon the self which was looked for through a prophet (one who was outside the self)?

Because each of the figures in Oedipus is mythic—appearing in different versions to different people—each of these "figures" is a condensation. In this respect, so too are the parents for the child, who has experienced them differently, radically—as well as himself—over the years.

These stories upon stories upon stories, with legends in different versions insist upon repression (due to the horror of mental content) and return in derivatives: in new but disguised form. The story of Oedipus shows this.

The oedipal child discovers his father, mother and self every day, as the dream restages them all at a time of conflict, when basic horrors are repressed.

A list of horrors:

1. killing one's child
2. eating one's child
3. matricide
4. incest

But of incest we could say it is a disguise—a false crime or fear. In fact it equals (or counters) the force of murder with the force (equally brutal) of this type of love. By pretending to escape this, it is murder that is denied.

Robert Graves' fascinating introduction to the Greek myths, on the struggles between matriarchal and patriarchal authorities, brings to my mind another side of the oedipal

327

complex: the distribution of power (sacrifice) between the mother and the father. And how the child, at the oedipal age, is between the waning of the mother's power (serpent part of the Sphinx) and the waxing of the patriarchal power (the lion part of the Sphinx's body). The body of the Sphinx is a condensation of the power struggle (environmentally and intra-psychically) of the parents. It is a bi-parental object. The primal scene—sexuality—is the wish (effort, desire) to bind these opposites through eros, rather than have each kill the other off. Does erotics (biting, sucking, struggling) ritualize, then, a true struggle that is erotically transformed?

Is there a fight for the child? Do mother and father struggle with one another for the right to be the identifying matrix? Is the child the narcissistic lake into which each parent gazes, putting the other parent into Echo's place?

Reading Graves' introduction[14] one sees that O, the play, can now easily be seen as an effort to establish sexual place, security, in a situation that the Greeks see as dangerous. Antigone's act (looking after father) is so unusual, as a legend.

T. Reik's analysis of the Sphinx as a condensation—therefore a dream—is interesting, if we see it as combined male and female and in Oedipus representing the conflict between the sexes that was very much upon the Greek mind. Certainly for the man, a question was, can the mother be left? Can the boy child become himself?

[undated]
"Genera and the O complex"

Is it possible that by making the Oedipus complex the center of psychoanalytical theory, it is actually a complex that is the discovery: that is of a psychical structure that generates new forms. The fact that the Oedipus complex generates many forms is of interest, as it is the psychoana-lytical paradigm, or discovery, of genera itself.

For example, Laplanche and Pontalis say of the Oedipus complex that one must consider the triangle from three points: "it is the different types of relation between the three points of the triangle which—at least as much as any particular parental image—are destined to be internalised and to survive in the structure of the personality"[15] referring to the elements of the unconscious desire of all, seduction, and the relation between the parents.

All these factors work their way into combinatory process, the child's psychic structure, exactly as a genera is formed. If the combinations are procreative then the structure is a genera; if not, a trauma. So it is possible, then, to see the Oedipus complex as the basics of genera formation in a person?

Further, what I regard as the categories of experience is an effort to widen the contributing-in elements (if you look at what would be there in the oedipal child, emerging out of relation to the mother).

"Blood bonds between us":[16] to what extent is this one of the aims of the Oedipus complex, to fuck the mother in order to be closer to the father by sharing the same object of desire?

Secrets: throughout the play Oedipus keeps his secret—that he left Cadmus because of an Oracle. This is the secret of private psychic life, which is abrupted (rupture) through action.

Solving the riddle. As Tiresias points out to Oedipus, his great good fortune was his ruin, because in solving the riddle he freed the city of the plague and was declared King. Then he slept with Jocasta. But I think he solved the <u>false riddle</u> and failed to see the true riddle: concentrate on the feet! By appearing to avoid the murder, the sphinx actually created a new riddle that pointed to the murdered. O solved the old riddle but everyone failed to see the new riddle. And there will be more new riddles: from Tiresias for example. The riddle, like the sphinx, is a condensation. But it is a dynamic process and <u>condensations change</u>. O cannot see the changes in or before him. He cannot truly see.

The chorus equals the third factor. In any two-person conflict or within one etc., there is always the reflections of the chorus: a kind of hysterical cant. It does not know where to go. The mind in flux. So, with heroes set on sometimes fated and determined courses one has a chorus quite the opposite.

Burn[17] writes (p. 56) that the legend of the return of the Herakleidai (the exiled descendants) is an <u>invention</u> to reconcile the claims of Dorian Kings to descent. So in the Oedipus myth the story encapsulates this political aspect of succession. Indeed is it possible that O's ignorance of Laius (of his not telling Jocasta about him, of Jocasta not telling O about Laius, of Oedipus not telling Jocasta about Polybus etc.) indicates the historical fact of a <u>true ignorance</u>, of not knowing much. There is little <u>historical sense</u>, or historicity in the play and we may wonder if Sophocles demonstrates the makeup of Greece as composed this way.

Burn says that by the end of the 8th century BC (700) kingship disappeared due to the collapse of trade (and therefore keeping retinues) to be replaced by a council of the "best men" (p. 66). Isn't it possible that the chorus is a manifestation of this new council, off stage, competing with the notion of the King's power, but is Sophocles also revealing a fear of the psychosis of group process?

Indeed doesn't this raise intriguing questions about the psychic nature of life in a democracy and life in a monarchy? Democracy is open to psychosis while monarchy may be a patriarchal system supporting the vertical topography of neuroses. Even something like repression recognizes a patriarchal order (law) and of putting down into the system unconscious, while psychosis speaks to a split when the mental contents live in a fragmented but democratic order.

Is it possible therefore that Sophocles was exploring (consciously or unconsciously) the change of psychic states between the neurotic structure (oedipal complex and law of the father) of the patriarchal order and the psychic anxieties released by the democracy? And Freud's *Totem and Taboo* is the killing of the father, the killing of the law of the father, with a group of sons important now as <u>the group</u>, the council, descended from the destruction of the warrior King structure.

Burn goes on to say (pp. 66–67) that often (as at Acropolis) what had been a Palace now became a temple of "the state's chief patron deity". In Athens the monarchy was abolished, replaced by the nine Archons, led by an Archon (a regent) which meant the King was reduced to a faux leader, but "continued to be the city's chief priest".

It was felt that the gods would feel an affinity with the Kings etc. But what if the gods (or new gods) are the dead Kings: ennobled but killed by displacement? The father (monarchy) is removed, but his palace—seat of his former power—is now occupied by the temple where dwells a patron deity: a dream object that is the ghost of the father generated by the wishes of the people for a father.

When a figure goes to consult an oracle, are they circuitously hearing from their own demise? The fate of fate? In other words, is construction of the oracle—the power vested in man intermediate between a King and his ghost—(therefore a god, a man/god etc.), a structural feature or representation of a prior historical development: the usurpation of the monarchy by the group (or the father by the sons).

Burn substantiates much of this on page 74. Homer's gods were comic figures: the old war lords now out of place. But mental stress is the outcome for the Greeks of the time, because they are "in this middle age between two civilizations" out of which emerged philosophy. Now I think this historic state parallels the psychic state of the oedipal child, who is between two civilizations (mother and father), of a first civics of formerly very powerful internal objects (mother and father) but now left with a sense of self in a place not dominated by such powerful beliefs. Freud's theory that the oedipal child now wishes to wed mother and to kill the father may be a last hurrah: a joke of sorts. The romance with mother is true, but now, because she is desirable in her own right, not so dominating. The father's presence—and powerful superiority—seems to create a mutilation anxiety. But he is desired because of it: namely as the law who renders the mother and father less powerful.

The child who engages this arrival may act out the O complex, but certainly with Sacha[iii] there was pleasure in my arrival and function, as I was the law. The child who cannot reach this is left still with the primitive gods, and mutilation anxiety increases. The outcome of the Oedipus complex however is philosophy: that is, reflectiveness about life. This is crucial! It is what O achieves at Colonus.

—the ghosts under the earth are simply carrying home contact with the killing of the fathers that is denied in the worshipping of the gods who are idealized.

—the preservation of the city offered the Greeks a sense of immortality: (cf. Burn, p. 75).

—Zeus/ Kronos.

Kronos (the father) eats his children because he fears they will kill him. His wife Rhea hides Zeus, giving him a stone instead, and when Zeus is grown up he forces Kronos to cough up his brothers and the stone. The mother saves the child from the father by giving the father something false to introject. It is a story of a mother/child complicity to escape murder and so forth.

I think some of the above works for the oedipal child like this :

1. the child has powerful legendary memories of the mother and the father. These are his primitive myths.

[iii] My son.

2. he is now aware of the family structures and the law of the father, which I think entitles him to desire the mother. The act of identification precedes the full complex, although it is, or goes through, a murderous phase. The structure here is of neurosis. Repression.
3. the family as group (the household: the democracy) is the final dissolution of the father-son or mother–son relation. Splitting usurps repression. Psychosis rather than neurosis is the ordinary structure.

Stage 3 is the synthesis of 1 and 2. In it the laws of the mother and the father are combined and now with the child the group is formed. The family usurps the two previous structures, borrowing on the third party as the ideal container for anything split off from the two to form a stronger bond.

[undated]
"Oedipus"

It is the group, and identification with the many different persons in the family, including one's awareness of one's own subjectivities that displaces the law of the father.

[20/7/90]
"Psychic life"

Psychic life depends on, or rather it is partly thought amidst, or engaged with unknowableness. The infant's psychic life is his effort to think something known but always beyond thinking, as in apprehending. Apprehensive thought—thought which brings knowledge to light—is rare. Even for the adult. We live with very real difficulty in being able to render our state of affairs into a subjective stance. Psychic life is subjectivity amidst (engaged with) complexity that is beyond it. Therefore much is filled in with fantasy or imagination.

[22/7/90]
"Borderline oscillation"

The movement to and fro as a pathology represents a disturbance in the ordinary movement, back and forth, between simple and complex self states: immersion in experience and objectification of the experience.

[22/7/90]
"Condensation as a model"

Freud's metaphor of the dream thoughts being under the pressure of the dream work which breaks the elements of thought into a kind of pack ice of fragments. "When the whole mass of these dream-thoughts is brought under the pressure of the dream-work, and its elements are turned about, broken into fragments and jammed together—almost like pack-ice" (SE4, 312).

It seems to me that the way we organize our thoughts is in this way of condensing and then dispersing (displacement, projection, substitution, symbolization).

So, is the oscillation at another level: of condensation followed by dispersion?

Dispersion or dissemination?

[22/7/90]
"Intuition in sessions"

The psychoanalyst's "feel"[18] in a session for "where" the patient is, is an intuitive act which is based on multimodal processing of the situation.

Is it possible that feelings are indications of our intuitive place vis-à-vis the world (other, state of affairs)? So my feelings express my self state (even to myself) and partly indicate my sense of my place/position at that moment in time. This really only holds in a small way, I think.

[22/7/90]
"Endowment not projection"

I think I should differentiate the subject endowing an object with meaning (thus making his physical world rich with psychical subjectifications) from projective identification, which still connotes loss of parts of the self.

[undated]
"Psychic complex"

Perhaps I should say that psychic complexes—nuclearities—form in and through trauma or in and through genera. But clearly trauma can be transformed into genera. Or, if not into genera, then into new complexes or rendered non-repetitive. Actually a new perspective on a trauma becomes a genera.

[23/7/90]
"Anzieu's work and genera"

Anzieu's "formal signifier"[19] which is a metaphor of psychic spaces ("envelopes") is a possible synonym for a genera: or its cousin rather. For a genera is a perspective latent with logical new views that develop themselves in the course of time and events sought out specifically to articulate the genera. So in a way, genera are like idioms that are constructed over time—enucleated—and once set become fully or partly conscious and they (that is the structure) are now object seeking and object perceiving, in a new way.

Anzieu (p. 14) on interpretation as transformation of pathological structure: the skin of words.

I think I should use my concept of the analyst's work as transformational object to indicate how a trauma is analytically divested of its force of repetition through the work of deconstruction, and how this does <u>not then</u> form a genera, it only makes it possible for psychic economy investment in genera formation.

The unconscious ego is a <u>form maker</u>. Freud's 1895 ego was concerned with the boundary, to stop free flow of excitations etc. But the structure—ego—does this by finding forms for the development of objects which serve to represent the internal states of the self.

1. excitation or anxiety or need
2. ego is boundary
3. ego unconsciously knows of forms for the channeling of one's self
4. it then serves the particular content to a form area, where it is most likely to be satisfied.

These form areas built first from the body areas:

1. the mouth
2. the anus
3. the eyes
4. the ears

Each of which develops its own psychic area or capacity:

1. mouth: sucking, eating.
2. anus: expelling, waste
3. eyes: taking in visually

Out of these psychic qualities emerge—or rather alongside them—representational mediums: imagining, wording, gesturing, etc.

[undated]
"The uncanny and the paranoid mother"

An example. A child looks at a pair of glasses, looks away at other objects, and during the period of hesitation the mother says "don't touch the glasses." For the child: how did she know I wanted to touch before I knew?

[undated]
"Functions of interpretation"

According to my theory, psychoanalytic intuition is, in part, the analyst's search to open up foreclosed representations, and therefore experiential means of experiencing and representing.

To visualize, to empathize (feel), to abstract, to reflect, to gesture, to word (as in signifier freedom): these are psychic abilities.

Each of these ways of being (or processing units of experience) increases different or enriched forms of <u>apprehension</u>.

To apprehend is to grasp, to get "life" in one's hands, yet it is not the same as to know. One may apprehend reality, insofar as one may act upon it. As an idiom of processing reality this is deeply unconscious, and we know little of what has been processed.

In psychoanalysis the analyst uses many means of processing a patient—word play, visualizing (imagining), feeling, abstracting, proprioceptive sensing, etc.—in which the analyst brings to bear the range of the unconscious ego's apprehension of the other.

The sense of intuition is the subject's sense—derived from the efforts of apprehending—of the work-play being accomplished in the pursuit of some conscious grasp of a situation or problem.

The analyst does not use the sense of intuition so much as intuition is a sense derived from the activity of the subject involved in solving a problem, as if one does possess a sense of being in more or less accurate pursuit of a solution.

In fact, this sense may be quite inaccurate as all that it registers is the psychic operation of a multifaceted effort of the many factors in apprehending "x". It announces the presence of a particular type of work going on in this psyche-soma.

This work is used by psychoanalysts, who, by their comments, indicate that they are operating from within that sense, which they gradually impart to the patients who release their functions into many different operations upon reality.

This is a psychic sense.

This part of what I am interested in is psychic knowing, which operates on the "x" with that kind of labile effort found in the theory of the dream work, only I add to this the specific categories of experience and representation, as they are inadequately represented there.

At last I can abandon the distinctions—categories of experience and modes of representation—as each of these is experience. So perhaps the forms of experience, to represent the form, the aesthetic which marks the different types of experience.

1. visual 2. auditory 3. linguistic 4. gestural 5. somatic 6. relational (person perception), etc.

Relational: person perception is a type of apprehension of the other by bringing one's idiom to bear on play-work upon the other.

[31/8/90]
"The California holocaust"

How is it possible to define the trauma of development, as in California, in which the environment is eradicated, leaving one with a sense of an underlying Hiroshima or Nagasaki (like the unconscious) but buried underneath a sparkling, clean, new city.

The trauma lives on in the minds of those who were there when the Holocaust came (a kind of urban AIDS: killing slowly yet methodically).

What is in the minds of those who do this?

Developers with their charts, narrowed in on their task are remarkably similar to the pilot/bombardier with his charts and his eradications.

But the bombing of California is not so disturbing as the material wealth to take its place, akin to the concentration camps being bulldozed over with spanking new shopping malls—keeping their old name. "Dachau Shopping Center", for example. What does that do?

[undated]
"Love silence/hate silence"

M's patient is silent with fury because she is punishing M for her failure to demonstrate love to the patient. Before, she was silently loving her analyst. In both eras she was silent, although now she is silent with hate.

I think a patient's silence can match the analyst's ordinary silence (from neutrality) to create a pair of silences that constitute a merging for the patient. Love is gratified through hate.

Erotic transferences are often gratified through hate, in which the patient marries the analyst's silence. The patient imagines the analyst to be equally furious.

[10/9/90]
"Transgression of the symbolic/real"

This emerges from work with "X" on the recognition that to work in a dangerous country would put him in true danger rather than metaphorical danger. Real danger (or danger in the real) versus symbolic danger (danger in the symbolic) is distinguishable if we think of an action that will result in someone aiming to kill us (real) versus an action resulting in someone speaking a devastating criticism (a murder in symbolic versus murder in the real). Salman Rushdie comes to mind.

Perversion and the real. Neurosis and the symbolic. Freud pointed the way here. But it is as if the pervert gains control of the signified (in its concrete status) and kills the signifier in doing so. So the word "shoo" as in "go away" is bypassed and the pervert collects the shoe. Or if one thinks or says "I could murder you", the moment in which one actually acts to do so is a transgression based upon the usurpation of the symbolic, specifically the right (or place) of the signifier (the word "murder") to re-present (i.e. "stage") the murderous. By acting one commits a transgression against language.

How is the above to be differentiated from "I love you" (utterance–symbolic) to fucking the other? Is this an allowed transgression? A symbolic violation of the symbolic—that is one reason why fucking is so exciting. A mutual violation. A partner in transgression, in which the object of the desire simultaneously objectifies the subject as the object of their desire. One is converted in such a moment to being the object, the impersonal, the convergence of two objects (other/internal object), an eradication of self that is a thrill.

But for some, the wish is to see, take possession of the signified. To engage the real—unmediated. This wish is acted out. It does not mean the real is engaged, it only means the wish to do so is enacted. The symbolic is eradicated and the real enacted: in murder, in perversion. All murders are preceded by murder of the symbolic.

In the erotic transference this question (to signify or to transgress and take possession of the object of the signified) is a formal incest. The erotic transference is the only self state which allows this problematic to be posed between the signifier and the signified.

The mother's tongue re-presents the child. Does she elaborate the child through speech? Or does she not? Does the child have an impact only upon the body and mind of the mother? To kick her, cause her to be angry and so forth? The same is later true of the father.

The child who only acts upon the mother and the father, rather than speaking to them; or the mother and father who refuse to elaborate the child's communications (and transform from body to mind) establishes a relation to the real rather than to the symbolic. Use of the body (the thing itself) is the paradigm of somatization, of the refusal to transform a self state into speech.

The patient rarely plays with the notion of murdering the analyst. But by falling in love and demanding completion, the patient in the erotic transference can pose this deep question. Mary is determined to transgress because the mother destroyed (i.e. never employed) the symbolic. Self states, then, can only be enacted in the real.

For the analyst, however, these acts have symbolic value and by putting it into speech, signifiers are created and an incest barrier is gradually established. This can lead the patient to the anguish that the patient is losing a primary contact with the body of the mother.

[11/10/90]
"Interpretation as paradigm"

Each time the analyst "gives" an interpretation he conveys a model of the conflict and an implied solution to it. Therefore, interpretation is structurally homologous to the symptom (a compromise formation) in that it is a compromise between the illness and its cure.

Over time, as the analyst works on several topics, in some areas he constructs an overlapping set of interpretations that begin to collect material. They also constitute an inner sensor of meaning, yielding a sense of intuition.

[16/10/90]
"Why Oedipus?"

It was the group that killed the father: i.e. the group of multiple identifications, the group of perspectives. The group enables one to truly see many things from many points of view.

In Sophocles, the story had it that the group did something to the King and O keeps changing it to the singular. He keeps moving back to the oedipal dilemma and away from the Oedipus complex. In *Totem and Taboo* it is not the sons who kill, but the group.

"One day the brothers who had been driven out came together, killed and devoured their father and so made an end of the patriarchal horde. United, they had the courage to do and succeeded in doing what would have been possible for them individually" (SE13, 141).

What kills the father is the arrival of a group. The first peer group. The group that kills. Because once one forms the group it kills the patriarchal power of the father.

[23/10/90]
"Being a character"

This will be for Boston in 1991 and at this point all I know is that it will be about the subjective experience of the unraveling of one's own idiom (character) which unfolds (activates-elaborates) in or through experience. With bits from my history. And using the concept of the experiencing self (simple self) and the complex self (reflection) which is the essential oscillation. And how this works in the transference.

Also on how character can be a theme but also how we disseminate our idiom into the unconscious (that is through its displacement of our self).

[undated]
"Experiencing the other's complexity"

What is it to experience another person's character? Take the phone call with S or B: how difficult it is to be.

Some people create generative silence or receptive areas. Others lay mines.

What is it to be drawn into the character, like into a foreign country etc.? What is the nature of such a drawing in?

[24/10/90 Heathrow]
"Freud's complexes"

Freud's theory of "personal complexes" are, in fact, hermeneutic idioms of the unconscious that organizes perception. It is a good example of a type of genera.

"Instead … the Greek chrysos obstinately forced themselves on him as substitutes" (SE6, 35, The Psychopathology of Everyday Life) and shows how an inner idea has a force, which opposes us. It is a good example of genera.

Interestingly, "here-and-now" [interpretations] transfers dimensions of a forgetting that do not occur to Freud. In what way does the final story behind a forgetting signify an aspect of the subject who forgets in the presence of a specific other?

The dreams of psychoanalysis: Freud's theory of forgetting takes an absence, and by association constructs a series of images, words, feelings, memories which do come eventually together. But in a way isn't this also a form of dreaming?

[24/10/90 New York]
"The fairy-godmother transference and the bulimic patient"

See analyst B on his patient "X". This is when the patient tells the analyst what she did: eating on Sunday night, sleeping late on Monday, dozing, and, and, and … A sequence of images. In the sequence there is the self doing something and the self being watched. Acting in the transference and being watched by the analyst.

337

Originally (and still so) watched by a split off part of the self, which I think is the "fairy godmother self": watching. A tear comes into the eye of the fairy godmother (in the background of the patient's unconscious mind) on Sunday when she binges. The fairy godmother is an alternate to the mother and father as psychic object. Technically the analyst may say:

1. "You describe these scenes very clearly and movingly."
2. "It is so well described, I think a part of you—or something—is watching."
3. "I think it is as if I/we are watching."
4. "like a fairy godmother."

The "palpable hate" this patient "X" feels—her self hate. This is <u>positive</u> in that at least now she can hate one object, when a problem with hate of any object, of ordinary hate is being brought into contact with an ordinary object.

So too with binging. Bingers do not binge on life, on life's psychical objects (experiences) but on <u>thing</u> alternates, when that is, they approach "it" as itself. Otherwise they create radically altered dreamworlds as ghostlines.

In the clinical hour this patient relates to the analyst as the fairy godmother who is <u>to see</u> <u>her</u> first, to note the tragic evidence which accumulates into a dense psychic gravity to become its own object: the alternative self (alter to true self or false self—the dead self or tragic self). The weight of this evidence (note the irony of bulimia) is to be passed on to the analyst. It is to sit inside the analyst as an unwelcome, sad mass.

The patient believes that at some point, having watched enough suffering, this might hearten the fairy godmother (a manic portion of the patient) who will feel the weight of the patient's despair and <u>do</u> something at last.

The magic wand is the act. A radical transformation. The intervention of a manic portion of the personality.

The analyst may feel this, may act on it, in the form of <u>granting</u> further sessions, openly bequeathing good words, perhaps holding the patient (therefore giving her the prince with the shoe). (Slip/her: to slip from her, the last slip/her. What is split off?)

The wish of Cinderella is to have this <u>alternate</u> object enter the real to find her there and to transform her in the real. Therefore the analyst is to find the right slipper, to slip it on her, and like the magic wand transform her, but now the transformation is from the imaginary to the real.

The fairy godmother's wand moved the child from the real to the imaginary. The slipper that fits moves Cinderella from the imaginary to a now transformed real. The story therefore is a saga of a double transformation.

I think the bulimic patient expects this contribution from the analyst.

Further, by maintaining herself as a <u>thing</u> who refuses to articulate her idiom—here meaning to be and to represent herself in the creation of effects—she adamantly remains larval (the larval self) awaiting the butterfly moment. Indeed the weight of the body is like a cocoon (or chrysalis) in which the to-be-transformed butterfly self is inside.

"Comic grief"

M's case of "X" who is an amateur stand up comedian. Her acts are occupied by poking fun at her former husband and their marriage. Initially I was concerned over the manic side of the performances and seeming lack of contact with herself. But her analyst worked well with her.

It raises interesting issues of differentiating the comic way of processing trauma from the tragic. In the tragic view of man, it is the hero who discovers that he has flaws in his character which have produced his trauma. In the comic view, the subject is a true victim of misfortune.

In "X"'s case her mother became psychotic and was hospitalized. As a small child she recalls the mother putting her in the broom closet where she thought she would be killed.

Let us assume therefore that there are people who suffer, not because of the effect of their psycho neurotic conflict but because of the actions of the other.

A stand up comic may be an isolate. Jokes are made against the other, but also against one's self; and actually against the self which is presented as ridiculous, infantile, or simply odd. The audience laughs but does not cry; it is not empathically involved. The scene is all on the stage—object of its amusement.

"X" knew she was an isolate in her family. Or, by virtue of maternal actions "X" was thrown back upon the self. She could not project aspects of herself into the mother but instead kept it all inside.

In tragedy the hero's plight is human and involving. The audience identifies. Or, we would say, the tragic hero projects himself into the receptive egos of the audience who now are part of it all.

The comic position achieves no such depth of involvement. Or should I say, the stand-up comic, which I should separate perhaps from other comedies. But Jacques Tati, Chaplin, Keaton are objects of our humor as they suffer in their isolation.

It is this isolation I find interesting.

By becoming a stand up comic "X" now masters the trauma. A victim, she is now the victorious. She turns her misfortune into her new life.

In this respect, her comic grief over having been left by her husband—"I just can't get over it"— is partly to do with the fact that she's actively thriving on the trauma, using it to fuel her comic material. So here is one unconscious motivation for the preoccupation with her husband leaving her: she returns to it because it is the psychic energy that fuels the transformation.

Secondly, however, her husband's betrayal is "a screen experience", the x factor, where x = all previous, repressed examples of trauma to the self. In other words, with a person who has suffered a series of traumas in childhood, later in life an event may become the focus of intense, prolonged, unresolvable rage and grief. This is because it serves to represent many prior injuries.

"X" became an isolate who also did so by denying the parental reality. In response to the husband leaving her she has said that she is sure if she had plastic surgery he would want her. But here I think she means "surely cracks in the other can be smoothed over by cosmetics", in this case by doing so to herself (a reversal of the true smoothing over of the other).

The psychic pain of the comic position—or of comic grief (a comic's grief) is that as a child and adolescent the patient perceived her parents' madness, but she was on her way up and out. When she married her husband she sealed over her past and it did not break out until she was traumatized by her husband's betrayal.

[26/10/90 New York]
"Adolescence, groups, Oedipus"

The adolescent era is as we know the best occasion to see what occurs in the child's earlier trauma.

My oedipal theory is that the group displaces the oedipal dilemma. Regard the adolescent!

His denigration of parents is partly accomplished by true perception of parental weakness. His group of fellows shares this new vision.

[3/11/90]
"Primary investiture"

Each person during childhood and adolescence (perhaps through university) invests the noumenal world with private significance. It is his dreaming and like the Australian aborigine he goes walkabout through it during his life.

It allows "imaginal perception" as the subject lives in his own metaphysical universe, populated by "noetic points" that provide epiphanic self experience.

We may speak of "primary investiture" as a mental act of projection in which a child puts his self experiences into an object. "Secondary investiture" is when he learns from such experiences distinct social, cultural, conceptual and other meanings.

I believe that there is a qualitative difference in a person's life between those who have engaged in primary investiture and those for whom it is damaged. For example: children who are moved around literally lose contact with objects (a particular stream, the neighborhood, a garden, a church) which are the objects of primary investiture formation.

Loss of such objects psychically deletes part of one's vocabulary.

Additionally, in the modern world we are aware of how the primary invested world is destroyed by material change.

Imagine a child plays next to a church. As he does so its mass and texture will precede his knowing what a churches is, or means. Imagine that as an adult this place is destroyed. No longer there. It is no longer possible for him to go walk about there, to participate in an object that transcends him, or gives him comfort with his own genesis.

It is not the same as with those who have, say, a good memory. We may not see this church again and yet we have it inside us as we age. We may not see a friend for a long time, if ever again, and yet the friend is inside us. It is important to have a friend and to see them, to experience them and, as importantly to be experienced or to experience ourself through them. In the West we have had to overvalue the concept of the internal object, because external objects are easily eradicated.

Violence and internality. If an expansionist and progressive culture erases its past, this landscape can live only in memory. Therefore there is a great emphasis placed upon memory and the internal. But there are other stationary cultures that do not destroy their landscape and who can reliably walk about in a culture of objects that is shared and at the same time enables imaginal perception. God knows, maybe television is an effort to establish this in our own culture.

But in more stationary cultures perhaps there is less emphasis on the notion of 1. separation 2. loss 3. formation of internal objects, because there is less violence committed against the landscape.

[undated]
"The commission of true damage"

The adolescent who must truly damage the parent. In this re-living of the pre-oedipal era the child shows that illusion (representation) fails as the areas within the parent (dialectic, empathy,) are truly destroyed—as they may have been for the child. When this happens the child will now put the parent in contact with a reality (the adolescent) that is truly destructive.

[undated]
"Analyst as 'the you'"

Of "I" speaking to "myself" or to the "you". A feature of the transference. I talk to myself. There is a type of silence in analysis when the patient speaks to the "me" through the analyst.

Analyst as imaginary companion.

[undated]
"The erotic transference"

With a choirboy the female analyst must put the erotic into words, as the assumption is that her silence speaks something of her submission to his dominance. While with the female erotic transference—with the male analyst speaking it—it may feel as if the patient is denied her own speech of it.

It is intriguing how the female's love becomes erotic, or how the erotic seems to be so problematic. Because in a sense it is the use of an object to conjure dense sexualities, usually highly specific. These erotic preoccupations involve verbalized "sexual play" with the analyst, which some analysts see as a defense against analysis when in fact it is a representation of desire.

Why shouldn't a woman eroticize the transference?

The notion of it as entrapment is based on a confusion: yes, if the aim is to actually possess the analyst sexually, but in the great percentage of cases it is more like creating a romance, a body romance expressing a woman's representational aggression.

But is she not denied the object of her desire, and, does not this denial become the basis of victimage? No, in fact, the unavailability of the erotic object, the "object noumena" (ON) enables her to be free to use object internal (OI).

In all of this, there is a deep question about possession of the real: making the imaginary *into* the real. By selecting the analyst as an erotic object the patient does put herself in a place where she believes she can possess the real. So this is an aspect of the dilemma.

[undated]
"The cultural unconscious"

How do we analyze a society's collective process of unconscious thought? What is a country thinking about? What are its mental contents?

Television and cinema (novels, newspapers)—in other words mediations of transmission—give clues. Through looking there we may see unconscious ideas.

How do these transmitters differ?

1. TV
2. film
3. radio
4. painting
5. literature
6. sport

Each of the above is an area of social representation which processes a society differently, with different areas able to contain and process different elements:

Seeing a film we gather 100 plus in a darkened room.

Seeing a football game we gather 35,000 plus.

Gaza, Dick Tracy, John Major, Saddam Hussein. Some assert themselves, but we pick the objects, we center ourselves (more or less) as a society on certain issues.

A one month's read of a society's papers, television, film indicates the work of the cultural unconscious. What is its ego work? How do its features inter-play?

[19/12/90]
"The abused child"

I think each of us is an abused child. We begin life within the illusion of understanding, resting on maternal provision, affective attunement, certain unconscious communicatings, but gradually from age 5 on we know how complex we are. At the same time we now feel alone, as no one knows this complexity. That is, we know our mother or father cannot know us there (in our internal world) where we live much of the time.

The family romance is the child's effort to be rescued from aloneness emerging out of recognition that we cannot be precisely understood. The child creates internal parents who display the actual parental others: these internal objects now "knowing" the child and rescuing him from aloneness. Behind the ego ideal is an ideal other (the parents) who witness and know us throughout the lifespan. As we grow, develop careers etc., we live inside the illusion of understanding, now reinforced by the internal parents who know us.

To return to the child, mental life abuses the self. The child who has a destructive fantasy about the mother or the father is shocked by this thought. Life then is internally traumatic and as this accumulates the child feels isolated from love objects by mental life, which emphasizes the absurdity of it all. Further, such internal traumas sponsor mental work, to repair, displace etc., the traumatizing impulse.

True abuse—when a mother or father is dreadful—can be a relief, as a child is removed from contact with his own endogenous destructiveness by a parent who now seems to warrant attack (the attack is authorized by the parent).

Malignant actual abuse is destructive, but it does not [necessarily] lead to mental conflict, but to psychic pain or anguish. It is not something mentally elaborated (or capable of elaboration) as it is an enclosed thing: a fact, an action, which is awful. In a way its facticity destroys mental elaboration. Actual others and the subject's instincts (of destruction) cannot be linked. One's own destructiveness is therefore not easily represented, indeed may be silenced as the mind is numbed.

Therefore mental life makes us ill. Actual child abuse makes us less human but, oddly, perhaps less disturbed. Abuse makes us into simpletons, not so capable of complexity.

[20/12/90]
"Wish versus enactment"

"X" cannot have intercourse. She is stubborn. But her power is not the result of a wish but of an ego attitude. Many enactments, object relations, express an ego position rather than a wish.

[20/12/90]
"Eroticism in the transference"

What exactly is this? Is there an erotics specifically for the analysis? Freud's instinct searches for any object to discharge excitation. But the analyst presents the patient with only one object (other). Is there an erotic relation to it?

How about eroticism of the transference or the transference as eroticism?

[25/12/90]
"Freud/Klein"

The controversy seems to be about the first year of life, the early ego and phantasies, but in fact it is about early meanings at the very beginning of adult analysis, when the Kleinians believe the patient is demonstrating complex aggressive fantasies in the transference which need immediate interpretation. The Freudians do not believe this.

The paranoid/schizoid position may express the analyst's vigilant (paranoid) perception which creates a split (schizoid) between patient and analyst, with the patient's emotional state split off by the analyst's mental acquisition of the contents.

What does it mean if I say that in work with X she destroys my capacity to dream, and that this capacity is vital to understanding her? It is as if we come full circle back to Freud's self analysis and the prominence of the analyst's mind and struggle as central to the analytical project.

What would it mean if at a certain point the analyst was to disclose his incapacities to the patient, such as telling an X that I can no longer dream the analysis. It bothers me that this is not possible, that "the analysis" could become a kind of redundant machine, burdened by its history of interpretations and their failures and the patients plotting incarceration in a dead world.

Endnotes

1974

1. By "functional tradition" I am referring to ego psychology which understands the individual in terms of how he or she functions. Hence the interest in ego functions and ego deficits.

2. In the British school of psychoanalysis the term "object" is intentionally ambiguous. Does it refer to the "other": to a person? Does it refer to the mental representation of someone? Might it simply be the mental construction of an imagined and otherwise non-existent other? Indeed, use of the term "object" allows it to simultaneously refer to all such possibilities without having to make a distinction. So, the maternal "object" or "the mother", although seeming to signify the actual mother in these notebooks always simultaneously understands that "object" to be the self's experience of her person. Such experience is always open to imaginary constructions just as it is to "perceptive identifications".

3. At the Institute of Psychoanalysis in London, part of one's training was in "infant observation". This meant weekly visits to observe a mother and her newborn, for one year. The trainees also met as a group with an expert in infant–mother observation. My seminar leader was Lydia James.

4. This refers to an unpublished paper (1974) on "examination anxiety" in which I maintained that for some students studying for an exam constituted an intolerable break from reality, as exam preparation is experienced as a false reality.

5. All the Freud references are from the "Standard Edition". The Standard Edition in English was edited by James Strachey with collaboration from Anna Freud and assistant editorial help from Alix Strachey and Alan Tyson. It was published by The Hogarth Press and The Institute of Psycho-Analysis in London. The first edition was published in 1957.

6. "Character: Language of the self", in *International Journal of Psychoanalytic Psychotherapy*, 1974.

7. Masud Khan had written an essay on "exorcism of the ego alien objects" or "introjects". See Masud Khan, "Exorcism of the intrusive ego-alien factors in the analytic situation and process" (1972), in M. Masud R. Khan, *The Privacy of the Self*. London; The Hogarth Press, 1974, pp. 280–293.

1975

1. This is a reference to my published essay "Character: Language of the self", *International Journal of Psychoanalytic Psychotherapy*, 1974.
2. Martin Heidegger, *Being and Time*. London: Blackwell, 1962.
3. See Roger Poole, *Towards Deep Subjectivity*. New York: Harper & Row, 1972.
4. A term coined by the Gestalt therapist Fritz Perls. See Arthur Janov, "Gestalt therapy: Being here now, keeping unfinished business unfinished", in *Grand Delusions*. Posted June 2005 on primaltherapy.com.
5. Use of the term "Other"—upper case "O"—refers to both the unconscious as other and any "object" it represents. So, "Other" is this internal structural other (our unconscious) presenting an object of thought—an "other"—to us.
6. Sigmund Freud, *Studies on Hysteria*, in *The Standard Edition*, Volume 2 (1893–1895). London: Hogarth, 1955, pp. 1–251.

1976

1. See Erving Goffman, *The Presentation of Self in Everyday Life*. New York: Anchor Books, 1959.
2. Heinz Lichtenstein, *The Dilemma of Human Identity*. New York: Aronson, 1977.
3. See Ian Donaldson, *The World Turned Upside Down: Comedy from Jonson to Fielding*. Oxford: Clarendon Press, 1970.
4. See Murray Krieger, *Theory of Criticism*. Baltimore: Johns Hopkins, 1976.
5. See René Descartes (1637), *Discourse on Method and the Meditations*. London: Penguin, 1974.

1977

1. See Angus Fletcher, *Allegory: The Theory of a Symbolic Mode*. Ithaca: Cornell University Press, 1964.
2. See Angus Fletcher, *Allegory: The Theory of a Symbolic Mode*. Ithaca: Cornell, 1964.
3. See Georges Poulet, *The Interior Distance*. Baltimore: Johns Hopkins, 1959.
4. See Masud Khan (1969), "On symbiotic omnipotence", in Masud Khan, *The Privacy of the Self*. London: Hogarth, 1974, pp. 82–92.
5. See *Poems in Persons*. New York: W. W. Norton, 1975.
6. This idea forms the nucleus of an essay on destiny and fate that will be written some ten years later.

1979

1. Some twenty years later this idea works its way into an essay, "Borderline desire", in *The Mystery of Things*.
2. This concept would not be published for twenty years, in an essay titled "Borderline desire". See *The Mystery of Things*.

1981

1. Notes toward an essay to be published in the *Nouvelle Revue de Psychanalyse*.
2. "Ego orgasm" is a concept of Masud Khan and may be found in his publications.

3. "Mentation" refers to the defensive use of cognitive processes aimed at over-mentalizing any emotional or psychic state in order to nullify it. To my knowledge, the term was first used by Masud Khan.

1984

1. This conceptualization reflects the pre-judgement of many an analyst—including myself—that autism could only be understood as a breakdown in the infant–mother relation.
2. See W. R. Bion, *Second Thoughts*. New York: Aronson, 1967, p. 106.
3. Reference to "Moods and the conservative process", in *The Shadow of the Object*.

1986

1. In working with a hysteric in hospital who believed all men were molesting her, I characterized her reticence to see me for her appointments as "coming to see the beast" to which she associated that she was therefore "beauty", and she often used this tale to frame our meetings.
2. The argument here is very different from the one put forward in *Forces of Destiny*.
3. See Ágnes Heller, *Renaissance Man*. New York: Shocken Books, 1981.
4. See Christopher Bollas, "Expressive uses of the countertransference", in *The Shadow of the Object*. New York: Columbia, 1987, pp. 200–235.
5. D. W. Winnicott, *Playing and Reality*. London: Tavistock, 1971.

1987

1. From Vergil, *The Aeneid* (tr. Robert Fitzgerald). New York: Vintage, 1984.
2. "L" was silent for long periods of time and would occasionally describe an event in the hospital that had upset or amused him. I would say "Well I imagine ..." and proceed to tell him what I reckoned he was "probably" dealing with in his mind. He would allow this to go on for some time, often say "nice try" or "that's close" but eventually he would pick it up and interrupt me to elaborate what he was thinking. He would look at me as I attempted these interventions with a an amused affection, and after while I was his "side-kick" as he called me. I think his attitudes brought up the notion of the therapeutic alter ego. This bears relation to Paula Heimann's concept of the "auxiliary ego" and also the concept of the "supplementary ego", both terms recognizing the fact that analyst may have to supply ego ability in analysis if the patient cannot provide it for him or herself. (CB)
3. See Wilfred Bion (1962), *Learning from Experience*. London: Karnac, 1977.
4. Trip to Warsaw revealed that in adolescence young men had dreams of success but as they entered the workforce and faced a future with a dead end they turned to drink, their marriages broke up, and they returned to their parental home broken and with no hope.
5. Wave Street, Alexander Road, Glomstad, were streets where we lived. My parents separated when at Alexander Road (I was 14). I left at 19 to attend the University of Virginia (from 1962–1964).
6. For some time in the Notebooks I had been using (M) or (F) as a shorthand for mother and father. Here, however, I am restoring the original notation as (M) and (F) refer increasingly to functions held

in the name of the mother or the father, but in accord with what later I will term the maternal order and the paternal order.

7. I was teaching a seminar on Freud's self analysis at the University of Massachusetts in 1986. See Didier Anzieu (1959), *Freud's Self Analysis*. Madison, Connecticut: International Universities Press, 1986.

1988

1. See James Baldwin (1957), *Giovanni's Room*. London: Black Swan, 1984.
2. See J.-B. Pontalis (1977), *Frontiers in Psychoanalysis: Between the Dream and Psychic Pain*. London: Hogarth Press, 1981, p. 57.
3. See *The Interpretation of Dreams*, SE4,15.
4. See Jorge Luis Borges, *Labyrinths*. New York: New Directions, 1962, pp. 165–168.

1989

1. See Ihab Hassan (1961), *Radical Innocence*. New York: Harper, 1966.
2. See Richard Poirier, "Learning from the Beatles" (1976), in *The Performing Self* by Richard Poirier. New York: Oxford, 1971, pp. 86–111.
3. See H. Stuart Hughes, *Consciousness and Society*. New York; Vintage,1958.
4. *Notebooks of the Mind: Explorations of Thinking*. New York; Harper & Row, 1985. This is a brilliant book, full of wide-ranging evocative ideas. Like the great poet critic, Helen Vendler, John-Steiner's work brings insights to psychoanalysis that the profession needs.
5. From *The Princeton Encyclopedia of Poetry and Poetics*. London: McMillan, 1974, p. 666.
6. See Rainer Marie Rilke (1903–1910), *The Notebooks of Malte Laurids Brigge*. New York: Norton, 1964.
7. I met Erikson in 1971 when he was on the staff of the Austen Riggs Center in Stockbridge, Massachusetts. He kindly offered to help me think out my future, and the above quote is in response to my asking him if he thought I should train in Great Britain or not.
8. Solnit interviewed me as part of the application process for analytical training. He later agreed to sponsor me for application to the Institute of Psychoanalysis. In those days, non-medical Americans seeking to train in the UK had to have two American psychoanalysts sponsor them for their application to be approved. The other analyst supporting my application was Heinz Lichtenstein of Buffalo.
9. A dream I had some five years after the premature termination of my analysis with my training analyst when I was in analysis with a new analyst. The blood-stained coat refers to a dream where I was back on my analysts couch, he tells me he has cancer, I see a new coat of mine covered in bright blood. My last session with my analyst took place when he coughed up a lot of blood into his white handkerchief before phoning for a doctor. The new coat was an important object in my analysis as my analyst had encouraged me to exchange worn-out clothing for new material that was more befitting.
10. In Vera John-Steiner, p. 113.
11. See Monique Wittig (1973), *The Lesbian Body*. Boston: Beacon, 1986.
12. See John Russell, *The Meanings of Modern Art*. New York: Harper & Row, 1974.

13. See Vera John-Steiner, p. 103.
14. See Vera John-Steiner, p. 142.
15. See Reginald Gibbons, *The Poet's Work*. Chicago: University of Chicago Press, 1979.
16. Allen Thiher, *Words in Reflection*. Chicago: University of Chicago Press 1984.
17. Roland Barthes, *The Responsibility of Forms*. Berkeley: University of California Press 1985.
18. See Malcolm Budd, *Music and the Emotions*. London: Routledge, 1985, p. 18.
19. The "Free Speech Movement" began in October 1964 in protest against the UC Chancellor's capitulation to former governor William Knowland (at the time, editor of an Oakland newspaper) who called for removal of tables disseminating political pamphlets at the entrance to the campus.
20. At a sit-in on the steps of Sproul Hall at UC Berkeley in 1964 I was adjacent to a group of students from Newport Beach. They came to observe not to protest. Then the police forces charged the crowd—all of whom were seated and peaceful—and took out their truncheons and began beating anyone and everyone they could including two of the Orange County students. They were beyond incensed: they transformed there and then from conservative and entitled apolitical youth to radical students determined to correct the wrongs they confronted.
21. See Ludwig Wittgenstein (1977), *Culture and Value*. London: Blackwell, 1980.
22. See Howard Gardiner, *Frames of Mind*. London: Paladin, 1984.
23. Paula Heimann was my first psychoanalytic supervisor and when discussing the transference she always asked the following question: "Who is speaking, to whom, about what, and why now?" Her views were to become widely known in the British Psychoanalytical Society.
24. Giovanni Zibordi, "Towards a Definition of Fascism" (1922, pp. 86–96), in David Beetham, *Marxists in the Face of Fascism*. Manchester: Manchester University Press, 1983.
25. Hampshire quotes are from Stuart Hampshire, *Innocence and Experience*. London: Allen Lane, 1989.
26. See Eric Brenman, "Cruelty and Narrowmindedness", in Elizabeth Spillius, *Melanie Klein Today*: Vol 1. London: Routledge, 1988, pp. 256–270.
27. See Leo Kuper, *Genocide*. London: Penguin, 1981.
28. Personal communication while touring Pompeii together. I did not know his work but after several hours of conversation it was clear there were many points of convergence.

1990

1. See "Edwardo Paolozzi, Interview, 1965", in Herschel B. Chipp, *Theories of Modern Art*. Berkeley: University of California Press, 1968.
2. All references to Chipp are from the same text. See Herschel B. Chipp, *Theories of Modern Art*. Berkeley: University of California Press, 1968.
3. See Paul Valery, "A poet's notebook", in Reginald Gibbons (Ed.), *The Poet's Work*. Chicago: University of Chicago Press, 1979, p. 70.
4. Refers to a swing in my childhood; initially—and most importantly—the swing at my pre-school in Glendora California when I would swing high in delight but the unoccupied and unused swing also became an unconscious thought objectified in the swing: dreams not fulfilled.
5. The discussion of Bowra's work is derived from his *The Greek Experience*. New York: Mentor Books, 1957.

6. See Walter J. Ong, *Interfaces of the Word*. Ithaca: Cornell University Press, 1977.

7. See Ralph R. Greenson, *The Technique and Practice of Psycho-Analysis*. London: Hogarth, 1967.

8. See Helen Vendler, *The Music of What Happens*. Cambridge: Harvard University Press, 1988.

9. See Vendler, *The Music of What Happens*.

10. See Vendler, *The Music of What Happens*.

11. See Robert Fagles, "Introduction: Oedipus at Colonus" in Sophocles, *The Three Theban Plays*. London: Penguin, 1982, pp. 255–277.

12. Fagles' edition, *The Three Theban Plays*.

13. Michael Grant, *Myths of the Greeks and Romans*. London: Penguin, 1995, p. 223.

14. Best to read the most current edition. See Robert Graves, *The Greek Myths*. New York: Viking, 2018.

15. See J. Laplanche and J.-B. Pontalis, *The Language of Psycho-Analysis*. London: Hogarth, 1973, p. 286.

16. What Oedipus says to the Leader, unknowingly rationalizing incest. See lines 295–300.

17. See Robert Andrew Burn. *The Pelican History of Greece*. London: Penguin, 1966.

18. Dennis Duncan, British psychoanalyst, delivered an important paper, "The feel of a session", in the mid-1980s, which influenced my own thinking.

19. See Didier Anzieu, *Psychic Envelopes*. London: Karnac, 1990, p. 15.

Index